ROY EDGLEY is Professor of Philosophy at Sussex University.
RICHARD OSBORNE is a worker on the *Radical Philosophy* collective.

Verso

Radical Philosophy Reader

Edited by Roy Edgley and
Richard Osborne

**British Library
Cataloguing in Publication Data**

A Radical philosophy reader.
  1. Philosophy
  I. Osborne, Richard   II. Edgley, Roy
  100   B72

First Published 1985
(c) Copyright in individual contributions
remain with their respective authors

Verso
15 Greek Street London W1V 5LF

Filmset in Baskerville by
PRG Graphics Ltd
Redhill Surry

Printed in Great Britain by
The Thetford Press
Thetford Norfolk

ISBN 0 86091 101 2
  0 86091 2 pbk

Contents

Introduction   *Roy Edgley*   vii

1. Philosophers   1

Kant as a Problem for Marxism   *Martin Baker*   3
An Introduction to Derrida   *D.C. Wood*   18
Personality and the Dialectic of Labour
and Property — Locke, Hegel, Marx   *Chris Arthur*   43
Birth of the Subject   *Colin Gordon*   69

2. Marxism and Social Science   99

On the Theory of Ideology — Althusser's
Politics   *Jacques Rancière*   101
Who Makes History? Althusser's Anti-
Humanism   *John Mepham*   137
Reason as Dialectic   *Roy Edgley*   158
Realism and Social Science   *Ted Benton*   174
Truth and Practice   *Andrew Collier*   193

Morality and Politics   215

Mental Illness as a Moral Concept: The
Relevance of Freud   *Sean Sayers*   217
Moral Philosophy without Morality?   *Richard Norman*   234
The Economist on Allende's Chile: A
Case Study in Ideological Struggle   *John Krige*   249

4. Philosophy and Gender   275

Feminism, History and Morality   *Jean Grimshaw*   277
Masters, Slaves and Others   *Genevieve Lloyd*   291
Did Man Make Language?   *Alison Assiter*   310

5. Confrontations 323

Discourse Fever	*Tony Skillen*	325
Marxist Modes	*Jonathan Rée*	337
The 'New Philosophers' and the End of Leftism	*Peter Dews*	361
The 'Real' Meaning of Conservatism	*Andrew Belsey*	385
Edifying Discourses	*Joe McCarney*	398
Videotics	*Richard Osborne*	406

Introduction

This volume is a collection of items from the magazine *Radical Philosophy*.[1] Published by the Radical Philosophy Group, the magazine began in January 1972 and has since appeared three times a year. It has some claim to having the biggest circulation of any philosophical journal ever, up to four thousand copies per issue. It is still going strong.

The frontispiece declaration of the first issue outlined the aims of the Group and its magazine: 'Contemporary British philosophy is at a dead end. Its academic practitioners have all but abandoned the attempt to understand the world, let alone change it. They have made philosophy into a narrow and specialized academic subject of little relevance or interest to anyone outside the small circle of Professional Philosophers . . . The Radical Philosophy Group has been set up to challenge this situation . . . But we do not want to become exclusively preoccupied with the inadequacies of this type of philosophy. Our aim is to develop positive alternatives. For this there are other traditions which may inform our work (e.g. phenomenology and existentialism, Hegelian thought and Marxism). However, the Group will not attempt to lay down a philosophical line. Our main aim is to free ourselves from the restricting institutions and orthodoxies of the academic world, and thereby to encourage important philosophical work to develop.'

Philosophy as an intellectual discipline exists centrally in academic form, the form of a 'subject' within the institutions of higher education. Membership of the Radical Philosophy Group, always loose and informal, is and has been mainly academic in that sense, largely involving professional philosophy teachers and students; and contrary to the emphasis in Martin Walker's favourable account of Radical Philosophy in his series of *Guardian* articles on 9, 10 and 11 January 1984, the universities have been as strongly represented as the polytechnics. As the report from Kent points out in *RP* 1, the formation of a Radical Philosophy Group was originally planned at a discussion weekend at the University of Kent in June 1971. Local groups were organized in universities and polytechnics, and from the start the intention was that editorship, production and distribution of the magazine, though cooperative tasks open to anybody's participation and in fact widely shared, should be centred on a particular local group and should circulate regularly from one such group to another. The first five issues were accordingly edited from Kent, and then the centre moved to the London group of Middlesex Polytechnic. At that point the original frontispiece declaration of aims was dropped, and from *RP* 10 a new one appeared, explicitly relating Radical Philosophy to the student movement of the 1960s, in particular to its discontent with 'the sterile and complacent philosophy taught in British universities and colleges' and to the 'revival of interest in theoretical work on the left'.

The *RP* magazine was thus conceived as the organ of a movement, a movement working to subvert the philosophy of linguistic analysis radiating since the end of the Second World War from its centre in the gigantic Oxford school of philosophy. This school, which trained such a vast proportion of the English-speaking professional philosophers involved in the great post-war expansion of the subject, including many of us in the Radical Philosophy Group, thought of itself as the outcome and bearer of a 'revolution in philosophy'. Linguistic analysis was the latest phase of the analytical movement started at Cambridge at the beginning of the century by Russell, Moore and Wittgenstein, and the 'revolution' had been brewing since then. It was a revolution in the conception of philosophy itself, in which traditional conceptions were repudiated as being the result of 'metaphysical' confusion. The truths of philosophy proper were now understood as solely about the meaning of words rather than the reality they refer to, and thus as purely verbal and tautologous, uninformative and empty of content about reality and practical affairs.

It followed that if philosophy was everywhere and always properly practised, it would have no implications for either substantive (including scientific) theories or practical morality and politics. As such it would become useless and pointless, and there would be an 'end of philosophy'. But while metaphysics survives, philosophy proper on this view has a substantive critical task, to change and improve thinking that is metaphysically muddled and meaningless. At this point two different possibilities arise, concerning the scope of such confusion and criticism. Is metaphysical muddle peculiar to the specialism of philosophy? If so, the critical task of philosophy is itself specialized and recondite, and of little relevance or interest to anybody outside that specialism. Or can metaphysical mystification occur in 'other' subjects and areas of discourse, in science, politics, religion, art, and in and about the everyday activities of work and leisure, buying and selling, eating and drinking? If so, philosophical analysis can be of some general social importance, at least an echo of the critical practice of the *philosophes* in the Enlightenment. This latter option was open to logical positivism and falsificationism, with their empiricist criteria of meaning and scientificity, and as part of their programmes for the purification of science from philosophical contamination both developed a campaigning spirit and occasionally, if not always prominently, political affiliations. Significantly, though empiricism is deeply rooted in the British tradition and was in fact widely, if more or less covertly, present in English-speaking analytical philosophy, this course was taken by the one part of the analytical movement chiefly identified not with Britain but with the European mainland, particularly Vienna. But in his later period Wittgenstein, who was also Viennese, gave post-war English philosophy, especially at Oxford, a powerful impetus towards the former option. Rejecting empiricist criteria of meaning, he declared that '. . . every sentence in our language "is in order as it is" ', that the task of philosophy 'is to bring words back from their metaphysical to their everyday usage', and that therefore philosophy 'leaves everything as it is' (*Philosophical Investigations*, paras. 98, 116, and 124). To some extent anticipated by Moore's defence of 'common sense', this was the explicit foundation of 'ordinary language philosophy'.

Radical philosophy refuses both of these alternatives. Empiricism, though developed historically in defence of science as part of the Scientific Revolution and the Enlightenment, is incapable of accounting for theoretical concepts, including those in scientific theories. It in fact expresses a hostility to theory that is typical of, though by no means confined to, British attitudes, and having played its part in the historical process of secularization by attacking metaphysics in its religious form, in the twentieth century its chief critical and ideological function, in a shift of target from religion to overt politics, has been to attack Marxism. As to the linguistic analysis of the analytical movement's last phase, distinctions have been drawn between Wittgenstein's practice and his theory of philosophy, and between Wittgenstein and the Oxford school. The question has been raised, moreover, whether there is a non-empiricist form of linguistic analysis capable of use on burning issues and even for radical purposes — one of the ideas behind the foundation of *RP*'s almost exact contemporary, the journal *Philosophy and Public Affairs*. Whatever the answers, what Radical Philosophy objects to is not the investigation of language and concepts but rather the assumption that for philosophers such study means professional isolation from the world of material reality and acceptance of the ordinary language criterion of meaningfulness. The overriding tendency of Oxford linguistic analysis was clear. In the middle of a century of unprecedented human upheaval, a century of scientific and political revolutions, world wars, tyrannies and terrorism, the philosophical virtue of detachment came to be identified with a posture that combined donnish remoteness from these matters with a philosophical acceptance of the ordinary concepts in terms of which they are commonly misunderstood. Philosophy dwindled into a position it considered to be neutral. The effect of this 'neutrality' was certainly conservative.

The 'revolution in philosophy' was politically a counter-revolution. Radical Philosophy has fought it not, in general, by direct, explicit and detailed criticisms of the particular ideas and arguments produced under its influence, but rather by undermining its restrictive practices through the constructive exploration of alternatives. Among the things at stake here are two different views of the philosophical tradition and its historical role.

In its relation to traditional philosophy the so-called revolution has not been even-handedly critical. Within modern European philosophy from Descartes onwards it has discriminated, notably, between the period from Descartes to Kant and the succeeding period, especially on the European mainland, from Hegel to the present day. The former, the age of the Scientific Revolution and Enlightenment, has been respected, particularly in its empiricist tendencies, and has been widely taught in academic courses and studied at the research level. The latter, the age of the Romantic Reaction and its aftermath, has been generally regarded, Mill, Frege, and the 20th-century Viennese connection apart, as too benighted to be worth much attention. For the founders of the analytical movement, Russell and Moore, were explicitly reacting against Hegelianism; and the change they brought about, in which language, meaning, and logic in its modern mathematical and symbolic form moved as more or less exclusive categories into the focus of philosophical attention, submerged Hegel from view in English philosophy, and with him most of the 19th and 20th-century philosophy characteristic of the European mainland. For the analytical movement the chief ancestral authorities in the tradition have been Hume in the movement's earlier phase and then Kant, both of whom, though thought to have been badly mistaken about the nature of philosophy itself, nevertheless managed, on this view, to see through many of the pretensions and absurdities of traditional philosophy, i.e. of metaphysics. Indeed, it was supposedly the failure of Hegel and his successors to take advantage of their critical insights that made necessary a 20th-century revival and development of the Enlightenment attack on metaphysics.

Confronted with the Radical Philosophy movement, some analytical philosophers have represented their position as defending the philosphical tradition against the radical challenge. In reply, members of the Radical Philosophy Group have pointed out that in some very basic respects the boot is on the other leg (see *RP* 3). On the crucial question of the relation of philosophy to the real world, it is the philosophy of linguistic analysis that repudiates the tradition and Radical Philosophy that defends it. In fact, given the cultivated ignorance of linguistic analysis about most of the philosophy distinctive of the Continental mainland from Hegel to the present day, its claim to be defending traditional philosophy is a ridiculous charade. It has always been a central policy of the Radical Philosophy Group to do what it can to redress this neglect of Hegel and the Continental post-Hegelians, and some credit is due to it for recent improvements in that situation.

However, it has not been the policy of Radical Philosophy to revive philosophy in the old style, as either traditional metaphysics or even political philosophy, nor simply to import foreign thinkers forgotten or unknown on this side of the Channel. Our aim has been to develop our own ideas from our own perspective, and this has involved replacing the orthodox view of the tradition, and our relation to it, with a very different conception. The orthodox neglect of 19th and 20th-century mainland philosophy, and the orthodox revival of Enlightenment themes, are not just innocent academic fashions, nor is Radical Philosophy's concern with that neglected period. The theoretical detachment of philosophy from reality, especially in conjunction with the use of 'ordinary language' as a criterion of meaningfulness, has had this real effect: it has discouraged the subjection of accepted ideas about reality to the fundamental questioning that has been the traditional task of philosophy. It is just such a fundamental questioning of Enlightenment rationalism that has been undertaken by the Continental mainland in the 19th and 20th centuries. The Enlightenment inherited the Scientific Revolution, in which natural philosophy began to give way to what we now recognize as natural science. The scientific study of society was a later development. It was in the transition from the 18th to the 19th century that social philosophy began to be superseded by the social and human sciences, including scientific history, and at the same time, and not by coincidence, the liberal political ideas of the Enlightenment began to be challenged by the socialism of the new working-class movement. If Descartes, Locke, Hume and Kant are worth studying for their roles in the intellectual and political revolutions of the 17th and 18th centuries, when the bourgeoisie was rising to power, and thus for the historical light they throw on their (and our) contemporary situation, is not something similar true of Hegel, Marx, Freud and Sartre? For mainstream linguistic analysis, of course, Hegel and Sartre are thoroughly confused metaphysicians, and Marx and Freud thoroughly confused pseudo-scientists. But apart from Popper, another representative of the Viennese connection and one who rejected the later Wittgenstein and Oxford philosophy, these attitudes have been almost entirely unsupported by any serious study of the thinkers concerned. In any case, throwing light on our contemporary situation is not the aim of linguistic analysis. Real situations are not an object of philosophical attention, not even, in general, as social contexts of thought. It is true that, like Marx, Wittgenstein asserts a strong connection between meaning and the use of language in practical forms of life, and it is also true that through followers like Winch Wittgenstein's work helped, with Popper's, to promote the growth of philosophical interest in the social sciences. But the Wittgensteinian tendency here has been to undermine a specifically critical approach to ordinary language and its related practices: philosophy 'leaves everything as it is'. Besides, for most analytical philosophers the idea of the practical context of language has remained a purely theoretical gesture, and in particular the orthodox involvement with the philosophical tradition (a matter of little interest to Wittgenstein himself) has tended to presuppose that the content of past thought can be understood independently of its historical context, assessed for its timeless truth or falsity, and appropriated or rejected accordingly.

In opposing the dominant philosophy of linguistic analysis, Radical Philosophy has challenged not only its explicit content but also these underlying assumptions and practices. It has aimed to unite its criticism of the general content of orthodox philosophy with understanding and criticism of its related context both of institutional practice in the education system, especially higher education, and of the wider overall structures of society. The magazine has discussed and criticized academic examinations, course material and design, and teaching methods, relating the standard forms of these to society's general hierarchies. In this way also it has drawn on and championed the tradition of modern European social science and philosophy. Inevitably, a central role has been played here by the rich vein of critical theory inaugurated by Marx, with its ramifications in 20th-century mainland philosophy. Marx's revolutionary ideas questioned and attacked the prevailing ideology at the most fundamental level, including the level of philosophy itself, where Marx was so deeply engaged with Hegel; and for the Radical Philosophy movement and magazine Marxism has been both a central object of philosophical study and an inspiring example of theoretical and social critique. In the process, we have contributed to the current revitalization of left-wing theory.

This subject of left-wing theory, with its corollary about the relation of *RP* to other left-wing journals, has been one of the most contentious in the Radical Philosophy movement. The Radical Philosophy Group has never supposed that it had any tablets of stone inscribed with eternal truths to deliver to the waiting multitudes. The movement has been in constant motion because its members have needed to educate themselves, using the magazine as a forum for discussion. The prevailing philosophy has been attacked less from the position of a positive alternative than from a felt need to explore possibilities blanked off by that philosophy. There have consequently been strong disagreements within the Group and struggles about the way the movement and magazine should develop. Most members, but not all, have been socialists. Most of the socialists, but not all, have been Marxists, or have recognized Marxism as the intellectually most powerful component of the socialist tradition. But how is socialism related to philosophy? Many of us, especially those trained in analytical philosophy, had been socialists and philosophers, but could there be any such thing as socialist philosophy? The socialist tradition, especially within Marxism, has provided and explored a range of possible answers. Our opposition to the narrowly specialist conception of philosophy, together with our awareness of Marx's famous theme, echoed in a very different key by Wittgenstein and the analytical movement, of the 'end of philosophy', have been pressures pushing *RP* towards the role of being simply another journal of left-wing theory. That tendency has been resisted in various ways.

For one thing, the unity of socialist theory cannot be undifferentiated, and the concept of philosophy still marks out, if not a well-defined body of systematic doctrine, a range of questions and topics, e.g. the relation of class division and class struggle to scientific objectivity. We have questioned and tried to develop the resources of the socialist tradition on such topics, bringing to bear our knowledge of the possibilities explored in philosophy and epistemology in general. So in attacking orthodox English philosophy we have also aimed to raise the level of philosophical clarity and coherence in contemporary socialist argument. In the process we have retained, within the revival of left-wing theory as a whole, something of our specifically philosophical identity.

Another form of resistance has centred on the temptations in the nature of theory. Theory needs some degree of detachment and abstraction from the concrete reality of practical affairs, but detachment can lead to remoteness and its attendant ills — a politics of knowledge that is elitist, a language that is obscure and jargon-ridden, a mood of scholarly solemnity and pomposity. We have recognized that the left as well as the right, especially the Marxist left with its commitment to theory, can suffer from academicism and scholasticism, that within theory philosophy is particularly vulnerable by virtue of its place at the more abstract end of the theoretical spectrum, and that for some of us *RP* has at times succumbed (see the editorial contributions in *RP* 20, 21, and 22). Nevertheless, this kind of shortcoming has been limited by some built-in safeguards.

In opposition to the publications of the academic establishment, *RP* has always been conceived of as a magazine rather than a learned journal. It has the shape and format of a magazine. It reports, analyses and comments on some current political events in higher education, such as the Swansea affair (*RP* 9). It reports on its own conferences and day-schools. It encourages and publishes letters from readers. It includes graphics and humour, especially satire. It prefers a combative style, and language that is as simple and direct as the difficulties of the subject permit. All of this adds up to a relationship with readers that by comparison with most academic journals, including some on the left, is open, receptive and democratic.

In the practical tasks of production and distribution also we have broken with academic convention and tried, with varying degrees of success, to make the magazine a cooperative socialist venture. Though we have recently introduced the idea of individual editors for specific issues of the magazine, there is no editor in the orthodox sense: no autocrat, that is. Editorial decisions are made by the editorial collective, a group of open and flexible membership that meets to discuss both business matters and, after receiving referees' reports, the composition of each issue. Moreover, as an alternative to employing professional specialists we have done as much as we can of the preparatory publishing work ourselves, including, during the first few years, layout and paste-up. One effect of this has been to keep the cost and price low; the first issue sold at 35p, the latest £1.50. On the distribution side we have always used, besides more conventional channels, a system of college sellers, enabling readers to buy copies of the latest issue direct from members of the Radical Philosophy movement on the campuses.

In the early days the excitement and vigour of Radical Philosophy gave it the feel of a genuine movement, especially at our massive open meetings. It was part of a more general tide, in which revolutionary possibilities seemed to be within reach. That tide has been stemmed, and we have not had the subversive success we hoped for. Local groups have dwindled, the open meetings have given way to more modest day-schools, production of the magazine has become more professionalized, college selling is less extensive: innovations have settled into routines, and the mood is more sober. It is hardly possible these days to think of Radical Philosophy as a movement. However, though we have no cause for complacency, or much of a tendency towards it, changes in English philosophy have occurred, some of them in the directions we have argued for and partly in response to our pressure. In some ways, as young Oxford philosophers of the fifties' 'revolution' have settled into their college headships, with their knighthoods and peerages and chairmanships of Royal Commissions, the philosophical establishment has become more closely consolidated with the administrative and political establishment. On the other hand, the philosophical adjustments that have occurred over the last 15 years look less like reconsolidation than fragmentation. In these circumstances Radical Philosophy intends to do more than just survive the backlash. Having for the first time in history secured a foothold for socialist philosophy in Britain, we propose to maintain a persistent and active subculture of philosophical radicalism, without illusions about our own particular power and influence but also providing more than simply one extra option among those now emerging on the philosophical agenda. The sickness of our time, with its drive towards nuclear annihilation, can be cured only by some form of socialism; and whatever the pathological fashions and fads of philosophy, it is our philosophical project alone that can have any assurance of a future. The general tide will return, and that next opportunity we intend to be prepared for, and to help prepare. It may come sooner than we think.

*   *   *   *   *

Preliminary selection of items for this anthology was carried out by a subcommittee of the editorial collective, and the collective then modified the subcommittee's proposals and authorized the final result. A glance through the 36 issues so far published, or more manageably through the Index for issues 1–30 in *RP* 31, will suggest some of the problems. We have aimed at an overall collection representing the dominant concerns and style of the magazine, and written mainly by members of the Radical Philosophy movement. For reasons of space we have not been able to do justice to a feature achieved sometimes but not often enough, namely sustained discussion of a topic over several contributions and issues. We have had to settle for article-length pieces sufficiently independent of others to stand on their own. Another criterion used to eliminate otherwise acceptable contenders was that we should not include more than one piece by any author. Finally, we have preferred where possible to avoid pieces already reprinted, or printed elsewhere, or substantially overlapping with other such publications. Among those items ruled out by this last criterion are the following:

M. Barker's 'Racism — The New Inheritors' (*RP* 21, see Barker's *The New Racism*, Junction Books, 1981);

R. Bhaskar's 'Scientific Explanation and Human Emancipation' (*RP* 26, see Bhaskar's *The Possibility of Naturalism*, Harvester Press, 1979);

P. Feyerabend's 'How to Defend Society Against Science' (*RP* 11, see I. Hacking's ed., *Scientific Revolutions*, OUP, 1981).

J. Krige's 'Revolution and Discontinuity' (*RP* 22, see Krige's *Science, Revolution and Discontinuity*, Harvester Press, 1980);

S. Kruks's 'The Philosophy of Merleau-Ponty' (*RP* 11, see Kruks's *The Political Philosophy of Merleau-Ponty*, Harvester Press, 1981);

J. McCarney's 'The Theory of Ideology' (*RP* 13, see McCarney's *The Real World of Ideology*, Harvester Press, 1980);

J. Mepham's 'The Theory of Ideology in *Capital*' (*RP* 2, see Mepham and Ruben's *Issues in Marxist Philosophy*, vol. III, Harvester Press, 1979);

R. Norman's 'On Dialectic' (*RP* 14, see Norman and Sayers's *Hegel, Marx, and Dialectic*, Harvester Press, 1980);

T. Pateman's 'Language, Truth and Politics: A Conception of Philosophy' (*RP* 3, see Pateman's *Language, Truth and Politics*, Jean Stroud and Trevor Pateman, 1975);

S. Sayers's 'The Marxist Dialectic' (as for Norman, above);

A. Skillen's 'The Statist Conception of Politics' (*RP* 2, see Skillen's *Ruling Illusions*, Harvester Press, 1977);

K. Soper's 'The Needs of Marxism' (*RP* 17, see Soper's *On Human Needs*, Harvester Press, 1981);

R. Taylor's 'The Marxist Theory of Art' (*RP* 5, see Taylor's *Art, An Enemy of the People,* Harvester Press, 1978);

R. Waterhouse's 'Heidegger: An Assessment' (*RP* 27, see Waterhouse's *A Heidegger Critique,* Harvester Press, 1981).

The sections into which the book is divided need little explanation. The first exemplifies *RP*'s interest in important aspects of modern European philosophy neglected by the analytical movement. The last shows that we have taken critical note of some contemporary tendencies, left, right and centre, and both English and Continental, of a more ephemeral sort. Between these two are sections on Marxism's claim to the status of scientific theory, on the more practical and specific matters of morality and politics, and on one of the most significant departures in modern radicalism, the feminist movement. In feminist matters we acknowledge a serious shortcoming. Only two or three women have been active members of the editorial collective, and the preponderance of men, itself reflecting the situation in philosophy in general, has had its effect. Though we have devoted a whole issue to gender problems (*RP* 34), overall there has been a disproportionately small allocation of space and time both to such problems and to the work of women authors on other topics. The section here on Philosophy and Gender is even smaller than it would have been if M. LeDoeuff had not refused us permission to use her 'Women and Philosophy' (*RP* 17).

Roy Edgley

1. Philosophers

Kant as a Problem for Marxism

Martin Barker

The relation between the thought of Immanuel Kant and the Marxist movement has been distinctly problematic. Kant, as the founder of the German idealist school, was recognized by Marx as one important precursor of his own theory in a general sense. But although Marx's appreciation of Kant's thought was generally full of insight, it involved at times an astonishingly harsh dismissal. In *The German Ideology,* where he came to terms with his 'philosophical conscience', he sensed quite correctly that the heart of Kant was his *Critique of Practical Reason,* not, as traditionally thought, the *Critique of Pure Reason.* Nevertheless, he treats Kant merely as the theoretical representative for 'the impotence, depression and wretchedness of the German burghers, whose petty interests were never capable of developing into the common national interests of a class and who were, therefore, constantly exploited by the bourgeois of all other nations.'[1] In keeping with this interpretation, he considers that Kant relegated the resolution of a conflict between individual and society to the world beyond.

The basic truth, however, is that Marx had very little to say about Kant. Lucio Colletti, who has recently tried to reconstruct the theoretical relationship between the two,[2] has had to rely heavily on Marx's critique of Hegel in arguing that he ultimately faced certain Kantian problems. He does not claim that there was any explicit reference to Kant in the formulation of these problems.

This blindness on Marx's part was not common. He was usually quick to grant recognition to important, or even minor forebears.[3] One might be tempted either to join Marx in dismissing Kant as a theo-

1. K. Marx and F. Engels, *The German Ideology,* Moscow 1964, p. 207.
2. See 'Kant, Hegel and Marx', in L. Colletti, *Marxism and Hegel,* NLB, London 1973.
3. *Das Kapital,* for instance, is strewn with footnotes in which he pays his respects to those he opposes fiercely in other ways.

retician, or to conclude with Kant:'I am a century too early with my works; it will be a hundred years before they are properly understood.' Neither course, however, would help us to grasp the essential elements in Kant's thought, and to judge whether the appearance of Kantianism in the Marxist tradition must always be a signal for political worries, as has often appeared to be the case in the past.

Marxist Critiques of Kant

If we consider the traditional images, and consequently the traditional objections to Kant as a theorist, they are as follows. He is seen, first, as providing a last-ditch defence of theism against the encroachments of science. In this view, he is in the tradition of Descartes, who, by positing a strict dualism of body and soul, was able to allow Newtonian mechanics full sway over the body, while leaving the soul to the governance of God. Kant, it is said, reproduces this dualism in his distinction between appearance and reality, or between phenomenon and noumenon as he calls them. For God is then sealed off in the noumenal realm, graspable only by faith.

Secondly, he is seen as introducing a hard separation of fact and value, to the point where they become irreconcilable contradictories. A sample of this approach — more an article of faith than a reasoned argument — may be seen in the following quotation: 'In the case of the natural world, Kant distinguished between things as they are (in-themselves) which are unknowable and the phenomenal world of appearances subject to causal laws. Correspondingly, man's existence has a similar dual structure: man as a phenomenal being is under the sway of unalterable causal laws, while the other aspect of his existence (the noumenal sphere) is characterized by freedom and self-determination. Thus any knowledge of man as a *social being* could only be achieved through the speculative methods of philosophy. The result of Kant's distinction was radically to separate fact from value, relegating the former to the domain of nature and the latter to the social.'[4]

Thirdly, Kant is seen as introducing a purely formal ethics, which can therefore be filled with any content, and as the theorist of the abstractly free individual. From the interstices of this analysis can come all forms of domination. This account of Kantianism as a simple variant of bourgeois individualism is connected with a further objec-

4. R. McDonough, 'Ideology as False Consciousness: Lukács', *Working Papers in Cultural Studies* No. 10, p. 33.

tion that it draws a rigid distinction between reason and emotion, making of morality a Puritan system of duties to be fulfilled through continuous acts of self-denial.[5]

Finally, Kant is regarded as having introduced a new form of fatalism which neatly matched the uncertainty and practical pessimism of the German burghers: 'So sharp was his distinction between appearance and reality . . . that reality ceased to be knowable, one could only act "as if" it existed at all. So radical was Kant's dualism that, paradoxically, his effort to save human freedom seemed to result in a new form of philosophical fatalism.'[6]

The key, in fact, to all the objections is embodied in Anchor's comment. For all of them derive from a claim about the relationship between appearance and reality, or the phenomenal and the noumenal. All the claimed dilemmas and oppositions dovetail into that distinction, or rather, into an interpretation of it. It is argued that Kant used the distinction to define God as a 'Regulative Idea' — that is, as something beyond the realm of appearance and therefore not capable of being proved *or disproved*. Thus Kant can make religion a matter of rational faith, safeguarded against any possible scientific development; for science is the method of comprehending appearance, not reality. The fact/value distinction is interpreted in the same light: Kant sees value, and all morality, as deriving from his concept of freedom which is only applicable as a noumenal category, while the phenomenal world is governed by mechanical causality. Morality as such, and therefore the moral laws derivable from the concept of freedom, can have no empirical content. Indeed, the pursuit of the formal requirements of duty demands the 'humiliation' of all empirical desires such as the desire for happiness or self-realization. Finally, Kant's fatalism is held to stem from the fact that, in his theory, the realm of freedom (the noumenal world) is out of all contact with the world as we experience it (phenomenally).

An Ahistorical Philosophy?

Traditionally, then, Marxists have denied the importance of Kant in the actual construction of a Marxist theory. He was significant as a precursor of Hegel, but was dedicated to ahistorical deductions of no

5. Durkheim seems to make a virtue of this. 'There is no moral act that does not imply a sacrifice, for, as Kant has noted, the law of duty cannot be obeyed without humiliating our individual, or as he calls it, our "empirical sensibility".' 'The Dualism of Human Nature', in K. Wolff, ed., *Emile Durkheim*, Ohio UP 1960, p. 323.
6. R. Anchor, *The Enlightenment Tradition*, London 1967, p. 119.

use to us: 'However we read Kant, Hegel and Marx could both argue that Kant's separation of the noumenal and phenomenal worlds made it impossible for him to discover the concrete historical mediations for the transvaluations of human practice.'[7]

Of course, not all have agreed. There have been serious attempts to make something more of Kantianism for the Marxist tradition. Lucien Goldmann, in his fine book, presses a Lukácsian mould out of Kant — not without success.[8] But apart from the fact that the book is marred by a strong idealist tendency, we are left at the end with little sense of the actual use that we can make of Kant for our own purposes. More, it seems like an exercise in historical honesty.

One of the recent revaluations that has done something to discover the historical and theoretical significance of Kant nonetheless concedes much to the tradition of anti-Kantianism. Sohn-Rethel, in his insightful studies on epistemology and ideology, argues:

> It is an essential condition of capitalism that the technology of production be founded upon knowledge of nature from sources other than manual labour. And how a knowledge thus defined and yet reliable, exact and objectively valid is constituted and indeed possible, is a question which must be answered, especially if we do not share the idealistic belief in the original theoretical capacities of a 'pure intellect'.
>
> The epistemological interest in science is clearly specified historically and economically by its tie-up with the capitalist mode of production. It is not Kant's ahistorical concern with the possibility of knowledge and of experience in general and as such. Still, even taking leave from Kant's philosophical apriorism, the questions he asks — how are pure mathematics and pure science possible? — look confusingly like the ones of concern to us. The reason for the similarity lies in the emphatically ahistorical or rather timeless, universal character of mathematics and science and indeed of all intellectual labour divided from manual labour. While Kant's answer is in line with this character and, correspondingly, implies the perpetual necessity of the division of head and hand and, hence, the impossibility for ever of social classlessness, the answer that we require must, on the contrary, be in historical and materialistic terms.[9]

In this reading Kant's account is not only unconcerned with a historical understanding of the possibility of knowledge, but actually *incompatible* with a historical account. In saying this, Sohn-Rethel has reintroduced the absolute antinomies which he had apparently over-

7. J. O'Neill, 'On Theory and Criticism in Marx', in P. Walton and S. Hall, eds., *Situating Marx*, London 1980, p. 77.
8. L. Goldmann, *Immanuel Kant*, NLB, London 1971.
9. A. Sohn-Rethel, 'Mental and Manual Labour in Marxism', in *Situating Marx*, op. cit.

come with his recognition that empirical knowledge has a priori grounds determining its form. Now, the opposition has become one between history and theory. He therefore concludes that Kant represents only the apex of bourgeois thought, to be taken over by Marxism via a critique which reveals it as the most systematic possible version of bourgeois thought. The problems, the concepts, and the system are all, according to Sohn-Rethel, those of the rising bourgeois class.

Who are the Educators?

What is particularly crucial about Sohn-Rethel's interpretation, is that he cites against Kant a problem which can be shown to be absolutely central to Marxism: the problem of the educators. He argues that there is a necessary distinction implicit in Kant between head and hand. This clearly recalls the problematic of the Third Thesis on Feuerbach: 'The materialist doctrine that men are products of circumstances and upbringing, and that, therefore, changed men are products of other circumstances and changed upbringing, forgets that it is men who change circumstances and that it is essential to educate the educator himself. Hence, *this doctrine necessarily arrives at dividing society into two parts*, one of which is superior to society.'[10]

This is a, even *the*, key point in Marxist theory, because it is the point of juncture between theory and practice. On the one hand, it derives its force as a question of theory from the possibility of a world which is, according to one's theoretical preferences, rational, non-alienated, planned, post-ideological, or whatever; in short, a socialist world. But it also immediately raises the total question of agency — which is at once a theoretical and a practical question. In what ways can organization and action by the working class be brought to bear upon the capitalist system, so that it can carry through its role of self-education? In that little question — who shall educate the educators? — is embodied a whole problematic.

If it were the case that Kant never saw a problem here, and that the problem cannot even be stated in terms of his concepts and theoretical outlook, then his significance for Marxism would indeed be minimal. He would be merely an important part of the history of bourgeois theory. *But the fact is that the problem was implicit in his whole theory: he directly posed it and worked hard to find a solution.* The most explicit discussion occurs in one of the most neglected of Kant's mature writings, an essay on history published in 1784.[11] But his proposed

10. Marx and Engels, op. cit., pp. 651–52.

solution, and its theoretical underpinning, are implicit in the whole of his work.

How Men Make History

In the 1784 essay Kant sets out nine Theses, which apply to history the results of his mature investigation into man's nature and capacity for knowledge and morality. The main argument essentially begins with the Third Thesis:

> Nature has willed that man shall produce wholly out of himself everything that goes beyond the mechanical ordering of his animal existence; and that he should partake of no other happiness or perfection than that which he himself, independently of instinct, has created by his own reason.[12]

The crux of this Thesis is the denial of any instinctual basis to man. We are given the opportunities and capacities in general to make of ourselves what we will:

> Man, accordingly, was not to be guided by instinct, not nurtured and instructed with ready-made knowledge; rather he should bring forth everything out of his own resources. Securing his own food, shelter, safety and defence (for which Nature gave him neither the horns of the bull, nor the claws of the lion, nor the fangs of the dog, but hands only), all amusement which can make life pleasant, insight and intelligence, finally even goodness of heart — all this should be wholly his own work.[13]

If it is to be man's own work, the risks are various. Kant discusses the theoretical possibility that we might have remained in a state of 'Arcadian bliss', at such a low level of development that human capacities are hardly developed at all. But, noting that massive development has in fact taken place, Kant seeks to explain the motive force behind change and human social growth. For Kant makes it clear that, even if theoretically 'men make themselves', nonetheless, they decidedly do it 'under conditions not of their own choosing'. In a statement that has all the appearance of paradox, Kant writes:

> The means employed by Nature to bring about the development of all the capacities of men is their antagonism in society, so far as this is, in the end, the cause of a lawful order among men. By 'antagonism' I mean the

11. I. Kant, 'Idea for a Universal History from a Cosmopolitan Point of View', in I. Kant, *On History*, Indianapolis. Henceforth abbreviated as IUH.
12. IUH, p. 13.
13. IUH, p. 14.

unsocial sociability, i.e. their propensity to enter into society, bound together with a mutual opposition which constantly threatens to break up the society.[14]

Thus, after the Third Thesis has denied the presence of significant instincts, the Fourth reinserts a social and an anti-social instinct. Without going into the whole argument, we can locate the resolution of the paradox in the fact that Kant sees social life as the precondition of being human at all. It is the tendency to socialize which makes man more than 'the developed form of his natural capacities'. Nor is Kant's anti-social tendency of the Hobbesian kind: it is a tendency not to disengage from society, but to enter into a specific form of antagonistic social relations. These constitute a specific way of becoming human. But the antagonism is not instinctual or rooted in any basic human nature. It stems from the limited experience of every particular individual, who therefore confronts the world with only a partial understanding. The antagonistic social relations are those in which each individual attempts to make use of other individuals to his or her own end. And that is attempted because the world beyond the individual *appears* governed by alien (social) laws.

This important point connects closely with Kant's ethical theory, which was then in the process of development. A prime version of the Categorical Imperative would be precisely that we should never treat others merely as means to an end, but always as ends in themselves. The substantive implications of this ethical statement need to be disentangled, but it is certainly very revealing for Kant's understanding of history, for his view of antagonistic social relations as decidedly immoral. This does not, however, lead Kant into a simple condemnation. On the contrary, first we must recognize the naturalness of such relations. And having done that, Kant actually applauds them for a most interesting reason:

> Thanks be to Nature, then, for the incompatibility, for heartless competitive vanity, for the insatiable desire to possess and to rule! . . . The natural urges to these, the sources of unsociableness and mutual opposition from which so many evils arise, drive men to new exertions of their forces and thus to the manifold development of their capacities.[15]

Towards a Rational Society

Kant is here taking an enormous stride forward. For his model of

14. IUH, p. 15.
15. IUH, p. 16.

history, deriving from his general philosophy, now admits the naturalness, but not the inevitability, of competitive social relations; recognizes the evil they embody, and also generate; but nonetheless develops a theory of social development. The theory, crudely put, is that even with antagonistic social relations, the degree and richness of social relationships determine the level of possibilities of any individual's personal development. In other words, in order to extend my 'exploitation'[16] of you, I need to *deepen* the social relations between us, not weaken them. Exploitation can increase, rather than reduce, social interdependence; can be the mechanism for the development of human capacities, rather than the source simply of mutual destruction.

Not only does Kant see this vital logic; he also adds the last dimension which is required to make him useful to Marxism. He posits as an essential element — both practically in terms of our acting in the present with an orientation of the future, and theoretically in terms of our capacity to grasp the essential nature of the present — that social antagonism should be capable of being superseded:

> What is the good of esteeming the majesty and wisdom of Creation in the Realm of brute nature . . . if that part of the great stage of supreme wisdom which contains the purpose of all the others — the history of mankind — must remain an unceasing reproach to it?[17]

Kant is insistent that a rational, non-antagonistic society must be possible, if only as a theoretical condition in the light of which we think and act now. Otherwise, he says, Rousseau would be right 'in preferring the state of savages, as long, that is, as the last stage to which the human race must climb is not attained'.[18] Kant's problem therefore was: how is a rational society possible, both theoretically and practically? It is my interpretation that the *Critique of Pure Reason* and the *Critique of Practical Reason*, were largely devoted to its theoretical possibility, and his 'Idea for a Universal History . . . ' to its practical possibility. It can, of course, be argued that Marx's scathing comment is true to the extent that, in the German conditions of the late 18th century, Kant was not really able to go beyond the theoretical possibility of freedom, his consideration of the practical-political mechanisms for its achievement being confined to one essay.

16. That is, my use of you only as means to my end.
17. IUH, p. 25.
18. IUH, p. 21.

The differences between a cooperative society and the present antagonistic society need to be restated. In the present, men form antagonistic social relations in which each attempts to use others to his own ends, that is, as means only. This has the effect of enforcing human development; we become increasingly socialized, and therefore in one sense more humanized, because humanity requires social relationships. But the cause of unsociable, antagonistic relations is not any innate drive; rather, it is that our understanding of the world is limited to the world as it appears. And it *appears* that any progress on my part requires the subjection of you to my will. But the very fact of this reveals a paradox which reason can disentangle. For in subjecting you to my will, it becomes evident that both I and you are conscious agents, more than mere objects of mechanical causation. Therefore, the greater the degree of antagonistic social development, the greater the possibility that reason will discover all the antagonism to be at the level of appearance. Thus reason can show us the possibility of mutual human development on the basis of co-operation — reason here understood as the capacity to have *insight into the way the world could be*.[19]

We are left with a problem of the relation between the world-as-it-is, and the world-as-it-could-be. It is in tackling this problem, which is immediately both theoretical and practical, that Kant predates Marx's statement of the 'educators' problem:

> Man is an animal which, if it lives among others of its kind, requires a master. For he certainly abuses his freedom with respect to other men, and although, as a reasonable being he wishes to have a law which limits the freedom of all, his selfish impulses tempt him, where possible, to exempt himself from them. He thus requires a master, who will break his will, and force him to obey a will that is universally valid, under which each can be free. But whence does he get his master? Only from the human race. But then the master is himself an animal, and needs a master.[20]

Of course the language is that of the 18th-century thinkers, but the problem is that of Marxism. Kant continues:

---

19. This interpretation of reason is also the signal for a whole reinterpretation. Kant's account of reason in the two main Critiques has been singularly misunderstood, almost as another mode of perception which, because it attempts to look at noumena, cannot really see anything at all. But in the case of humanity, the noumenal character to be grasped is a series of *potentials:* man is capable of being free, and rational, and moral. Reason is then a faculty for grasping what is materially possible.
20. IUH, p. 17.

Let him begin it as he will, it is not to be seen how he can procure a magistracy which can maintain public justice and which is itself just, whether it be a single person or a group of several people. For each of them will always abuse his freedom if he has no-one above him to exercise force in accordance with the laws. The highest master should be just in himself, and yet be a man. This task is therefore the hardest of all . . .[21]

. . . but *it is still a task.*

Kant in the end finds the practical achievement of it impossible, or nearly so. He posits its possibility as a necessary condition of living; but finds the difficulties of realization overwhelming. It is in fact quite noticeable how his certainty diminishes at the end of the article, as he tackles the transformation issue. Statements become questions; questions become hesitant, even querulous:

Would it be expected . . . that states . . . should form all sorts of unions which in their turn are destroyed by new impacts, until once, finally, by chance a structure should arise which could maintain its existence — a fortunate accident that could hardly occur? Or are we not rather to suppose that Nature here follows a lawful course in gradually lifting our race from the lower levels of animality to the highest level of humanity . . ? Or perhaps we should prefer to conclude that . . . absolutely nothing, at least, nothing wise, is to issue?[22]

It would indeed be amazing — if I am right that Kant correctly identified a major practical/historical paradox in advance of Marx — if he had gone on to provide a solution.[23] For what enabled Kant to discover the dimensions of this problem was an emergent philosophical anthropology of 'man the maker', still conceived in a partly idealist manner. He lacked all the derived categories of labour, production and class which gave Marx his solution.

There is, of course, a great deal more that needs to be said about Kant's notion of the human construction of history. But we can already see the falsity of Sohn-Rethel's argument that Kant was a metaphysical idealist whose thought, because it was ahistorical, could not encompass the problem of the educators. He is wrong

21. IUH, p. 17.
22. IUH, pp. 19–20.
23. It has been said that Rousseau, who greatly influenced Kant, also found himself in this situation. His General Will, with its metaphysical bases, had to become the theoretical substitute for a practical political will embodied in a specifiable group, precisely because his experience of the world revealed no group or class with the characteristics of both universality and sectional power.

because he has partly misunderstood what Kant was attempting in his Critiques. In particular, both Sohn-Rethel and others who find fatalism and suchlike in Kant wrongly construe the noumenon/phenomenon relation in his thought.

Without going into a long account, we should recall that Kant saw himself as an idealist. We should therefore expect to find a theoretical imbalance between the possibilities of knowledge of the natural and the human world. Benton's sharp remark will only hold against Kant's concept of natural science: 'Kant's distinction between a phenomenal world, open to perception and to knowledge through scientific concepts and methods, and an unknowable world of free subjectivity is, of course, open to serious philosophical objections. The principal difficulty is that the resolution of the problem of freewill and determinism (as well as the other problems of speculative metaphysics) require a good deal to be *said* about the nature of the supposedly unknowable things-in-themselves.'[24]

As I shall show, the world of free subjectivity can have a lot said about it. Kant is insistent upon the special position of the concept of freedom in this respect. And Benton is only partly right in his consequential comment: 'Accordingly, attempts to modify, or even altogether to abandon, Kant's noumenal/phenomenal distinction played a vital role in the development of German philosophy following Kant's death.'[25]

Now, the reasons for the attempts to modify or reject the distinction are not purely philosophical: it was his phrasing of the distinction that enabled Kant to see the possibility of a free, rational world: he *did not* draw a crude separation between them. Indeed, for Kant practical (that is, moral) action could in a sense break down the boundaries between freedom and causality. Thus he writes: 'The concept of freedom is meant to actualize in the sensible world the end proposed by its laws.'[26] Kant specifically connects the possibility of this, and the impossibility of knowing the noumenal character of non-human nature, with his idealism:

Properly, therefore, it was *understanding* — which insofar as it contains constitutive a priori cognitive principles has its special realm and one moreover in the faculty of knowledge — that the Critique, called in a general way that of Pure Reason, was intended to establish in secure but particular possession against all other competitors. In the same way, *reason*, which contains constitutive a priori principles solely in respect of the

24. T. Benton, *Philosophical Foundations of the Three Sociologies*, London 1977, p. 104.
25. Benton, p. 104.
26. I. Kant, *The Critique of Judgement*, Oxford 1952, p. 14.

faculty of desire, gets its holding assigned to it by the Critique of Practical Reason.[27]

Understanding is the Kantian faculty for grasping the world of appearance, by analysing concepts and their relation to experience. Reason is the faculty that can give us insight into the noumenal nature of things, because it analyses and synthesizes concepts in their relation to the totality. But reason is here specifically limited to the faculty of desire, that is, to man as actor.

This demand for a reinterpreation of Kant is not an idle matter. For, as has already been suggested, Kant's system is primarily one of practical, rather than theoretical, reason. He saw the *Critique of Pure Reason* as an exercise in clearing an obstacle from the ground ('like a stone from the path'[28]) before his essential job. And that job was to construct a scientific and human ethic, rooted in the nature of man and the possibility of a rational world. Right at the start of his Practical Reason he insists that the whole of reason is practical. His own preferences were clearly stated: 'Then I will go on to metaphysics, which has only two parts: the metaphysics of nature, and the metaphysics of morals, of which I shall publish the last part first, and I rejoice over it in anticipation.'[29]

The moral philosophy was the heart of Kantianism; and it was a very special moral philosophy. Not at all the formal, contentless Puritan self-flagellation most interpreters would have us believe. On the contrary, as Cassirer notes: 'What is truly permanent in human nature is not any condition *in which* it once existed and *from which* it has fallen; rather it is the goal *for which* and towards which it moves. Kant looks for constancy not in what man *is* but in what he *should be*.'[30] And, more importantly, as I have tried to show, *'could be'*.

The second *philosophical* reason for misunderstanding on this score arises from a failure to appreciate the force of the terms 'noumenon' and 'phenomenon'. It is not simply the case that they designate two alternative worlds; rather, the one is an ordered version of the other. The problem, then, is to trace the way in which *reality appears*. (This, in Marxist terms, is none other than the problem of ideology.)

27. Ibid., p. 4.
28. I. Kant, letter to Herz, quoted in F. van de Pitte, *Kant as Philosophical Anthropologist*, The Hague 1971, p. 37. This excellent book is one of the first to grasp that at the centre of Kant's thought is a perception of a possible future.
29. Quoted in van de Pitte, p. 37.
30. E. Cassirer, *Rousseau, Kant, Goethe*, Princeton 1945, p. 20.

Kant's Legacy for Marxism

Why does all this have to be said in an article on Kant's relation to Marxism? As I argued before, I believe that in many senses the Third Thesis on Feuerbach constitutes the heart of the Marxist problematic. And it is not accidental that Kant discovers the problem, and has at his disposal the theoretical means to move towards a solution. Within the rich texture of Kant's thought there are elements, and in particular a structure, which need preserving in the transformation from idealism to materialism. If we agree with Lukács that Marxism is the theory of proletarian revolution, then two points from Kant become essential to us:

(1) The theory has to contain the possibility of liberation. It is worth recalling Marx's insistence that he had surpassed theoretically not merely Hegelianism, but also the metaphysical materialists of the Enlightenment. And it was the metaphysical materialists who had created the impassable dichotomies of the sort that 'man is born free, but is everywhere in chains'. Who put them on him? Who can take them off? Marxism, as the theory of the liberation of the working class, supplied the answers to these questions. For the working class is the creator, in a crucial sense, of its own exploitation, and therefore has the potential capacity to end it — and thereby free the whole of humanity.

But Marxism has to work as a theory, not just as an assertion; and Kant supplied the essential premises for it to work. These lie within the distinction, and the relation, that Kant draws between noumenon and phenomenon. Freedom in man is both *ground* and *end*: ground, in that, as he says, freedom is the *ratio essendi* of morality; end, in that morality is the *ratio cognoscendi* of freedom. The possibility and realizability of a moral social order is what gives content to freedom, turns it from a mere absence of instinctual determination into a freely constructed social system. What is needed therefore is the materialist equivalent of the concept of freedom in this Kantian sense.

However, the dismantling of the noumenon/phenomenon distinction and relation effectively demolished Kant's solution to empiricism. In empiricism, the present judges the future. The given world is the source of our understanding of possibilities. In Kant, the materially possible future judged the present, and specified the action to be taken in it. It is this fact that re-emphasizes my objection to Benton's suggestion that philisophical faults alone led to the post-Kantian rejection of the distinction and relation. On the contrary, if we take two highly perceptive post-Kantians who make use of Kant in entirely contrary ways — Weber, and Durkheim — we find that it is possible to understand their pessimism and conservatism, and opposition to Marxism, only by tracing their rejection of the Kantian distinction and relation between noumenon and phenomenon.[31]

I believe also that it can be shown by careful 'immanent criticism' (to use an important idea of Lucio Colletti's) that a number of modern interpretations of Marxism fail as possible theories of revolutionary socialism, precisely because they have no materialist equivalent of this concept of freedom, with its intricate theoretical and practical logic.[32]

These are claims, and I am not trying to substantiate them here. But, even if there were not other powerful reasons for re-evaluating the tradition of Kantian interpretation, this would surely be more than enough.

(2) It is perhaps not a trite thing to say that Marxism is a *theory* of revolutionary socialism. As a theory, it must pass critical tests of adequacy; it must also live in a world of competing theories, and have much to say about them.

Since Marxism is opposed to all variants of empiricism, one of whose chief tenets is the preconceptual availability of the world, it needs a theory of concepts, of understanding. As Gramsci put it:

> An enquiry into a series of facts to discover the relations between them presupposes a 'concept' that permits one to distinguish that series from another possible series of facts. How can there take place a choice of facts to be adduced as proof of the truth of one's own assumption if one does not have a pre-existing criterion of choice? But what is this criterion of choice to be, if not something superior to each single fact under enquiry? An intuition, a conception which must be regarded as having a complex history . . .[33]

. . . but also as having *a logical structure.*

In fact, one of the lessons we should draw from Kant is the requirement of systematic structure. Marxism as a theory creates by its

31. I have in fact carried out this exercise for both thinkers, but space obviously forbids its inclusion here.

32. If we take, as a central example, the Althusserian system, I am struck by Simon Clarke's argument ('Althusser's Marxism', circulated in CSE but so far unpublished) that Althusser is in fact a metaphysical materialist, returning to Montesquieu, Smith, and so forth. But it is worth recalling that it was precisely against such that Marx directed the Third Thesis; they had not solved, could not solve, the 'educators' problem. In a sense, then, Althusser is a pre-Kantian, except that, ironically, his thought owes a heavy debt to Hegelian inevitabilism.

33. A. Gramsci, *Selections from the Prison Notebooks*, London 1971, p. 461.

central concepts a number of dilemmas, the compatibility and possibility of historical movement between the apparent contradictories of determinism and freedom, alienation and self-realization, ideology and science, and so on. As a theory, therefore, it needs a structure of concepts that admits and resolves these contradictories into practical historical problems.

Conclusions

Kant is wrongly regarded as a fatalist: he thought of freedom not merely as a Regulative Idea, guiding our penetration of the world of appearance, but also as a material possibility imposing on us the duty to try to realize it. He was not a 'defender of the faith' (though he was religious); and in considering his views here, we should recall the extent to which he was regarded in his own time as atheistically inclined. But most importantly, the positive point in his theory of religion was that God can have ascribed to him/her/it only those characteristics which are derived from our moral life; our perception of God reflects our understanding of morality.

Kant did not draw a rigid distinction between fact and value; he worked theoretically to merge them. He did not produce a timeless, contentless ethic: on the contrary, he showed the necessity for a substantive concept of freedom and social morality. More than that, he was the first to make a clear analysis of 'evil' and to integrate into his theory an understanding of it as a not unnatural aspect of human development. (There is no socialism without capitalism.)

In the light of these and many more points that deserve to be brought out, it should be possible to reconstruct, by way of a materialist critique of this real Kant:

(a) a theory of ideology (which is already implicit in many of Kant's comments, particularly in the *Critique of Practical Reason*);

(b) a theory of science, resolving both logical and historical dimensions;

(c) a resolution of the apparent shifts within the theory and practice of Marxism between inevitabilist and voluntarist orientations;

(d) a powerful base for the critique of specific ideological views.

An Introduction to Derrida

D. C. Wood

In 1967 Derrida made an impressive entrance onto the French intellectual stage by publishing two collections of essays and a short study
of the early Husserl.[1] The importance of this intervention stemmed
from the fact that while he endorsed the critical distance from phenomenology that was de rigeur for all pan-structuralists, he simultaneously developed a critique of the Saussurean concept of the sign
on which 'structuralism' rested. And as he considers his work political
and 'not inconsistent with Marxism', while maintaining a carefully
tuned distance from any particular Marxist or radical texts, he has
posed a considerable problem of assessment ever since.

To understand the position from which this tissue of distances was
set up, we need to appreciate how he appropriated and fused into a
new way of reading, the work of a number of his predecessors. These
include the accounts of the closure or exhaustion of metaphysics
developed by Nietzsche and Heidegger, the radical critique of the
concept of meaning that Saussure's semiology implicitly opens up,
and the Freudian critique of the enthroned subject of consciousness.

As formative intellectual elements these do not, however, pick out
Derrida from the Parisian crowd. What does distinguish him is the
way he organizes these elements. He uses the critique of metaphysics
to develop, by rethinking the classical concept of the sign, a new
'concept' of *writing,* which functions as the basis of a new diagnostic
programme. What he gains from it is a more direct access to the
metaphysical alignments and commitments both of his con-
temporaries (Lévinas, Foucault, Lacan, Lévi-Strauss) and of many
'classic' texts (including those of Plato, Rousseau, Hegel, Husserl and

---

1. *La Voix et le Phénomène*, Paris 1967 (E.T. *Speech and Phenomena*, 1973); *De la
Grammatologie*, Paris 1967 (E.T. *Of Grammatology 19*, 1976); *L'Ecriture et la Différence*,
Paris 1967.

Heidegger).

Derrida's position is based on the belief that there are two radically different ways of understanding language which parallel Husserl's distinction between indication and expression.[2] One can understand language as deriving its 'meaning' from some underlying semantic layer, such as experience, consciousness, or even the Platonic world of forms. Or one can understand its meaning as self-constituted, brought about by the play of differences between terms, by their repetition, without reference to some field of sublinguistic guarantees.[3] The alternative to an expressivist or foundationalist account of language is one that treats meaning not as the basis of language but as an effect of language. On such a view language is understood 'primarily' as *writing*.

Now, this term has been the source of a certain misunderstanding, or non-understanding. It does not in principle involve any claim about the relative ranking of the spoken or written word.[4] Derrida's championing of *writing* is an intervention that opposes itself not to speech but to speech considered (however silently) to be privileged, as linked by a hot-line to meaning.[5] To announce that speech is a form of writing is simply to deprive it of this metaphysical status, and to assimilate it to the articulatory condition of all meaning, for which the term 'writing' stands. The violence done to our linguistic reflexes by the apparently perverse inversions found in Derrida's discussion of the relation between speech and writing is strictly therapeutic. When we discuss his procedure of *deconstruction*, we will gain some idea of the general strategy involved.

But if Derrida is not in principle committed to a concern for the sort of writing found in books, it is to this area that his work is largely confined. To say that his work is heavily parasitical on other writing is not just to utter a truth about all writing, but to say something special about his. Other thinkers have intellectual debts, take issue with the published views of others, even try to refute them. And even if, like the later Wittgenstein, one is concerned to come to terms with people's linguistic intuitions in the field of everyday speech, one is still using a public language. But Derrida's modes of parasitism are quite other. In a whole series of texts, of which *Marges* and *Glas* are the prime examples, he doesn't just feed off his prey, he hatches his eggs inside

2. See *Speech and Phenomena*, op. cit.
3. Cf. the distinction between logical and rhetorical modes of language in Newton Garver's preface to *Speech and Phenomena*.
4. See, for instance, Plato's *Phaedrus*, the locus classicus of this view.
5. See, e.g., *Of Grammatology*, p. 55 of French edition.

their flesh. Sartre once talked about the worm at the heart of Being. The possibility of a Derridean inworming lies at the heart of every text.

If there is one principle behind this inworming it is a basic questioning of authorial identity. What is put in question is any principle that (a) guarantees the distinction between the writer and critic, host and parasite and (b) guarantees the unity through time of the critic himself. This questioning has its origin (and not just a temporal one) in the philosophical problem about the nature of personal identity (the theological problem of the nature of the soul). In France this problem appears not only in a defence of the concept of a person as an ethical a priori — in the Christian tradition especially — but also in the phenomenological concept of the subject, which in either its transcendental form (Husserl) or its existential version (Sartre) seems to embody a commitment to the a priori unity and continuity of the subject which, to many a post-Nietzschean nose, is something short of metaphysical. Identity is the atheist's plastic soul.

By using the term 'writing', Derrida is bringing the problem of meaning back to language for its solution. (*Back* to language because it started as a problem about general names.) It is by a parallel 'linguistic turn' — that is, a turn towards language — that we can understand the transformation being performed on the metaphysical problem of personal identity. We can understand Derrida as endorsing, at the level of 'writing', the criticisms that Heidegger had already made of the classical Subject. These criticisms included a rejection of the subject's a priori unity through time and of its metaphysical independence from the 'external' world. What now replaces the problem of personal identity, in the new linguistic idiom, is the problem of textuality. The fact that dreams display such textual articulation is a symptom of the theoretical displacement of the 'enthroned conscious subject'[6] that this linguistic turn involves. Indeed, even consciousness will be seen to have a structure based on the sign. This is the theme of Derrida's first book, and I shall now begin to explain in more detail how some of the ideas I have discussed have been presented in specific Derridean texts.

The Text and Meaning

Derrida's first published work of importance was devoted to the work

6. On this displacement Lacan is the obvious source. See also *Speech and Phenomena*, op. cit.

of Husserl, whom Oedipal fingers point to as the father of phenomenology. His first unostentatious foray into the field of Husserl
criticism began with an introduction of 171 pages to his accompanying translation of Husserl's late, and much shorter essay, *The Origin of
Geometry*. The key word in the title that attracted his interest was
'origin', and it is no coincidence that he should also write on
Rousseau's *Essay on the Origin of Languages*, and, later, an introduction
to Condillac's *Essay on the Origin of Human Knowledge*.[7] The English
reader may not know quite how to assess Derrida's selection of objects
of interest. Many of us will never have looked at Condillac, and
neither Husserl's nor Rousseau's essay is the first piece one would
normally read in trying to understand their work. Matters are a little
different in France. But even if Condillac is the Locke of French
philosophy, Derrida focuses on parts of the 'essay' which are not
normally taken as central. We can understand Derrida's purpose,
however, without great prior knowledge of these texts. They are
simply vehicles by which he exemplifies his practice of reading.

In each case the reference to an origin, even when it is presented in
a historical context — and after all geometry, one supposes, did start
sometime — is a reference to a point or a site possessing a primary
epistemological power, a pure source of meaning, a ground with
which we can come into direct contact. Under the guise of a history we
find metaphysics. They trace the past to find a *presence*, a point beyond
which we need not go in trying to give a foundation to language, to
geometry, to knowledge, a point which it may still be possible to
reactivate. What Derrida shows is that in each case the theories and
models employed are shaped by this theme of *presence*.[8]

One of the interests of this analytical procedure is that it allows
Derrida to assimilate rather different, indeed otherwise opposed
points of view. Husserl's position, for example, founds meaning on
intuition, while Rousseau founds it on feeling. Yet they still share a
common assumption about what ranks as an adequate account. In
fact, such an assumption is the basis of their conflict. An adequate
account of meaning has to discover a source which is non-
conventional, non-artificial, non-constructed, but primitive. For
Rousseau this means 'natural', and for Husserl it means 'pure'.
Rousseau posits a natural language of cries, Husserl a pure order of
experience. Derrida is offering us here not a scholarly summary of
their theories but a metaphysically symptomatic *reading* in which he

7. See, respectively, *L'Ecriture et la Difference* and *L'Archeologie du Frivole*, Paris 1973.
8. See *Of Grammatology*, p. 12, for the manifold meanings of 'presence'.

displays certain forms of theoretical appeal. It would be a mistake to think of this discovery of a ground, of a centre, of what Derrida calls a *presence* simply as a detached interest in the form of theories. The metaphysical or, as he calls it, the logocentric tradition can be seen as a tradition of inviable textual *authority*. We are referring not just to the traditional authoritative texts such as bibles, law books, rule books etc, but to the legitimation structure of certain apparently innocent texts. The tracing back of conclusions to points, or presuppositions that cannot be questioned because of their privilege, hidden by the metaphysical value that they embody, is in fact the exposing of a textual power, a power given authority by the metaphysical privilege of presence. We can perhaps understand metaphysics in Derrida's account as the legitimation of textual power. The attack on the privilege of presence parallels the political attack on the divine right of kings. I take up this line of thought again later.

What I have said so far is thoroughly schematic. I do not apologize for this and I shall return with another simple schematism a little later, but we still ought to give some illustrations of how Derrida actually goes about the business of uncovering logocentrism in his chosen texts. I will take two classic cases, of Husserl and Saussure, for his account of these thinkers explains how he is situated in a complex space between and beyond both phenomenology and structuralism. Derrida began his patricidal exercise on Husserl, as I have mentioned. Husserl's *Logical Investigations*,[9] a long and systematic attempt to provide for logic and what was called logical grammar (the supposed a priori structure of language) a foundation that is neither purely formalistic nor psychological, begins with what Derrida rightly calls a 'portentous distinction' between two different senses of the word 'sign'. We can understand by 'sign' both 'expression' and 'indication'.

Before we explain what Husserl means by this distinction, it is worth recalling the theoretical commitments he had already made. He had been attacked by Frege for the psychologism of his first work, and was trying this time to ensure that no traces of the empirical remained in his account of the foundations of logic and language. Later in *Ideas* (1912), the exclusion of the merely empirical was to be accomplished by a kind of epistemological screening procedure, the phenomenological reduction. Here, with regard to what we might call the raw material of logic — relations of signification — the distinction he draws between two sorts of sign serves the same function at the

9. E. Husserl, *Logical Investigations*, London 1970.

semantic level.

Those signs he calls 'indications' include both natural and conventional signs, that is, both causal or similarity relations (smoke/fire is a causal example) and arbitrary linguistic relations (like that of 'chair' to a chair). These cannot be the basis of the ideal 'sciences' with which he is concerned because they lack *necessity*. They are just links by which the mind happens to move from one thing to another. Husserl thinks of relations of indication as external, superficial, so much epistemological dross. What has to be carefully separated and described phenomenologically, is that class of signs he calls 'expressions'. These have an intimate relation of direct acquaintance with what they 'mean', and the paradigm of such an acquaintance is our own inner experience on uttering words to ourselves, perhaps silently.

This involves Husserl in a view of the social employment of language as a derivative and secondary phenomenon with no contribution of its own to the production of meaning. As the public formulation of one's ideas in language involves one in the use of indicative signs (a public language consisting of arbitrary relationships between words and things), Husserl insists on the need to conduct his enquiry into ideal meanings at the level of the expressive signs constituted in 'solitary mental life', prior to their taking on an external linguistic form, however necessary that might be for communication. Husserl, in summary, thinks he can and must bracket out the impure, external, empirical aspects of signification, leaving the pure ideal aspects available for internal and immediate inspection by a pure consciousness. If we appear to be making a great deal of the indication/expression distinction, it is because Husserl devoted the first of his *Logical Investigations* to the distinction, and hung the rest of them on it. And Derrida hangs Husserl on it.

Derrida approaches Husserl's position here at two levels. The first is an ironic one: to insist that the separability of the ideal from the empirical in the form of these two types of signification is a *presupposition* that Husserl makes. And as phenomenology takes presuppositionlessness to be a founding value, there is something of an inconsistency here. Derrida also recognizes in this presupposition, and particularly in the way Husserl appeals to a privileged sphere (pure consciousness) to establish the independence of expression from indication, the most basic metaphysical theme of presence, in its particular form of the presence of meaning to consciousness. As Husserl is dedicated to the elimination of metaphysics, which he thought of as the cause of most of the sterile debates in the history of philosophy, this criticism is one to which phenomenology is peculiarly sensitive.[10]

Derrida does not just assert the metaphysical nature of Husserl's appeal, he argues for an alternative account of the sign and of meaning, which would destroy the credibility of Husserl's privileged 'presence'. The idea of presence is a very powerful one. Its power rests on the way it combines a spatial and a temporal sense, a here and a now in a single value. And the appeal to it as an epistemological ultimate has, dare we say it, an immediate plausibility. We usually rely on what we can see in front of us. If the literal visual cases of seeing are subject to sceptical doubts, we would eliminate these doubts, it might seem, if we restricted ourselves to the kind of 'seeing' with which consciousness apprehends its objects. And the problems scepticism has with memory (what is only remembered is not immediately available and so subject to doubt) can be solved by sticking to what *is* immediately given at an *instant* of time. Derrida demonstrates, however, that the immediate plausibility of the value of presence does not survive closer inspection.

Central to Husserl's account of the non-empirical status of language, logic and philosophy — all of them 'ideal' disciplines —was the concept of ideality. He understood the ideality of a term, say, or a sentence, as the possibility of its infinite repetition. Derrida, however, interprets the notion of infinite repeatability extensionally —that is, he insists on chasing it out into a real infinity of operations, which of course can never be 'given'. And so it follows that we can never be acquainted with 'ideality'. If we then say, as Husserl does, that series are completed in the imagination, then we are faced with a problem that the imagination is linked to the very empirical world Husserl has fought to exclude. The final blow is struck when Derrida juxtaposes Husserl's assumption that there could be an instant, a pure temporal presence in which this confrontation with meaning takes place, with Husserl's own fully developed account of time-consciousness.[11] And here a real inconsistency appears. Husserl gives us an account of the

10. It is worth pointing out that Derrida is not the first French philosopher to have criticized Husserl's account of a purified consciousness. Sartre and Merleau-Ponty both made this a measure of their distance from transcendental phenomena. Derrida's distinction is to have undertaken this criticism by an appeal not to the impossibility of 'bracketing out' existence, but to the irremediable other-relatedness (in many different senses) of the sign, which is the structure of consciousness. Derrida would claim a common inspiration in Heidegger, but I cannot help wondering about a more direct relationship to the 'vulgar' Sartre.

11. See E. Husserl, *The Phenomenology of Internal Time Consciousness*, Indianapolis 1966.

purified structure of time which makes quite clear that there can be no pure present. Any 'now' is shadowed by the past, and casts a light forward on the future. The 'now' is from the outset structured in terms of the past and future. There is no pure present. Consequently there is no temporal site, says Derrida, for the privilege Husserl has accorded to presence.

As well as pointing out internal flaws in Husserl's analysis, Derrida introduces an account of the nature of signs which is thoroughly at odds with the view that they are merely the external form given to meanings. Signs relate to other signs, by opposition, by derivation, by a whole 'play' of differences. All these 'horizontal' relationships make nonsense of the 'vertical' model of Husserl's which ties signs down to individual meanings. To retain that model, we would have to suppose that the 'horizontal' relationships we have mentioned, such as opposition, are to be found at the level of meanings, but in that case it would be impossible for them to be discretely grasped in conscious acts, because in the act of immediate grasping, their relationships to other, absent signs would have been excluded.

Meaning for Derrida is always mediated, never immediate. And by mediation is meant not just a deferred presence which finally comes, but a permanent state of deferment. The play of differences that Derrida substitutes for Husserl's immediacy of presence can never be captured in a system, can never be represented.[12] The wish for such a structured semantics is nothing but the reappearance of the belief in presence at another level.

Derrida has cut a great swathe through Husserl. One could argue that he has not given Husserl a fair run for his money — perhaps Husserl could have reconciled the two accounts of time, drawn after all from different periods and contexts; perhaps he would have disputed the whole extensionalist interpretation of ideality by a more careful account of the idealizing functions of the imagination. Perhaps Husserl was saying many other things that Derrida has missed. But there is no doubt that Husserl, as they say, will never be 'the same' again.

In his critique of Husserl, Derrida used not only the Heideggerian view of metaphysics as the interpretation of Being as presence, but also the Saussurean account of the sign. It was the externality of the

12. Can it even be captured in a single article? A number of Derrida's essays are dedicated to an interventionist exposition and elaboration of a substitute of non-meaning, or difference. *Difference* (in *Speech and Phenomena*, op. cit.), Derrida's 'answer' to Heidegger's 1929 text *What is Metaphysics?*, is the classic case.

sign to itself, the claim that all signs are what they are by their relation to other signs, that Derrida finally substituted for Husserl's account of language. And this is essentially a Saussurean doctrine. But how can this be if Derrida, as we have said, also attacks Saussure? The time is ripe for an account of Derrida's Saussure.

Saussure is the main focus of the essay *Linguistics and Grammatology*.[13] The way Derrida begins his study of Saussure is characteristic. If we grant the expanded scope of the concept of writing that we have already introduced, then one might imagine that just as semiology, for instance, is the general science of signs, there could be a *science* of writing. This, however, raises certain reflexive problems, problems that the subject matter of such a science throws up for the status of the enterprise *as* science. Firstly, might it not be that the rigour and objectivity of science as such presuppose writing as 'the condition of the possibility of ideal objects'? Secondly, if we grasp the appearance of the science of writing as the product of particular historical conditions, are we not then confronted with the dependence of history on the possibility of writing? Thirdly, a brief exploration of the subject would reveal that the concept of science is dependent on a highly determined relationship between speech and writing. The general difficulty, then, is that writing does not simply serve to define the scope of its science as an obedient subject matter should, but is the problematic ground for the idea of science as such.

Given these problems — which are genuinely fascinating — we might perhaps wonder whether linguistics, supposed after all to be a general science of language, might not be some help.

On the contrary, as the reader may have guessed, the hope that Saussure might be able to come to our rescue is doomed to disappointment. What is at stake in understanding Husserl is the status of Saussure's work as science. And Saussure is immediately suspected of having made a grave though not original assumption about the relationship between speech and writing, a presupposition which is nothing short of metaphysical. It is not the first time that Saussure has been charged with having invented a pseudo-science.[14] But Derrida's reasons for making this charge are original. He shows that the scien-

---

13. In *Of Grammatology*, op. cit.
14. To give a home-grown example: we find Ogden and Richards opening *The Meaning of Meaning* (London 1923, p. 4) with the objection that Saussure's *langue* — the supposed object of linguistics — is a fiction, created by the 'primitive impulse to infer from words some object for which it stands'. Despite the real differences from Ogden and Richards, it is fascinating that Derrida also attributes to Saussure an error based upon a metaphysical conception of language.

tificity of Saussure's choice of an object of study — which turns out to be *spoken* languages — rests on his identification of the spoken sound with meaning (thought). This phonocentrism can achieve the integrity of its object only by treating writing as merely an external, secondary, supplementary addition to the spoken word. What Husserl claimed about language as such — its externality (to thought/meaning/consciousness/expression) — appears in Saussure as the relationship of writing to speech. Writing is just an external notation. Derrida shows that this exclusion of writing from linguistics is the product of an attempt to draw the boundaries of linguistics in such a way that it be a closed system. But the principle on which writing is excluded from consideration — its mere externality — is one which is contradicted by the extraordinary sixth chapter of the *Course in General Linguistics*,[15] in which Saussure inveighs against the damage done to language by its transcription into writing, a sort of dead skin that corrupts. Writing is seen as a danger to the purity of the system of speech. Derrida points out, too, the extraordinary language of contamination, pathology, perversity associated with writing, in opposition to the natural purity of spoken language. This contradiction — between writing as empty externality and writing as source of contamination — is symptomatic. Saussure is unable consistently to theorize the primacy of speech over writing. For Derrida this ranking is based on the privilege of presence that Saussure as a representative of the logocentric tradition accords to the spoken word.

What is Derrida's response? Saussure is part of a tradition that needs deconstruction. This consists of: 'Deconstructing this tradition will therefore not consist of reversing it, of making writing innocent. Rather of showing why the violence of writing does not *befall* an innocent language. There is an originary violence of writing because language is first, in a sense I shall gradually reveal, writing.'[16]

The rejection of a simple reversal is a lesson learned from Heidegger and Nietzsche. If we are trying to change the framework within which opposed terms appear, then a mere reversal will not be adequate, it will merely be a repetition of the original structure. So when Derrida shows how language is 'first . . . writing', it is 'in a sense' he must explain, a new sense.

To explain it, we might look at some of the patterns of Derrida's thought so far. In the texts we have already referred to, what is particularly striking is that he is constantly pointing to ways in which

15. F. Saussure, *Course in General Linguistics*, London 1974.
16. *Of Grammatology*, op. cit.

these texts are organized according to metaphysically loaded patterns of space and time. He defines logocentrism, for example, as 'the exigent, powerful, systematic and irrepressible desire for a "transcendental signified" '.[17] A transcendental signified is a meaning which would exist outside any system of signs, and 'would place a reassuring end to the reference from sign to sign'. In other words, it would end regresses in the search for the real meaning. A philosopher's stone. When Nietzsche said that we had not got rid of God if we still believed in grammar, it was just this structure of a privileged first point to a series that he was talking about. Here Derrida has located a constitutive feature of metaphysics — the metaphysical organization of an ideal temporal series so as to produce a meaning, at the level of the text. And in the same way, he shows how one of the most basic topological structures — the relationship between inside and outside — is loaded to carry a metaphysical weight. If it is the case (and it would take me an argument for which I have neither time nor space to develop here) that there are such analogues of spatiotemporal organization in, at least, all theoretical texts, then the assignment of a privilege, or an orientation to such structures, silently, or invisibly, allows them to carry a metaphysical message.

If this sort of analysis is correct, one would expect Derrida to have something to say about space and time in the textual sense, and of course he does. Most of his 'constructive' as well as his deconstructive essays contain some account of, or at least a trace of an allusion to, an alternative theory of language, one which can only function as a substitute for the one he is dismantling for those who have managed to shake off the 'powerful desire' to which we have just alluded. Kant's solution was to demonstrate to us the proper limits of reason, so that reason would then cease to stray with the slightest hope of success beyond those bounds, like a trained dog that will not pass an open gate. Derrida's solution is to intervene with a new set of terms, and a new account of the spatiotemporality of the sign to 'underpin' it. Some of this can be found in the remainder of this essay on Saussure. But the best source is the essay *Differance*. It is a difficult essay and not a little eccentric, but with some priming it is well worth reading. His explanations of the packing and unpacking of the term 'differance' allow one to locate him in a history of 'influences'[18] and to grasp his alternative spatiotemporalization of the textual meaning.

I said above that *Differance* is Derrida's answer to Heidegger's

17. Ibid., p. 49.
18. In *Speech and Phenomena*, p. 130.

lecture *What is Metaphysics?* I did not mean that it was a conscious reply, but that it occupies a parallel place in his writing, that it is even more outrageously 'brilliant', and that it presents many of the same problems of assessment. The Heidegger lecture is all about *Nothing* (which is neither a thing, nor simply nothing), while Derrida's lecture is about Differance (which is neither a word nor a concept). And both offer accounts of the role of their 'terms' which sound like new transcendental roles, while this status is vigorously denied. There are many more things which should be said about the influence of Heidegger here, but they will have to be deferred for the time being. Let us now try to summarize what is going on in this essay.

We must understand that 'difference' (with an 'e') is itself derived from the French word 'différer', which already embodies a combined spatiotemporal sense in its two meanings 'to differ/differentiate' and 'to defer'. 'Differ' or 'differentiate' are understood as spatial in the sense of involving differences that are most naturally represented on some sort of spatial grid. Derrida transforms 'difference' (with an 'e') into 'differance' with an 'a' to mark a difference between his term and the one he is modifying. Marking the difference with an 'a' is something of a serious joke. If we remember that Derrida's project can be viewed as the establishment of the primacy of 'writing' over 'speech', when the latter is understood logocentrically, then the fact that the difference between 'difference' and 'differance' is only visible and not audible is Derridean wit. Why 'a'? Think first of the ABC . . . Has not 'a' a sort of privilege? And Lacan's 'a' for 'autre' (otherness). Or 'a' for 'arche' — origin or first point. 'a' may not be defined, but it is not unmotivated and such an unfinished series of allusions is just the sort of 'meaning' that 'differance' allows. If we are not happy with the sort of ways in which he introduces 'differance', it is because we hanker after something which could be properly defined like a concept. But that is to fall back into the logocentrist account of language of which differance announces the limit, if it cannot tell the end. With all the subtle reflexivities and theoretical embodiments of the term differance, it is really a very brutal way of nose-rubbing in the materiality of language. But at the same time it clearly does connect to all the themes we have described. The way Derrida puts it, it sounds like a tin-opener: 'it opens up the very space in which . . . philosophy produces its system and its history.'[19] It performs this role by being carefully used in such a way that it cannot be thought in terms of the traditional oppositions constitutive of that space, so that it can never

19. Ibid., p. 135.

legitimate those forms of blindness that philosophy has necessarily taken so seriously.

Derrida distinguishes the two senses of differance as spacing and temporizing.[20] Insofar as the traditional concept of the sign has involved the representation of a presence (e.g. a thing or a meaning) in its absence, breaking out of that conception will involve us in dropping our commitment to that presence which is deferred, and in understanding deferment without implicit reference to a final realization. We can understand differance in its sense of 'spacing' by referring to Saussure's account of the differential character of signs. Signs have their value by the differences that relate them to other signs, an explanation dispensing with any fixed or privileged point. Or 'in language there are only differences and no positive terms', as Saussure put it. What Derrida extracts here is the odd way in which Saussure's principle of difference seems to be of a different order from that of the signs that it accounts for. As differance incorporates this Saussurean sense, we can understand it as a 'play of differences', a play which, while making concepts possible, is not itself a concept.

Derrida cannot, however, bring himself to say that it is an activity, nor that it has effects. That would be to attribute to it the function of a new ground or founding principle of a metaphysical order. And then all would have been in vain, the game lost. He christens the non-effect of this non-cause the 'trace'. He cannot avoid the use of metaphysical terms to explain himself, but his commitment to them is only an expediency, part of a deconstructive strategy. It is impossible to do without them, but the implication is that one can use them to contest the very system of which they are a part. This reference to strategy is cashed out not only in relation to the future but also in terms of the whole chain of terms with which differance can already be linked, drawn from his other texts.[21] So differance, neither a word nor a concept, takes its place in a guerrilla army of similar 'terms' none of which are exactly synonyms, but each of which shares the job of displacing the logocentric competition and disordering the field in which they are placed. Summaries, strictly writing, are impossible, and summaries of summaries are subject to the law of even more diminishing returns. For that reason I shall leave the very rich second part of *Differance* for unguided exploration. What Derrida does is to

20. The English translator entirely misses the distinction that Derrida makes between *temporizing* (playing for time?) and *temporalizing*. Compare *Speech and Phenomena*, p. 136, n. 7, with *La Voix et le Phénomène*, p. 47.

21. For a very useful list of references to Derrida's terminological exposition, see *Speech and Phenomena*, p. 142, n. 6.

reveal the campaign contributions of Hegel, Nietzsche, Heidegger, Freud and Levinas, in a tantalizing collection of trailers for more important occasions.

So far we have concentrated on some of the more accessible routes to the Derridean heights. But this does not exhaust the field. In particular, it should be stressed that Derrida writes texts in which the classical authorial function is abandoned, in which the author as friend who explains what he is doing, who presents his ideas with ease of comprehension in mind, who at least plays at producing a classical text — this author has left the scene. *Glas* is the extreme case,[22] but the principle of withdrawing guarantees of unambiguous textual identity is one distributed throughout his work. The further principle of *exemplifying* his theory of writing in his practice of writing is inevitable given its radical nature, and yet makes for considerable difficulty in reading him. The reason he has to exemplify his theories performatively is to be found in his sympathetic account of Hegel's problems with prefaces.[23] Prefaces to philosophical texts attempt the impossible, for texts cannot be summarized.[24] The summary is simply a different text. There is no *meaning* that can be boiled down. The attempt to do so just leads to its evaporation. Consequently there is an irreducible aspect of demonstration or 'showing' or *practice* about Derrida's work, and a showing in the form of an articulated doing.

I have so far tried to keep fairly close to the ground. But now I would like to take up a certain distance from Derrida, and pose some questions for him, to which I shall offer certain answers. There is no pure distance, however, only distance within a particular space.

Deconstruction and its Implications

Where does Derrida stand in relation to other sorts of radical theory and practice? I shall raise some general problems based on the work we have already considered, and try to answer them in part by reference to his published interviews. In trying to come to terms with the political dimension of Derrida's writing, I will make a provisional distinction between on the one hand the question of Derrida's theory of reading, and its relationship to a Marxist reading of philosophy, and on the other, the wider political relevance of Derrida's work. I will begin with the first question.

22. *Glas*, Paris 1974.
23. See 'Hors Livre', in *La Dissemination*, Paris 1972.
24. Cf. R. Barthes, 'Writers, Intellectuals, Teachers', in *Image, Music, Text*, London 1977: 'The summary is a dislike of writing.'

I will take it for granted that if there is any single method that captures Derrida's theory of reading, it is the practice of what he calls 'deconstruction'. While accounts of this can be found in a number of places in his work, perhaps the most important is an account of what he calls its 'general economy' in the title interview of *Positions* with Jean-Louis Houdebine and Guy Scarpetta.[25]

The subject matter of deconstruction on any particular occasion is a text, either a philosophical text in the traditional sense, or a theoretical text with critical pretensions such as Saussure's *Cours*. The local aim is to display the latent metaphysical structure of the text, according to a theory of what constitutes metaphysics (the privileging of some 'presence' or other) and then to transform it. The deconstruction of a particular text derives its wider meaning from a neo-Heideggerian account of the history of Western thought, in which it is claimed that this entire system of thought, with a few heroic exceptions, is a kind of internal debate employing certain fixed conceptual oppositions, and is essentially *finite*, that is to say, has describable limits. Derrida's forte is to apply his method to texts which themselves take up a severely critical attitude to their own tradition, and to show that these texts are nonetheless naive in their understanding of that tradition, that they repeat the errors they criticize in a disguised way.

Deconstruction is a critical method of displaying the latent metaphysical structure of texts, which is distinctive in the way it tries to avoid falling into the same traps itself, even if this is to some extent unavoidable. In the interview we mentioned above Derrida's account of deconstruction is directed to this complex problem of how to transform a text without merely endorsing the wider framework to which its terms belong: 'One would have to avoid, at one and the same time, a simple *neutralization* of the binary oppositions of metaphysics and simply remaining (*résider*) inside, and so confirming the closed field of these oppositions.'[26] In many respects this is just updated Nietzsche so far. In order to prevent one's critical enterprise from being aborted in this way, Derrida distinguishes two phases of the deconstructive strategy. The first he gives a name to — *reversal*. The second we will call *transformation*.

1. Firstly, why 'reversal'? What is reversed? 'In a classical philosophical opposition [and it is out of oppositions that texts are structured — DCW] we do not find a peaceful co-existence between the two sides, but a violent hierarchy. One of the two terms dominates

---

25. *Positions*, Paris 1972. English translation in *Diacritics*, Winter 1972 and Spring 1973.
26. Ibid. My translation.

the other (axiologically, logically, etc) occupies the higher place. To deconstruct the opposition one must first of all, at a given moment, reverse the hierarchy.'

So, if we were confronted with a text promoting idealism, working with a loaded opposition between the ideal and the material, the first move would be to reverse this hierarchy, to argue for the priority of the material, etc. If instead of doing this one were merely to transcend the opposition straight away, then: 'One passes too quickly without giving the first opposition much consideration, to a neutralization which, practically speaking, would leave the first field as it was, depriving one of any means of effectively intervening in it.'

Reversal, even if naive in the last analysis, is at least a move *in the game*. It is strategically justified if one can use it as the first move in changing the game. It is important that Derrida finds it natural at this point to draw a practical analogy: 'We know what the practical (and, in particular, the political) effects have been of leaping immediately beyond all opposition, and of protests in the simple form of neither/ nor . . .' Derrida is not in favour of transcendental politics. And yet this determinate negation of the hierarchical organization of one concept's relation to another is useless by itself. 'The hierarchy of the dual opposition always reconstitutes itself. To hold onto this stage one needs the second stage.'

2. The second stage — transformation — corresponds to what I earlier described as Derrida's hatching his eggs in his host. The aim of stage two is to prevent the old opposition from simply re-establishing itself, by putting a conceptual spanner in the works. 'This involves operating further on the terrain and in the interior of the deconstructed system. One must also, by this double writing, carefully stratified, displaced and displacing, mark the distance between the inversion which, by deconstructing the sublimating or idealizing genealogy, brings it lower, and, on the other hand, the irruptive emergence of a new "concept", one which no longer allows itself (not that it ever did) to be understood on the earlier ground.' So it becomes clear that inversion or reversal is only a preliminary to a more radical reorganization of the conceptual field brought about by the introduction of a new term.

Derrida's concept of 'writing' is a good case in point. The first stage of his deconstruction of the privilege of speech is to privilege writing instead. The second stage is to redefine writing, if only by use, so as to include speech and indeed any other such articulation. The first stage brings about an engagement with the present field, the second stage aims at transforming it so that it cannot re-form into the old pattern.

He imports into the field concepts which are 'indecidables' from the point of view of the old field, and which, to be handled at all, require that the work of deconstruction be left intact.

Many of his essays place these new terms into a new textual practice, so that they acquire by example imitable patterns of use, recognizable functions, if not quite meanings. 'Differance', which he originally claimed was neither a 'word' nor a 'concept' because of the unwanted presuppositions that can be read into these innocent terms, he now concedes has become a word!

But if we now have a clearer picture of least the 'general economy' of deconstruction, how should we assess it? I would first like to point out two quite contrasting aspects of this method, which, united, give it power. Firstly, it is a highly *formal* method of criticism, and second, it is nonetheless guided by considerations of strategy which are thoroughly *practical* (in a limited sense). It is formal in the sense that Derrida is concerned with the *structure* of philosophical texts, or with reading a structure in them which betrays the imbalances and hierarchies that are grist to his mill. At this level there is not much to choose between Derrida and other philosophers with a general view of the history of philosophy, except perhaps the ingenuity and originality of his analyses. The difference comes at the second level, with his strategies for forcing a permanent change in the ways we read not just the texts he has chosen but theoretical texts in general, including, as we shall see, the texts of the Marxist tradition. For it is clear that these strategies have analogues, not to say models in what seem to be extra-textual struggles. But are they? There is nothing, Derrida has said, 'hors texte'. We will return to this question.

My analytical separation of the formal and practical aspects of deconstruction has severe limits. One of the most revealing features of Derrida's writing is the use he makes, even in describing what I have called the formal strands of this method, of militaristic and 'political' language. 'Peaceful co-existence', 'violent hierarchy', 'dominate', 'structure of conflict' even 'strategy' itself. We have already learned from Derrida that metaphors are never innocent.

We can perhaps understand the force of these terms, but how do we assess them? One might think of them simply as a rhetorical enhancement, which perhaps reflects Derrida's own unhappy consciousness of his own political irrelevance or impotence. But more plausible is the view that politics and struggle are inseparable from the rethinking of language and writing on Derridean lines, and that one can use the sharpened sense these terms can acquire in their use to describe a strategy of interventionist reading, to reaccentuate their relevance in conceptualizing and structuring other forms of political action.

If not wholly accurate, this second reading of Derrida's language is closer than the first. It is clear that he thinks the form in which certain problems of radical transformation occur at the level of rethinking writing is one from which we can learn a great deal. Let me illustrate this point further. At the end of his paper *The Ends of Man*[27] he gives us a distinction between two deconstructive strategies: the first, which he associates with Heidegger, involves the kind of inworming or internal subversion we have just described; the second involves a kind of break, a standing apart, a refusal to participate, the invention of one's own dance, laughter . . . There is something of Nietzsche in this account (and a bit less in the first). Derrida suggests that both can be used, and even intermingled. The point is that both are solutions to a problem, of how to overcome what I would call the conservative logic of system recuperation, that has a very distinct political analogue. The absorption and toleration of dissent characteristic of Western 'democracy' and the development of strategies to prevent such recuperation has, for example, been one of the central themes of the post-war Frankfurt School. Indeed, Derrida's remarks about the illusions of freedom of speech at the beginning of his delivery of that paper could have come straight from Marcuse, for all their other differences. The illusions of opposition, originality, 'revolution' which litter the history of logocentric philosophy offer Derrida an ideal field in which to develop the vocabulary of escape from the seemingly inescapable, the very predicament so often felt by those engaged in radical politics. This account does not, however, go far enough. It still makes the relationship between the practice of deconstruction and of radical political action just one of analogy. Derrida would contest that limitation, as I shall explain shortly.

Derrida says at one point that he does not think he has ever said anything inconsistent with Marxism. However, this remark, which could have come straight from a heresy trial, requires considerable unpacking. In order to understand Derrida's relation to Marxism, there is no substitute for at least a glance at his relation to Heidegger (see below) and Hegel. First of all, with all his rejection of humanism as a form of metaphysics,[28] Derrida has a certain sympathy with

27. In *Philosophy and Phenomenological Research* No. 30.
28. See 'The Ends of Man', in ibid. Criticizing the latent humanism in Sartre, for example, he says: 'Everything takes place as though the sign "man" had no origins, no historical, cultural, linguistic limit, not even a metaphysical limit.' (In this assessment of Sartre he is closely following Heidegger.)

Althusser. But Derrida has a different reading of Hegel, and great debts to Nietzsche and Heidegger. Derrida's Hegel, if we can discount his eschatology, his teleology, the final return of presence in that terminus he calls Absolute Knowledge, has a profound understanding of writing as such, of philosophy as textuality. Even if this thought is finally a testimony to the logocentric tradition, Hegel's system is an account of the progressive discovery of the limits of other philosophical systems, the destruction of their finite forms, the instability of their oppositions, and perhaps most important, the understanding of any 'knowledge' as a mnemonic 'trace' which is never purely present except 'at the end'. The journey from the Hegelian concepts of dialectic and Aufhebung (overcoming, sublation) to 'differance' is a journey through mined territory, fraught with complications. Merely to stand Hegel on his head would be to continue to work within the same metaphysical space. One does not escape a frame of reference by negating someone else's terms. Derrida tries to produce from Hegel a new text free from logocentrism. If Marx found Hegel a representative of German Idealism, Derrida sees him through the spectacles of the logocentric tradition. The relationship between logocentrism and idealism? Derrida tries to explain this in the course of answering the criticism that he 'under-estimates, even ignores the struggle between materialism and idealism'.[29] His answer is complex. He argues that if he neglected that problem, it is because he thought that the most necessary and urgent task was to give a 'general determination of the conditions of emergence and of the limits of philosophy and of metaphysics', and all that it entails. But in principle he has not neglected it, because (a) logocentrism is also fundamentally idealism; (b) it is the matrix of idealism; (c) idealism is the most direct representation of logocentrism; and (d) logocentrism is a larger concept than idealism. These variants are trying to capture the fact that one need not be an idealist to be logocentric, but all idealists are logocentrists. He goes on to insist that as the deconstruction of logocentrism is at the same time the deconstitution of idealism, he has not 'ignored' (*effacé*) the 'struggle' against idealism. In saying that, however, he has not actually said where he stands in the struggle against idealism; he has left out the questioner's reference to materialism. And the reason must be that materialism too, in any ordinary sense that opposes it to idealism, must itself be exposed as metaphysical. Indeed he goes on to say that certain so-called nonidealist and anti-idealist philosophies are part of this tradition.

29. See *Positions*, op. cit., p. 69.

Two questions arise from this account. The first is the status of the *necessity* and *urgency* of the task of delimiting philosophy. This surely poses the question: necessary or urgent for what? But Derrida will not stay for an answer. Secondly, we are not much closer to understanding what he thinks of Marx. His questioner obviously thought the same, because the status of the problematic of writing in relation to dialectical materialism is raised a few pages later. Derrida talks like a lawyer. Insofar as dialectical materialism is a critique of idealism, he agrees with it. What he doesn't say is which parts he rejects.

Derrida shows himself extremely reserved about Marxism. He claims that his thought is not incompatible with Marxism, but insists that if there are gaps in his work about his relationship to Marx, these are deliberate. That is work yet to be done. He cannot spell out in any simple way what that relationship is. And he concludes by indicating the sorts of reservations with which he would read Marx. He does not think of the texts of Marx, Engels or Lenin as homogeneous, and in reading them he would necessarily transform them, as Althusser has already demonstrated.

Derrida's reserve is not hard to understand. He cannot abandon his critical perspective, and that is constituted by a whole apparatus for the dismantling of philosophical and indeed any theoretical texts. From that vantage point, Marxism appears as a series of texts with debts to the past, with internal conflicts, limitations etc — i.e. as complex objects for analysis. To set up Marx's or anyone else's writing as an ultimate point of reference is to repeat an old error. And if one wanted a concrete example as to why, he would point to the pervasive concept of 'contradiction', which has not yet been freed from its 'speculative, teleological, eschatological horizon'.

Another crucial influence on Derrida is Heidegger — the same Heidegger for whom Marxism is 'the spirit taken (= falsified) as intelligence'.[30] Derrida's debt is both to Heidegger's understanding of the history of philosophy as the metaphysics of presence — what Derrida calls logocentrism and the problematic of the limits of philosophy — and to the development of a language that might take one beyond those limits — of 'difference', 'appropriation' etc. Derrida is no simple disciple — he accuses Heidegger of bringing back presence in the shape of the problematic of Being. But what he does seem to accept is the possibility of what we might call an 'internal' audit of the history of philosophy, an assessment which confines itself to the field of its texts. Derrida, like Heidegger, will tell us about the relationship

30. See Heidegger, *Introduction to Metaphysics*, New York 1953, p. 39.

between Marx and Democritus before he will mention capitalism. It is important to realize that neither Derrida nor Heidegger thinks that in having these priorities he is failing in his duty. One can understand this in Heidegger's case, because he allows himself the language — at least — of German idealism. The term 'spirit' gets one a long way in being able to write about thought, culture and politics in the same 'breath', but that language is not available to Derrida. Does he nonetheless harbour the same generalizing confidence about the scope of the logocentric tradition? And the effects of dismantling it interminably?

If we bear in mind the influence on Derrida of these theorists of metaphysical closure — and of the illusions of escape, of the snares, the traps and the ironies — we can at least appreciate, if we do not accept, why the question of strategy is so central for Derrida, and why the question of political commitment is so difficult for him.

Before I conclude with an assessment of the political directions in which his work could lead us, I would like briefly to consider some previous assessments of his political significance.

Christine Buci-Glucksmann[31] has drawn a basic distinction between a 'political' reading of a text and a Derridean reading, and describes the commitment latent in Derrida's practice of deconstruction as, in so many words, intellectualism. At its sharpest points, she says, deconstruction bears witness to the division of intellectual labour, the hierarchical ordering of languages in society (she refers here to Barthes), and to the division of the human sciences into separate disciplines. She asks, moreover, whether we can really be happy with a theory of the effects of a philosophical discourse which is only concerned with the theoretical practice of the text.

Much the same criticism is made by Frederic Jameson. He draws certain parallels with Marx: the givenness of the past built into the idea of a 'trace' corresponds to Marx's (but equally Heidegger's or Sartre's) account of the givenness of social existence; the attack on logocentrism is seen as a sort of demystification. But his final analysis is that Derrida falls into a kind of text-centrism: 'In the very act of repudiating any ultimate or transcendental signified, any concept which would dictate the ultimate or fundamental content of reality, Derrida has ended up inventing a new one, that of the script itself.[32]

Finally, after the Althusserian and Hegelian Marxist, we might

31. In the special Derrida issue no. 54 of *L'Arc*. Her essay is entitled *Déconstruction et Critique marxiste de la philosophie*.
32. See F. Jameson, *The Prison-House of Language*, Princeton 1972, pp. 182–3.

perhaps recall Foucault's drops of acid.[33] Foucault's main objection is again to Derrida's text-centredness. He reduces 'discursive practice to textual traces'; 'It is a historically sufficiently determined little pedagogy . . . that tells the pupil that there is nothing outside the text.' It is a pedagogy, he thinks, because it gives the maître the power to license his pupils in endless readings. The archaeologist of the 'document' must be peculiarly aware of the problems of this sort of reduction. But is he right to claim that Derrida offers no account of discursive practice? Derrida's answer must be that writing is a practice, that he does not distinguish theory and practice in the way implied, and that all discourse has the form of writing, a point that takes us back to our earlier point about the non-privilege, on Derrida's analysis, of either speech or writing (in the old sense) as such. But it does raise an important point: although Derrida ascribes' no *metaphysical* privilege to writing (old sense) — for he does not simply invert the classical privilege of speech — and although all that he says about writing (new sense) is applicable not only to speech but also to consciousness (if we take his account of Husserl seriously), Derrida nonetheless specializes in the analaysis of writing in the old 'literal' sense. That is, he concentrates on what people have written in books in a way that Barthes, for example, does not. Now, there are many reasons for this. We need only recall the urgency he claims for a rather special project — that of delimiting the boundaries of philosophy. And yet that need not confine one to the analysis of written texts (old sense), as Wittgenstein demonstrated. Indeed, the latter's later work is a rejection of such confinement on philosophical grounds. Might it not be that the focus on the text, which Derrida repeats, is the basic presupposition responsible for the continuation of the metaphysical circus? Even if one limits oneself to the study of written texts (such as books) without claiming any completeness of purpose, does one not still presuppose the adequacy of an analysis restricted to the level of the text, an adequacy which would be challenged by anyone for whom the non-philosophical nexus within which philosophical texts are produced, is important? Derrida can recognize this only in the abstraction of an 'outside'. How important or urgent is the limited project that concerns itself only with the classical philosophical tradition?

In short, the belief that one can come to understand the logocentric commitments of particular texts would seem to involve a number of

33. See M. Foucault, 'Mon Corps, ce papier, ce feu', in *Histoire de la Folie*, Paris 1972; cited and discussed in Spivak's introduction to Derrida, *Of Grammatology*, p. lxi.

highly dubious assumptions. The tracing of a universal theme like this is blind to the particular contingent conditions to which such a theme may on each occasion be responding. To talk about logocentrism as an irrepressible desire and to relate it to anxiety reduction, as Derrida does, is to psychologize metaphysics. There is an alternative: without naivety, to historicize it.

In the abstract, Buci-Glucksmann's objections to the intellectual division of labour that Derrida's practices involve could equally apply to her critique. But if we concretize it, it is worth reminding ourselves that Derrida does have to (!) teach philosophy at the highly traditional École Normale. And for at least some of his courses, the topic is laid down by a higher educational authority, as is the method of textual exposition. In that context, a radical reading of texts is the obvious answer to keeping one's job and one's sanity at the same time. But this surely does not endorse Foucault's 'little pedagogy' accusation.

What we seem drawn to ask is whether there might not be other ways of raising the question about the limits of philosophy, quite different from the textual/metaphysical ones with which Derrida chiefly concerns himself. These different ways would relate to philosophy as a practice.

A Linguistic Politics?

I would like to conclude this introductory paper with some positive remarks about the application of Derrida's work, in such a way as to try to answer some of the questions and doubts I have raised or ventriloquised.

I think that the most obvious uses to which one can put Derrida's work in political practice are in those areas with a strong linguistic infrastructure. I would pick out three main areas: educational institutions, other linguistically dependent institutions, like mental hospitals and families, and everyday ideological struggle.

1. The role of some version of the strategy of deconstruction in schools, polytechnics and universities seems to me clear. Deconstruction illuminates, in previously innocent books, structures of presupposition, structures of authority which run diagonally across the logical order of argument. Derrida's commitment to liberating educational practices and the role of philosophy in that liberation is clear in his founding support for Greph, a group of lycée philosophy teachers formed to fight the Haby 'reforms', which would substitute job-

oriented school-teaching for such endless games as philosophy.[34] I am also convinced that Derrida has something like the Leninist view of philosophy as class struggle at the level of theory, and consequently of the value of doing battle at that level. There does seem to be some point in this, if only a limited one, in that the effect of Derrida's readings on intellectuals/academics is to make considerably less plausible naive appeals to philosophy's treasurehouse of ultimate justifications. Kant's arguments against masturbation will fall on sterile soil.

2. Derrida's strategies can, I think, be adapted for use in challenging the linguistically embodied structures of power in such institutions as families, factories, mental hospitals and, at a different level, schools (as above). How this should be performed is a difficult question. One would need to adapt the insights about the ways in which oppositions are so loaded as to give one side a 'privilege' — and to do it in such a way as to provide a theory of the hidden use of power in discourse. What we are not in a position to settle is the degree of importance of the linguistic dimension of power, in relation to, say, the powers of physical confinement, which are exercised by all these institutions.

These remarks about institutions are partly based on remarks I have heard Derrida make about the use of deconstruction in disrupting conventions of discourse, and hence in challenging the structures of power that depend on those conventions. I would suspect that the problem of handling *system recuperation*, as I have called it, would require in these linguistically 'impure' areas, where power is of many kinds, a different analysis, one which Derrida has not given.

3. This reference to the relation between power and convention brings me to the last category of the direct political application of Derrida's ideas. I have called it 'everyday ideological struggle'. My point is simple. That struggle takes the form of intervention, almost entirely linguistically mediated, into what are often our own practices and habits. These interventions often take the form of questioning language, questioning assumed patterns of domination. Derrida has given us techniques for the contestation of linguistically rooted domination, and they can be applied.

Derrida once gave the example of a press condemnation of foreign workers as 'parasites' on the French economy — the same term often applied in Britain to the unemployed. He has on a quite different occasion attempted to challenge the appearance of one-way depen-

34. See Godon and Rée, 'The Philosopher in the Classroom', *Radical Philosophy* 16.

dence implied in the judgement of parasitism (in the context of the philosophical claim that an unusual use of a philosophical term is 'parasitical' on the standard case, in discussing Austin). His philosophical deconstruction of the concept of 'parasite' is given a new lease of life in a political context.

To give another concrete case: the fight against sexism has a very important linguistic element and involves the perpetual exposure of the privilege language accords men in its most habitual practices. The complicity of language with phallo-centrism is the perfect target for a Derridean-inspired assault. It is no accident that very many of Derrida's most serious 'disciples' are women. It is also worth stressing that one of the most common and important discursive practices is that of justification — of actions, 'states of affairs', etc. Philosophy does not rule the world, and never will, but crude versions of the principles it sometimes manufactures, and often cleans and perpetuates, are inseparable from the public world of discourse. Insofar as the metaphysical ground of these principles is an appeal to 'presence' — and Derrida specializes in diagnosing such appeals — he has an important contribution to make to everyday argument.

The attempts at presenting Derrida may, when all is said and written, be utterly misguided. Both when reading Derrida and listening to him reply to questions, one can see why he claims that all that he does is a risk, a gamble, that it demands his constant vigilance to ensure that he is not misunderstood. I have been as tempted as others to conclude that what Derrida is *actually* offering, however surrounded by disclaimers, warnings, reminders, signposts, are new sorts of transcendental arguments which would take us back — perhaps even deeper — into the metaphysical mire. Is there any reason to suppose that he would be spared this sort of misunderstanding if he was used as the basis for a new form of extratextual political practice? Texts have controls (indeed *are* systems of control) that speech does not have. That is something of the secret of Derrida. But might not his 'text-centrism' be his Achilles heel?

Reprinted from *RP* 21

This paper was one of the first attempts to introduce Derrida to the English speaking philosophical world, but it should not be taken to be the author's last word on the subject. See also (1) 'Style and Strategy at the Limits of Philosophy: Heidegger and Derrida', *The Monist*, vol. 63 No. 4 Oct. 1980; (2) 'Derrida and the Paradoxes of Reflection', *JBSP* vol. 11 No. 3, Oct. 1980; (3) 'Time and the Sign' *JBSP* vol. 13 No. 2, May 1982; (4) 'Derrida and the Question of Strategy' in *Derrida and Differance*, ed. Wood and Bernasconi. University of Warwick: 1984.

David Wood

Personality and the Dialectic of Labour and Property — Locke, Hegel, Marx

Chris Arthur

One of the earliest objections to communism claims that 'the complete abolition of private property' makes no sense because people have an inalienable property in their own *individuality*, which comprises all those features that are *peculiar to the person* who has them.[1] This objection flows from the fact that the bourgeois critic construes all personal relationships in terms of the language of property; but if he then marks off one sphere as *inalienable property*, he misses the *point* of the property relationship; for, as Marx says: 'In reality I possess private property only insofar as I have something vendible, whereas what is peculiar to me may not be vendible at all.'[2]

This confusion illustrates the complexities in the relationship of property and personality. This paper takes up a tradition of discussion of this issue, especially in connection with property in a person's labour. We shall see that, according to Locke, property is founded on personal labour; according to Hegel it is the expression of the person's will; while, according to Marx, it is a realm of estrangement — in it is manifested the alienation of labour.

After a section on John Locke, I contrast Hegel's and Marx's fundamental ontological determinations before going on to deal more specifically with Hegel's account of wage-labour in his *Philosophy of Right*,[3] and with Marx's theory of alienation in his 1844 *Manuscripts*. I end by suggesting some clarifications of Marx's concept of alienated labour.

---

1. See *The German Ideology*, in *Marx-Engels Collected Works* Vol. 5, London 1976, pp. 228–29.
2. Ibid., p. 231.
3. For a brief discussion of the role of labour in his *Phenomenology*, see my 'Hegel's Master/Slave Dialectic and a Myth of Marxology', *New Left Review* 142, November/December 1983.

1. John Locke

Locke's justification of property right in his *Second Treatise of Government* trades on a confusion of two senses of *'property'*. The first sense he employs is that in which property is inseparable from its possessor; it is *essential* to that person's being the person he is; and, so far, *inalienable*. The second sense of property refers to something immediately *external* to its possessor, held by him as a matter of right (rather than identical with his person) — hence disputable, and hence alienable.

Let us now consider Locke's argument, bearing this distinction in mind. He sets out from the problem: How can *individuals* legitimately appropriate materials to satisfy their needs if God gave the world to mankind *in common*? It would seem that one would have to await the consent of the rest of mankind before appropriating anything. Locke wishes to convince us that it is not necessary to await the constitution of a *social* process of allocation because there is a *natural* (pre-political) *right* to *private property*, rooted in our persons and labours:

> 'Every man has a property in his own person; this nobody has any right to but himself. The labour of his body and the work of his hands we may say are properly his. Whatsoever, then, he removes out of the state that nature hath provided and left it in, he hath mixed his labour with and joined to it something that is his own, and thereby makes it his property . . . For this labour being the unquestionable property of the labourer, no man but he can have a right to what that is once joined to . . .
>
> He that is nourished by . . . the apples he gathered from the trees in the wood, has certainly appropriated them to himself. Nobody can deny but the nourishment is his. I ask, then, When did they begin to be his? . . . And 'tis plain, if the first gathering made them not his, nothing else could. That labour put a distinction between them and the common . . . and so they became his private right . . .
>
> Thus the grass my horse has bit, the turfs my servant has cut, and the ore I have dug in any place . . . become my property. The labour that was mine removing them out of that common state they were in, hath fixed my property in them' (paras. 27–28).

It is clear that Locke's intention here is to specify criteria whereby property (in the second sense) may *rightfully* be held. Something in the state that nature left it in — that is, external to the individual — becomes 'his private right' (even though it was originally 'common' and could in principle have been appropriated as private property by someone else) in virtue of the fact that he has mixed *his* labour with it; 'for this labour being the unquestionable property of the labourer, no man but he can have a right to what that is once joined to'.

The premise of the argument — that 'the labour of his body and the work of his hands are properly his' — is ambiguous. On the one hand, if this is property in the second sense, one cannot assume that it *is* his; the legal title to it may be held by a slave-owner, a feudal lord, or a capitalist employer; that Locke assumes such labour *is* alienable is evident from the striking interpolation of 'the turfs my servant has cut' among those things in regard to which 'the labour that was mine . . . hath fixed my property in them' . On the other hand, our readiness to accept the premise is due to our reading it as if the labour mentioned in it is 'the unquestionable property of the labourer' in the first sense of the term, that is, *inseparable* from him. That Locke is trading on this sense is evident from the discussion of gathering apples: 'Nobody can deny but the nourishment is his.' If nobody *can* deny it, it must be because the nourishment is *essentially* his (the first sense of ownership); but then Locke goes on to ask, 'When did they begin to be his?' — and in asking this clearly conjoins the sense 'rightfully his' with 'essentially his' in order to end with the conclusion that 'gathering' made them 'his private property' — property in the second sense, obviously.

Locke's argument trades on this shifting between the two senses of ownership. His procedure is fallacious in that, if property is alienable, there is only ever a contingent relation between a man and the property he holds at any given time; so if the power to labour is such a property, it undercuts the argument based on the mixing of such labour with the natural material; alternatively, if labour provides a natural foundation for property right because it is *'unquestionably'* the labourer's then it should not also be alienable; yet, besides the notorious turf-cutting servant, there is general evidence in Locke's text that he takes for granted that it is natural for labour-power to be alienable.[4]

Locke presupposes a thoroughly bourgeois view of the individual as standing in a property relation to himself; he attributes to a man property in 'his life, liberty and estate' (para. 87). He also says: 'By property I . . . mean that property which men have in their persons as well as their goods' (para. 173). Yet, if an individual stands in a property relationship to his *person* and his *labour* in the *same* sense as he does to his *goods,* then he must treat them as external to him and

4. See K. Marx, *Capital* Volume One, Harmondsworth 1976, pp. 1083–84. For these moves in Locke, see also C.B. Macpherson's careful analysis in *The Political Theory of Possessive Individualism*, Oxford 1962.

alienable; if this is so, there is nothing 'natural' about the characterization of labour as property of the labourer — still less about his 'private right' in the product of 'his' labour. In the end, for Locke, the only thing inseparable from a person is the abstract capacity to hold property.

This is also inherent in the views of such an apparently dissimilar thinker as Hegel, to whom we now turn.

2. Property and Personality in Hegel's Ontology

The central organizing idea of Hegel's *Philosophy of Right*[5] is *Freedom;* the book is designed to show that it is actualized in the life of the modern *state*. The first part — entitled *Abstract Right* — introduces the notions of personality and property. According to Hegel, the person demonstrates his inherent freedom through embodying his will in an external thing, immediately *different* from him, thereby making it his. If we compare Hegel with Locke, we find that there is a deeper contrast than that between Hegel's talk of 'putting one's will into a thing' and Locke's talk of 'mixing labour with it'. For Hegel stresses that the rational ground of property lies in its relation to freedom: 'If emphasis is placed on my needs, then the possession of property appears as a means to their satisfaction, but the true position is that . . . property is the first embodiment of freedom and so is in itself a substantive end' (para. 45R).

Hegel postpones discussion of the relationship of property to *need* to later sections which *presuppose* the rational basis of private property. Locke, to the contrary, starts from needs rather than freedom, and this is why he must immediately add limitations to rightful appropriation with respect to 'spoilage', and to 'enough, and as good, being left for others' (*Second Treatise*, paras 31 & 33). He *presupposes*, rather than deduces, the property of individuals in their persons; but then faces a problem, granted the contingencies of need, in that the earth is supposed to be given to mankind in common. For an individual to satisfy needs without 'express consent of all the commoners' (para.

5. G.W.F. Hegel, *Grundlinien der Philosophie des Rechts*, Leipzig 1921; *Hegel's Philosophy of Right*, trans. T.M. Knox, Oxford 1952. Paragraph numbers in the text are given from these editions; 'R' = Remark by Hegel, in smaller print than the main paragraph; 'A' = Addition, culled from notes taken at Hegel's lectures, appended to relevant paragraphs by Gans in his 1833 and 1854 editions but relegated to an appendix in Lasson's 1921 Leipzig edition and in Knox's translation. I restore many emphases omitted by Knox.

28), a transition to private property must be effected on the basis of pre-political claims. The founding of private property on the labour 'that is his own' gives a person such rights and enables him to satisfy his needs. Since it is assumed that others have the same sort of needs, and the movement from common property in the earth to private right in its useful produce is based on 'natural reason' (para. 25), it is against such reason to appropriate so much that some would spoil; and from further contingencies making possible monopolization is derived the natural limitation that enough be left for others.

Hegel, on the other hand, refuses to discuss the question of the *extent* of ownership at this point: 'The rational aspect is that I possess property . . . What and how much I possess is a matter of indifference as far as rights are concerned' (para. 49). It seems, nevertheless, that Hegel should have introduced analogous limitations to those of Locke insofar as his own justification of property might run into problems over monopolization. However, it should be understood that Hegel in this first part of his book is talking to *the* person (para. 49R); the moment of *differentiation*, and hence the positing of *many* individuals and their relationships, arrives only with *Civil Society* — discussed by Hegel in the third, and last, part.[6]

According to Hegel, then, property is no mere social convenience giving people access to means of subsistence as of right; it is a 'substantive end' in virtue of its role in giving personality objectivity. He argues for its necessity by pointing out that 'a person in making decisions is related to a world of nature directly confronting him, and thus the personality of the will stands over against this world as something *subjective*'. In reacting to this situation 'personality . . . struggles to lift itself above this restriction and to give itself reality, or in other words to claim that external world as its own' (para. 39).

In this way personality can express its inherent freedom, Hegel believes, and he develops this idea as follows:

> 'A person must translate his *freedom* into an external sphere . . . *immediately different* and *separable* from him. What is immediately different from free mind is that which, both for mind and in itself, is the *external* pure and simple, a thing, something not free, not personal, without rights . . .
>
> A person has as his substantive end the right of putting his will into any and every thing and thereby making it his, because it has no such end in itself and derives its destiny and soul from his will. This is the absolute *right of appropriation* which man has over all things' (paras. 41, 42, 44).

6. In this connection, see especially paras. 195, 244-45.

It seems curious to speak of a *'right'* of appropriation man has over 'things', without conceiving of it in terms of the relationships *between persons with respect to* the things appropriated. However, the point Hegel is driving at is that, from his philosophical standpoint, a thing can be appropriated rightfully, and constituted as the content of a right which prohibits any other attempting to appropriate it, if, and only if, it is not itself 'substantive', in that it 'has no ends of its own to realize' because it is *external* 'both for mind and *in itself'*. How can there be a realm of such things? What is its significance in Hegel's problematic?

His problematic is one in which personality overcomes the limitations of subjectivity by appropriating an external sphere as its property; but the way in which this problematic is articulated is significant, for personality (in the phase of its 'elementary immediacy' (para. 43) claims the world of nature ('what is immediately different and separable from him' (para. 41)), not as its *proper* realm, but *in spite of* its being 'immediately *different'*. Hegel feels it necessary to apologize: 'Even if my freedom is here realized first of all in an external thing, and so *falsely realized,* nevertheless abstract personality in its immediacy can have no other embodiment save one characterized by immediacy' (para. 41A, emphasis added).

Why does he hold freedom is debased when realized in 'things'? It depends upon the concept of 'the external' being given a sense peculiar to Hegel's idealism in this problematic: 'From the point of view of free mind, which must, of course, be distinguished from mere consciousness, the external is external absolutely, and it is for this reason that the determinate character assigned to *nature* by the concept is *inherent externality.*

[For], since a thing lacks subjectivity, it is external not merely to the subject but to itself' (para. 42 Remark and Addition).

Hegel on Nature

This doctrine (a truth of Speculative Reason which passeth Understanding (see 44R) 'of course') depends upon Hegel's general system, of which the *Philosophy of Right* is only a part. This is expounded in his *Encyclopaedia of the Philosophical Sciences,* which moves from Logic, through Nature, to Spirit. The various moments of thought outlined in the *Logic* are internally connected through the self-determination of the concept in its development. The categories cannot be external to each other — they form a mediated whole. However, at the end of the *Logic* the absolute *Idea* freely posits itself in the form of *otherness*, 'as Nature'.[7] 'Since therefore the Idea is [presented as] the negative of itself, or is *external to itself*, Nature is not merely external in relation to this idea (and to its subjective existence, Spirit), but *externality* constitutes its specificity, as Nature'.[8]

Nature is an external world of objects externally related to one another; it is unconscious of its concept, external to its own truth. It is absolute externality because the internality to which that externality is related can only be reconstituted through the medium of *thought*. As Marx points out, the form of the dialectical deduction in the *Encyclopaedia* renders Nature, as such, *senseless;* it 'only has the sense of an externality to be superseded [*aufgehoben*].'[9] When Hegel characterizes Nature as 'externality', this sounds innocent enough; but, as Marx explains, externality should not be understood as a sensuously accessible world exposing itself to the light of day; rather, he says, 'it is to be taken in the sense of alienation [*Entäusserung*], a flaw, a weakness . . .' 'For the abstract thinker Nature must therefore supersede [*aufheben*] itself, since it is already posited by him as a potentially *superseded* being'.[10] Because *Nature* is posited as the exoteric form of *Logic,* with the consequence that 'the truth about things is that as such immediately single, i.e. sensuous things, they are only a show [*Schein*],[11] —they have no substantive independence from the Speculative viewpoint. Nature is a realm of immediacy in which immediately single things positively cry out for mediation, as it were.

For Hegel it is not a question of natural objectivity *of which man is a part* and in and through which his existence is *naturally* mediated; it is a question of *mind* positing the realm of nature (including the body, as we shall see below) as immediately *other* (i.e. opposite, antithetical, not merely difference within a unity), and hence being moved to idealize this actuality, since, as inherent externality, Nature lacks ideality itself (in spite of its 'show of self-subsistence for consciousness, intuition and representative thinking' (para. 44R)) and must submit to its incorporation as a moment in Spirit's actualization.

One sees now why, for Hegel, the central instances of free action in

7. *Hegel's Logic,* trans. W. Wallace, Oxford 1975, para. 244.
8. *Encyclopaedia,* para. 247. Two English translations exist of this part of the *Encyclopaedia* (paras. 245–376): *Hegel's Philosophy of Nature,* ed. and trans. M. J. Petry, Vol. 1, London 1970; and *Hegel's Philosophy of Nature* (being Part Two of the 'Encyclopaedia of the Philosophical Sciences'), trans. A.V. Miller, Oxford 1970.
9. 'Ökonomisch-philosophische Manuskripte aus dem Jahre 1844', in Marx-Engels *Schriften bis 1844,* Vol. 1, Berlin 1968, p. 587; Karl Marx, *Early Writings,* Harmondsworth 1975, p. 399; Marx-Engels, *Collected Works* Vol. 3, London 1975, p. 346.
10. *Schriften bis 1844,* p. 588; *CW*3, p. 346.
11. *Encyclopaedia (Enc.),* para. 246A.

the world are not bodily labours, but turn out to be 'judgements of the will on the thing' (para. 53), because it is free-*will* that characterizes spirit; certainly, when he touches on a material content, the importance of such moments is presented merely as a spur to an ideal upshot.

The Ideality of Property

Let us look at the material content touched on under the head *Property* and how this reality is idealized.

Hegel admits that, since property is to be the '*embodiment* of personality, my *inward* idea and will that something is to be *mine* is not enough to make it my property' (para. 51). *Occupancy* is necessary — not least in order to make my property recognizable by others. However, in the discussion of occupancy, Hegel overcomes 'the matter of the thing' only in ideality; for since 'matter offers resistance to me, . . . occupancy, as an external activity whereby we actualize our universal right of appropriating natural objects . . . involves . . . restriction and contingency'; hence 'mastery and external possession of things becomes . . . indeterminate and incomplete'; yet (Hegel consoles us) 'this actual occupancy is different from property as such because property is complete as the work of the free will alone' and 'in relation to the will and property . . . this independence of matter has no truth . . . even though there still remains in possession, as an external relation to an object, something external' (para. 52 & Remark).

Hegel then turns to the 'further determinations' of property actualized in three moments of 'the will's relation to the thing' (para. 53). The *positive* moment is signified by '*taking possession* of the thing immediately' whereby one becomes objective to oneself *in* one's property. This sinking into the *particular* inadequately realizes the *universality* of the will. Thus we move to the moment of *negativity* whereby the will *distinguishes* itself, through the '*use*' of the thing for one's own ends, from the thing itself. Even in this relation the will is still debased (see above discussion (of para. 41A)) by its involvement with the particularity of the objects and their use-value (see below on *exchange*-value). Hence the will must be asserted *as the will absolutely* and not in connection with the particularity of its objects. This is realized in '*alienation*' (*Veräusserung*) of the thing whereby is accomplished 'the reflection of the will back from the thing into itself' (albeit through the mediation of things still). Hegel says: 'These three are respectively the *positive, negative,* and *infinite judgements* of the *will* on the thing' (para. 53; see Enc para. 172–3).

Let us examine the actual content of these 'judgements' more closely. The positive judgement is signified by 'taking possession' of the thing '(a) by directly grasping it physically,[12] (b) by forming it, and (c) by merely marking it as ours' (para. 54). The extraordinarily idealist manner in which Hegel 'shows his mastery over things' through taking them into possession is well exemplified in the following passage: 'The notion of the mark . . . is that the thing does not count as the thing which it is but as what it is supposed to signify . . . By being able to give a mark to things and thereby to acquire them, man just shows his mastery over things' (para. 58A).

No comment seems necessary — except to say that thus clothed with a costume not its own the individuality of the natural object is estranged. The negative judgement of the will on the thing is signified in its use to satisfy needs (and this is 'a still more universal relation to the thing' (para. 59A) than marking); yet, lest we should be tempted to look here for a material content, Hegel reminds us that use is only a moment in the development of 'the will's relation to the thing' (para. 53). For example, 'squatting' is rejected thus:

> The fact that property is realized and actualized only in use floats before the minds of those who look upon property as derelict and a *res nullius* if it is not being put to any use, and who excuse its unlawful occupancy on the ground that it has not been used by its owner. But the owner's will, in accordance with which a thing is his, is the primary substantive basis of property; use is a further modification of property, secondary to that universal basis, and is only its manifestation and particular mode (para. 59R).

It is also very striking that Hegel considers that it is not the specific utility of a thing as related to a definite need but its universality as *value* ('abstracted from the thing's specific quality') 'wherein its genuine substantiality becomes determinate and an object of consciousness' (para. 63). He comments further on the commensurability of values: 'The advance of thought here therefore is from the specific quality of a thing to indifference to this specificity, i.e. to Quantity' (para. 63A). One cannot but agree with Knox[13] that it is because 'value is a concept existing for thought, not sensation,' that it 'is the genuine substance of the thing' for Hegel, in spite of (or rather because of?) the fact that: 'If we consider the concept of value, we

12. Marx makes fun of all this in *Capital* Volume 3, Harmondsworth 1981, p. 752.
13. *Hegel's Philosophy of Right*, p. 326.

must look on the thing itself only as a symbol; it counts not as itself but as what it is worth' (para. 63A).[14]

Commodity Fetishism confuses this peculiar social form — value — with the body of the commodity and hence naturalizes it. Hegel goes one better by declaring this social form *form as such* — as immediate the thing is formless, a mere 'show'. Hegel lifts himself above the fetishism of the commodity-*body* when he declares the value form to be a *social mediation;* but then, instead of affirming the natural form of the object, he declares this social form itself to *be* the substantive actuality of the thing, thus fetishizing the commodity-*form*. It would hardly be an exaggeration to see in Hegel's Absolute, in which activity is ultimately self-related, the reflected form of capital's pure movement (M — M') which abstracts itself from use-values and the specificity of their production.

In the dialectic of 'the will's relation to the thing' as property, the moment of *alienation*, rather than posing any problem for Hegel, is seen by him as the most complete *actualization* of ownership. By a typical idealist twist, it is precisely in this 'negatively infinite judgement' on the thing ('in which the subject has no relation whatever to the predicate'[15]) whereby my will is reflected 'back from the thing into itself' (para. 53) that, in rigorously distinguishing myself as an owner from any particular content to this proprietorship, I become a real proprietor!

Possession and use are limited, finite, relations of the will to property in which its movement runs aground; but through treating things merely as exchangeable objects, in the endless circle of acquisition and alienation, the will is reflected into its own self — without getting bogged down in the natural features of the alienated objects; in this way, the dialectic progresses to *'contract'* where the will is dealing with its *own* other. 'This relation of will to will is the true and proper ground in which freedom is existent' (para. 71).[16]

In conclusion: the overriding moment in the 'mastery of things exhibited by free-will' is that which is most removed from their useful material character, namely the process of their *alienation*. This pushes forward the actualization of the will to the form of contract whereby it achieves recognition in another person. Only as a proprietor among proprietors am I free!

We will come back to Hegel after we have spent a little time

14. This remark of Hegel's is cited by Marx in *Capital* Vol. One, p. 185.
15. *Enc.*, para. 173A.
16. See para. 74. Cf. R. Plant, *Hegel*, London 1973, p. 155, who is good on the dialectic of unity and difference.

developing the positive content of Marxian materialism.

3. Marx's Ontology

Marx uses a *materialist* criterion to distinguish the fundamental specificity of human being in Nature (and — let it be said — insofar as it is a practical and historical criterion also, it is more *dialectical* than anything in Hegel):

> Men can be distinguished from animals by consciousness, by religion, or anything else you like. They themselves begin to distinguish themselves from animals as soon as they begin to *produce* their means of subsistence'.[17]

The fundamental human relationship to Nature lies therefore in labour. Nature is the objective sphere in which labour realizes itself through its objectification in a product worked up out of natural objects; as the object of his activity and the basis of his subsistence, Nature is constituted for and by man as his 'inorganic body'.[18] *Industry* is the mediation in which is united both the identity and difference of human nature with so-called 'external' Nature: 'the celebrated "unity of man with nature" has always existed in industry and has existed in varying forms in every epoch according to the lesser or greater development of industry, just like the "struggle" of man with nature'.[19]

In Marx's materialist ontology, there is an affirmation of the *inter*dependence of Man and Nature. The object of labour, for example, is as 'self-subsistent' as the labourer himself, and proves it through its resistance to his labours. Man cannot pose as an autonomous being over against a dependent objective world; even with extensive development of the productive forces, the 'cunning of reason'[20] remains mired in the 'realm of necessity'.[21] The proprietor's 'absolute mastery over things' (from the point of view of legal ideology) is cruelly complemented by the subordination of labour to the natural recalcitrance of objects, which exhausts it. Furthermore Marx, unlike Hegel, recognizes particularity *as such* (not purely as a moment to be sublated). He emphasizes that, when the objective world becomes the

---

17. Marx-Engels, *CW*5, p. 31.
18. *Early Writings*, pp. 324, 325, 328; *Capital* Vol. One, p. 285.
19. *CW*5, p. 40.
20. *Enc.*, para. 209A; Marx, *Capital* Vol. One, p. 285.
21. *Capital* Vol. Three, p. 959.

objectification of man and the realization of his powers, the *manner* in which the object becomes his depends on the *specificity* of the relation that constitutes its *particular* mode of affirmation.[22]

The significance of human acitivity is by no means limited to the production of utilities in the narrow sense. Marx points to its fundamental ontological significance:

> By producing their means of subsistence men are indirectly producing their material life . . . This mode of production must not be considered simply as being the reproduction of the physical existence of the individuals. Rather it is a definite *mode of life* on their part. As individuals express their life, so they are. What they are, therefore, coincides with their production, both with *what* they produce and with *how* they produce. Hence what individuals are depends on the material conditions of their production.[23]

This ontological framework stayed constantly at the basis of Marx's work. In *Capital* he sketches the fundamental bases of man's production of himself through labour:

> Labour is, first of all, a process between man and nature, a process by which man, through his own actions, mediates, regulates and controls the metabolism between himself and nature . . . Through this movement he acts upon external nature and changes it, and in this way he simultaneously changes his own nature.[24]

The difference between Marx's materialist problematic and Hegel's idealist one, turns crucially on the relationship of the object of activity to that activity. A materialist point of view, of course, cannot accept Hegel's characterization of Nature as external to itself. Nature is not *in itself* external to anything — least of all to *itself*. It is a mediated whole in which, if single *isolated* things only have a 'show' of self-subsistence, it is not because they require spirit to incorporate them in its logical totality, but rather because on investigation they will be found to depend on larger natural complexes.

The problem now is: to conceptualize the status of such things as natural objects taken up by human activity. The struggle to wrest the means of subsistence from Nature grounds that activity in an internal differentiation in which, from the side of man, Nature is a means of life

22. *Schriften bis 1844*, p. 541 (and 562–63); *Early Writings*, pp. 352–53 (and 375).
23. *CW*5, pp. 31–32; *Early Writings*, p. 355.
24. *Capital* Vol. One, p. 283.

only as *transformed* (in accordance with its *objective* possibilities in relation to the current historically developed powers of man) by productive labour; and *for his labour* Nature is now posited as the moment of *immediate material* — labour's *object*. In this sense, Nature as a realm of essential objects for labour is man's 'inorganic body'. However, there is np reason why these essential objects for man should have man as *their* essential object![25] Labour's object may be posited as immediate *by labour* but it is not so *inherently*. It is of course true that (whereas the animal's activity is bounded by particular pre-given relationships to its environment) man's activity, and his relationship to Nature, is *universal*. From this point of view an object can be put to *new uses* which — if you like — are 'unnatural' to it. So, abstractly considered (and especially from the point of view of certain social relations which posit activity as abstract, whether it is Hegel's 'free-will', or, more concretely, the production of value by 'abstract labour') Nature is reduced to immediately existing material divorced from any specific internal connection (its *own* mediatedness in natural ecology) or from *particular* labour processes. The abstract identity in labour's material disappears, however, when any *concrete useful labour* is actually embarked upon. As Peter Ruben points out, it cannot then be considered merely 'naked matter';[26] for in showing its specific resistance, it requires specific adaptations of labour based on knowledge of its objective specificity. As a corollary we can understand that labour's object is posited as *immediate* material *only* as it is taken up as a moment in the production of values.[27]

A further important consequence is that, in the outcome of labour's mediating activity, we find that natural objectivity and particularity are by no means *negated* — as they are for Hegel when the mediation of mind idealizes the 'external sphere'. *Productive consumption* reposits the object *as an object* in that: in consuming the material it makes use of *this consumption itself* in order to transform, while preserving, the material, and the materialized labour, into the form of a product; and, while treating the given form of the object merely as the immediate material moment in production, it reduces *this sublation* (of the objective character of the thing) *itself* to moment, and is hence the *positing of the object*, but in a new objective form. (The dialectical

25. But compare *Early Writings*, p. 390.
26. Ruben's critique ('Problem und Begriff der Naturdialektik', in *Dialektik und Arbeit der Philosophie*, Cologne 1978), which we have drawn on here and below, is actually directed against A. Schmidt. But since the latter is accused of Hegelianism, the points may be taken as applying to the master himself.
27. Ruben, p. 156.

negation of the negation is not of course the restoration of the origin of the movement.) On the basis of this new *determinate* objective form, the product, as a particular object, becomes a *definite use-value*, more *specifically adapted* to human requirements.[28]

Marx and Hegel

If we compare this with the Hegelian philosophy of property, we recall that when the object acquires the 'mark' of private property it is posited as other than itself, and that the most significant use then made of it is the suspension of its use for the purposes of exchange, in which its abstract universality as a value negates the particularity of its natural form (para. 77)[29] and it becomes the mere bearer of the identical wills of the proprietors. Free-will posits the object as *other than itself* in that: in marking, using and alienating it, freewill makes the matter of the thing its property; and in treating the object as *inherent* externality it overtakes the 'unmediated' (para. 44R) objective character of the thing in this movement and hence posits *itself*, but as objective rather than subjective will.

Because Hegel remains uncritically within the camp of private property, he cannot conceive the (first-order) mediations of man and nature in industry except through the prism of (second-order) property relations. Thus he presents private property as a fundamental ontological dimension of the concrete totality manifested in Spirit's actualization. For Marx, it is a derived second-order mediation with the fundamental ontological framework of objectification — it is a determinate mode of externality of man to himself and to the conditions of his labour. Marx does not consider the natural conditions of labour as immediately external to man and his powers (except in the sense that all of nature, *including* man and his work, participates in a sensuously manifest whole). However, if Nature is man's 'inorganic body' because it has been constituted as the *essential object* of his activity through the mediation of labour, then to separate labour-power from its conditions of realization by constituting the latter as private property (whether or not the means of production are in fact monopolized in consequence) is really to constitute the object as external both to itself ('land has nothing to do with rent . . .'[30] —

28. *Grundrisse*, Harmondsworth 1973, pp. 300–301. See also *Capital* Vol. One, pp. 287–90.
29. Compare *Capital* Vol. One, p. 179, with para. 77.
30. *CW*5, p. 230.

Marx) and to labour-power —which latter is now thrown back (because of the *contingency* of this external relationship to the means of production) into '*subjectivity*' estranged from its *objective realm of expression*. (Here is an *inversion*, if you like: for Hegel, private property is the mediation through which subjectivity *claims* the external, thus *constituting* personality; for Marx, private property is the mediation whereby personal powers *separate* themselves from their objective conditions of expression — one might almost say they are *de*-mediated — thus *introducing* an external relation between them requiring sublation in further mediations — exchange, wages, etc. — of the estranged moments.) If the potentially monopolizable means of production are in fact monopolized, the *subjective moment too* has to become external to itself, since labour-power can now realize itself in objective activity only insofar as it is *alienable*. The consequence is that, in Marx's striking phrase, the worker is no longer at home in his work.

We now turn to Hegel and Marx on alienated labour.

4. Hegel on Personal Powers

Like Locke, Hegel considers the relation between persons and their labour-power to be one of property, and also recognizes that as such labour is alienable. Unlike Locke, he recognizes that there is a problem in accounting for the justification and even the very possibility of such alienation — because he sees that labour-power is not immediately 'external' in the same sense that other alienable things are. Before taking up the question of labour's alienation, then, we must review Hegel's account of bodily power. Hegel considers that men, while free 'in their concept', are not free in their immediate natural existence. Hegel emphasizes that it is necessary for this concept of human freedom to be actualized through a *process* whereby the *natural* basis of human existence is sublated through the mediation of free mind. This mediation turns out to be the evolution of a *property* once again! He speaks of 'the possession of our body and mind which we can achieve through education *(Bildung)*, study, habit, etc., and which exists as an *inward property* of mind' (para. 43R). *Immediately* my 'bodily organism' is merely 'my external existence' (para. 47) so that it has to 'be taken into possession by mind' (para. 48) through the mediation of the will.

Man, pursuant to his *immediate* existence within himself, is something natural, external to his concept. It is only through the *development* of his own body and mind, *essentially* through his *self-consciousness's apprehension of itself as free*, that he takes possession of himself and becomes his own property and no one else's (para. 57).

We find that for Hegel, just as the world of nature, as an 'inherent externality', is to be ideally subsumed under the concept of property, so too our own natural existence is 'external to its concept' and likewise to be sublated through this same mediation. We are to own ourselves! One of the results of developing our powers is that we have the power to treat our powers as mere legal 'things'! The phrase 'he becomes his own property' is explicitly given the significance that one can take self-consciousness and its powers 'as one's object', and, logically therefore, one's self-consciousness becomes thereby 'capable of taking the form of a "thing"' (para. 57), like any other, held as property, and, if suitable mediations may be found (see below), alienated as such. However, here Hegel runs into insoluble problems: how can essentially *inward* property be held as a 'thing' of this kind? On the one hand it seems that such substantive characteristics of the person should be inalienable[31]; on the other hand, Hegel (in an earlier section) recognizes that alienation penetrates this sphere insofar as mental aptitudes, erudition, skills, attainments, inventions, and so forth, are 'brought on a parity through being bought and sold, with things recognized as things'; and yet it seems difficult to speak of *legal* possession of such 'things' for 'there is something inward and mental about it' (para. 43R). Hegel attempts to rationalize this situation as follows:

> Attainments, erudition, talents, and so forth, are, of course, owned by free mind and are something internal and not external to it, but even so, by expressing them it may embody them in something external and *alienate (veräussern)* them . . . and in this way they are put into the category of *'things'*. Therefore they are not immediate at the start but only acquire this character through the mediation of mind which reduces its inner possessions to immediacy and externality (para. 43R).

This does not seem very satisfactory, but instead of amplifying the point Hegel backs away from it:

> In this sphere we are concerned with mental aptitudes, erudition, etc., only in so far as they are possessions in a legal sense; . . . it is not until we come to deal with *alienation (Veräusserung)* that we need begin to speak of

31. Paras. 65–66.

the transition of such mental property into the external world where it falls under the category of property in the legal sense (para. 43R).

Nevertheless, Hegel was forced eventually to recognize that he fails to cope with a new problem here — that of *externalization* — for he notes in the margin (that is, *after* publication of the book) with respect to the use of the word 'alienation' here: 'It would be better to speak here of a mode of externality. Alienation is giving up something which is my property and which is already external, it is not to externalize.'[32] In other words, we cannot cheerfully subsume the problem away under the process of 'alienation' for, if alienation is of something 'external by nature', then it has to be shown how my 'inner possessions' acquire the 'mode of externality', and whether or not this is contrary to their concept. It would seem that we require a particularly subtle 'mediation of mind' whereby these inner possessions, acquired so that I become 'my own property', achieve a 'mode of externality' on the basis of which they are alienable on a par with 'things' yet without estranging personality from itself.

The Sale of Labour-Power

At all events, Hegel certainly regards spiritual possessions, such as conscience, as inalienable, while cheerfully accepting the alienation of external things embodying a person's powers (paras. 43 and 67). The former are supposed to involve the *substance* of personality, whereas the latter are merely *particular* single objectifications of my powers. Leaving aside any problems that might arise with a person's products, what of the alienation of personal material powers themselves? The alienation of material powers ought to pose difficulties for Hegel, for, in spite of his identification of the person with 'self-consciousness', he admits the peculiar status of *the body* once the will has taken posession of it, and says clearly that I, and my freedom, exist for others only as embodied (para. 48R). Hence it would seem to follow that the worker lacks freedom while labouring for another, albeit that he might 'abstract himself' from the routine of production and absorb himself in dreaming up dirty jokes, for example. If I

32. *Hegels eigenhändige Randemerkungen zu seiner Rechtsphilosophie*, ed. G. Lasson, Leipzig 1930, p. 29. Quoted from Knox's note 16 to *Hegel's Philosophy of Right*, p. 322. The German is readily available in Hoffmeister's edition of the *Grundlinien der Philosophie des Rechts* (Hamburg 1955): 'Wäre besser hier als Art von Ausserlichen aufzuführen — *Veräusserung* ist das Aufgeben eines *schon Ausserliechen*, das mein Eigentum ist, — nicht erst das Aussern' (p. 330).

possess my labour-power only because I have made my body my own in such a way that its powers only exist as powers developed by my will, Hegel should find it paradoxical that my abilities could yet be posited in the mode of exteriority required for their alienation.

Hegel certainly regards slavery as incompatible with the Idea of Freedom, but he makes an ingenious distinction between wage-labour and slavery, whereby the former may be endorsed by 'the concept':

> *Single* products of *my particular physical and mental skill* and of my power to act I can *alienate (Veräusserung)* to someone else and I can give him the use of my abilities *for a restricted period,* because, on the strength of this restriction, my abilities acquire an external relation to the *totality* and *universality* of my being. By alienating the *whole* of my time, as crystallized in my work, and everything I produced, I would be making into another's property the substance of my being, my *universal* activity and actuality, my personality (para. 67).[33]

And he explains in the *Remark:*

> It is only when use is restricted that a distinction arises between use and substance. So here, the use of my powers differs from my powers and therefore from myself, only insofar as it is quantitatively restricted.

It seems, then, that Hegel admits that my labour-power is part of the substance of my personality — an essentially inward property insofar as I am in possession of myself. However, as he noted earlier (para. 43R), it might be possible that in expressing my powers I reduce them — 'through a mediation of mind' — to 'immediacy and exter-nality'. Although not immediately external at the start, labour-power may be *externalized* through some mediation. Here, in this discussion of the alienation of the use of my powers, the mediation required is identified with the time-limit which creates a distinction between use and substance even though the substance of my power is nothing but 'the totality of its manifestations' (para. 67R): 'On the strength of this restriction, my abilities acquire an external relation to the *totality* and *universality* of my being.'

The trouble with Hegel's distinction between entire alienation and alienation piece by piece — a distinction which is supposed to guarantee the independence of the worker's personality — is that it breaks down when one considers the possibility (which is effectively

33. Marx quotes this approvingly in *Capital* Vol. One, p. 272.

realized in the case of modern wage-labour) that, through *successive* piecemeal alienations of my time, my *entire* labour-time is appropriated by others. Either Hegel must take his equation of the totality of the manifestations of my labour-power with that power itself in a material sense and criticize wage-slavery; or else he will have to posit that from an idealist standpoint the *substance* of my power is its status as *property* rather than the totality of its potential manifestations. For the powerful person there is substituted the legal person who remains himself alone even when effectively relinquishing his entire power to others. Legal ideology in its pure form would accept the substance itself as external property like other 'things'. It is only Hegel's instinct for the non-legal essence of possession based on *Bildung* that prevents him assuming that; but he capitulates to piecemeal reification. What is a 'thing' in pieces is all of a piece a 'thing'. Only the position that the substance of labour-power is itself alienable property will justify wage-slavery; and if that is reificatory because it treats inward property as an external 'thing', then the pieces are inwardly 'substantive' as well, and their alienation is an offence against personality. The substance of the coalminer thrown on the scrap-heap with 'black lung' has certainly wasted away in the service of the employer, notwithstanding that 'a distinction between use and substance arises' in virtue of the miner's selling himself piece by piece instead of into explicit slavery. If the worker's entire labouring time is alienated, then his distinction from a slave is surely reduced to his legal status, while materially he is in slavery to capital.

However, these quantitive considerations may be left at this point; for there is a deeper, qualitative, incoherence in Hegel's endorsement of wage-slavery.

To say that the time restriction effects an 'external relation' between the use of my powers and my substantive possession of them is inadequate, because Hegel fails here (para. 67) to deal with the same point that was missed in the earlier (para. 43R) discussion. Even if the time-limit may satisfy the criterion for the continuation of an independent legal personality throughout piecemeal alienations of labour-power, it does not deal with the problems arising when the transition of such personal power into the 'mode of exteriority' is attempted such that 'it falls under the category of property in the legal sense', that is (having been 'reduced to immediacy and externality') alienable to another to be made use of by him for however limited a period. Hegel says, at one point, that if I am given the use of something that remains the property of someone else 'there would remain in the thing something impenetrable by me, namely the will, the empty will, of another' (para. 62). Does the alienation of labour-power reduce the status of its original possessor to that of an 'empty will'? The situation is clearly more complicated; with wage-labour the worker is present in his work as much more than an empty will; for, since his power *only exists* insofar as he is 'in possession of himself' and he has developed it as essentially 'inward property', it is not a 'thing external by nature' but is itself will-with-thing, so to speak. In developing the powers of my 'brains, nerves and muscles', I remove their immediately external character and they become my inward possessions (to use Hegel's terminology). The mediation by which my labour-power is yielded 'to the will of another as a *res nullius*' (para. 65) cannot consist, therefore, in my *withdrawing* out of myself, leaving behind only my 'empty will' to mark my right to recover my powers. The powers of my brains, nerves and muscles exist only insofar as I am present in exercising them. If they are to be alienated, these powers must be *externalized*. But they can be externalized only if they are objectified in production, and this latter requires, not the *exclusion* of my will, but my own use of my powers, however grudgingly. The worker's will is not in his powers like a squatter in a house — to be ejected or ignored. Getting him to exercise those powers in the service of another therefore requires the *subordination of his will* to the other's.

There are two problems with labour's externalization that arise from this fact. One is a problem for the purchaser of the use-value, labour-power: how is he to effect its externalization if this must involve subordination of the worker's will? (We advert to this central question below, after we have raised it on the basis of Marx's work.) The other problem arises for Hegel's apologetic. At this point there comes home the contradiction implicit in Hegel's view of personal powers as, on the one hand, inward property actualizing freedom, and, on the other, potentially externalized property held mediatedly as an alienable 'thing'. If this second relation is realized in the alienation of labour the will exists in contradiction with itself: for, in Hegel's *general* theory, the moment of alienation establishes the will as will through its *reflection from the thing;* in the contractual relation with the other's will, *symmetrically* mediated in the 'thing', it becomes *'identical'* with *its* other and both equally achieve objective *recognition: but,* since the 'thing' here *itself embodies the will,* as we have seen, the externalizing mediations presuppose an *asymmetrical* relationship, in which one will bends to the other, being thus 'refracted' rather than 'reflected' (so to speak) in this alienation. This is nothing less than self-estrangement.

5. Marx's Theory of Alienated Labour

The contradiction between the symmetry of the wage-labour contract effected by autonomous, juridically equal persons, and the asymmetry of the employer's relationship during the working day to his 'hands' (to employ the striking vernacular of capital), finds its way into the textbooks of the bourgeois ideologists from *reality*. This reality disguises the relations of personal dominance inherent in wage-slavery by reifying the personal powers of the labourer to that they become a 'factor of production' like any other. The factors of production themselves are posited as inherently external to one another and mediatable only through the valorization process brought about within the movement of capital. What lies at the basis of all this is the estrangement of labour from its conditions of actualization and itself. This was first brought to light in that extraordinary text of Marx's: the chapter on *Estranged Labour* in his *1844 Manuscripts*. Let us review that, very briefly. The poor situation of the modern wage-worker is reflected first of all in the fact that the objectification of his labour in the product is no confirmation of his powers, but their estrangement, in that the product is not his but the property of his employer.

Furthermore:

> The *externalization (Entäusserung)* of the worker in his product means not only that his labour becomes an object, an *external* existence, but that it exists *outside* him independently of him and alien (*fremd*) to him, and begins to confront him as an autonomous power; that the life which he has bestowed on the object confronts him as hostile and alien.[34]

Moreover, if we are concerned about the estrangement between the worker and his product, it is necessary also to look at the character of the activity that effects it.

> How could the product of the worker's activity confront him as something alien (*fremd*) if it were not for the fact that in the act of production he was estranging himself from himself. After all, the product is simply the résumé of the activity, of the production. So . . . production itself must be active *alienation*, the alienation (*Entäusserung*) of activity, the activity of alienation. The estrangement of the object of labour merely summarizes the estrangement (*Entfremdung*), the alienation in the activity of labour itself.[35]

34. *Schriften*, p. 512; *Early Writings*, p. 324.
35. *Schriften*, p. 514; *EW*, p. 326; *CW3*, p. 274.

Marx describes the situation in the following striking terms:

> Labour is *external* to the worker, i.e. it does not belong to his essential
> being; . . . he therefore does not confirm himself in his work but denies
> himself . . . Hence the worker feels himself only when he is not working;
> when he is working he does not feel himself. He is at home when he is not
> working, and not at home when he is working. His labour is therefore not
> voluntary but forced, it is forced labour. It is therefore not the satisfaction
> of a need but a mere *means* to satisfy needs outside itself . . . In it he belongs
> not to himself but to another.[36]

In sum: the worker views his product — and his very labour — as
external to him; his production is the activity of externalization; his
objectification of his powers is their alienation; and his activity is
'directed against himself' insofar as it produces and reproduces his
'self-estrangement' — his estrangement from himself, his work, and
his world.[37]

Terminological Excursus

I am going to argue that Marx's theory is insufficiently clarified
conceptually. But to introduce this point, it will be useful to examine
some of the terminology employed and the difficulties that have faced
translators — difficulties which, I will argue, flow from a certain
condensation in the employment of the expressions themselves.

There are three key terms:

(1) *Vergegenständlichung:* objectification.

(2) *Entfremdung:* estrangement; alienation.

(3) *Entäusserung*: alienation (of property); parting with; renunciation; relinquishment; externalization.

Let us examine these in turn:

(1) 'Objectification', as should be clear from our earlier discussion,
is employed when Marx is dealing with the natural and essential
expression of labour in its product. In the context of the first-order
mediations (logically prior to the second-order mediations: alienated
labour and private property) it is confirmation of man's activity:
'through it nature appears as his work and his reality . . . he can
therefore contemplate himself in a world he himself has created'.[38]

(2) *'Entfremdung'* has the sense of 'making strange'. It is used in

---

36. Loc. cit.
37. *Schriften,* p. 515; *EW,* p. 327.
38. *EW*, p. 329.

cases of inter-personal estrangement for which English also uses 'alienation' (following Latin: alienare = (a) to make another's, transfer ownership; (b) to cause a separation, interpersonal estrangement). *However,* it should be noticed that whereas English, following Latin, uses the term 'alienation' in the sense of transfer of ownership in legal-commercial contexts, *'Entfremdung'* would *not* be used in such contexts and therefore its meaning maps more naturally on to 'estrangement'. I agree with Istvan Meszaros[39] that Marx uses *'Entfremdung'* to express the fact that man is being *opposed* by a hostile power *of his own making.*

(3) *'Entäusserung'*: one should note here that the root *'äusserung'* means 'manifestation' and that the prefix *'ent'* indicates establishment of, or entry into, a new state or relinquishment of an old state. Thus, in combination we see that the sense is that something is manifested in such a way as to change its state. The sense of relinquishment comes out strongly when Marx makes the following contrast between the root and its modification in connection with life: *'Private property* is only the sensuous expression of the fact that man becomes *objective* for himself and at the same time becomes an alien and inhuman object for himself, that his expression of life (*Lebensäusserung*) is his alienation of life (*Lebensentäusserung*).'[40]

'Entäusserung' would naturally be translated as 'alienation' in legal-commercial contexts involving transfer of ownership. The problem is that unlike 'alienation' it also has the sense of 'externalization' and appears therefore in other contexts besides.[41]

It will be noted that, with regard to the *two* crucial terms (*Entfremdung* and *Entäusserung*) which may be translated as 'alienation',[42] we have *three* concepts: (a) estrangement; (b) alienation of

39. I. Meszaros, *Marx's Theory of Alienation*, London 1970, p. 313.

40. *CW*3, p. 299; *EW*, p. 351.

41. According to Lukács, Fichte originated its philosophical career. G. Lukács, *The Young Hegel*, London 1975, p. 538.

42. To complete the picture we should note: (4) *Veräusserung* is another, more usual equivalent of the English legal-commercial term 'alienation', which could be translated simply as 'sale'. In Hegel's *Philosophy of Right,* he uses it interchangeably with *Entäusserung,* so much so that whereas in para. 53 we are promised a threefold dialectic of the will's relation to the thing as property ending with 'a) die Reflexion des Willens in sich aus der Sache — *Veräusserung',* the relevant final paragraphs of the section on property refer to 'C. *Entäusserung* des Eigentums'! (In the English translation, of course, both terms appear as 'alienation'.) However, it is noticeable that when Hegel speaks of alienation in a critical context, he chooses *Entäusserung:* for example, in the remark to para. 66, 'Alienation (*Entäusserung*) of personality'. In *On the Jewish Question* Marx writes: 'Die Veräusserung ist die Praxis der Entäusserung' (*Schriften,* p. 376, *EW*, p. 241).

property to another; (c) externalization.

In my view, the problem is not simply one of translation, but that this reflects a certain fuzziness in Marx's own expressions. The problem for translators appears as 'three into two won't go', but it really comes down to the rendering of *Entäusserung*. There is no good reason not to select 'estrangement' for *'Entfremdung'*, except that the adjectival usage is not very idiomatic: 'The product becomes strange to the worker' sounds 'strange' to be sure! More idiomatic is 'alien to'. Nevertheless, the conceptual content of *'Entfremdung'* is univocal and maps on to 'estrangement' as we have argued above.

The problem remains that we have to choose between 'alienation' and 'externalization' for *'Entäusserung'*. Milligan and Benton, who both prefer the former, nevertheless occasionally feel forced to resort to the latter, thus indicating a genuine ambiguity. If all alienation were of 'things external by nature', then all occurrences would be equivalent in that the change of state implicit in the term could only refer (in the conditions dealt with by political economy) to the transfer of ownership. This is indeed how the matter appears to the ideological consciousness caught up in the toils of reification. It knows of no problematic of 'externalization' as a *presupposition* of alienation. However, if we penetrate this reification then we understand that, whatever the case with the means of production (see above), labour-power is surely *internally* related to its owner as his peculiar possession. We must therefore *distinguish* the moment of *externalization* from the moment of *alienation*, for to *alienate* is to treat something as *already* external property, it is not to externalize. The use of *'Entäusserung'* in Marx condenses these two moments and they need to be separated.

I suggest that the problem of 'alienation' comprises *three* distinct moments. We need the following three terms:

(1) *'Externalization'* — for the process whereby a person's labour-power is expressed in such a way as to be treated as immediately external property.

(2) *'Alienation'* — for the transfer of such property to some other agency.

(3) *'Estrangement'* — for the consequences of the subordination of the person to his own externalized powers. Objectification of my powers in working up nature becomes at the same time estrangement in the conditions dealt with by political economy, i.e. wage-labour.

Alienated Labour and Private Property

This clarification of the conceptual framework of Marx's theory of alienation helps us to understand that passage in the *1844 Manuscripts* which has mystified many commentators[43] — that in which private property is posited not as the *cause* but as the *consequence* of labour's estrangement. It seems that it is the movement of private property which separates the worker from his means of production and constitutes his labour-power as a commodity like any other, thus estranging him from his labour. Marx says that this view inverts the real relation.[44] I suggest that this is because the estrangement inherent in the capitalist labour-process is not an epiphenomenon of the property relations of the wage-contract but a *precondition* of its making sense to posit labour-power as alienable property; before anything can be alienated an external relation must exist, or be potentially realizable, between it and its present owner. The estrangement of labour-power from its conditions of expression, and its own self, is presupposed by such private property. In order to uncover the real relationship, 'alienated labour' must be given conceptual priority over 'private property'.

As far as the material practice is concerned, the interest of the capitalist in appropriating the use-value of labour means that labour-power is alienable only if the capitalist is confident he has ways and means of externalizing this labour-power in an appropriable form. No capitalist would buy my immortal soul — for such alienation would remain notional without the possibility of introducing the relation of externality required for the realization of another's property in it. The devil alone knows how such a purchaser would occupy, use, or even mark, it as his.

With most commodities the contract of sale, and acquisition of the use-value, are concluded more or less at the same time. In the case of wage-labour there is a problem for the capitalist in that, after hiring the worker, he must find ways of enforcing performance of work with desired quality and in maximum quantity. For labour-power to exist as alienated property, an external relation between the worker and his work must be set up; but this is not *given* in the wage-contract itself; it

43. R. Schacht (*Alienation*, London 1971), unable to believe Marx means what he says, goes to the length of misquoting him: 'And he contends that the dominance of the institution of private property "is the basis and cause of alienated labour" . . . ' (p. 108); the alleged quote from Marx actually reads 'appears to be (*erscheint*) the basis and cause', as the Bottomore translation cited by Schacht in fact says (p. 131).
44. *EW*, p. 332.

must be *realized in the labour-process*. The history of the capitalist labour-process is not merely one of increasing efficiency through technical improvements but also one of the increasing subordination of labour to the will of the capitalist. From this point of view capitalist exploitation is not a merely quantitative matter of getting something for nothing — analogous to merchant profit — it is a qualitative matter of subordinating the worker to the aims and methods of the capitalist, so that surplus labour can, in Marx's graphic phrase, 'be pumped out of him'. The problem of management is to assure this 'pumping out', through all sorts of controls and pressures which tend to supplant the worker's autonomous exercise of his powers. The factory organization constitutes a collective worker which is under the sway of capital and in the face of which the personality of the individual worker is effaced.

The worker reproduces his estrangement every day insofar as his externalized labour accumulates as 'dead labour' at the pole of capital, reconstituting its domination over his living labour, and the necessity for him to alienate his labour-power piece by piece.

Conclusion

Private property is the mediation in and through which labour is estranged from itself; it is the expression of the estrangement of labour from its objective conditions and itself.[45]

In the works of the bourgeois ideologists such as Locke and Hegel the estranged consciousness expresses in an uncritical way the external relation thus established between the person, his powers, and his world. In their eyes, a person appropriates this world as private property, and is even presented as the owner of his individuality; but since the actualization of the property relation presupposes *alienability*, no coherent account of personality can be given; a person both is, and is not, constituted through the development of his powers and their objectification through activity in the material world.

For Marx the critique of private property leads to the unveiling of its secret: that it is the historically developed form through which the development of human powers, and the humanization of Nature, has been realized, but an estranged form. The abolition of private property is significant for him insofar as it amounts to the reappropriation by humanity of their essential powers and essential objects.[46]

Reprinted from *RP* 26

45. Ibid., p. 332.
46. Ibid., p. 375.

Birth of the Subject — Foucault

Colin Gordon

Since 1970 Michel Foucault has published three books, *L'Ordre du Discours* (The Order of Discourse), *Surveiller et Punir* (Surveillance and Punishment) and *La Volonté de savoir* (The Will to Knowledge), none of which has yet appeared in English in this country.[1] This body of untranslated work, which is likely to be rapidly augmented in coming years, establishes Foucault not only, as was already evident from his *Madness and Cilization*, *The Birth of the Clinic*, *The Order of Things* and *The Archaeology of Knowedge*, as being one of the most original and exciting writers on history, science and discourse, but also as one of the most politically important and radical theorists currently working. The theoretical conditions which would permit an assessment of the full significance of these writings have yet to be realized, and my purpose here is simply to give a rudimentary outline of the contents of *Surveiller et Punir* and *La Volonté de Savoir*. However, it seems already clear that the present chronological threshold of English translation coincides, if not with a radical break or change of direction, at least with a major turn in Foucault's work; the turn being marked by the explicit and central thematization in *L'Ordre du Discours* of the question of power.

Like its predecessor *The Archaeology of Knowledge* (1969), *L'Ordre du Discours* is a systematic reflection on the principles governing a programme of historical description of the production of 'discourses'. The difference between the two books can be baldly expressed by saying that, whereas in the *Archaeology* the focus is on the identification of 'rules', in *L'Ordre* Foucault speaks of the operations of a discursive 'police'. The immanent ordering of the discourses is represented as the effect of an immanent power. The *Archaeology* largely consists of a systematizing, retrospective commentary on Foucault's earlier studies of the discourses of psychiatry (*Madness and Civilization*), medi-

1. *L'Ordre du Discours*, Gallimard, 1970; *Surveiller et Punir*, Gallimard, 1975; *La Volonté de Savoir*, Gallimard, 1976.

cine (*The Birth of the Clinic*), general grammar, natural history and analysis of wealth with their respective precursors and successors (*The Order of Things*). It identifies four modes of concrete 'historical a priori' which regulate the conditions of possibility of these organized historical collections of statements and practices: the constitution through discourses of certain possible objects of knowledge (mental illness, the clinical case, the table of species . . .); the social, political and epistemological determinations of the possible place that can be taken up by the subject of a particular discourse (alienist, clinician, economist . . .); the modes of possible conceptual ordering local to specific discourses (taxonomies, aetiologies, semiologies . . .); lastly, the strategic principles governing the possible options and transformations within discourses of themes and theories, and the strategic effects of their articulation on to non-discursive social practices. A year later, Foucault gave the inaugural lecture at the Collège de France of which *L'Ordre du Discours* is the expanded text. The lecture is a theoretical, programmatic prospectus for his subsequent researches. Here, the theory of discourse is located for the first time within a theory of power. A fundamental theme emerges which Foucault has since repeatedly stressed:[2] the intimate connection between the production of knowledge and the exercise of power. The means of regulation of discourses are exhibited as permeating effects of control and delimitation. The boundaries of discourses are demarcated by practices of exclusion: certain topics and objects of discourse are prohibited (politics, sex); certain individuals are radically disqualified as speakers (the heretic, the madman); certain statements are rejected as false by the competent social instances. The status of statements is controlled by structural principles interior to discourses: the relationship of text and commentary, the unities established by the identity of an author and the coherence of a discipline. Qualifications are demanded of the speaker in a discourse: participation in a ritual; admission to a group; adherence to a doctrine; acceptability, for example in terms of class, under a social regime of appropriation of discourse. Finally, Foucault notes the power of particular philosophical concepts such as 'ideality', 'subject', 'experience' and 'mediation' to limit the possible form of production of statements within the discourses where they hold sway. For instance: the category of original experience carries the implication that discourse is to function essentially as a recognition and repetition of pre-given significations; 'a primordial complicity with the world is taken as founding for us the possibility of speaking of it . . . If there is

2. Cf. 'Prison Talk', *Radical Philosophy* 16, pp. 14–15.

discourse, what can it then be in its legitimate form except a discreet reading?'[3]

This development in Foucault's theory did not amount to an overall rejection of his earlier work, but was rather an explication of its implicit orientations — no doubt with a little help from the May *événements*. 'When I think back now, I say to myself, what could I have been speaking about in *Madness and Civilization* and *Birth of the Clinic*, if not power? Now, I'm perfectly conscious of not having used the word then and of not having had this field of analysis at my disposal.'[4] The tentative remarks in the *Archaeology* on the strategic ordering of discourses and their articulation on the non-discursive already opened the way towards the thematization of power. In *L'Ordre du Discours*, discourse is viewed 'from outside' as a social entity which implicates power because of its essential attributes to scarcity, instability and desirability. But the operation of power in and upon discourse is still not theorized here in a form which integrates it with the principles of discursive *production*: power canalizes, controls and delimits production, but these operations appear as essentially negative and mediated in their relation to production: the historically constituted forms of '*will to truth*' and '*will to knowledge*' which animate discourse appear in the form of 'something like a system of exclusions.'[5] The discursive deviation, like the mediaeval leper or madman in *Madness and Civilization*, is expelled from the city. The dialectical pathos of domination and repression which informed Foucault's early masterpiece is still perceptible in this formulation of 1970.

Surveiller et Punir and *La Volonté de Savoir* advance, for the first time, a set of general theses on the history and nature of power itself, with a critique of the ideology of power as repression: an ideology whose dominance extends to the radical left. They examine the histories of two social/discursive complexes where the language of repression has customarily found its themes and materials: the prison system and sexuality. Their common thesis is that the play of power in these complexes has not, in the modern world, consisted primarily in the negative procedures of repression and prohibition, but is characteristically positive, productive, and creative: a continual process of proliferating tactics and techniques, which functions in capitalist society by reinforcing both the relations and the forces of social production, manufacturing, at the concrete physical level, docile utilizable social individuals and, at the 'ideological' level, consti-

3. *L'Ordre du Discours*, p. 53.
4. MF quoted by Pascal Werner, *Politique Hebdo* 247, pp. 30–31.
5. *L'Ordre du Discours*, p. 16.

tuting individuals as subjects.[6] Foucault is to this extent in agreement with Althusser in regarding *assujettissement* in capitalist societies as meaning not only subjection to, but also, necessarily, subjectification. In this respect it would be true to say that Foucault has shown with greater correctness and historical specificity than anyone else how (and why) 'Substance' becomes 'Subject'. Moreover, if one can take Foucault's genealogical method as correctly positing that, in history, genesis is always also constitution, then his examination of *assujettissement* may provide us with some insights into the true stakes and dramatis personae of all past and present versions of the 'problem of the subject'.

General Theory of Power

Foucault argues in *La Volonté de Savoir* that the structure of social power since the emergence of the European nation-states has had two distinct and consecutive organizing principles, that the former of these regimes of power has continued, in the capitalist period, to determine the ideology of power, and that up to the present time this *'inverted representation'* of power has pervaded political discourse, including that of the left. *Surveiller et Punir* traces, across a relatively narrow chronological threshold before and after 1800, a transformation in the *power to punish*; *La Volonté de Savoir*, in a wider-ranging, preliminary survey, outlines an ever-proliferating process of investment of the modern regime of power in an unprecedented *'apparatus of sexuality'*.

'By power, I don't mean "Power" in the sense of a set of institutions and mechanisms which guarantee the subjection of the citizens of a given State . . . An analysis in terms of power should not postulate as initial data the sovereignty of the State, the form of the law or a global unity of domination; these are rather only the terminal forms of power. By the term power it seems to me that one must understand first of all the multiplicity of relations of force which are immanent to the domain where they are exercised, and are constitutive of its organization . . . The omnipresence of power: not at all because it might have the privilege of regrouping everything under its invincible unity, but because it produces itself at each instant, at every point, or

6. It being a condition and a consequence of these productions of power that individuals in general are made, for the first time, objects of knowledge. (The use of the term 'ideology' here in a loose, untheoretical sense is mine and not Foucault's; his work is not directed towards the construction of a theory of ideology. Cf. *The Order of Things* p. 328; *The Archaeology of Knowledge*, p. 184–62.)

rather in every relation from one point to another. Power is every-where — not because it encompasses everything, but because it comes from everywhere . . . Clearly it is necessary to be nominalist: power is not an institution, a structure, or a certain force with which certain people are endowed: it's the name given to a complex strategic situation in a given society!'[7] Foucault affirms the priority, in the order of exposition, of power over politics. Politics, like war, is a particular, derivative figure produced in the play of power. Power is exercised, rather then held: it is a general form of relations rather than a privileged possession, a form of relations which are immanent to social relations of other kinds — economic, cognitive, sexual — and which are productive, rather than superstructural. Power 'comes from below': relations of global domination are effects of, and are sustained by, the play of power in small, local groups, families and institutions. The intelligibility of the field of power relations consists in their being 'at once intentional and non-subjective'; they are imbued by a calculation, intrinsically oriented to aims and objectives, but this form of immanent rationality is not the effect or creation of a calculating will, that of a class or an oligarchy. They are made up of local tactics of power which are often perfectly explicit, even cynical; but they combine and compose into co-ordinated strategies without a strategist, anonymous systems possessing an unstated, yet clearly decipherable, rationality. Finally, there is no power without resistance as well; indeed points of resistance are internally related to the operation of power. This is not to say that power is essentially relational in character. In the words of Nietzsche, 'The will to power can manifest itself only against resistances; therefore it seeks that which resists it' (*The Will to Power*, p. 656). Resistances are constituted as resistances by the effect of power, but this does not mean that they are eternally passive or hopeless; like power, resistances are essen-tially dispersed, mobile, local and heterogeneous, and it is in this shape that they form the base and the precondition for occasions of global, revolutionary rupture and confrontations.

'The study of this microphysics assumes that the power which operates in it is to be conceived not as a property, but as a strategy, that its effects of domination be attributed not to an 'appropriation', but to dispositions, manoeuvres, tactics, techniques, functions; that one deciphers in it more of a system of relations always in stress, always in activity than a privilege to be captured; that one gives as its model perpetual battle, rather than the contract which effects a

7. *La Volonté de Savoir*, pp. 21–23; for the following cf. pp. 123–7.

cession, or the conquest which takes hold of a domain . . . This power, moreover, does not impose itself purely and simply, as an obligation or a prohibition, on those who "haven't got it"; it invests, traverses and works through them, just as they themselves, in their struggle against it, draw support from the very hold power exercises on them. Which means that these relations reach deep into the texture of society, that they aren't localized in the relation of State to citizens or at the boundaries between classes, and that they don't merely reproduce at the level of individuals, bodies, gestures and behaviour the general form of the law of government; that if there is a continuity (these relations are indeed articulated on this general form of power through a complex series of interactions), there is no analogy or homology between the global and the local, but instead a regional specificity of mechanisms and modalities.'[8]

The development of this theory of power in the specific investigations of these two books concerns the interrelated problems of the forms of appearance of power (which are also the forms of its acceptability) and of the modes of its real operation within and on a particular privileged focus, namely the body of the individual member of society, on the one hand through the institutional discipline and surveillance of her/his physical existence, and on the other through the organized questioning and supervision of her/his 'sexuality' — in both these cases operating through a regime which is constantly maximizing its power by functioning at the same time as a production of knowledge of the individual.

La Volonté de Savoir contains a sustained attack on the dominant notion that the relation of power to sex is essentially repressive. Foucault argues that to break away from this conception means at the same time discarding a certain general view of power which is prevalent in political analyses and deeply rooted in European history. This view is represented in discourse on sexual repression in a number of ways. First, the relation of power to sex is *negative*: power has no hold over sex and its pleasures, except that of saying no to them. It produces only absences and lacunae, its effects have the forms of limit and lack. Secondly, power acts by pronouncing a *rule*; the grip of power on sex is in this way linguistic and discursive; the purest form of power is that of the legislator. Thirdly, power takes the (paradoxical) form of *prohibition* of its objects: 'renounce yourself on pain of being suppressed; don't appear, if you don't want to disappear; your existence will be prolonged only at the price of your annulment'.[9] Fourthly, power operates a *logic of censure* with three

8. *Surveiller et Punir* pp. 31–32.
9. *La Volonté de Savoir*, p. 11.

principal terms: affirming that something is not permitted, preventing its being spoken, denying that it exists. Each term supports the other in a circular system, 'linking the non-existent, the illicit and the non-formulable so as for each to be at once the principle and effect of the other'.[10] Fifthly, power is a *unitary apparatus*; its form of unity is that of the law, operating in the mutual play of licit and illicit, transgression and punishment. In all the power-figures of prince, father, censor, master, 'power is schematized under a juridical form; its effects are defined as those of obedience. In the face of a power which is law, the subject is constituted *as* subject — subjected subjectified; the one who obeys.'[11]

Such are the elements of what Foucault calls the 'juridico-discursive' representation of power. How is it that such a curiously restrictive representation of its operation is accepted? Foucault suggests two reasons. First, power in general needs an element of secrecy; only by a partial masking of its operations can it be rendered tolerable for its subjects. 'Power as a pure limit traced to freedom is, at least in our society, the general form of its acceptability.' No doubt Kant's equation of moral freedom with the categorical imperative is the masterpiece of this jurido-discursive language. Moreover, the language of rights and freedoms (not forgetting duties) is, as Foucault points out in *Surveiller et Punir* (Pp. 223–5), consonant with a system of maximizing disciplinary controls. The greater the valorization of the individual as ideal subject (and the intensification of his real technical-economic value), the greater is the demand and the legitimation for techniques of individual training and re-training.

The second reason is historical. The monarchical state apparatus triumphed in the Middle Ages in the guise of an instance of regulation, arbitration and limitation of the previous tangle of economic, civil and military rights and obligations; monarchical law imposed itself as a principle of order and hierarchy for other, pre-existing instances of power. 'Its formula *pax et justitia* denotes, in this function to which it laid claim, peace as the prohibition of private and feudal wars, and justice as the way of suspending the private settlement of claims in law . . . Law (*droit*) was not simply a weapon skillfully deployed by the monarchs; for the monarchical system it was the mode of its manifestation, and the form of its acceptability. Since the Middle Ages, in Western societies, the exercise of power has always been formulated through the law.'[12] Although correct in its substance, the critique of monarchy dating from the 17th century

10. Ibid, p. 111.
11. Ibid, p. 112.
12 Ibid, pp. 114–5.

which portrays the king as an arbitrary power setting himself above the law, neglects the fact that the principles of universal justice by which it condemns the monarchy are the same principles which the monarchy used to gain acceptability for itself and to curtail the rights and freedoms of classes. These principles themselves were never called in question by the anti-monarchist. 'At bottom, despite differences between periods and objectives, the representation of power has remained haunted by monarchy. In political analysis and thought, we have still not cut off the king's head.'[13] At the present time the 'hypothesis of repression' concerning sexuality envisages and directs its liberationist critique under the guidance of a conception of the hold of social power over sex which is framed in terms of law. *La Volonté de Savoir* suggests that the historically rooted form of this critique permits it to be incorporated in and exploited by a regime of power which it has profoundly misrecognized. The real character of this regime is the question to which these books propose an original and radical answer.

Birth of the Prison

Surveiller et Punir, subtitled 'Birth of the Prison', traces the transformation in penal theory and practice in France between 1780 and 1840. The narrative has three main phases: the style of criminal trial and punishment under the *ancien régime*, the programme of penal reform advanced by Ideologue writers in the revolutionary period and their Enlightenment precursors, and the new penal institutions established after the Revolution with their associated police and legal apparatuses. The socio-historical scope of the book, however, ranges beyond this domain and period because Foucault shows that the new prisons do not correspond to the penal theories of the first generation of reformers, but are rather the successor and the apotheosis of a complex of disciplinary procedures evolved over the preceding three centuries in a variety of different social institutions; the prison is the focus of the synthesis of disciplinary techniques with the reformers' ideology of punishment, and of their intensification and transformation into a new type of apparatus of political and social power which, transcending particular institutions, functions as a paradigm for modern society in some of its fundamental aspects: the 'carceral society'. *Surveiller et Punir* links up with Foucault's work of the 1960s by presenting the genealogy of one of the 'human sciences' — penology/

13. Ibid, p. 117.

criminology; and by reconstructing the formation of one of the seminal incarnations of the modern 'soul', the Man of the human sciences — the criminal. Before we attempt a summary of the book, it should be said that Foucault here shows himself once again to be a virtuoso of the archive; his extraordinarily rich and dense text is stunningly documented from original sources, deployed in a subtle and complex exposition.[14]

Readers will perhaps be surprised by the problematization of a 'birth of the prison' dated at the beginning of the 19th century; the prison as such is not after all an invention of the Napoleonic period. But in fact confinement was not primarily conceived in the *ancien régime* as an instrument of judicial punishment, and it occupied at best a marginal place in its penal system. In 1767 Serpillon writes in his *Code Criminel* that 'prison is not regarded as a punishment in our civil law'; a statute of 1670 does not mention imprisonment among the penalties of law. In France, imprisonment was either an obsolescent, or a local and regional practice numbered among the range of trivial penalties. Execution, corporal punishment and mutilation, the galleys, fines, public exposure occupy the major penal roles. 'Prisons, in the intention of the law, being destined not for punishment but only for assuring oneself of their persons . . .'[15] The 'general hospitals' of Paris and the provinces indeed make up, as was shown in *Madness and Civilization*, a massive system for the extra-juridical confinement of troublesome and deviant individuals; but in law the prisons function primarily as a place of detention for accused persons, as well as, for instance, juvenile convicts not yet old enough for the galleys.

The place of the prison is only one of the radical differences between the criminal law of the 18th and 19th centuries. Foucault begins by characterizing the forensic practices of the *ancient régime* in France (which resembled those of most other European countries, with the exception of England). Crucial is the relationship of the judicial process to the accused. In the 18th century judicial investigation is conducted secretly and in writing as an assembling of 'proofs'; as the instrument of kingly sovereignty, the court retains sole and absolute power over the investigation and its truth. Proof of guilt is arrived at additively: a combination of 'half-proofs' is reckoned to equal a 'full proof'; moreover a 'partial proof' in itself signifies a partial culpability and justifies a partial punishment; a suspect is already, as such,

---

14. Foucault himself summarizes some of the principal themes of *Surveiller et Punir* in 'Prison Talk' (*Radical Philosophy* 16). I try here to avoid duplicating this material.
15. *Surveiller et Punir*, p. 122. Cf. pp. 119–22.

culpable to a certain degree which merits a degree of punishment — custodial imprisonment, interrogation administered in the course of the trial itself. The accused himself enters the procedure directly only at the stage where he is confronted by the proofs of guilt and induced to make a confession by an institutionalized and carefully regulated use of torture. A confession has the virtue of being the completest possible proof, making other proofs superfluous; on the other hand, a prisoner who does not confess under torture is (normally) exempted from the maximum penalty he would otherwise suffer.

This physical, corporal struggle for the truth, and overlapping of trial and punishment, extends to the execution of the penal sentence *par excellence,* the *supplice* (contemporary definition: 'A corporal, painful, more or less atrocious punishment'). The explicit rationale of the *supplice* is as an act of royal vengeance on one who by his crime (whatever its other consequences) has violated the sovereignty of the king. Conceived metaphorically as an assault on the physical form of the sovereign,[16] crime is repaid literally, in kind, in a form whose greater intensification reaffirms the absoluteness of the violated royal power. The execution of sentence is commonly accompanied by a display of military force, while the executioner acts as the champion of the king who, if he fails in his duties, may be penalized in place of the prisoner. This procedure of penal torture has a number of additional features and functions. The display of symbolism accompanying the ceremony makes the convict into 'the herald of his own condemnation . . . the convict publishes his crime and the justice he has been made to render by bearing them physically on his own body';[17] his public confession before execution prolongs his trial through a climactic revelation of judicial truth; the place and means of execution can be used to establish an immediate symbolic, even theatrical, correlation between the crime and the punishment; the protraction and gradation of torture, finally, serve as an ultimate extraction-revelation of truth through the victim's public contrition. 'Judicial torture, in the 18th century, operates in this strange economy where the ritual which produces truth goes together with the ritual which imposes punishment. The body interrogated in the *supplice* constitutes the point of application of punishment and the place of extortion of truth. And just as presumption is an integral part of the trial and a fragment of guilt, the regulated suffering of the interrogation is at once a measure of punishment and an act of

16. Foucault cites on this E. Kantorowitz, *The King's Two Bodies.*
17. Kafka's story 'In the Penal Colony' contains an ingenious elaboration of this theme.
18. *Surveiller et Punir,* p. 46.

inquiry.'[18] The precise function of torture/*supplice* is that of 'a revealer of truth and an operator of power. It assures the articulation of the written on the oral, the secret on the public, the procedure of enquiry on the operation of the confession . . .' Nothing is more foreign to 19th-century justice than this intimacy between the court of law and the punishment it prescibes.

It is thus clear why Foucault regards the history of punishment as needing to be located within a 'history of the body'; the central peculiarity of classical penal practice is not so much its singular exploitation of corporal violence as the role which it assigns to the body of the criminal as the point of integration of power and truth. With the ending of the *supplice*, penal practice does not migrate from the corporal to a disembodied field of moralization, but transforms the value, the place and the fate of the body within a new regime which is none the less still centred on it. It produces 'the soul, prison of the body'.[19]

The 'Ideology' of the reforming literature which mediated this transformation proposed effectively to elide the physical dimension of punishment in favour of a 'penal semiotics', a 'technique of punitive signs'; its punishments were to consist in the public display of convicts in a manner calculated to act as a prophylaxis for the minds of the populace. The ideas of crime and punishment must be tightly connected and 'succeed each other without interval . . . When you have thus formed the chain of ideas in the heads of your citizens, you may then pride yourself in being their guide and master. An imbecile despot can bind his slaves with iron chains; but a true politician binds them more tightly with the chain of their own ideas, its end attached to the solid base of reason — a bond which is all the stronger because we are ignorant of its substance and believe it to be of our own making; time and despair can wear down bonds of iron or steel, but can do nothing against the habitual union of ideas, except tie them more firmly still; and it is on the soft fibres of the brain that the unshakeable base of the strongest empires is to be founded.'[20] Punishment as terrorism is to be replaced by punishment as moral representation; it continues the form of the public and the theatrical but changes the tone from the horrific to the 'picturesque'.

The reform programme of the Ideologues rested on a multiple critique of the *supplice*, for its dangerous ambiguity (liable to induce outrage and rebellion as easily as political edification); for its ineffec-

19. Ibid, p. 34.
20. *Surveiller et Punir*, p. 105, quoting from J.M. Servan, *Discours sur l'administration de la justice criminelle*, 1767, p. 35.

tiveness (because of an imagined upsurge of violent crime, and of a real and economically unacceptable increase in crimes against property); and for the irregularity of its convictions and penalties. It substituted for the deliberate excess of the *supplice* a technique of measure and calculation. Excessive punishments are politically and morally dangerous; 'it is necessary to punish crime exactly enough in order to prevent it: just enough to outweigh the hope of criminal gain.' 'What is to be maximized is the (public) representation of punishment, not its corporal reality'; the physical person of the criminal is the least significant object of the spectacle; the 'representation' of justice necessitates its perfect certainty and truth; the procedure of judicial investigation must follow the pattern of research, not that of inquisition, and judicial judgmeent must approximate to *judgement* pure and simple. The penal code calls for a sort of double taxonomy, a 'Linnaeus of crimes and punishments':[21] crimes must be exhaustively classified and specified, while penalties are individualized according to the nature of the criminal, his wealth, his class. The casuistic tradition of ancient jurisprudence and the confessional, whose object of knowledge was the illicit act, begin at the same time to give place, in penal concern with recidivism and the *'crime passionnel'*, to the investigation of the criminal *individual* as a delinquent subject, a criminal will. The discourse of 'Ideology'[22] utilized by the reformers is in this respect a partial precursor of criminology. This discourse 'provided in fact, through the theory of interests, representations and signs, through the series and genesis (of ideas) which it reconstituted, a sort of general recipe for the exercise of power over men: the "spirit" as the surface of inscription for power, with semiology as the instrument; the subjection of bodies through control of ideas; the analysis of representations, as the principle of politics of bodies far more effective than the ritualized anatomy of the *supplices*.'[23]

This reforming literature was directed *against* punishment by imprisonment; the secrecy of the prison was associated, as in the flagrant example of the Hopital Génèrale, with the arbitrary royal power of the *lettre de cachet*. The new prison system in France, therefore, depended on other methods and examples in the field of penitentiary technique. Foucault cites as the earliest such initiative in correctional confinement the Rasphuis and Spinhuis founded at Amsterdam in 1596, which practised a form of pedagogical and spiritual transformation of the individual by the imposition of a system of continuous

---

21. Cf. *Surveiller et Punir*, p. 102.
22. (Whose 'Newton', according to Condillac, was John Locke.)
23. *Surveiller et Punir*, p. 105.

exercise. In the 18th century three important foundations introduced a number of new themes into penal technique. The Ghent reformatory (1749) stressed the function of the restraining of the prisoner as labourer: the reconstruction of a 'homo economicus'; in England Hanway's proposals (1775) and Howard and Blackstone's Act (1779), implemented notably in Gloucester prison, emphasized *solitary* labour as the optimal method of individual correction; the Walnut Street prison in Philadelphia specified the non-publicity of punishment as a requirement for its effectiveness as a process demanding a rigorous surveillance and classification of the individual prisoner — 'a sort of permanent observatory which permits the separating out of the varities of vice and weakness'. These experiments shared the Idéologues' concern with the role of punishment as prevention, the specificity of penalties and knowledge of the individual, but differed from them fundamentally at the level of technique — and therefore of policy. To the reformers' fantasies of a public domain saturated by moral representations, there is opposed the necessity of closed institutions in which the delinquent, instead of being placed on display as a social enemy, is 'taken in charge' in the totality of his physical daily existence, and made, by the operation of an absolute institutional power, the subject not of an ideal and generalized but of a concrete, individualized, 'orthopaedic' process of correction. The pure legal subject thus becomes the real human individual, according to Foucault, in the shape of a body to be trained.

Discipline

The question of precisely how and why this institutional technique conquered the field of penal practice is the fulcrum of Foucault's exposition. He does not, as with the hospital in *Birth of the Clinic*, relate the political struggles through which this penal policy was adopted after the Revolution. In point of fact his treatment indicates that the question of the systematic adoption of imprisonment as penal policy is perhaps wrongly posed; the problem is the wider and profounder one of the constitution of punishment as discipline,[24] of the prison as the

---

24. The problematic here is formulated by Nietzsche: cf. *On the Genealogy of Morals*, II, p. 13. "To return to our subject, namely punishment, one must distinguish two aspects: on the one hand, that in it which is relatively enduring, the custom, the act, the "drama", a certain strict sequence of procedures; on the other hand, that in it which is fluid, the meaning, the purpose, the expectation associated with the performance of such procedures. In accordance with the previously developed major point of historical method, it is assumed without further ado that the

point for the totalization and perfection of a polymorphous disciplinary technique previously elaborated within a variety of other institutions. It is not surprising that this is also the point where 'questions of method' separate Foucault from more 'orthodox' social historians; the elaboration of control through discipline is a paradigm case of Foucault's 'intentional but non-subjective' regimes of power whose institution cannot be reconstructed as a history of conscious individual or collective choices.

Marx noted in *Capital* how the development of a disciplinary apparatus (and penal code: 'the law-giving talent of the factory Lycurgus') is an essential part of the social regulation of the labour-process in the capitalist mode of production. Foucault's genealogy of discipline stands in close continuity with Vol. I, part 4 of *Capital*; he refers explicitly to Marx's discussion there of the relations between technology, the division of labour, and the elaboration of disciplinary procedures.[25] But Foucault contributes an added dimension to the study of 'the production and reproduction of the capitalist's most indispensable means of production: the worker'.[26] The worker as such is not produced solely through his insertion into large-scale industry as a 'living appendage of the machine', or by his 'mutilation' and 'crippling' through the division of labour imposed by manufacture. The positive, productive arts of discipline function as an analysis and transformation of the individual as human machine — both morally and physiologically — and construct a macroscopic model of social mechanics complementary to that of industrial technology. In the 19th century, 'the prison is not a factory; it is, it must be in itself a machine of which the prisoner/workers are at once the cogs and the products'[27] — or, in the words of a contemporary reformer, 'Labour

procedure itself will be something older, earlier than its employment in punishment, that the latter is projected and interpreted into the procedure (which has long existed but been employed in another sense), in short, that the case is not as has hitherto been assumed by our naive genealogists of law and morals, who have one and all thought of the procedure as invented for the purpose of punishing, just as one formerly thought of the hand as invented for the purpose of grasping . . . the previous history of punishment in general, the history of its employment for the most various purposes, finally crystallizes into a kind of unity that is hard to disentangle, hard to analyse and, as must be emphasized especially, totally indefinable. (Today it is impossible to say for certain why people are really punished: all concepts in which an entire process is semiotically concentrated elude definition; only that which has no history is definable.)' Translated by Kaufmann and Hollingdale, Random House, 1969.

25. And also to F. Guerry and D. Deleule, *Le corps productif*, Paris 1973.

26. *Capital* Vol. I, Pelican, p. 718.

27. *Surveiller et Punir*, p. 245.

should be the religion of the prisons. For a society-machine, purely mechanical methods of reform are needed.'[28]

During the 17th century, concomitantly with the use of large standing armies, the 'soldier', as specified in his necessary bodily characteristics, ceased to be a recognizable type identified and selected from among a population, and became a type to be produced through military training. The elaboration of this science was coeval with the influence of Descartes' mechanical speculations on physiology and La Mettrie's *L'Homme-Machine* ('at once a materialist reduction of the soul and a general theory of training (*dressage*)'; both drew inspiration from the celebrated clockwork automata of the period, which 'were not just a way of illustrating the human organism; they were also political dolls, miniature models of power: the obsession of Frederick II, the scrupulous king of little machines, well-trained regiments and long exercises.'[29] The focal concept of 'docility' designates this dynamic and constantly intensifiable interrelation of the attributes of knowability, malleability and utility of individuals. Foucault notes the general concern, throughout the 18th century, with the knowledge of the infinitely small and the 'discipline of the miniscule'. La Salle's rules for the Christian Brothers' schools stress 'how dangerous it is to neglect the little things . . .'; the young Bonaparte dreamed of becoming the Newton of the microscopic. This military pedagogy was characteristically 'analytic/specific', analysing physical manoeuvres into their smallest temporal segments, and scientifically founding uniform regulations on the study of individual anatomical variations, operating the repetition of precisely defined exercises and achieving its results within an uninterrupted, calibrated temporal continuum. With the stop-watch and the parade ground, knowledge and power elaborate the structure of a 'disciplinary time'. This 'analytical pedagogy' foreshadows the paramilitary social regimes of prisons and other 'total institutions', and in turn draws upon and refines the disciplinary traditions of Christian monasticism, which received a new impetus and elaboration with the Jesuit colleges in the 16th century. Foucault proposes a general analysis of the common disciplinary regime of armies, schools, workshops and reformatories (whose inherently multipurpose character is reflected in the curious hybrid foundations of the 18th and 19th centuries, such as convent-prisons and convent-factories, and reaches its apogée in the penitentiary school at Mettray (founded in 1840), 'the model which

28. Cited in *Surveiller et Punir*, p. 246.
29. Ibid, p. 138.

concentrated all the coercive technologies of behaviour', those of family, workshop, army, school and judicial/penal system: 'the first normal school of pure discipline'). Discipline involves a typical spatial as well as temporal technique: an enclosed site (barracks and factory follow, in this,. the model of the convent), a cellular geometrical organization and subdivision (classroom, workshop), a mobile assignment and ordering, in a space at once ideal and real, of hierarchical ranks (the 'legions' of the Jesuit schools, the complex seating plans of classrooms) — visible taxonomies like those of botanical gardens, making possible 'at once the characterization of the individual as individual, and the ordering of a given multiplicity'. Individuation as a technique of discipline.

These procedures are supported by specific techniques of enforcement. Firstly, 'apparatuses of hierarchical surveillance': the style of 'architecture' of the military camp, 'diagram of a power which acts by the effect of a general visibility'. Hospitals, military schools and factories adopt a spatial plan which ensures the complete visibility of their inmates; a new intermediary class of specialized overseers, like the 'student/officers' of the mutual schools, takes up the functions of surveillance. Secondly, an apparatus of 'normalizing sanctions': miniature institutional penal systems develop, in which quasi-juridical constraints exist to enforce natural norms, punishments themselves take the characteristic form of exercises and repetitions isomorphic with obligatory behaviour itself, and individuals are continually graded on a bi-polar continuum between reward and punishment as members in a parareligious economy, a moral accountancy of 'penances' and 'exemptions'; the knowability of the individuals is maximized at the same time as control, and assignment of visible rank can count as a reward in itself; the essence of normalization consists in its power simultaneously of homogenizing and individualizing its subjects. Thirdly, the special ceremonies of inspection and examination — the origins, for Foucault, of the methods of the 'human sciences' with their questions, notations and classifications. In the schools, examination is integrated with teaching through daily, competitive tests; education takes the form of a continuous two-way exchange of knowledge, a mutually reinforcing cycle of learning and surveillance.

The Carceral Archipelago

Given, then, the prior emplacement, by the period of penal reform, of a system which superposed the functions of discipline, pedagogy, surveillance and punishment, it becomes intelligible how, once it was politically established that the judicial power to punish in a constitutional state must take the form of reformation, not revenge, there rapidly appeared a new empire of penitentiary institutions in which punishment meant placing under surveillance. Foucault's fascinating and many-faceted reconstruction of this process cannot adequately be presented here. What is perhaps most worth bringing out is the epoch-making significance of the thematization and elaboration of the technique of surveillance itself.

(1) It signifies an *'inversion in the political axis of individualization'* and *'transforms the whole social body into a field of perception'*. It has not always been the subject, rather than the ruler, whose individuality is of primary concern, nor the child who has always been more intensely individualized than the adult. The beginnings of the institutional practice of documenting 'cases', 'keeping files' on individuals, goes together with a 'deglorification' of writing and biography; no longer are the personal lives of kings the only ones worthy of written description. This shift from the visibility of the ruler to the visibility of the subject appears in the reign of Louis XIV in the shape of the mass military review as a power-display which inverts the form of the Roman triumph. The individual as subject is not just the 'fictive atom' of a mercantile ideology, but a fabricated reality — the work of a productive power. 'Knowable man (soul, individuality, consciousness, behaviour, no matter which) is the object-effect of this analytical investment, this domination-observation.'

The theme of visibility is elaborated in specific historical models, both real and imaginary. Foucault cites from the late 17th century the rules for plague towns in France — a total administration which immobilizes and isolates each street and household, imposing a regular, compulsory inspection of their inhabitants; at the opposite pole from this state of exception, contemporary with the penal reforms, is Bentham's project for a 'Panopticon', a circular building composed of cage-like cells whose occupants can be continuously observed from a single closed and darkened tower at its centre: visibility as a trap. Whether implemented in the form of a factory or a prison, the plan synthesizes the productive function of the institution with a power of minimal effort and maximal effect: the model for a disciplinary society.

(2) The archipelago of institutions of surveillance is the base for the disciplinary colonization of a whole society. In the 18th century the schools, the hospitals and the public charities began to extend their surveillance to the families of their subjects. With the prisons, the

police, and the new juridical-penal conception of criminality, a whole social class is opened up to institutional management and observation which extends political power to embrace the smallest details of social life — the police were early exhorted to keep an eye on 'everything which happens'. (As Foucault explains in 'Prison Talk' — *Radical Philosophy* 16 — the bankruptcy of the reformative functions of the prisons by no means impairs their usefulness as instruments for the extraction of surplus power, and it is an indication of the over-determined potentialities of the disciplinary regime that, as he remarks, it is always the prison which is proposed as 'its own remedy' by reformers of the reformatory.) The criminal is henceforth understood not through his act, but through his life, which becomes the object of the combined curiosity of the law and the object of the combined curiosity of the law and the criminologist, and which receives the correlative ideal form of a 'disciplinary career'. The continuum established between discipline, law and punishment and the scientific normalization of the legal has the effects of 'lowering the threshold of social tolerance of penality' and of creating 'not just a new right to punish, but a new acceptance of punishment'.

It was said above that for Foucault the 'juridico-discursive' form of appearance of power has ceased to represent its essence but continues to provide it with its acceptable mask. Here, it seems that the inalienable power of civil society to punish its members continues to serve as the underlying 'natural' legitimation of the penal principle, while at the same time the 'purpose' of intensified disciplinary control is able to invest the 'custom' of judicial punishment, eliminate the appearance of violence previously inseparable from it, and fabricate an acceptable procedure of normalization and power which it can bequeath to the nonpunitive social institutions of medicine, psychiatry, education, public assistance and 'social work'. Perhaps it is part of the strategic role of the prison in transmuting the mode of production of power that the disciplinary regime makes possible techniques of power in which discipline itself becomes barely recognizable.

Sexuality and the Will to Truth

'The will to truth, which is still going to tempt us to many a hazardous enterprise; that celebrated veracity of which all philosophers have hitherto spoken with reverence: what questions this will to truth has already set before us! What strange, wicked, questionable questions! It is already a long story — yet does it not seem as if it has only just begun? Is it any wonder that we should at least grow distrustful, lose our patience, turn impatiently away? That this sphinx should teach us too to ask questions? *Who* really is it that here questions us? *What* really is it in us that wants "the truth"?' Nietzsche, *Beyond Good and Evil* (1885).[31]

Michel Foucault, following no doubt in Nietzsche's footsteps, proposes an interrogation of the will to sexual truth. He uses the metaphor of Diderot's 'Les bijoux indiscrétes'. 'This magic ring, this jewel which is so indiscreet when it's a matter of making others speak, but so ineloquent about its own mechanism, it's this which we must now make loquacious in its turn, it's of itself that it must be made to speak . . .'[32]

La Volonté de Savoir is the introduction to a projected six-volume *History of Sexuality*, at once a theoretical preface and an overview of the terrain to be covered by the subsequent volumes. Its central thesis amounts to something of a Copernican revolution — the denial that the development in the politics of sexuality for the past three or more centuries in the West can be adequately understood in terms of repression and censorship, and the assertion that the 20th century's talk of sexual repression, the 'great sexual evangelism' which prophecies an emancipated future and denounces a past which 'sinned against' sex, is in reality a historically determined tactic within a strategy of power whose essence is, not the suppression, but the proliferation and incitement of sexualities and the multiplication of discourses about sex. Foucault proposes to examine the origin of the modern 'question' of sex, of a double process of questioning — the extraction from sex both of its truth, questioning which is now posed by Foucault. What is the origin and meaning of this 'speaking sex', this 'fantastic animal housed in us', and of this 'game of truth and sex', which the 19th century has bequeathed to us, in which 'pleasure mingled with the involuntary, and consent with inquisition'?

If surveillance is the central device in the genealogy of prisons, the confession has a similar place in that of the 'apparatus of sexuality'. It is with the mediaeval development of the confessional that the modern interrogation has its origin. The changing meaning of the word 'aveu' follows the changing meaning of the 'truth' to be spoken — from the 'authentication of the individual by reference to others and his ties with others' (the *aveu* of the feudal bond), to 'the

---

31. *Part One: On the Prejudices of Philosophers* 1 (translated by R.J. Hollingdale, Harmondsworth 1973).
32. *Histoire de la Sexualité*, Vol. 1: *La Volonté de Savoir*, Gallimard, 1976, p. 104.

discourse of truth he is capable of conducting about himself'. 'The avowal of truth is inscribed at the heart of procedures of individuation by power.' Where Nietzsche spoke of Western history as breeding an 'animal with the right to make promises',[33] Foucault speaks of modern man as a '*bête d'aveu*' — a confessing animal. The problematic of repression articulates on to, and is perfectly compatible with, the strategy of confession. Repression implies a secret, hidden and guilty: this theme of the enigmatic truth which it is for us to uncover, the secret of sex, 'is not the fundamental reality in relation to which all the incitations to speak about it are situated — whether they really attempt to resolve it, or whether they somehow prolong it through their very way of speaking. It is more a question of a theme which is part of the mechanism of these incitations: a way of giving form to the requirement to speak of it, an indispensable fable for the indefinitely proliferating economy of discourse on sex.'[34] We no longer perceive the obligation of confession as the effect on us of a constraining power, but as a demand of our own secret truth to reveal itself; 'if it does not do so, we believe that some constraint is holding it back, that the violence of some power is weighing upon it, and that it will only be able finally to articulate itself at the cost of a kind of liberation. Avowal frees, power reduces to silence . . .'[35] This modern philosophy of truth through self-interrogation is an 'inverted representation' of the real operations of the 'political history of truth', a ruse of power — of the strategy of subjectification — belonging to the essence of the confession. The avowal, as it determines the constitution of sexuality as an object of knowledge, is defined by Foucault as a ritual of discourse in which the subject who speaks coincides with the subject of the statement; which is deployed within a power relationship; where truth is authenticated by the obstacles and resistances it must lift in order to be formulated; and where the utterance itself produces intrinsic changes in the utterer. Foucault stresses repeatedly that the reason for the constant valorization and sensitization of the truth of sexuality is not to be sought in the preeminent intrinsic significance of the pleasures of bodies or the functions of reproduction, but in the multiple challenges and opportunities for invention and exploitation which the question presents for the economy of knowledge/power.[36]

33. *On the Genealogy of Morals*, II, p. 1 ('Man himself must first of all have become *calculable, regular, necessary*, even in his own image of himself, if he is to be able to stand security for *his own future*, which is what one who promises does!' (ibid))
34. *La Volonté de Savoir*, pp. 48–9.
35. Ibid, p. 89.
36. 'In ever narrowing circles, the project of a science of the subject has tended to gravitate around the questions of sex . . . not by reason of some natural property

In the 19th century, the fear of impending scandal which accompanies the project of a science of the sexual, and the initially paradoxical appearance of a theory centred on the individual reflect the magnitude of the task of creating a *'confessional science'* and the massive consequences of the postulates upon which the science was founded. Among these postulates Foucault numbers: the clinical synthesis of examination and confession, of visual observation of pathological symptoms and verbal interrogation of their subject; the positing of a generalized and diffuse sexual causality, as manifested in the astonishing 19th-century proliferation of sexual aetiologies; the postulate of the 'intrinsic latency' of sexuality, of that which is hidden from the subject himself — hence the need for constraint to a difficult avowal; the necessity for an interpreter who can 'duplicate the revelation of the confession with the decipherment of what it says'; the postulate of a morbidity proper to the sexual, of the essential sexual duality of the normal and the pathological, with the therapeutic correlate of a cure accomplished purely through the eliciting of sexual truth.

If 'sexuality' is indeed constituted by a complex of discursive practices involving the scientific deployment of the confession, the genealogical importance of the historical derivations linking the penitential with Krafft-Ebing is evident. The confessional was first instituted in a compulsory annual form in the 13th century; during the Counter-Reformation it underwent both an intensification of its frequency and an evolution of method and emphasis, which 'makes the flesh into the root of all sins, and displaces its most important moment from the act itself to the perturbations, so difficult to perceive and formulate, of desire.'[37] Increasing discretion about direct reference to the bodily act, but also increasing pertinacity in probing and rendering into discourse and concupiscence of the soul. An infinite task; and an illustration of the thesis that a partial censorship can serve an overall process of incitement to discourse.

The terrain of the confession of sex widens again with its gradual 'emigration' from the sacrament and the bond with moral theology to the relationships of pedagogy, adult and child, family, medicine and psychiatry. 'The confession opens out, if not on to new domains, at least to new ways of traversing them. It is not simply a question of saying what has been done — the sexual act — and how; but of reestablishing in and around it the thoughts which double it, the

---

inherent in sex itself, but as a function of the tactics of power immanent in this discourse' (ibid, p. 99).

37. Ibid, p. 28.

obsessions that accompany it, the images, the desires, the modula-
tions and quality of the pleasure that inhabit it.'

Parallel developments took place in the social principles of regulating sexual practices. The triple mediaeval system of canon law,
civil law and pastoral supervision concentrated its attention on the
marriage relationship and its infringement. The criminal status of
'sodomy' was vague and uncertain, the sexuality of children a matter
of indifference; there was no clear discrimination in terms of culpability between the 'illicit' and the 'unnatural', between marriage
without consent and bestiality, copulation during Lent and rape —
or rather the 'against nature' was only the extreme form of the
'against the law'. (The hermaphrodite was a constitutionally criminal
being.) From the 18th century on, this pattern is progressively transformed. The normality of the heterosexual monogamous marriage is
increasingly shrouded in privacy and discretion, while attention shifts
towards more marginal infractions. An increasing separation appears
between the instances which detect and sanction on the one hand
breaches of the legislation and morality of marriage and the family,
and on the other infractions of natural sexual functioning. Beneath
the libertine appears the pervert. But what Foucault particularly
emphasizes is that the phenomenon is not solely one of a redirection of
attention, of a more discriminate visibility, but also of a production of
sexualities, an 'implantation of perversions'. Where only acts are in
question, we can perhaps speak of perversities; the language of perversions — and the reality — become possible only when, beyond
and through the act, the individual is seized in his totality.

Foucault distinguishes four of the 'implantations of perversities'.
Firstly, particularly with the emergence of the campaign against child
masturbation, the contradiction in the practice of prohibiting something whose (natural) existence is at the same time denied gives rise to
the constituting of 'perverse' pleasures as secrets, making them
conceal themselves in order to be then uncovered. Within the strategy
of 'anchoring on the family a whole medico-sexual regime', the vice of
masturbation figures in reality more as the support of the campaign
against it than as its enemy. What appear to be barriers to the
pleasures of the body function in fact as the lines of their penetration
by power.[39] Secondly, and following on from this policy of pursuit,

39. This illustrates the essentially subordinate function of a censorship within the
    'apparatus of sexuality'; on one level schools endeavour to eliminate the sexual
    component of children's language, while on another they erect a pedagogical
    discourse about their (non-) sexuality. Foucault suggests that the former may have
    been a necessary condition for the latter. Possibly it is a general condition of the

there is the process of 'incorporation of perversions', the formation of a new principle of specification of the individual. To the juridical subject of the illegal act of sodomy there succeeds the 'homosexual personality', a perverted essence pervading the subject's entire being and consubstantial with his person: his homosexuality (as with the voices of the Baron de Charlus in Proust) becomes a secret which his body betrays in his every act and gesture. This discourse of specification flowers in the bizarre 19th century taxonomies of sexual perversion, and the appearance in 1870 of the concept of 'inversion' engenders the concept of the homosexual as a distinct human 'species' — marked by a 'hermaphroditism of the soul', and 'inner androgyny'. Thirdly, the technology of sexual health and pathology, as it takes it upon itself to 'grapple with the sexual body', creates a new form of interplay between power and pleasure, a game of hide and seek in which 'pleasure diffuses itself on the power which pursues it, while power anchors the pleasure which it has uncovered' — 'the "pleasure of analysis", in the widest sense of the phrase'. Lastly, Foucault numbers the bourgeois family itself among the principal sites for 'apparatuses of sexual saturation': the multiple relationships between parents, children, nurses and domestics create a proliferating system of sexual power, danger, surveillance and deviation.

The historically determined characters of sexuality 'correspond', Foucault argues, 'to the functional exigencies of discourse'.[40] 'The various sexualities are all correlates of precise procedures of power.' The proliferation of perversions is 'the real product of the interference between a type of power and bodies and their pleasures.'[41] Hence, 'the history of sexuality — that is, of what functioned in the 19th century as a specific domain of truth — must be undertaken, to begin with, from the point of view of a history of discourses.'[42] The multiplication of these discourses derives from the position occupied by sex as a particularly rich and fruitful nexus for relations of power. The last four of the six volumes of Foucault's *History* are planned to examine in detail four distinct 'strategic ensembles' in the creation around sex of apparatuses of knowledge/power.[43] These are:

---

constituting of a subject as *'bête d'aveu'* that (because of this discursive 'cordon sanitaire') the subject is one who can only confess.

40. Ibid, p. 91.
41. Ibid, pp. 65–6.
42. Ibid, p. 92.
43. The titles of the five further volumes to be published are (2) La chair et le corps (the flesh and the body); (3) La croisade des enfants (the children's crusade); (4) La femme la mère et l'hystérique (the wife, the mother and the hysteric); (5) Les pervers (the perverts); (6) Population et races.

(1) The *'hystericization' of the woman's body*: the analysis of the woman's body as one which is 'saturated with sexuality', integrated by its inherent pathology into a field of medical practices, socialized and familialized by the discourses of fertility and nurture. 'The Mother, with her negative image, the "nervous woman", constitutes the most visible form of this hystericization.'[44] (2) The *'pedagogization of the child's sex'*. The child, biologically susceptible to an activity 'at once "natural" and "against nature"', becomes an ambivalent and marginal social being, the object of the pedagogical concern and attention of every institution into which she/he is inserted. (3) The *'socialization of procreative conduct'*: a developing medical/fiscal/economic/political apparatus for the control and/or stimulation of the birth-rate. (4) The *'psychiatrization of perverse pleasures'*: the isolation of a biological-psychic sexual instinct which becomes the index for the normality/abnormality of the whole individual and the target of a corrective technology.

Family, Class, Race

These themes are given by Foucault a number of further elaborations which are of immense interest and significance, but can only be outlined here in the briefest summary.

Firstly, the domain of the family (which covers three at least of the above four strategies) stands at the heart of the problematic of sexuality because it marks the point of articulation of two historical/ethnographic structures regulating the relations of bodies and their sex: the *alliance*, a system centring on the homeostasis of kinship structures, on the themes of blood and ancestry, where questions of sex (as in the mediaeval confessional) are predicated on the axis of the matrimonial alliance; and the more recent system of sexuality, oriented towards maximization rather than stabilization, 'linked from the start to an intensification of the body', relating sex to a problematic of sexuality, substituting the valorization of sex for that of blood, preoccupied with heredity rather than ancestry. For Foucault it is the family which acts as the integrating 'exchanger' between the structures of sexuality and alliance; and this is why since the 18th century 'the family has become a place of obligatory affects, sentiment, love', why 'sexuality has the family for its privileged point of emergence', and why, because of this, sexuality is *born "incestuous"*.

44. Ibid, p. 137.

Hence the early preoccupation of ethnography with the incest-taboo. 'To affirm that every society . . . and hence our own, is subject to this rule of rules, guaranteed that this apparatus of sexuality . . . couldn't escape from the old system of alliance.' 'If one admits that the incest-prohibition is the threshold of all culture, then sexuality finds itself placed since the depths of time under the sign of the law.'

As the family came to be penetrated by the discourse previously developed at its margins in the confessional and the school, its position as the centre of sexual danger took visible shape in the new gallery of sexual characters: 'the nervous woman, the frigid wife, the mother indifferent or beset with murderous obsessions, the impotent or perverted husband, the daughter hysterical or neurasthenic, the child precocious, already exhausted, the young homosexual who refuses marriage or neglects his wife . . . the mixed figures of dis-ordered alliance and abnormal sexuality.' Hence the mounting chorus of cries for help addressed from the family to clinical experts. Hence, again, at the end of the 19th century, the apparent paradox of psychoanalysis, which 'uncovered the sexuality of the individual outside of the family, but rediscovered at the heart of this sexuality, as the principle of its formation and the core of its intelligibility, the law of alliance, the mixed games of marriage, kinship and incest.'[45] The problematic of sexuality, after being grafted on to the system of alliance, now comes to the latter's therapeutic aid. (This is not, Foucault however adds, to deny that psychoanalysis set itself in radical opposition to the discourses of sexual heredity and degener-acy, with their eugenically-minded therapeutics and fantastic aetiologies, spuriously buttressed upon advances in the biology of animal reproduction, which prepared the way for the state racisms of the 20th century.)

A critique of 'the repressive hypothesis' must take into account the counter-criticisms that psychoanalysis can make of it; Foucault indeed does so, and his responses connect with both his remarks on the 'juridico-discursive' image of power and his observations con-cerning the genealogy of psychoanalysis.[46] But there is also to be considered the objection that the strategy of sexual repression has had a major historical function in the service of capitalism, parallel to that of the techniques of popular moralization, described in *Surveiller et Punir*, of disciplining and controlling the poorer classes. Foucault argues, however, that the construction of the 'apparatus of sexuality'

45. Ibid, p. 149.
46. On this, see also *Madness and Civilization*.

had the initial and primary sense of a self-affirmation of one class, the bourgeoisie, rather than of an enslavement of another, the proletariat. The 'question of sex' is originally posed — beginning with the confessional — by means of subtle techniques available only to restricted groups. The sexual family is the bourgeois family; the nervous woman is the leisured woman; the deviant youth is the college pupil. It is its own heredity, the safety from degeneration of its own intellectual and moral powers, the 'important, fragile treasure, the indispensable secret' of its own sex which concerns the bourgeoisie: 'the high political price of its own body'. 'There is a bourgeois sexuality, there are class sexualities, or rather sexuality is originally, historically, bourgeois, and induces in its successive displacements and transpositions specific class effects.' Foucault identifies three stages in which sexuality is generalized and transposed to the masses: the late 18th-century anxiety about popular infertility;[47] the beginnings, around the 1830s, of campaigns of popular moralization in favour of the canonical family; the emergence at the end of the 19th century of mass medico-juridical measures against perversions, in the interest of the general biological protection of society and the race. Foucault remarks on two class effects of this generalization of sexuality: on the one hand, the persistent suspicion of the proletariat that 'sexuality' is the bourgeoisie's affair, not theirs; on the other, the point of origin of the discourse of repression as a new principle of sexual differentiation of the bourgeoisie — no longer in terms of the sexuality of its body, but of the intensity of its repression. 'Those who have lost the exclusive privilege of concern with their sexuality have henceforth the privilege of experiencing more than others what prohibits it, and possessing the means of lifting its repression.'[48] Hence the possibility of an archaeology of psychoanalysis as a historic 'displacement and realignment of the great apparatus of sexuality'; hence also the reason for doubting whether the post-Freudian critique of repression, even in the politically radical form given to it by Reich, can serve either as a principle for understanding the history of the apparatus in which it is itself embedded, or as a means towards dismantling it.

Instead, the questioning of the 'question of sex' has to be located, as Foucault's concluding chapter argues, within a historical horizon

47. 'The discovery that the art of tricking nature, far from being the privilege of city-dwellers and debauchees, was known and practised by those who (being so close to nature itself) ought to have been more than all others repelled by it' (ibid p. 161).

48. Ibid, p. 172. Cf. how the bourgeoisie appropriates to itself the art of the master criminal. See 'Prison Talk' in *Radical Philosophy* 16.

where societies appropriate the power not only to destroy the bodily life of its members, but to manage it: the era of 'the entry of life into history' in the sense that the human species itself appears as a stake in its own strategies. The political importance of sexuality consists in its being the point of intersection between two extreme levels of power over life — the discipline of the individual body, and the regulation of the life of the population.[49] The strategies of sexual power enumerated by Foucault have the function of integrating these dimensions of 'discipline' and 'regulation'. It is in this framework, and that of the tension between 'alliance' and 'sexuality', that Foucault situates both the route to genocidal racism and the contemporary and expressly anti-racist Freudian quest for the 'law' of sexual desire.

La Volonté de Savoir ends with a confrontation of the objection that Foucault has obliterated the fundamental, material fact of sex in favour of a history of discourses, thereby instituting just one more form of repression: castration, once again. His uncompromising response to this is to deny that the materiality of our bodies and their pleasures is to be identified with the 'sex' of sexuality. It is part of the armature of the 'general theory of sex' that it 'permits the inversion of the representation of the relations of power and sexuality, and makes the latter appear not in its essential and positive relation to power, but as anchored in a specific and irreducible instance which power seeks to subject as it may; thus, the idea of "sex" allows one to evade the issue of what makes the "power" of power — allows one to think of it only as law and interdict ... Sex is only an ideal point made necessary by the apparatus of sexuality and its functioning.'[50]

Hence one can elicit the message — which is unlikely to be universally welcomed — that the struggle against sexism (to which, without overtly referring itself to it, Foucault's present undertaking makes an important contribution) can be effective only if it addresses itself to 'sexuality' itself — to the sexism of sex. Foucault has remarked upon the characteristic mobility of power relationships, citing in particular the instance of homosexuals who, since the 19th century, have seized upon the pathologizing discourse of 'perverse implantation' and reversed it into a discourse of defiant self-affirmation; but he has

---

49. What Foucault says here about discipline (cf. pp. 184–5) is in complete continuity with *Surveiller et Punir*; he adds here that the reformist theories of 'Ideologues' (discussed in that book — see above) are an early attempt, but at an abstract and speculative level only, at the problem of the integration of these two axes of power: a problem to whose solution in the 19th centruy the 'apparatus of sexuality' was to make a crucial contribution.

50. Ibid, pp. 204–5.

recently added that 'liberation' movements are under the necessity of displacing themselves in relation to the apparatus within which they come into being, of disengaging from and moving beyond it.[51] As he says in *Surveiller et Punir* about the prisons, his historical inquiry is indeed inspired by contemporary struggles. An anachronistic history, then? 'No, if one means by that to do the history of the past in the terms of the present. Yes, if one means by that to do the history of the present.'[52]

Foucault says that his theoretical postulates about sex and power stand in a circular relationship to the historical inquiry which he has undertaken. In a less defensive spirit, he has said that the questions of philosophy and history are inseparable.[53] Partly because I share this view, I am not offering here a 'philosophical assessment' of Foucault's recent work.[54] However, one consequence of both this and his earlier writings is of some philosophical interest. This is that it unmistakably points towards the final bringing down of the curtain on the theatre of psychological interiority, and on the latter's leading player, 'the subject'. Probably we have yet to fully register what it means not to think of human individuals as 'subjects', and (of course) one condition for doing so is the settling of our accounts with moral philosophy; in any case, 'the individual' itself might have a less hegemonic part to play in a different form of knowledge.

Utilizing Foucault

Perhaps it is sufficiently clear that, if we choose to accept and utilize the substance of what Foucault is saying, this may have immediate consequences for the way we situate ourselves in relation to questions of power. These texts, which harp on the themes of 'bodies', 'discipline' and 'power apparatuses', in the absence of any prior statement of political position, are perhaps still apt to offend against our political good taste, our libertarian prudery, our sense of decency

51. *Le Nouvel Observateur*, 12 March 1977, p. 95.
52. *Surveiller et Punir*, p. 35.
53. 'The question of philosophy is the question of the present which is ourselves. That's why philosophy today is entirely political and historical. It is the immanent politics of history, and the history which is indispensable to politics.' *Le Nouvel Observateur*, ibid, p. 113.
54. One condition for a discussion of this would be an enquiry into the knowledge/ power structure involved in the production of 'history' — both the object and the discourse. (Cf. Michel de Certeau, *L'Écriture de l'Histoire* (Gallimard, 1975) and Jean-Pierre Faye, *Théorie du Récit/Langages Totalitaires* (Hermann, 1972–3).) The need for a theory of the relationship between the standpoint, 'method' and object of history is, of course, particularly pressing when it is the history of power which is in question. The theory has yet to be produced.

about discussions of power. One can simply note that Foucault puts on to the agenda the question of the political as such, of the relationship, that is, between our conceptions of 'politics' and our 'political' practices. 'What strikes me in Marxist analyses is that it is always an issue of "class struggle", but that if there is a word in this expression to which less attention has been paid, it is "struggle". Here again one must be more precise. The greatest of the Marxists (beginning with Marx) have insisted on "military" problems (the army as a state apparatus, armed insurrection, revolutionary war). But when they speak of "class struggle" as the general outcome of history, they are chiefly worried about knowing what a class is, where it is situated, who it encompasses, but never what in concrete terms the struggle is. With one exception (near to hand, in any case): not the theoretical, but the historical texts of Marx himself, which are finer in a different way.'[55]

Postscript (1984)

Surveiller et punir appeared in English translation as *Discipline and Punish* (Peregrine, 1979), and *La volonté de savoir* as *The History of Sexuality, Volume 1* (Pelican, 1981). Background material to these books may be found in M. Foucault, *Power/Knowledge: selected interviews and other writings* (Harvester, 1980). See also Foucault's important Afterword, 'The Subject and Power', in H. Dreyfus and P. Rabinow, *Michel Foucault: Beyond Structuralism and Hermeneutics* (Harvester, 1983).

Foucault's work after 1976 moves in two new directions. The first is an exploration, complementary to his study of the micro-politics of discipline and normalization, of the 'macro-political' history of transformations in techniques and rationalities of government, from the early modern police State to the advent of neo-liberalism. Some research by Foucault and others in this field is collected in *The Foucault Effect: Studies in Governmental Rationality* (ed. G. Burchell et al, Harvester, 1985), and in *I&C*, issues 4 to 11. The second of Foucault's shifts of perspective is an extensive recasting of his original plan for a History of Sexuality, resulting in the three new volumes *L'Usage des plaisirs*, *Le Souci de soi*, and *Les Aveux de la chair* (Gallimard, 1984). Foucault's attention focuses here on the development, from classical antiquity to the period of the early Church, of a 'culture of the self', a phenomenon which he regards as distinct from and irreducible to what he had termed *assujettissement*, the constitution of subjectivity as an effect of normalizing techniques of power.

55. Ibid, p. 130.

2. Marxism and Social Science

On the Theory of Ideology — Althusser's Politics

Jacques Rancière

Foreword

The following text was written amid the political and academic debates of the immediate post-'68 period in France. In one respect, therefore, it is an occasional piece. In another respect it is also a first clearing of the terrain for a longer-term reflection on the philosophical and historical relations between knowledge and the masses, pursued most notably in *La Nuit des Proletaires* and *Le Philosophe et ses pauvres*. I believe it was absolutely necessary to begin by clearing away the impoverished theoretical conceptions and political consolations conveyed by this unfortunate 'theory of ideology'. This critique did not develop without some extreme simplification concerning the masses, knowledge and the class struggle. I have tried, since then, to correct these as I go along. During the same period our politicians, for their part, were doing their best to get up to date. With the aid of an army of sociologists and educational theorists they finally discovered that the best means of reducing inequalities in the face of formally transmitted knowledge was to cut back on this knowledge itself. Those who thought like me in 1969 are today nearly unanimous in denouncing this 'perverse effect' of our former struggles.

> *'Certainly it is an interesting event we are dealing with: the putrescence of the absolute spirit'*
> (Marx: *German Ideology* Part I)

'All the mysteries which lead theory into mysticism find their rational solution in human practice and in the understanding of that practice.' For a long time the main mystery as far as we were concerned was this sentence itself. We gave it a not unmystical solution: like the young theologians of Tübingen seminary, scouring the undergrowth to discover new 'faculties', we would multiply 'practices', each endowed with specific laws. In the forefront of course lay theoretical practice, containing the principles of its own verification. This was how we interpreted the question — the more so as its own opponents could only counter with a practice reduced, in the name of 'praxis', to the invocation of itself.

In May 1968 things were suddenly thrown into relief. When the class struggle broke out openly in the universities, the status of the Theoretical came to be challenged, no longer by the endless verbiage of praxis and the concrete, but by the reality of a mass ideological revolt. No longer could any 'Marxist' discourse keep going on the mere affirmation of its own rigour. The class struggle, which put the bourgeois system of knowledge at issue, posed to all of us the question of our ultimate political significance, of our revolutionary or counter-revolutionary character.

In this conjuncture, the political significance of Althusserianism was shown to be quite different from what we had thought. Not only did the Althusserian theoretical presuppositions prevent us from understanding the political meaning of the student revolt. But further, within a year we saw Althusserianism serving the hacks of revisionism in a theoretical justification for the 'anti-leftist' offensive and the defence of academic knowledge. What we had previously chosen to ignore thus became clear: the link between the Althusserian interpretation of Marx and revisionist politics was not simply a dubious coexistence, but an effective political and theoretical solidarity.

The following remarks seek to indicate the point in the Althusserian reading where this interdependence is established: namely, the theory of ideology.

The Analysis of Ideology

The specificity of the Althusserian theory of ideology can be summarized in two basic theses:

1. In all societies — whether divided into classes or not — ideology has a common principal function: to assure the cohesion of the social whole by regulating the relation of individuals to their tasks.

2. Ideology is the opposite of science.

The critical function of thesis (1) is clear: it is directed against ideologies of 'de-alienation' according to which the end of capitalist alienation would be the end of the mystification of consciousness, the advent of a world where the relations of man to nature and of man to man would be perfectly transparent — in a certain sense, the Pauline transition from indistinct perception in the mirror to direct perception. Against these ideologies of transparency, Althusser sets the necessary opacity of every social structure to its agents. Ideology is present in every social totality by virtue of the determination of this totality by its structure. To this there corresponds a general function: that of supplying the system of representations which allow the agents of the social totality to accomplish the tasks determined by this structure. 'In a society without classes, just as in a class society, ideology has the function of securing the *bond* between men in the ensemble of the forms of their existence, the relation of individuals to their tasks fixed by the social structure.'[1]

So the concept of ideology can be defined in its generality before the concept of class struggle intervenes. To some extent, the class struggle will subsequently 'overdetermine'[2] the principal function of ideology.

We would like to examine how this thesis is established and how it is articulated with the second in a particularly explicit text:

> Ideology, in class societies, is a representation of the real, but a necessarily false one because it is necessarily aligned and tendentious — and it is tendentious because its goal is not to give men objective knowledge of the social system in which they live, but on the contrary to give them a mystified representation of this social system in order to keep them in their 'place' in the system of class exploitation. Of course, it is also necessary to pose the problem of ideology's function in a society without classes — and this would then be resolved by showing that the deformation of ideology is socially necessary as a function of the very nature of the social whole: more specifically, as a function of its determination by its structure which renders this social whole opaque to the individuals who occupy a place in it determined by this structure. The representation of the world indispensable to social cohesion is necessarily mythical, owing to the opacity of the social structure. In class societies, this principal function of ideology still exists, but is dominated by the additional social function imposed on it by the existence of class division. This additional function thus by far outweighs the first. If we want to be exhaustive, if we want to take these two

1. Théorie, Pratique Théorique et Formation Théorique: Idéologie et Lutte Idéologique, p 29.
2. N. Poulantzas, *Political Power and Social Classes*, NLB, London 1973, p. 207.

principles of necessary deformation into account, we must say that in a class society ideology is necessarily distorting and mystifying, both because it is made distorting by the opacity of society's determination by the structure, and because it is made distorting by the existence of class division.[3]

Our first problem is the nature of the concepts put forward to define the general function of ideology: the notion of 'social cohesion' echoes the formula used above — 'the bond between men in the ensemble of the forms of their existence'. Is this 'bond' or 'cohesion' of the 'social whole' really the province of Marxist analysis? How, after having proclaimed that the whole history of mankind is that of the class struggle, can it define functions like: *securing social cohesion in general*? Is it not precisely because Marxist theory has nothing to say on this subject, that we have shifted our ground and moved onto that of a Comtean or Durkheimian type of sociology, which actually does concern itself with the systems of representation that secure or break up the cohesion of the social group? Is it not this phantasm of 'the social group' which is outlined here in Althusser's analysis? We can see an index of this displacement in the status Althusser here accords religion: 'In primitive societies where classes do not exist, one can already verify the existence of this bond, and it is no accident that its reality has been detected in the first general form of ideology, religion. (It is one of the possible etymologies of the word *religion*.)'[4]

By inverting the analysis we can pose this question: when ideology is conceived in general, before conceiving the class struggle, is it not necessarily conceived on the model of the traditional analysis of religion — that of a sociology which has inherited metaphysical discourse on society?[5] The *superimposition* of two functions of ideology

3. Théorie, Pratique Théorique . . ., pp. 30–31.
4. Ibid., p. 26.
5. [Note added in Feburary 1973:] The vague use of 'metaphysical discourse' subsequently inherited by sociology (social cohesion, the bond between men, etc . . .) loses the specificity of the concepts involved here, the fact that they belong to a historically determined *political* problematic. It was this problematic which, in the second half of the 19th century, gave sociology its status and position in the ensemble of practices then introduced by the bourgeoisie to mould the men necessary to the reproduction of capitalist relations of production. It was a time when, after the establishment of those relations, the bourgeoisie had twice faced the possibility of its extinction as a result of the proletarian riposte. More astute than 'Marxist' scholars who prate endlessly about the 'spontaneously bourgeois' ideology of the proletariat, the bourgeoisie recognized in 1848 and 1871 that, even if they used the same words (order, republic, ownership, labour . . .), the workers were thinking *differently*. Hence the necessity for the bourgeoisie to strengthen the *ideological* weapons of its dictatorship. The political threat

(maintenance of social cohesion in general; and exercise of class domination) may thus signify for us the *coexistence* of two heterogeneous conceptual systems: that of historical materialism and that of a bourgeois sociology of the Durkheimian type. Althusser's special trick is to transform this coexistence into an articulation, which implies a double subversion.

First, ideology is defined not on the terrain of Marxism but on that of a general sociology (theory of the social whole in general). Marxist theory is then superimposed on this *sociological* theory of ideology as a theory of over-determination specific to class societies. The concepts defining the function of ideology in a class society will therefore depend on concepts from this general sociology.

But, secondly, the level of this general sociology is itself claimed to

---

gave the new human sciences their place among the techniques for moulding the 'normal' man necessary to the system; a moulding which encompassed the detection of criminals or the prevention of suicides, as well as the selection of the cadres or parliamentary education of the masses (i.e. the parliamentary and electoral repression of the autonomous political practice of the masses). It also gave them their problematic as a science of the phenomena which consolidate or break up social cohesion. Its characteristic questions were: What principles strengthen the cohesion of a group? What criteria allow the most suitable ones to be chosen for such and such a position? Or, more crudely still: how can one identify in the physiognomy of a crowd, or in the dimensions of someone's skull, the danger that they represent for the social order? It is not difficult to spot behind the elaboration of the 'sociological method' the preoccupations of the detective Bertillon, author of anthropometry, or of the military doctor Lebon, theoretician of crowds and their 'ring-leaders'.

The important thing here is that Althusser separates these concepts of the bourgeoisie's 'police-reason' from the political dangers and manoeuvrings of power which underlie them, in order to relate them to a function of the social whole in general. This is naturally complemented by a conception of science above and beyond classes, which reproduces precisely the 'scientistic' ideology that crowns the edifice of 'police-reason'. If a direct line leads from this abstract conception of ideology to the validation of Kautsky's thesis of 'the importation of Marxism into the working class', it is perhaps because this line reproduces in theory the historical collusion of social-democracy in the bourgeois attempt to domesticate the working class, to wipe out its cultural identity. The pitiful bankruptcy of social-democracy must indeed have something to do with this 'importation of consciousness'. In practice, it has come to mean the containment of the working class by electoral parties which, while spreading parliamentary illusions, repress the political practices and pervert the organizational forms of the proletariat. At the same time a 'science' and a scientistic ideology are propagated which help to wipe out the traditions of autonomous popular expression, and so on. Conversely, the assertion that it is necessary to bring *consciousness* to a working class involuntarily trapped within bourgeois ideology, may really indicate the part played by social-democracy in the attempt to integrate the working class into bourgeois political life. If the working masses have been able to find the means to resist this kind of 'Marxism' in their practice, the intellectuals generally discover in it the form and substance of their 'Marxist' theoretical discourse.

be a level of the Marxist theory of ideology, despite the fact that Marxism has nothing to say about it. This reverses the process: the analysis of the alleged general function of ideology will be made on the basis of the concepts and analyses by which Marxist theory has thought the function of ideology in class societies. Marxist concepts defining class societies will be used to define society in general.

The mechanics of this subversion are clearly revealed when Althusser describes the double determination of ideology in class societies: 'In a class society, ideology is necessarily distorting and mystifying, both because it is made distorting by the opacity of society's determination by the structure, and because it is made distorting by the existence of class division.'[6]

What is this structure, whose level is here distinguished from that of class division? In Marxist terms, the determination of a social totality by its structure means its determination by the *relations of production* characterizing a dominant mode of production. But 'relations of production' refers to the social forms of appropriation of the means of production, which are class forms of appropriation. Capitalist relations of production exhibit the class opposition between those who possess the means of production and those who sell their labour power. The distinction between the two levels disregards the fact that the level of the 'structure' is strictly the level of a class relation.[7]

6. Ibid., p. 31.

7. Naturally this class relation has to be carefully distinguished from the forms (political, economic, ideological) in which the class struggle is fought, which are its effects. It nonetheless remains that the relations of production can only be understood as class relations, unless they are transformed into a new 'backstage-world'. It is just such a transformation which results from the distinction made by Poulantzas (in *Political Power and Social Classes*) between the relations of production and 'social relations'. Starting from the correct idea that the relations of production are not 'human relations', Poulantzas falls into the dilemma indicated above: transparency or opacity. As a result, the relations of production appear withdrawn into that exteriority represented by the 'structure'. The analysis of Althusser and Poulantzas ultimately results in a truism: the structure is defined by no more than its own opacity, manifested in its effects. In a word, it is the opacity of the structure which renders the structure opaque.

This quasi-Heideggerian withdrawal of the structure could in no way be politically innocent. The French Communist Party is happy to argue thus: the struggle of the students only concerns the effects of capitalist exploitation; the grass-roots struggles in the factories against the job hierarchy, automation and victimization also deal only with effects. It is necessary to come to grips with the very cause of exploitation, the capitalist relations of production. But to this dimension of the problem, only Science has access, i.e. the wisdom of the Central Committee. The withdrawal of the structure thus becomes a *focus imaginarius* in the Kantian manner, an inverted image, reduced to a point, of a future without limit: France's peaceful road to socialism.

The analysis of fetishism demonstrates this point very clearly. For it is not enough to say that fetishism is the manifestation-dissimulation of the relations of production (as I did in *Reading Capital*). What it specifically conceals is the *antagonistic* character of the relations of production: the Capital/Labour opposition disappears in the juxtaposition of the sources of revenue. The structure is not concealed because, like Heraclitan nature, it simply likes to hide. It disguises its *contradictory* nature, and this contradiction is a class contradiction. So the manifestation/dissimulation of the structure does not imply an opacity of the 'social structure in general': it is the effectivity of the relations of production; that is, of the class opposition 'labourers/non-labourers' which characterizes all class societies. Extended beyond class societies, this effectivity of the structure becomes a completely undetermined concept — or alternatively, it is determined by standing in for a traditional figure of metaphysics: the evil genie or the cunning of reason.

Ideology and Struggle

The distinction between two levels of ideological disguise is thus highly problematic. It clearly functions by *analogy* with Marx's analysis of the two-fold nature of every production process (the labour-process in general, and the socially determined process of production). But the analogy is clearly illegitimate. By transferring the law of the last instance to the superstructures, by making the effects reproduce the law of the cause, it posits the social whole as a totality of levels each of which expresses the same law. It is easy to see the absurdity that would result from an application of the same principle to the political superstructure: one might then say that the 'social totality in general' requires the existence of a political superstructure and define the general functions of a State before touching on the class struggle. This comparison of ours is more than a mere joke: ideology for Althusser may well possess the same status as that conferred on the State by classical metaphysical thought. And it may well be that his analysis reinstates the myth of an ideological state of nature — a myth whose theoretical and political meaning we must now make clear.

First we have to appreciate the irrevocable consequence of the distinction between two levels. Ideology is not seen from the start as the site of a struggle. It is related not to two antagonists but to a totality of which it forms a natural element: 'It is as if human societies could not survive without these *specific formations*, these systems of representations (at various levels), their ideologies. Human societies secrete ideology as the very element and atmosphere indispensable to their historical respiration and life.'[8]

To put the myths of origins (or ends) in the restrictive form of 'as if' is a standard act of philosophical modesty, perfected in Kant; and this is not the only time we shall come across Althusser's Kantianism. In the traditional 'as if', ideas of origin preserve their political function of concealing division. Ideology will thus be established not as the site of a division, but as a totality unified by its relation to its referent (the social whole). At the same time, the analysis of the second level will focus not on the ideological forms of class struggle, but on the 'over-determination of Ideology' (in the singular) by class division. One will speak of the ideology of a class society, not of class ideologies. Only at the end of the analysis is the division of ideology into 'tendencies'[9] admitted. But at this stage its introduction is no longer of any use: ideology, not having been initially posited as the field of a struggle, will in the meantime have surreptitiously become one of *the participants in the struggle*. The class struggle in ideology, forgotten at the start, reappears in a chimerical, fetishized form as a class struggle between ideology (weapon of the dominant class) and science (weapon of the dominated class).

Before commenting on them in detail, let us indicate the stages in this logic of forgetfulness:

1. Ideology is a system of representations controlling, in all societies, the relation of individuals to the tasks fixed by the structure of the social whole.

2. This system of representations is thus not a system of knowledge. On the contrary, it is the system of illusions necessary to the historical subjects.

3. In a class society, ideology acquires a supplementary function of keeping individuals in the place determined by class domination.

4. The principle which undermines such domination therefore belongs to ideology's opposite, i.e. science.

The strategic move in this proof is that which articulates the function of ideology with the domination of a class. 'Ideology, in class societies, is a representation of the real, but a necessarily false one because it is necessarily aligned and tendentious — and it is tendentious because its goal is not to give men *objective* knowledge of the social system in which they live, but on the contrary, to give them a

---

8. *For Marx*, NLB, London 1977, p. 232.
9. Théorie . . . etc., p. 32.

mystified representation of this social system in order to keep them in their "place" in the system of class exploitation.'[10]

By articulating two theses (ideology as the opposite of knowledge; ideology in the service of a class) which were previously only *juxtaposed*, Althusser sets forth the mechanism which, at a deeper level, ties them together: ideology is a false representation because it does not give knowledge. And it does not give knowledge because it is in the service of the ruling class. But what ideology is involved here? Would the ideology of the dominated class have the function of keeping the exploited 'in their place' in the system of class exploitation? What is defined here as a function of *Ideology* is the function of the *dominant* ideology. To conceive of a general function of ideology, Althusser has to present the domination of *an* ideology as the domination of *ideology*. The trick has been played: the general function of ideology will be said to be exercised to the profit of a class domination, and the function of undermining this domination, will be conferred on the Other of Ideology, that is, on Science. The initial suppression of the class struggle leads to a particularly interesting game of theoretical hide-and-seek. The 'Ideology/Science' couple proceeds to reintroduce the class struggle. But the latter also comes to the assistance of the 'Science/Ideology' opposition — ideology had at first only been posited as *other than science;* by being articulated with class domination, with the radical opposition 'dominant class/dominating class', this *other than science* has become the Other of Science. Difference has become contradiction.

What is this but the very process established by metaphysics and consistently repeated throughout its history: the process which answers the old problem of the *Sophist* — how, in the figure of the Other, to conceive difference as contradiction?[11] That here Marxism serves to accomplish this necessary yet impossible task of philosophy, is something to which we will have to return. It is enough for the moment to point out the significance of the displacement which has taken place in the conception of ideology. Ideology is firstly an instance of the social whole. As such, it is *articulated* with other instances, not confronted with any opposite. It is within ideology itself that the oppositions that concern it are determined: above all, that which opposes the ideology of one class to the ideology of another. How then can the 'Ideology/Science' couple become the pertinent opposition with which to grasp ideology? Only by a process which

10. Ibid, p. 30.
11. A substitute conception for the contradiction which is based, of course, on the misunderstanding of the real contradiction.

detaches ideology from the system of instances, and erases the main division of the ideological field to create a space in Marxist theory which it then shares out between science and ideology. The functioning of the 'Science/Ideology' opposition depends on the re-establishment of a space homologous to that of the whole metaphysical tradition: it supposes the closure of a universe of discourse, divided into the realms of the true and the false, into the world of Science and that of its Other (opinion, error, illusion, etc). If ideology is not fundamentally grasped as the site of a struggle, of a class struggle, it immediately slips into this place determined by the history of metaphysics: the place of the Other of Science.

Teachers and Students

We have so far shown only the general form of this displacement. We will now specify its functioning, by showing how the Science/Ideology couple works in a *political* analysis. Two of Althusser's texts — the article 'Problèmes Étudiants' and the text 'Marxism and Humanism'[12] — are in fact devoted to the political consequences of the theory of ideology.

The article 'Problèmes Étudiants' was an intervention in the conflict that had arisen between the French Communist Party's (PCF) theses on the university, and the theses then dominant in the National Union of French Students (UNEF). The latter sought to oppose the simply 'quantitative' demands of the PCF (increase in the number of universities and academic staff, etc.) with a 'qualitative' questioning of the teaching relationship, conceived, through the concept of alienation, as analogous to a class relation. Althusser's intervention was meant to draw the real lines of demarcation for the political and trade union action of the student movement. It was therefore not so much a text on the situation of time, as an article drawing the strict consequences of the Althusserian theory of ideology. These have since provided the framework, whether admitted or not, of the revisionist analysis of the university.

The principle of the article is to shift the line of class division from the teacher/student relation (where it had been drawn by the UNEF theorists) to the content of the knowledge taught. The dividing line does not appear in the transmission of knowledge between teacher and student; it lies in the very content of knowledge, between science

12. 'Problèmes Étudiants', *Nouvelle Critique*, No. 152, January 1964; 'Marxism and Humanism', in *For Marx*, op. cit.

and ideology. Althusser's argument involves a whole system of implication which we think it useful to state explicitly at this point.

Althusser bases himself on the distinction between the technical and social division of labour: 'What are the Marxist theoretical principles which should and can intervene in scientific analysis of the University? . . . Above all the Marxist concepts of the *technical* division and the *social* division of labour. Marx applied these principles in the analysis of capitalist society. They are valid for the analysis of every human society (in the sense of a social formation based on a determinate mode of production). These principles are *a fortiori* valid for a particular social reality like the university, which, for various essential reasons, belongs to every modern society, whether capitalist, socialist or communist.'[13]

A first reading reveals the same mechanism that was at work in the analysis of Ideology: suppression of the class struggle, and its replacement by the generality of a function necessary to the social whole. But the concepts here require particular attention. Althusser says he is undertaking to *apply* the Marxist concepts of technical and social division of labour. But these are in no way given as such in Marx's analysis. Rather, he demonstrates the two-fold nature of every production process, depending on whether one considers it as the labour process in general, or as a socially defined process of production, reproducing the relations of production which determine it. While a distinction between 'technical division' and 'social division' of labour can be deduced from this analysis, it is not a real distinction but a merely *formal distinction* corresponding to two ways of conceptualizing the same process. Technical division and social division are two aspects of a *single division*. The functions which assure the technical reproduction of the process are the same as those which determine its social reproduction.

Now, in Althusser's analysis there is a real distinction of places and functions which correspond to one or other of the divisions. Thus 'the technical division of labour corresponds to all the "posts" of labour, whose existence is exclusively accounted for by the technical necessities defining a mode of production at a given moment of its development in a given society', while the social division 'has the function of ensuring that the labour process of this society continues in the same forms of class division and of the domination of one class over the others'.[14]

13. 'Problèmes Étudiants', p. 83.
14. Ibid., p. 84.

Technical and Social Division of Labour

Formulated in this way, the distinction is enigmatic: how is one to define exclusively technical necessities in a mode of production? These would have to be independent of its social goals, of the re-production of the social relations of production which determine them. And conversely, does not the 'technical' functioning of the process of production already imply the reproduction of the relations of production, and hence of the forms of class division and domination?

To resolve the enigma, we must once more reverse the argument. The technical division of labour is supposed to throw a light on the function of the university. But in point of fact, the status accorded to the university will enlighten us as to the function of the concept 'technical division of labour'. Althusser tells us that the university 'for various essential reasons, belongs to every modern society, whether capitalist, socialist or communist'. So the technical division of labour, which at first seemed to correspond to the requirements of a determinate mode of production, now corresponds to the technical necessities of a 'modern' society: i.e., in Marxist terms, of a society having reached a certain level of development of the productive forces. The distinction thus becomes somewhat clearer: the technical division of labour corresponds to a given level of development of the productive forces; the social division to the reproduction of the relations of production of a determinate mode of production.

It all works 'as if' a certain number of necessary places and functions of a modern society in general could be defined exclusively in terms of the level of development of the productive forces. This conclusion will not fail to surprise the reader of Althusser. Did he not elsewhere devote all his energy to freeing Marxist theory from every ideology that views history in terms of evolution and linear development? Does not his new concept of 'modernity' absolutely contradict such an attempt? To explain this contradiction, we must ask what is at stake here politically. The significance of Althusser's backsliding is clear: it leads one to attribute to the technical division of labour — i.e., to the objective requirements of science or 'modern' rationality — that which belongs to the social forms of the capitalist mode of production.[15]

15. Thus it is that in the same article, Althusser deduces the 'technical' necessity of the whole industrial hierarchy. As for the 'essential reasons' which necessitate the existence of the university in a socialist society, their discussion will have to be left for some other occasion.

The concept of the technical division of labour appears, then, to be merely the justification for revisionist slogans based on 'the real needs of the nation', 'the real needs of the economy', 'modernization', and so forth. We know that the PCF has replaced the Marxist dialectic with a type of eclecticism resembling Proudhon's which distinguishes the good and the bad side of things. The revolutionary necessity to destroy bourgeois relations of production in order to free the productive forces, is reduced for the PCF to the job of suppressing the bad (the domination of the monopolies) to preserve and advance the good (the forms of the 'technical division of labour' corresponding to the requirements of every 'modern' society). But since Marx, we know that the 'real' needs of society always serve to mask the interests of a class; in this case, they mask the interests of the class which the PCF tends increasingly to represent: the labour aristocracy and the intellectual cadres.[16] The functioning of the concept 'technical division of labour' succeeds in justifying revisionist ideology in its two complementary aspects: a theory of 'objective needs' and a defence of the hierarchy of 'skills'.

The backsliding and the contradictions are explained as follows: Althusser has simply moved from the terrain of Marxist theory to that of its opposite, the opportunist ideology of revisionism. This displacement of Marxist analysis onto the eclectic ground of the good and the bad side is not new to us: it describes the same movement as that which shifted the theory of ideology towards the metaphysical relationship between Science and its Other. The core of Althusserianism undoubtedly lies in this articulation of the spontaneous discourse of metaphysics with revisionist ideology — an articulation that is perfectly demonstrated in the development of Althusser's argument. The distinction between the technical division and the social division of labour is expressed in the University as a distinction

---

16. [Note added in Feburary 1973:] These brief remarks will lead one astray, should they be thought to trace revisionist ideology back to the interests of the intermediary strata. What this ideology basically represents is the ideology of a power structure which already contains the prefiguration of a social order to come. The reaction of the PCF and the CGT to the corpse of Pierre Overney [a Maoist militant shot dead by factory security guards] expresses less the cadres' terror or the condemnation by members of the professions, than how it appeared to the occupants of an alternative State apparatus, who, moreover, were already participating as such in the bourgeois State apparatus. At Renault, the cadres of the Party and the CGT do not defend the interests of an intermediary class, but their own participation in the power of the employers. By taking up the position it did, the PCF was representing not the interests of its electoral following, but its own interests as an apparatus sharing in the management of capitalist power in the factory.

between science and ideology. In other words, the theory of ideology, the foundations of which seemed problematic, is now grounded on the theory of the twofold division of labour. But as the latter is but a scholarly justification for revisionism, the theory of ideology here proclaims its political basis. Mafxist theory at first acted as a solution to a problem within metaphysics; this problematic, in its turn, acts in the service of revisionist ideology. The analysis of knowledge will make this trajectory explicit: 'It is in the knowledge taught in the university that the permanent dividing-line of the technical division and the social division of labour exists, the most reliable and profound line of class division.'[17]

The strategem is here made perfectly plain: the science/ideology distinction is what allows the technical/social division to pass for a line of class division; which means that in Althusser's discourse, metaphysics arranges the promotion of revisionist ideology to the rank of Marxist theory. Only through this device does Althusser's thesis retain its 'obviousness'. For in fact it implies a double distortion: the first, already noted, concerns the status of ideology; the second bears on the effectivity of science, which is alleged to be automatically on the side of the revolution. 'It is not accidental if, in every matter, a reactionary or "technocratic" bourgeois government prefers half-truths, and if, on the other hand, the revolutionary cause is always indissolubly linked to rigorous knowledge, that is, to science.'[18]

We in turn will suggest that it is not accidental if Althusser's thesis appears here in its inverted form. It is both necessary for Althusser's argument — and impossible, without revealing what underlies it — to state in its direct form the thesis that scientific knowledge is intrinsically subversive of bourgeois domination. Such a problematic thesis is only comprehensible through a process which extends Marx's theses on scientific socialism outside their proper field. It is clear that the liberation of the proletariat is impossible without the theory of the conditions of its liberation; that is, without the Marxist science of social formations. The bond uniting the revolutionary cause and scientific knowledge is guaranteed in this case by their common object. But one has no right then to impute a revolutionary

17. 'Problèmes Étudiants', p. 89.
18. Ibid, p. 94. It is not uninteresting to note the agreement, at the very level of rhetoric, between the metaphysical formulation 'as if' and the classic rhetorical figure employed in the PCF: 'It is not accidental if . . .' Popular common-sense is not mistaken when it says that chance does many things.

character to science in general. In any case, one has only to apply this thesis to the reality of the teaching of science in order to see its inanity. The bulk of the courses given in medical schools or the big Colleges of Science undoubtedly have a perfectly valid scientific content. If this education nevertheless has an obviously reactionary function, it is not simply because the sciences are taught there in a positivist way, but because of the very educational structure of determinate institutions, selection mechanisms, and relations between students and staff (in which the latter not only possess a certain knowledge but belong to a social hierarchy — cf. the role of consultants in medicine). The dominance of the bourgeoisie and of its ideology is expressed not in the content of the knowledge but in the structure of the environment in which it is transmitted. The scientific nature of the knowledge in no way affects the class content of the education. Science does not stand confronted by ideology as its other; it resides within institutions and in those forms of transmission where the ideological dominance of the bourgeoisie is manifested.

'At least,' it will be said, 'the second element of the thesis is confirmed: ideology reinforces the power of the bourgeoisie —witness the role played by the "human sciences".' But the problem is badly posed. These disciplines owe their role to the fact that they constitute the place in the system of knowledge where the confrontations of the class struggle are most directly reflected. The problem is not their more or less 'ideological' nature, but the ideology which is trans-mitted in them. The psychology, sociology, law or political economy taught in higher education has a reactionary function not because it, wholly or in part, lacks scientificity, but because it spreads the ideology of the bourgeoisie. The point is not whether it falls under 'ideology', but whether it falls under *bourgeois* ideology. The task of revolutionaries is not to confront it with the requirements of scienti-ficity, nor to appeal from these pseudo-sciences to the ideal scienti-ficity of mathematics or physics. It is to oppose bourgeois ideologies with the proletarian ideology of Marxism-Leninism.

The most elementary concrete analysis of the university institution reveals the metaphysical nature of Althusser's division. The Science/ Ideology couple is nowhere to be found in the analysis of the univer-sity, where we are concerned with the ideology of the dominant class, not with 'ideology'. And the ideology of the dominant class is not simply — let us even say, not essentially — expressed in such and such a content of knowledge, but in the very division of knowledge, the forms in which it is appropriated, the institution of the university as such. Bourgeois ideology has its existence not in the discourse of some ideologue, or in the system of the students' spontaneous notions, but in the division between disciplines, the examination system, the organization of departments — everything which embodies the bourgeois hierarchy of knowledge. Ideology is not in fact a collection of discourses or a system of ideas. It is not what Althusser, in a significant expression, calls an 'atmosphere'. The dominant ideology is a *power* organized in a number of institutions (the system of knowledge, the media system, etc). Because Althusser thinks in the classic metaphysical terms of a theory of the *imaginary* (conceived as a system of notions separating the *subject* from the *truth*), he completely misses this point. The result is a complete distortion of ideological struggle, which comes to have the function of putting science where ideology was before. Bourgeois academic discourse is countered with a Marxist academic discourse; and the 'spontaneous, petty-bourgeois' ideology of the students is in turn countered with the scientific rigour of Marxism, incarnated in the wisdom of the Central Committee. The struggle of science against ideology is, in fact, a struggle in the service of bourgeois ideology, a struggle which reinforces two crucial bastions: the system of knowledge and revisionist ideology.

There is no ideology in the University which could be the Other of science. Nor is there a science which could be the Other of ideology. What the University teaches is not 'science' in the mythical purity of its essence, but a selection of scientific knowledges articulated into *objects of knowledge*. The transmission of scientific knowledges does not proceed from the concept of science. It forms part of the *forms of appropriation* of scientific knowledge, and these are *class* forms of appropriation. Scientific theories are transmitted through a system of discourses, traditions and institutions which constitute the very existence of bourgeois ideology. In other words, the relation of science to ideology is one not of rupture but of articulation. The dominant ideology is not the shadowy Other of the pure light of Science; it is the very space in which scientific knowledges are inscribed, and in which they are articulated as elements of a social formation's knowledge. It is in the forms of the dominant ideology that a scientific theory becomes an object of knowledge.[19]

19. [Note added in February 1973:] The formulation of the problem seems to have gone astray, because it somewhat diplomatically restricts the question of 'class science' to what is clearly the safest ground — the *teaching* of scientific knowledges — in order to avoid the shifting sands of 'proletarian' geometry or genetics. Although laudable, this restraint has the drawback of failing to deal with precisely what is in question: namely, the place of a scientific practice which would only be affected by the class struggle at the level of the transmission of its *results*. It would be advisable therefore to look more

The concept of knowledge, in fact, is not that of a content which can be either science or ideology. Knowledge is a system of which the 'contents' cannot be conceived outside their forms of appropriation (acquisition, transmission, control, utilization). The system is that of the ideological dominance of a class. It is not 'science' or 'ideology'. In it are articulated the class appropriation of science and the ideology of the dominant class. There is no more a class division in knowledge than there is in the State. Knowledge has no institutional existence other than as an instrument of class rule. It is not characterized by an

---

closely at what is involved in this representation of a 'pure' scientific practice.

What is the 'rational kernel' in the idea of the university of scientific practice: It is that propositions exist whose modes of verification seem valid for all existing classes and social systems. Let us note in passing that this universality of the modes of verification does not, for all that, place the practice which produces these propositions *above classes*. (Such developments in arithmetic as took place in the 19th century can be universally acknowledged, but this does not eliminate the political problematic of *order* which supports them.) Above all, let us note that, except in the treatises of philosophers, no science is ever reduced solely to the ordering of universally verifiable propositions, nor any scientific practice solely to the process of their production. Scientific practice is never 'pure', as it has its forms of existence in a system of social relations of which propositions, formal proofs, experiments (on the basis of which the *ideal of science* is established) are only elements. The class struggle can manifest itself at different levels: present even in propositions, proofs, a field of application, the methods and occasion of their elaboration, and so on. One can see from this that scientific propositions and theories can, at one and the same time, keep their power of verifiability and yet belong to bourgeois science. The Chinese mathematicians who made their self-criticism during the Cultural Revolution, were not accused of having produced false theorems, but of having practised in their ivory towers an academic's science, looking only for personal prestige. Similarly, they did not replace their 'bourgeois' theorems with 'proletarian' ones, but altered the relationship to the masses which had been implied in their practice. This is because the social nature of a science essentially depends on the two-fold question; *who* practises science and *for whom*? To conceal this double question is to vindicate, under cover of the universality of the modes of scientific verification, the universality of the bourgeois division of labour.

What was the basic flaw in the arguments about 'proletarian science' and 'bourgeois science' before the Cultural Revolution? Precisely that they neglected the question: who practises science? Not by accident, but because these arguments were based on a system of the division of labour which, keeping science out of the hands of the masses, entrusted the responsibility for judging its bourgeois or proletarian character to the functionaries of power and the experts on knowledge. Proletarian science will certainly never be created by a patent from the Academy of Proletarian Science and, as long as proletarian biology is the concern of Messieurs Besse, Garaudy et al., this science above classes will be in clover. As the Cultural Revolution has shown, proletarian science means essentially — and this can only be the work of a lengthy mass struggle — the suppression of a science which is the business of specialists beyond the reach of the masses. A proletarian science which distinguishes itself from the other not only by producing different propositions, but by virtue of the overthrow of the masses' age-old relation to knowledge and power.

interior division reproducing that which exists between the classes — on the contrary, its characteristics are determined by the dominance of a class. So the system of knowledge is, like State power, the stake in a class struggle, and, like State power, must be destroyed. The University is not the site of a class division, but the objective of a proletarian struggle. To transform this objective into the neutral site of a division, is quite simply to conceal the class struggle. Once it was finally grasped that there is not a bourgeois science and a proletarian science, it was thought possible to infer that science is intrinsically proletarian, or, at the very least, that it is an area of peaceful co-existence. But if science itself, at the level of its proof, cannot be bourgeois or proletarian, the constitution of objects of scientific knowledge, and the mode of their social appropriation, certainly can be. There is not a bourgeois science and a proletarian science. There is a bourgeois knowledge and a proletarian knowledge.

The Function of Teaching

The heart of Marxism is concrete analysis of a concrete situation. Now it is clear that the Science/Ideology opposition is unfit for such an analysis, class providing no more than a repetition of the classic dichotomy of metaphysics. It draws an imaginary line of class divisions for no other reason than to ignore class struggle as it really exists.[20] Althusser's misconception of the function of knowledge, and of the struggle which takes it as an objective, rests on this primary suppression. The position of the political having been misunderstood, it can only reappear in the wrong place; hidden in the alleged neutrality of the technical division of labour, or shifted into the hypothetically revolutionary function of science. We have already seen what the 'technical division of labour' represented. It remains to look more closely at the concept of science, at what gives it the specific function of concealing the class struggle.

To do this we must examine the second central thesis in Althusser's argument: 'The function of teaching is to transmit a determinate knowledge to subjects who do not possess this knowledge. The teaching situation thus rests on the absolute condition of *an inequality*

20. The characteristic of a metaphysical conception is that it tries to draw a line of class division in realities (institution, social groups) which it views in a static way. Thus the revisionists list social groups in terms of whether they are revolutionary or not. The dialectic teaches that, on the contrary, there is knowable unity and division only in struggle. One cannot draw a line of class division in the university, but only in the struggle which puts it at stake.

between a knowledge and a non-knowledge.'[21]

One can see the logic which articulates this thesis with the previous one. The first indicated the real line of class division: science/ ideology. The present thesis exposes the false dividing line: teaching/ taught. The teaching relation has the function of transmitting knowledge to those who do not possess it. It is hence based exclusively on the technical division of labour. The two theses complement each other, but absolutely contradict each other as well. For the first presents knowledge as *determined* by the difference between science and ideology, whereas the second suppresses every determination other than the opposition of knowledge to non-knowledge, of the full to the empty. The dividing line had been drawn solely between the concepts 'science' and 'ideology'. It is obliterated as soon as the reality of the teaching function comes into play. Althusser declares that students 'very often risk alienating the good will of their teachers who are unjustly held in suspicion over the validity of their knowledge which is considered superfluous'.[22] But did not the science/ideology distinc- tion precisely imply the deepest and most justifiable suspicion towards the knowledge of teachers? To remove that suspicion, it is necessary to give knowledge the status of science — to make the relation of science to non-science intervene a second time, not now in the shape of error (science/ideology) but in that of ignorance (knowledge/non-knowledge). The concept of science now appears in its true light: the science/ideology distinction ultimately had no other function than to justify the pure being of knowledge — more accur- ately, to justify the eminent dignity of the possessors of knowledge. To understand this reversal of quality into quantity, we must here again recognize the voice of the revisionist prompter: what is required is an education 'of quality', 'of a high cultural level'. As far as the teachers are concerned, in their double role of scholars and wage-earners they are objective allies of the working class. So in whose interest would it be to criticize them, if not that of provocateurs in the pay of the bourgeoisie? It is not accidental if etc., etc . . .

But it would be wrong to see Althusser's discourse as a simple piece of hack-work in the service of revisionism. On the contrary, its interest lies in the fact that it reproduces the spontaneous discourse of meta- physics, the traditional position of philosophy with respect to knowledge. Althusser indicates this position, while at the same time concealing it, when he defines philosophy as follows: 'Philosophy

21. 'Problèmes Étudiants', p. 90.
22. Ibid., p. 94.

represents politics in the domain of theory, or to be more precise: *with the sciences* — and *vice-versa*, philosophy represents scientificity in politics, with the classes engaged in the class struggle.'[23]

Althusser's thesis fails to recognize that this double representation — of the scientific with the political, and of the political with the scientific — already exists precisely in *knowledge*. Knowledge constitutes the system of appropriation of scientific conceptions to the profit of a class. It is a remarkable fact that philosophy has been established and developed in a definite relation to knowledge, but without ever recognizing its class nature. So when Plato attacks the Sophists, or Descartes scholasticism, their criticism functions largely as a critique of knowledge: that is, not simply of an erroneous discourse, but of a certain social and political power. But even when they grasp the properly political dimensions of this knowledge (Plato), they cannot attain to the level of the cause — that is to say, to the articulation of knowledge with the rule of a class. Unable to see knowledge as the system of the ideological dominance of a class, they are reduced to criticizing the effects of this system. Philosophy thus develops as a criticism of false knowledge in the name of true knowledge (Science), or of the empirical diversity of knowledge in the name of the unity of science. The criticism of knowledge, failing to recognize its class function, is made in the name of an Ideal of Science, in a discourse which separates the realm of science from that of false knowledge (opinion, illusion, etc). The opposition of Science and its Other has the function of misconceiving the class nature of knowledge. And the discourse of metaphysics propagates this misconception inasmuch as it presents itself as a *discourse on science*. What, it asks, constitutes the scientificity of science? The act of modesty characteristic of the 'epistemological' tradition to which Althusser returns, consists in believing that this question is produced at the very request of science. Thus for Althusser, a new science (Greek mathematics, Galilean

---

23. *Lenin and Philosophy*, NLB, London 1971, p. 65.

24. In his *Cours de Philosophie pour les Scientifiques* (a course run at the École Normale Supérieure in 1967–68), Althusser develops the idea that philosophy is not concerned with Science — an ideological concept — but with *the sciences*. Balibar, in *L'Humanité* of 14-2-69, mocks those who talk about science as if it were a 'Speculative Holy Spirit' incarnated in the different sciences. But one might well ask what this strange concept of *the sciences* is. Can one say anything about it which does not pass through the mediation of the concept *Science*? The nature of a concept is not changed by putting it in the plural — it can be all the more hidden. This is just what is involved here: to replace science by the sciences, is to conceal the proper object of philosophy (Science) as produced by the denegation of knowledge. The proclaimed anti-speculative act of Althusser and Balibar has the sole effect of strengthening the philosophical denegation of knowledge.

physics, etc. would call for a discourse defining the forms of its scientificity (Plato, Descartes, etc.). Is this not to play the question at its own game? In actual fact, the question may well exist *in order not to pose* the question: what is the basis of knowledge? It is produced not at the demand of Science (even if it voices this demand) but by knowledge's concealment of itself.[24]

Philosophy thus traditionally practises a critique of knowledge which is simultaneously a denegation[25] of knowledge (i.e. of the class struggle). Its position can be described as an *irony* with regard to knowledge, which it puts in question without ever touching its foundations. The questioning of knowledge in philosophy always ends in its restoration: a movement the great philosophers consistently expose in each other. Thus Hegel criticizes Cartesian doubt, which only results in re-establishing the authority of everything it pretended to reject. Feuerbach isolates the same pretence in the Hegelian 'path of despair'. 'The non-knowledge of the idea was only an ironic non-knowledge.' And this is what we rediscover in Althusser: the line of division is scarcely drawn before it is erased. Doubt about knowledge only existed the better to establish the authority of a knowledge elevated finally to the rank of science.

In repeating this manoeuvre, Althusser reveals its political significance, clearly showing that what is at issue is the status of the *possessors of knowledge*. Any serious doubt about the content of knowledge vanishes as soon as the question of its subject is raised, as soon as the very existence of a group possessing knowledge is at stake. Here again, there is an evident homology with that classic philosophical figure of which the Cartesian *cogito* provides a model illustration: the challenging of the object of knowledge aims at confirming its subject. Doubt about the object is only the obverse of the certainty of the subject. It is precisely this contradiction which gives philosophy its status: philosophy is constructed against the power of the false possessors of knowledge, or, more accurately, of the possessors of false knowledge (sophists, theologians, etc.). But it cannot go so far as to put at issue the very existence of knowledge as the instrument of a class. Against the object of false knowledge, it invokes the subject of true knowledge; which, in the final analysis, strengthens the grounds for dominance of those possessing (true) knowledge, and thereby justifies class domination. This passage from the object of false

25. Denegation is a word used by Freud to designate an unconscious denial masked by a conscious acceptance, or *vice versa*. It is used here in the sense of an ostensible criticism concealing a strengthened affirmation. The affirmation is '*misrecognized*' as criticism. (Translator's note.)

knowledge to the subject of true knowledge would consequently correspond to the political demand of a class excluded from power, lending this demand the form of universality. (The Cartesian 'good sense'.) This movement has ultimately no other end than to bolster the privileged position of the possessors of knowledge — a form of class domination.[26]

The Althusserian theory of ideology describes this same movement, and we now see how the spontaneous discourse of metaphysics comes to be articulated with revisionist ideology. Only one more mediation is required for this: Althusser's *academic ideology*. In it, the spontaneous discourse of metaphysics assumes the function of justifying the teachers, the possessors and purveyors of bourgeois knowledge (knowledge which includes academic Marxism). Speaking in their name, defending their authority, Althusser quite naturally adopts the class position expressed in revisionist ideology — that of the labour aristocracy and the cadres. The spontaneous discourse of metaphysics is thus the necessary mediation enabling Althusser to recognize his own class position in that expressed by revisionism. This convergence is located in the question of knowledge and the defence of academic authority. At this point, the Althusserian theory of ideology functions as the theory of an imaginary class struggle to the profit of a real class collaboration, that of revisionism. The transformation of Marxism into opportunism is complete.

The Analysis of Humanist Ideology

This concealment of the class struggle displays its most profound effects in the analysis of humanist ideology[27] — an analysis produced

26. [Note added in February 1973:] This bird's-eye view of the history of philosophy will no doubt seem insubstantial. Let me briefly state:

(1) It restricts itself to challenging, within his own terms of reference, Althusser's even more offhand interpretation of this history.

(2) Nevertheless, I have no more intention of reproaching Althusser for his casualness than of excusing myself to the punctilious historians of philosophy. The day that these historians are as scrupulous in making the voice of the masses heard, as they are in establishing the sense of a line in Plato, it will be time to see, in their respect for the great philosophers, something other than simple respect for the *Great*. As far as I am concerned, Althusser's casual treatment of Plato or Descartes seems quite pardonable compared with his nonchalant endorsement of the official history of the labour movement (both social-democratic and revisionist), which adds the weight of its falsifications to the firing-squads and prison-sentences of the bourgeoisie.

to answer the question: what is the function of the humanist ideology currently proclaimed in the USSR? To answer this question; that is to say, in fact, *not to pose it*. For the only way of posing it would be to enquire as to its class meaning. Instead we find it subsumed under another, more general question, whose answer is already laid out beforehand: since the USSR *is* a classless society, all we have to do is to apply the theory of ideology minus that which deals with the exercise of class rule. We know the conclusion all too well: ideology is not science, and it enables men to live their relation to their conditions of existence. 'Socialist humanism' thus designates a set of new problems without giving a strict knowledge of them. And what are these problems? Precisely those of a classless society: 'In fact, the themes of socialist humanism designate the existence of real problems: *new* historical, economic, political and ideological problems that the Stalinist period kept in the shade, but still produced while producing socialism — problems in the forms of economic, political and cultural *organization* that correspond to the level of development attained by socialism's productive forces; problems of the new form of *individual development* for a new period of history in which the State will no longer take charge, *coercively,* of the leadership or control of the destiny of each individual, in which from now on each man will *objectively* have the *choice,* that is, the *difficult task,* of becoming by himself what he is. The themes of socialist humanism (free development of the individual, respect for socialist legality, dignity of the person, etc.), are the way the Soviets and other socialists are *living* the relation between themselves and these problems, that is, the *conditions* in which they are posed.'[28]

We have three elements in this text: firstly, a series of very general remarks about the transition from a class society to a classless society; namely, that this transition poses a certain number of economic, political, ideological problems, and so on. Secondly, some generalities concerning the function of ideology with which we are by now quite familiar. And finally, in the hide-and-seek played by these two generalities, the absent object which was going to be analysed — the reality of the Soviet Union. But the absence of this reality is due to the solid presence of its image. What in fact is this 'new' reality which, in Althusser's view, must explain the new recourse to an old ideology? Nothing but the image which Soviet society presents of itself or, to be more precise, which its ruling class presents of it: 'a new period of

27. 'Marxism and Humanism', in *For Marx*, op. cit.
28. Ibid.,

history in which the State will no longer take charge, *coercively,* of the leadership or control of the destiny of each individual . . .', 'a world without economic exploitation, without violence, without discrimination . . .' etc. The 'explanation' for Soviet humanist ideology is really only its reduplication. The whole chicanery of the theory of ideology ends in this naivety which destroys any analysis of ideology before it has begun: an ideological discourse is taken to be the adequate expression of what it purports to express; the discourse which claims to be that of a classless society is taken at its word. It is clear that this reduplication is not a superfluous act, since it strengthens the inevitable effect of such discourse: that of concealing the class struggle in the assertion that it has been superseded.

The circularity of the analysis also closes the circle of the Althusserian theory of ideology, which returns here to its starting point. This return must be understood in two senses. On the one hand, the 'concrete' analysis of ideology in a classless society brings us back to the generalities dealing with the function of ideology in general. The theory offers its own repetition as the analysis of its object. But on the other hand, the political significance of the theory is shown up in its encounter with the object which it is its precise function not to think. Revisionism is not simply the object that the Althusserian discourse conceals or hesitates to think; it is strictly *its unthought,* the political condition of its theoretical functioning. While Althusser claims to be explaining Soviet ideology, it would seem to be much more revisionism which explains and founds the Althusserian theory of ideology. A theory which posits, even before the existence of classes, the necessity of a function for ideology — is this not the expression, the interpretation, of a politics which claims to have gone beyond classes?

If the Althusserian theory of ideology ends with this theoretical suicide, it is precisely on account of the prohibition which prevents it from thinking of ideological discourses as discourses of the class struggle, and only allows it to relate them to their 'social function' and their non-scientificity. So the critique of humanism leaves its object intact, since it cannot conceive it other than by reference to the scientificity from which it is excluded. The concept of man is that of a false subject of history, a new form of the idealist subject (spirit, consciousness, *cogito,* or absolute knowledge). Such a critique leaves aside the main problem: what does humanism represent politically? What does the concept man designate? Experience enables us to reply that humanist theory has always had the goal of protecting, under the disguise of universality, the privileges of a specific set of men. *Man* is always the Prince of the Bourgeoisie. It can as easily be the cadre —

the Party leadership. But it can also — according to a necessary law of ideology — be the concept in which those who rebel against their power make their protest and assert their will. Humanism always functions as the discourse of a class in struggle. And such must be the case for the various forms which humanist ideology has taken in the USSR. Stalin can put us on the right track here: is the famous formula 'Man, the most valuable capital' not the other side of the slogan which proclaims that 'the cadres decide everything'? And can one conceive of the present 'humanism of the individual person' other than by reference to the process of the restoration of capitalism? Is it not the equivalent in ideology of the 'State of all the people' in the political sphere? The recent history of the USSR and the people's democracies shows us how it can act both as the discourse of the new ruling class, which denies that classes exist in these societies, and as the expression of the rebellion of classes or peoples oppressed by revisionism. Now, it is noticeable that Althusser relates the ideological forms of humanism not to the reality of struggle or division, but to the unity of a *problem* which exists for the unity of a *group*: 'What need do the Soviets have for an *idea of man*, that is, an idea of themselves, *to help them live their history?*'[29]

The answer to this question is given by the relationship between the *tasks* to be accomplished (those of the transition to communism) and the *conditions* in which they have to be accomplished ('difficulties due to the period of the "cult of personality" but also . . . the more distant difficulties characteristic of the *"construction of socialism in one country"*, and in a country economically and culturally backward to start with'). Problems that men have to resolve, objective conditions, backwardness, exceptional phenomena — these are the ingredients of Althusser's recipe. There is one thing he absolutely refuses to understand, and that is contradiction. As a result he moves completely off the terrain of Marxism onto that of bourgeois sociology. We indicated the form of this shift at the beginning — we now know its political function.

A theoretical platitude to complement a political naivety: this is how every theory of ideology must inevitably end if it fails to make the class struggle its starting point.

Ideology and Class Struggle

In order to understand this original omission, we must return to

29. Ibid.,

Althusser's targeting of theories of transparency and de-alienation. To resist them, it was necessary to show that the world is never transparent to consciousness, that even in classless societies there is 'ideology'. At this point we began to suspect that the argument might actually have a quite different aim, and that the choice of enemy might have been made to suit its purposes. But, to be fair, the relation was two-sided. If Althusser's discourse on ideology is governed by the concern to justify revisionism, it could just as well be said that it is because Althusser remains prisoner of a classic philosophical problematic that he is situated in the camp of revisionist ideology. In fact, by struggling against ideologies of alienation, caught in the dilemma of transparency (idealist) or opacity (materialist), Althusser is led to fight on the ground of his opponent. The characteristic of the para-Marxist theories he criticizes (Lukácsian, existentialist, and the rest) is to identify the Marxist theory of ideologies with a theory of the subject. Yet Althusser does not sever the knot which ties Marxist theory to the idealist philosophical tradition. He only attacks one particular aspect of it: the interpretation of Marxist theory in terms of a theory of consciousness. His criticism fixes the status of ideology according to two basic determinations. On the one hand, the theory of ideology is a theory of the illusion of consciousness; on the other, ideology is not just 'false consciousness' but must be granted an objective status — it is a system of representations (images, signs, cultural objects) which extends beyond the sphere of consciousness and has an objective social reality. But this double correction leaves out what was specific to the Marxist theory of ideologies: the 'ideological forms' which the *Preface to the Contribution to a Critique of Political Economy* talks of are not merely social forms of representation, *but the forms in which a struggle is fought out.*[30] The realm of ideology is not that of subjective illusion in general, of the necessarily inadequate representations men form of their practice. Ideologies can be given an objective status only if they are considered in terms of the class struggle. Ideology does not just exist in discourses, not just in systems of images, signs, and so on. The analysis of the University has shown us that the ideology of a class exists, first and foremost, in institutions — in what we can call *ideological apparatuses,* in the sense in which Marxist theory talks about the State apparatus. Because of the point from which he starts, Althusser can only give to ideological forms the spectral objectivity of systems of 'signs', 'cultural objects', etc. In other words, a metaphysical theory of the subject (in the form of a theory of illusion) is linked with a sociology of 'systems of representations'. We have seen how the two are articulated within a conception of ideology which is wholly metaphysical, in the strict sense that *it cannot understand contradiction:* and only the ability to understand contradiction would allow it to quit the metaphysical ground on which its opponent stands.

The consequence of this is that the political problem designated by the 'end of ideologies' problematic, is conjured out of existence. 'Only an ideological world-outlook,' says Althusser, 'could have imagined societies *without ideology* and accepted the utopian idea of a world in which ideology (not just one of its historical forms) would disappear without trace, to be replaced by *science*.'[31] The problem is here posed entirely in the terms of the ideologies being criticized: the end of ideologies is identified with the reign of science, that is, with the disappearance of subjective illusion in general. On this basis, it is easy to show that the world of transparency cannot exist, and that classless societies can never do without ideology, so defined. We have seen how, in practice, this critique of utopia was revealed as the most fatuous naivety — not surprisingly, for its way of posing the problem meant concealing precisely what had to be thought: the pursuit and the end of the class struggle in the realm of ideology. It is impossible to understand this problem — and hence to produce any concrete analysis — if *ideology* is conceived as illusion, however much the 'social' necessity of this illusion is stressed. To understand it, *ideologies* must be conceived as systems that represent class interests and the waging of the class struggle. The end of ideologies then appears not as an eschatological concept but, like the withering away of the State, as a function of the end of the class struggle. We know that end to be still distant after the dictatorship of the proletariat has been established. The experience of the cultural revolution has taught us a little about this. It showed us that the forms supposedly taken by ideology in classless society were in fact the forms in which class struggle was being relentlessly pursued in a socialist society. The rejection of the 'ideological' theme of the end of ideologies stops one from considering the essential problem of the forms of class struggle in socialist societies. The Chinese experience has shown us the crucial importance of the ideological forms taken by this struggle. The socialist revolution involves struggle against the various forms of bourgeois ideology which continue to exist after the seizure of political power:

21. *For Marx*, p. 232.

traditional ideologies of individualism or obedience, or modern ideologies of skills and technicality. *All these problems concern the ideological effects of class division.* They have nothing to do with the disappearance of subjective illusion. Not that this problem should remain unposed; but it does not belong to the problematic of the Marxist theory of ideologies, which is no more a theory of the subject than it is a theory of science or of 'society'. Althusser sets out to attack the anthropological ideologies which make the theory of society into a theory of the subject; but his discourse has no more subversive effect than to re-establish a theory of science, as the mediation governing the relation between these two terms.

This theory of science rests on the same ground as the ideologies it claims to resist; which is to say that it reflects, in its own particular way, the class position of the petty-bourgeois intellectual oscillating between two camps.[32] On the one hand, the petty-bourgeois intel-

32. [Note added in February 1973:] We will have made some progress in the analysis of class struggles and their ideological components, the day we turf out these mechanical conceptions of the 'oscillation' of the petty bourgeoisie, which are based on heaven-knows what 'oscillatory property' of its intermediary position. Generally speaking, all the concepts which revolve around the notion of a petty bourgeoisie have become, for numerous 'Marxist' intellectuals, the refuge of blissful ignorance. What has not been explained by the oscillation of the petty-bourgeoisie? Gaullism, fascism, leftism — everything under the sun, and a few others as well . . . Thanks to this, one can dispense with analysing the particular factors which produce the adherence or partial resistance to bourgeois ideology of a particular, non-proletarian stratum. The closeness or distance from manual labour, existence or absence of traditions of collective struggle, social future, relation to State power, position in the relationships of authority, etc. — all the determinations are obliterated in this 'oscillation' which, in a single movement, alters the position of the student and the small shopkeeper, the ruined peasant and the consultant engineer, the teacher and the shop-girl in Prisunic. 'Petty bourgeoisie' is thus the *flatus vocis* which hides — badly — the inability to articulate the contradictions proper to each class or class fraction.

The concept of petty bourgeoisie has doubtless always had a certain power of camouflage. It is already visible in Marx where it serves, in particular, to conceal the contradictions within the proletariat, thought of as a contamination of the budding modern proletariat by the artisanal dreams or peasant frenzies of the bankrupted small proprietors. But on this point, as on many others, the academic reading of Marx has been powerfully supported by the practice of the 'workers' State apparatuses — primarily by the practice of the Stalinist apparatus, where the struggle against the 'petty-bourgeoisie', while concealing the inability to recognize and resolve contradictions among the people, serves simultaneously as the 'proletarian' justification for establishing a new bourgeoisie of planners, inspectors, prosecutors, and so forth.

A deliberate failure to recognize contradictions among the people, the concealment of new class contradictions: the concept of petty bourgeoisie must be numbered among those which have helped a State power to conceal what it does not wish to know — a 'theoretical' laboratory which has been found to be well equipped for this universal function of non-thought, the effects of which can be spotted as much in the discourse of Marxist scholars as in that of professional revolutionaries.

lectual is associated with the camp of the bourgeoisie, not only through class situation, but through the very sphere in which he works, through his theoretical problematic which reflects his function within the bourgeois ideological apparatus. On the other hand, he would like to join the camp of the proletariat, but he can only adopt its interests by assimilating them to the objectivity and universality of 'science'. Thus, insofar as he remains a petty-bourgeois intellectual — insofar, that is, as he does not participate *materially* in the proletarian struggle — he can only unite with the interests of the proletariat in a mythical fashion, by making the revolutionary objective coincide with that ideal point in striving towards which he justifies his own practice as a petty-bourgeois intellectual: the Ideal of Science. In other words, he adopts the 'positions of the proletariat' at the level of the denegation of his own class practice. To join the proletarian struggle at this level is to join the camp of bourgeois politics disguised as proletarian politics — the camp of revisionism. It is an ideal convergence, which in a country like France corresponds to a precise reality. For the petty-bourgeois intellectual, access to the working class is doubly guarded: by his own integration into the system of bourgeois ideological dominance; and by the revisionist apparatus, 'representing' the working class, which stands between him and the proletariat. So on both sides, the 'Marxist' petty-bourgeois intellectual sees himself excluded from participation in that proletarian struggle which, in the last instance, can alone guarantee the Marxist rigour of his discourse.[33] The operation which transforms Marxist theory into a discourse on science reflects this double limitation: a general limitation coming from the position of an intellectual divorced from the masses, and integrated into the bourgeois ideological system; and a particular limitation stemming from the revisionist encirclement of the proletarian struggle. The 'scientific' rigour of this discourse is thus only the obverse of the impossibility of its functioning as rigorous Marxist theory; in other words, of its being revolutionary. This 'scientific' rigour does not enable it to escape its double set of limits; quite the opposite — only by virtue of its own lack of coherence can a petty-bourgeois ideology acquire, in given circumstances, a progressive function. Once its basic rigour is attained, it is shown up for what it is — a bourgeois rigour. This is why the Marxist

---

33. [Note added in February 1973:] To go into this in any depth, it would be necessary to demonstrate the interrelation between this theory of ideology and the police-revisionist conspiracy theory. The theory states that workers do not have the capacity to produce an anti-capitalist ideology, and hence an *autonomous* anti-capitalist practice. So if this worker claims to speak and act for himself, he immediately reveals himself to be a false worker, and thus a real police-agent.

discourse on science ultimately dissolves into a two-fold justification for academic knowledge and the authority of the Central Committee. 'Science' becomes the watchword of the ideological counter-revolution.[34]

Without revolutionary theory, there can be no revolutionary movement. We said it till we were sick of it, hoping in this way to set our minds at ease. It is time now we learnt the lesson that the Cultural Revolution and the ideological revolt of the students have taught us. Divorced from revolutionary practice, all revolutionary theory is transformed into its opposite.

Jacques Rancière July 1969

34. Let us specifically state, should it still be necessary, that what is in question here is not Althusser's personal position in a particular set of circumstances, but the political line implied by his theory of ideology. Rarely has a theory been more rapidly appropriated by those who have an interest in it. In the name of science, the workers' struggles against wage-scales are resisted — don't they misunderstand the scientific law which says that each is paid according to the value of his labour-power? In the same way, the anti-hierarchical struggles in the university fail to understand that 'the ultimate nature of the staff-student relation corresponds to the advance of human knowledge, of which it is the very foundation'. (J. Pesenti: 'Problèmes de méthode et questions théoriques liées à la refonte des carrières', July 1969.) One could not admit in a more ingenuous manner what constitutes the 'foundation' of the theory of science to which one lays claim.

The impasse in which Althusser finds himself is demonstrated in a recent article in *La Pensée* 'A propos de l'article de Michel Verret sur Mai étudiant' (June 1969). In it, Althusser affirms the basically progressive character of the May student movement, and denounces the reactionary interpretation of it by an over-zealous defender of 'Science'. But he cannot — or will not — see in this the simple justification of a reactionary politics. He only sees the mark of an *inadequacy:* the Party 'has not been able to' analyse the student movement, to keep in touch with student youth, to explain the forms of working-class struggle to it, and so on. The conclusion of the article shows that he is thus still limited to the twin recourse to science and the Party apparatus. It is on the latter that he relies 'to furnish all the *scientific* explanations which will allow everyone, including the young, to understand the events they have lived through, and, if they wish, to grasp on a correct basis where they stand in the class struggle, by revealing the correct perspectives to them, by giving them the political and ideological means for correct action.'

Afterword — from the French edition

We must get rid of this habit of only criticizing after the event.

Mao Tse-Tung

The following text makes its appearance in France after a delay of four years. It was drafted in 1969 for an anthology on Althusser published in Argentina. I did not at that time think it worth publishing in France: for those who witnessed and took part in May 1968, the practical demonstrations of the mass movement seemed to me proof enough that the question of Althusserianism could be considered historically settled. And while it was useful as a means of clarifying my own ideas, as far as the anti-revisionist education of the masses went, this kind of theoretical refutation seemed laughable compared with the lessons of the struggle. When at every stop the autonomous initiative of the masses was finding itself policed by revisionism, it would have seemed anachronistic to settle accounts with a theoretical police whose headquarters May has sent up in flames.

Subsequent events have shown the idealism involved in such a position. It is true that refutation is of little weight compared with the transformations produced in people's minds by mass movements. But so long as the apparatus of bourgeois domination remains in place, the base survives for the reproduction of ideologies which the movement of the masses appeared to have utterly destroyed. And given that the university machine was working again, it was necessary that its role of keeping order — its police-role — should be restored to life, and that it should re-erect the scholarly, theoretical scaffolding designed to shore up the tottering maxim: 'it's always wrong to rebel'. Of course, this reconstruction is not exactly the same as the original, since it is produced in conditions modified by the effect of the movement. Thus the *experimental* forms of the post-May university (of the Vincennes type) tried to transfer the university's police-role from the authority of the teacher to the authority of knowledge; to transform professorial despotism into an egalitarian republic of petty mandarins — precisely the problematic set out in Althusserianism. In the immediate post-May period, moreover, Althusser's discourse recedes into the background, while at the same time his theses are appropriated by the combined forces of young bucks of revisionism and petty mandarins of the re-modelled university. This appropriation is perfectly illustrated by that literature student at Vincennes, a young PCF member, who was delighted that his teacher, by beginning a course on Racine with a posing of Althusser's problematic of reading, should enable students of an insufficient standard to be eliminated from the start.

So the very difference in formation between the ideas of revolt, produced by mass *movements,* and the ruling ideas, constantly re-produced by the ideological *apparatuses* of the bourgeoisie, determines the position of this type of ideological struggle which fights on its opponent's ground. It is a position strictly subordinate to the ideological transformations produced by the struggle, but nevertheless now impossible to abandon. Limited as the usefulness of this text would have been in 1969, it was wrong to restrict knowledge of it to those who could, in some private and roundabout way, get hold of it in Spanish or Portuguese.

All the same, its present publication in a different context of ideological struggle, poses new problems and necessitates certain rectifications.

Firstly, the passage of time will undoubtedly make my criticism seem one-sided. To which I shall reply that it was aimed at a specific target: the appropriation of Althusserianism after May 68 in the interests of revisionist and mandarin reaction. Hence, it concentrates on a specific articulation of Althusserian discourse: that which, in the theory of ideology, expresses the class position of 'Marxist scholars' confronted with the 'ideological' voice of revolt. With regard to this fundamental dividing line, my criticism was — and still is — correctly one-sided. But it is self-evident that a complete history — that is, a 'fair' evaluation of Althusserianism — would have to take account of its other modes of political appropriation, and indicate the points in the Althusserian text at which one can anchor a left Althusserianism that should lead a certain number of intellectuals to Maoism. If I have concentrated on its right-wing effect, it is because the mass movement established that this was its *dominant* character. But the attitude of the UJCML (Marxist-Leninist Union of Communist Youth) towards the student revolt at the beginning of May 68 is enough to demonstrate the hold which these events exercised even over 'left Althusserianism'.

Objections will also be raised against the early date (1964) of the texts criticized, and much will no doubt be made of the *self-criticism* by which Althusser, beginning with 'Lenin and Philosophy', is said to have broken with his previous 'theoreticism' in favour of a philosophy conceived as *political intervention.* Unfortunately for this idyllic vision, it is just these 'theoreticist' texts and problematic of the 1964 period which are found to have produced political effects, of the left as well as of the right. And if the 'new practice of philosophy' promised by

'Lenin and Philosophy' has paradoxically produced no noticeable effect in the field of class struggle, it is precisely because it turned its back on the *political* problems in which Althusserian theoreticism had been laid bare. The supposed politicization of philosophy was really more of a *denegation* of the foundations and the political effects of Althusserianism, which left philosophy as a field of political intervention, with the scarcely burning question of the reality of the object of knowledge.

I feel, then, that the concepts at issue here really do constitute a 'rational kernel' which has given Althusserianism the systematic character of an ideology independent of Althusser's personal history. His later contributions to the question of ideology are in my view of two kinds:

1. The texts of 1968 ('Lenin and Philosophy', *Cours de Philosophie pour les Scientifiques*) crystallize the science/ideology relation into a conceptual multiplicity (sciences, ideologies, the spontaneous philosophy of scientists, conceptions of the world . . .) in which the theoretical scheme of Althusserianism is retrieved unaltered. Thus the correct ideas which the researcher draws from his scientific practice are, by a complex mechanism, subject to interference by different systems of representation (a conception of the world, spontaneous philosophy, etc.) produced elsewhere. But the complexity of this mechanism conceals the question of this practice itself, of its forms of social existence and of the class struggle which puts it at stake. The class struggle is thus relegated to the level of the *representation* of a practice, in the traditional figure of the dislocation beween the production of an object and the production of the consciousness of it.

2. The 1970 text 'Ideology and Ideological State Apparatuses' introduces some ideas and a problematic produced by the Chinese Cultural Revolution and the anti-authoritarian revolt of May. But the Althusserian system cannot be 'set back on its feet' by these conceptions, which, if taken to their logical conclusion, could only smash it. So Althusser introduces them only in isolation from their mode of production; presenting as the surprising and paradoxical discovery of research ('I believe I am justified in advancing the following thesis. . . This thesis may seem paradoxical . . .') that truth about the dominant character of the educational ideological apparatus which was produced in such a profoundly unambiguous manner by the mass-movement. In this way, Althusser can bracket together in the same text analyses produced by two conflicting problematics (a problematic of subjective illusion and a problematic of State Apparatuses); can casually mention in a Party publication that political parties and

trades unions are State apparatuses; and can without danger — if not without malice — discuss the class function of education in a periodical devoted to the glorification of universal science and the state school. Nothing can be built on this ironic discourse, where what is stated, and the very statement of it, is constantly given the lie by the mode in which it is stated. Althusser can always adopt such or such a new notion, draw such or such a lesson from practice, but cannot set Althusserianism back on its feet — the complete and autonomous model of revisionist reason.

This text will have a negative effect if it joins the game of building up and knocking down monuments to great men. Yet it can still prove useful if, by depersonalizing the criticism, it allows the accent to be put on the ideological mechanisms of power which constrain the discourse of intellectuals in our societies. The criticism I make of Althusser's analysis of 'socialist humanism' in *For Marx* will lose its point if it should be thought, by a scorn that is all too easy with the benefit of hindsight, to attribute to the blindness or guile of an individual a type of *relation to power* firmly anchored in the practice of intellectuals; if it should be thought to exorcise, in the shape of the Althusserian devil, the temptation provided by this practice to transform the chains of power into the interconnections of theory. What was it that was always involved in the Althusserian seminars, and that is still involved in many a seminar even now? The *interrogation* of concepts, demanding their *authorization*, questioning their *identity*, restraining those which have wandered without a passport outside their *proper province*, etc . . . Proofs of identity, preventive detention — the vast network of philosophy's police mentality, for which Althusser is no more responsible than the capitalist, exists, according to Marx, for the relations of production of which he is the support. The apprentices of bourgeois knowledge are trained in a universe of discourse where words, argument, ways of questioning, deduction are prescribed by the discursive forms of the repressive practices of power. What is ultimately at issue here is the effect of this system of constraints, that I will call police-reason, on a particular philosophical discourse. And ultimately there is no paradox if the strength and relevance of this discourse ends up revealing on its surface the subterranean network of constraints in which the half-wits of academic philosophy romp, free from all problems.

It is also necessary to refer to the conjuncture and the aim of this text in order to prevent the lapse of time distorting the use it makes of the couple 'bourgeois ideology/proletarian ideology'. In opposition to Althusserianism, it was important to affirm at a theoretical level the capacity of subordinate classes to forge the ideological weapons of their fight, and hence to establish their right to rebel regardless of whether it suited the political and trade-union apparatuses 'of the working class'. This was particularly vital at a time when, from all quarters, the diehards, drawing the 'lessons of May' after their own fashion, were entering into a war against 'spontaneism' — i.e. against the revolt of the masses which they pretended to criticize — in order to supply it with what, according to them, had been missing in May: a vanguard, party, science, proletarian discipline, or a consciousness imported from the outside. The voice of the masses or the discourse of the scribes? The alternatives required that, faced with those pedlars of vanguards, the 'bourgeois ideology/proletarian ideology' opposition should be clearly put forward, without any hair-splitting, insofar as it signified the right of the masses to autonomous speech and action. But at the same time, the opposition was employed in a traditional form which concealed its fundamental originality. It refers not to two homogenous realities distinguished by a plus or minus sign, but to two *modes of production* of ideology which are profoundly hetero-geneous. Bourgeois ideology is a system of power relations daily reproduced by the ideological apparatuses of the bourgeois state. Proletarian ideology is a system of power relations established by the struggle of the proletariat and other subordinate classes against all the forms of bourgeois exploitation and domination; forms of resis-tance to the ideological effects materially produced by the bourgeois division of labour, forms of systematization of anti-capitalist strug-gles, forms of control over the superstructure by the masses. It is a system of power relations that is always fragmentary, because it defines a certain number of conquests and always provisional because it is produced not by apparatuses but by the development of struggle. Proletarian ideology is neither the summary of the repre-sentations or positive values of the workers, nor the body of 'prole-tarian' doctrines. It is a stopped assembly-line, an authority mocked, an abolished system of divisions between particular jobs of work, a mass fight-back against 'scientific' innovations in exploitation: and it is the 'bare-foot doctor' or the entry of the working *class* into the Chinese university. Mass practices produced by the anti-capitalist struggle whose uniqueness is missed as soon as one tries to set a proletarian philosophy, justice or morality against the philosophy, justice or morality of the bourgeoisie.

Now, this heterogeneity is habitually concealed by traditional dis-courses on proletarian ideology, which only establish its reality at the cost of an ambiguous oscillation which continually relates the positivity of texts (the ideology of the proletariat is Marxism-Leninism) to the positivity of the *characteristics* which belong to members of a class (proletarian ideology is the discipline of the factory-worker as against petty-bourgeois anarchism, or shopfloor solidarity in contrast to bourgeois individualism etc.). In this gross theoretical deviation the justification has traditionally been found for the manifold practical deviations of revisionism. Either the scientificity of *proletarian theory* has the job of marshalling the 'spontaneity' of the workers' wild reactions; or else the *proletarian characteristics* (order, labour, discipline . . .) serve to recall the anarchism of 'petty-bourgeois' rebellions to order. These are twin incarnations of law-and-order which lead us back to the source of the binary representation of proletarian ideology. A creation of neither working-class consciousness nor Marxist theory, but of the Stalinist State machine, this representation is supported on the power relations which define the functioning of the revisionist 'workers' parties and states. As *science*, proletarian ideology is the symbol of this power: as the sum of proletarian characteristics, it defines, for the workers, so many *reasons* for *obeying* 'their' power: 'a spiritual point of honour', with the concrete reality of the 'workers' militia opening fire on the workers of Gdansk.

Every critique of the 'science/ideology' couple which relies on the shifting meanings assembled beneath the concept of proletarian ideology, thus stays sunk in ambiguity. And this ambiguity doubtless does no more than translate the continuing ability of revolutionary organizations to rid themselves of the politico-organizational forms and the ideological effects bequeathed to us by the revisionist and Stalinist State machines. Here again, it is for the *practical* criticism of the mass movement to sweep away the 'proletarian' phantasms invoked by the sorcerer's apprentices of the State apparatuses.

Many other points in this text I feel to be subjects for discussion. But one does not correct the texts of the ideological struggle when the conditions of the struggle change: one writes new ones. So I have altered nothing in the original text; I have simply added this afterword and some additional notes to emphasize the conditions in which it was drawn up, and to forestall distortions in its reading which the delayed publication might otherwise produce.

Jacques Rancière, February 1973

Reprinted from *RP* 7

Who Makes History?
Althusser's Anti-Humanism

John Mepham

I am very much aware that in what follows I solve no philosophical problems. I attempt some conceptual clarifications and I propose some interpretations of theses of Louis Althusser. I hope this will at least make it possible to pose some problems more clearly than they are posed in Normal Geras's article 'Marxism and Proletarian Self-Emancipation'. I think that those of us who are Marxist philosophers can learn from Althusser. It is important that his work be debated, discussed, criticized and rectified. It is very important that we do not dismiss it. Norman Geras knows this, and his very useful article 'Althusser's Marxism: an Account and Assessment' is a good example of a thoughtful study of Althusser.[1] However, it contains certain misunderstandings of Althusser's theses, which are also present in his more recent essay. Moreover, Geras's comments are based on his interpretation of Althusser's work up to 1965. As Geras himself points out, Althusser has rectified his own work in many respects since that date: he has warned us against certain interpretations of that earlier work, he has engaged in self-criticism, he has moved on. Geras seems not to have kept up with him. He seems no longer willing to learn. Now, instead of discussing him, he dismisses him.

Geras makes three comments about Althusser. Each of these is either false or is the kind of oversimplification which impedes theoretical research. They are as follows:

(1) He claims that the doctrine that 'it is men who make history' is 'theoretically indigestible for the Althusserians'.

(2) He says that Althusser's view that 'men are nothing more than the supports/effects of their social, political and ideological relations' is to be identified with 'the view of the masses as the true objects of their

1. See *New Left Review* 71, January/February 1972.

circumstances'.

(3) He attributes to Althusser the view that the masses can only destroy and transform these relations 'by the power of a knowledge (Theoretical Practice) brought to them from elsewhere'.

In what follows I discuss these three comments in the order given.

The Humanist Formula

Geras's first remark is filled out as follows: 'It is *men* who make history, albeit on the basis of objective conditions which they have to take as given.' Let us label this formula for convenience The Humanist Formula (HF). This 'significant truth' is said to be decisive because it 'represents Marx's break with the whole problematic I have just surveyed, and it informs all of Marx's more concrete and specific theoretical constructions . . . Men are neither passive effects nor omnipotent wills, but at once the subjects and objects of a practice which generates and transforms social and ideological structures, and transforms men themselves in the process.'

Now it is true that the formula 'It is men who make history on the basis of objective conditions which they have to take as given' is significant by virtue of being a rejection of several alternative approaches to the problem of human history. It is a denial of the crude environmentalist thesis that circumstances make men, and also of the idealist thesis that men are masters of their circumstances. It is a rejection, therefore, as Geras points out, of a huge variety of positions of both the *'man* makes history' kind and of the 'legislators/educators make history' kind (Rousseau, Robert Owen). The trouble is, however, that this rejection is not, in the above formula, achieved by the elaboration of concepts which are fundamentally different from those involved in these other (idealist, materialist) formulae. It simply takes the old concepts, designating sources of determination (men, circumstances), and instead of asserting the primacy of one source of determination over the other, it says that history comes about as a result of a *mixture* of the two, a bit of one (men, not passive effects, subjects) and a bit of the other (objective conditions, not omnipotent wills, objects). It therefore is significant at an ideological level (and that is important), but it contains no new knowledge. It does not tell us how to think about history, about men, about 'social conditions'. The important question is, does Marx provide other concepts which *do* constitute an important advance in understanding history, and are they such as to allow the formula 'men make history' to be replaced? Althusser's research has been based on the belief that the 'men make history' formula represents a 'break with the old problematic' only in the sense that it is a denial of positions taken within that problematic by other social theorists and philosophers: but it remains *within* that old problematic because the terms of the denial are still the terms of the old problematic. A genuine *break* is only achieved when old formulae are not simply *denied* but *replaced*.

Althusser argues that Marx did *replace* the old problematic, did *break* with it, did therefore provide *new* concepts. He also believes that it is important, both in theory and in politics, to identify the new concepts as clearly as possible and to learn how to operate with them rigorously. It is important because the old formula and the old concepts both impede theoretical research and are politically and ideologically dangerous. The old formula is one with which Sartre, for example, can happily operate. It is not rigorous enough to *demarcate* between Marxist and non-Marxist theory. Althusser's arguments history' are equally applicable to the formula 'men make history'. Philosophers who use this formula 'mix everything up' and disarm revolutionary philosophers, theoreticians and militants. They disarm them because in effect they deprive them of an irreplacable weapon: the objective knowledge of the conditions, mechanisms and forms of the class struggle . . . If the workers are told 'it is men who make history', that helps to *disarm* them. 'It tends to make them think that they are all-powerful as men, whereas in fact they are disarmed as workers in the face of the power which is really in command: that of the bourgeoisie', which controls the *material* and *political* conditions determining history. 'The humanist line turns the workers away from the class struggle, prevents them from making use of the only power they possess: that of their organization as a class', by means of their class organizations (the trade unions, the party).[2]

What then of the claim that this formula, which has been used by 'all of the greatest Marxist thinkers and revolutionary militants' (Geras) is 'theoretically indigestible for the Althusserians'? This claim amounts implicitly to saying that any formula used by Marx, Engels and Lenin must not be tampered with. I, as a Marxist, reject this and so, of course, does Norman Geras. The formula was used, in fact, as an important political weapon by Marx, Engels and Lenin. It was used to combat, for example, certain forms of crude mechanical determinism (and revisionist politics) within the Second International. But it is not philosophically, scientifically or politically

2. L. Althusser, 'Reply to John Lewis' (1972), in *Essays in Self-Criticism*, NLB, London 1976, pp. 63–4.

adequate, and it is important to find a better weapon if we can.

This is clearly illustrated by one of the most famous of the texts in which HF occurs — Engels's letter to Bloch of 21 September 1890.[3] In this letter Engels also refers us, for confirmation, to perhaps the most famous of all the occurrences of HF in Marx's writings, that in *The Eighteenth Brumaire of Louis Bonaparte*. In the letter Engels says 'We make our history ourselves, but, in the first place, under very definite assumptions and conditions. Among these the economic ones are ultimately decisive.' Engels's explicit concern here is to combat 'economic determinism'. He does this by emphasizing that *political* and *ideological* elements 'also exercise their influence upon the course of the historical struggles'. So far so good. The trouble is, however, that Engels is in the position of having set up a thesis (a correct one) in a form that invites more questions than he can answer. The 'economic element is ultimately determining' but the superstructure also 'plays a part'. There is scarcely a text in all of the works of Marx and Engels which has suffered so many different interpretations, most of them bourgeois and incorrect, or which is so obviously open to the charge of evading all the issues. The questions of how it is possible for 'economic elements' and superstructures to be in such a combination, of just what they are and how they function, are not answered here, and the interpretation to be given to HF is therefore not specified.

In the next paragraph of the letter Engels attempts a brief philosophical exposition of the way in which men are agents in the historical process. That is, he attempts to explain HF. He does this in terms of the metaphor of the parallelogram of forces. The combination of individual wills produces a process which works unconsciously so that the overall effect is something that no individual has willed. In this exposition Engels in effect falls back into the old problematic in which individual wills are determined by the combination of micro-contingencies ('circumstances') and combine in a way that seems to be pure magic to produce intelligible history. The fact that this is a 'classic text' has not prevented Althusser from demonstrating its philosophical weakness, the way it fails to give a historical materialist account of the determination of 'individuality', and of the way in which men are the makers of history. In the appendix to his article 'Contradiction and Overdetermination',[4] Althusser raises these problems, without making any attempt to solve them. Of the general problem of the relation between Marxist theory and philosophy,

3. Contained in *Marx-Engels Selected Works*, Moscow 1968, pp. 682–84.
4. In *For Marx*, NLB, London 1977.

which underlies these particular questions, he says: 'But perhaps we may have to be convinced of the existence of the problem before we will find either the will or the way to *pose* it correctly and then resolve it.' And this, I think, is my position also on Geras's article. What he takes as *solutions* (which at a certain level, against certain enemies, as weapons, are 'solutions') rest on a philosophical basis which is no solution at all. We need to be convinced of the fact that Marxist philosophy is in an embryonic state, and we need to discover the will and the way to develop it beyond the state in which it has been left to us by Marx, Engels and Lenin.

Althusser's Anti-Humanist Formulae

Does Althusser provide us with a replacement for the formula 'men make history'? In fact he has provided *two*. They are both 'anti-humanist', and I will label them for convenience AF1 and AF2. They are as follows:

AF1 'It is the masses which make history. The class-struggle is the motor of history'. AF1 occurs more frequently in Althusser's more recent work: for example, the 'Reply to John Lewis'. But it is also present in *For Marx* for example (p. 215). The question is whether it is compatible with AF2. This occurs only in scattered passages and is never given systematic exposition. Because of this I give two versions of it which may not in fact be equivalent.

AF2 'The "subjects" of history are given human societies' (*For Marx*, p. 231). 'The true subjects of the practices of social production are the relations of production. Men are never anything more than the bearers/supports/effects of these relations.'

The second version is not a direct quote from Althusser but is an attempt to state clearly what is meant by the *only* passage in his work in which he offers a general formula (a formula not related only to the analysis of theoretical practice) to express the implications of his theory of the social totality for the problem 'Who makes history?'. The direct quote is as follows:

> The structure of the relations of production determines the *places* and *functions* occupied and adopted by the agents of production, who are never anything more than the occupants of these places, insofar as they are the 'supports' (*Träger*) of these functions. The true 'subjects' (in the sense of constitutive subjects of the process) are therefore not these occupants or functionaries, are not, despite all appearances, the 'obviousnesses' of the 'given' of naive anthropology, 'concrete individuals', 'real men' — but the definition and distribution of these places and functions. The true

'subjects' are these definers and distributors: the relations of production (and political and ideological social relations).[5]

We are on difficult ground here for various reasons. (1) There are very few passages in which Althusser uses the concept of *Träger* in relation to the problem of how we are to understand history. In fact the only other discussion of the concept in this relation seems to be in *Reading Capital* (pp. 111–112) where he attempts to replace the 'false problem' of 'the role of the individual in history' with the problem of 'the historical forms of existence of individuality'. (2) The relation between his various uses of the concept is that they are all in one way or another based on a generalized concept of 'practice', as forms of production in which specific forms of work transform material to produce new objects. For a clear exposition of this concept see Norman Geras's *NLR* article. The problem is that in spite of the fact that this concept is central, it nowhere receives anything like adequate presentation or justification. For example, it is not at all clear what might be meant by 'the places and functions determined by the social relations of ideological practice', or what the relation is between the concept of social relations and that of theoretical practice. That is, there is at work here a half-cocked analogy in which certain concepts derived from the analysis of the process of material production are generalized to cover other processes (object, material, work, transformation); and other concepts, with a different origin, are associated with them in a way that leaves them more or less totally obscured (functions, places, distributors, supports/effects). Some other concepts (structure, relations) occur sometimes as part of the half-cocked analogy and sometimes independently of it. (3) This structuralist terminology (the second group of concepts above) has more or less completely disappeared from Althusser's later work and was more or less absent also from his work prior to *Reading Capital*. It should be noted in what follows that Althusser's anti-humanism is not specifically dependent on his use of the concepts of this analogy (the first two groups of concepts above). This is true not only of his anti-humanism but also of his analysis of the dialectic inasmuch as this relies on the concepts, contradiction, overdetermination, conjuncture etc. In fact *almost* everything in *For Marx* survives a criticism of the structuralist generalized concept of practice.

5. L. Althusser, *Reading Capital*, NLB, London 1970, p. 180.

The First Anti-Humanist Formula

I imagine that Norman Geras would not want to deny the truth of
AF1. The question is: in what relation does AF1 stand to HF?
Althusser claims that it is an advance on HF, that it captures an
essential truth of Marxist theory, whereas HF does not, and that it is
important to insist on a rigorous exclusion of HF in favour of AF1. Are
the two formulae incompatible (in spite of the fact that many people
have asserted them both)? Or is it merely a matter of emphasis which
has ideological importance? Since Althusser claims that the formulae
have effects both in politics *and* in science, he clearly regards the two
competing formulae as incompatible and not just differing in ideological or pedagogical power or usefulness. But he also clearly regards
them not as incompatible in the logical sense that they could not both
be true, but as existing within different problematics. They are conceptually incompatible — the concepts cannot coherently coexist
within a discourse. Why?

If you want to engage in political practice, what kinds of knowledge
do you need? Knowledge of *What?* The formula 'men make history
under definite objective circumstances' suggests that you would need
to know about *men,* and this in two senses. You would need to know
what men are — that is, you would need to know *human nature.* And
you would need to know what men are in the particular situation. You
would need to know their subjective states, beliefs, attitudes, prejudices etc. This is how political economy thought about men. And
also empiricist philosophy, utilitarianism etc. This is how 'politicians'
talk about men. Listen to them talking about the crisis in the British
economy — listen to Jenkins and Maudling. 'The trouble is that we
do not have confidence in our ability to compete in world markets.'
'We need a new attitude to work and a new sense of responsibility
towards the less well off.' They believe that men make history and
that if only Englishmen, and especially English workers, had a different attitude the crisis would disappear. And it's not just that we
must defend *the workers* against this rubbish because they're too dumb
to know any better. On the contrary, they are by and large more likely
to be suspicious or spontaneously cynical about such talk, than are
'the intellectuals'. There was hardly ever an intellectual who sold
himself to a TV discussion programme without talking rubbish like
this. Of course I'm not accusing Norman Geras of talking in such a
way. What I'm saying is that the formula 'men make history' *invites*
such talk (and also much more sophisticated talk of course; existentialist talk, libertarian utopian talk, *Telos*-talk). And it does not

immediately hit such talk over the head with the decisive and all-important counter-concept: the *class-struggle*.

Then one would need to know about 'the objective conditions'. And one enormous problem here is to know what on earth this means. It does in fact seem more like a vacant space, in which any old bourgeois concept could settle, than a concept. One would then have to try to understand in what way these 'objective conditions' somehow leave 'causal gaps' within which individual men can operate; what room there is for the play of individual wills; how individuals might intervene so as decisively to alter the historical outcome which is otherwise inscribed in the determination of the 'objective conditions'. You might see it as impossible for men (all men) to intervene, but only possible for some man (Rousseau's Legislator) or some group of men (the educators in Robert Owen). The formula does not tell one *which* men it will have to be. How is it possible in these terms to think of men acting as *members of a class* engaged in class-struggle? How does the decisive fact discovered by Marx that society is class society enter? Does it enter as a fact about men (individual men aggregated)? Or as a fact about 'objective circumstances' (acting on men who are somehow ontologically prior to their class-membership)? Classes are not reducible to their individual members plus the 'human relations' between them. Nor are they circumstances external to their members which those members take as given. Social relations of production are reproduced continually, but the agents of this process of reproduction are not men *simpliciter*. The wage-labourer who sells his labour power for a wage thereby reproduces the relation in which he stands to capital because he produces surplus-value which the capitalist can use as capital, to pay his wage next time round, or to buy raw materials or whatever. But it is the fact that the labourer is a wage-labourer, that he sells his labour power to the owner of capital, that labour power is precisely a commodity that sells for less than it can produce, it is these *relations* that reproduce themselves (over the process of social production as a whole) in the production and appropriation of surplus value. We have here an example of process in which a social relation reproduces itself, although the individual's agency — in this case his human labour power and all the specific skills, techniques and knowledges that constitute it in the particular case — while being indispensably involved in the process of reproduction, is not the agency which affects the reproduction.

In other cases — cases of political relations, for example — we might not be able to present what is involved in quite the same way (on this more below). But we could at least say this. An individual

man is always some determinate kind of man (a proletarian, a func-
tionary in the State apparatus, a petty bourgeois etc), not in the sense
that men are the kinds of beings who always exist already-deter-
mined-internally by virtue of the fact that they occupy some place in a
system of social relations. I think that in this restricted sense it is true
that men are 'representatives' or 'personifications' or 'effects' of
places in a system of social relations; and that the formula 'men make
history' is conceptually incompatible with this important assertion.

Political practice guided by the formula 'The masses make history;
the class struggle is the motor of history' is different from the political
practice suggested by HF. The central concept of the theory of
political practice is the concept of the conjuncture. The concept
conjuncture replaces the concept 'circumstances' (although not
always the *word*) in the writings of Lenin and Mao. Althusser has
done more than any other contemporary western philosopher to
clarify the concept of conjuncture and to locate it within the science of
historical materialism. As far as knowledge is concerned, the task in
political practice is the analysis of 'the present situation', and that
means an analysis in terms of classes, fractions of classes, alliances
between classes, primary and secondary contradictions, tendencies,
and so forth. On the basis of this knowledge, which is not, incidentally, the kind of knowledge produced by professional bourgeois intellectuals, which is not the kind of knowledge that they are trained or
equipped to produce, political practice can transform the balance of
forces and ultimately the system of social relations. This practice is
possible only by class organizations, by cooperative and combative
class action. Althusser has never denied, as far as I know, that
individual agents are operative within the class struggle, nor that the
subjective conditions of the various members of the different classes
are an important aspect of the balance of class forces. On the contrary
he has often asserted precisely that. For example, in *For Marx* he
explains just *why* no theory of imperialism (or of the capitalist mode of
production in *Capital*, come to that) could replace the specific
knowledge and other aspects of political practice. 'As if a single word
(imperialism) could thus magically dissolve the reality of an ir-
replaceable practice, the revolutionaries' practice, their lives, their
sufferings, their sacrifices, their efforts, in short, their concrete history,
by the use made of another practice, based on the first, the practice of
a historian — that is of a scientist, who necessarily reflects on necessity's *fait accompli;* as if the theoretical practice of a classical historian
who analyses the past could be confused with the practice of a
revolutionary leader who reflects on the present in the present, on the

necessity to be achieved, on the means to produce it, on the strategic application points for these means; in short, on his own action, for *he* does act on concrete history' (p. 179).

What *has* been denied is that it is these individual agents *who make history*. It is not just that individual agents very often do not know what they are doing, do not understand the meaning or consequences of their actions (this is what is involved in the Engels metaphor of the parallelogram of forces mentioned above). It is that they, as individual agents, *could not* do what in fact gets done. No individual worker could be said to be the agent who by his actions reproduces the social relations of the capitalist mode of production; nor could individual workers taken together, aggregated, be said to be this agent. No individual revolutionary militant, not even Lenin or Mao, could be said to be the agent who transformed the social relations of production; nor could all the revolutionary militants taken individually and aggregated be said to have been this agent. And yet the social relations of production are reproduced and are transformed and will be transformed.

It is worth noting here that AF1 is not only preferable to HF but also to the formula 'The self-emancipation of the proletariat'. This for two reasons. The first is that 'proletariat' is not the name of a *self* but of a *class*. The second is that emancipation is to be achieved not by the proletariat but by the 'masses'. This is an important political reminder of how these abstract formulae are to be applied in particular, concrete historical situations. In concrete, revolutionary political practice it is important to identify 'the masses' or 'the people', i.e. to discover which classes and fractions of classes are or could be *in alliance* with the proletariat (poor peasants, petty bourgeoisie, sub-proletariats). 'As long as you can't answer the question: What, today, comprises the people in a given country (*today*, because the composition of the people varies historically; *in a given country*, because the composition of the people changes from place to place), you can't do anything in politics. Only by knowing what 'the people' means can you then develop: (1) a mass political line; (2) corresponding political actions.'[6] So, even abstract formulae can be more or less rigorous and can point the way more or less clearly to correct political practice.

The Second Anti-Humanist Formula

What is the difference between what I above called the restricted

6. Althusser in Macciocchi, *Letters from Inside the Italian Communist Party to Louis Althusser*, NLB, London 1973.

sense in which men are 'personifications' or 'effects' of places in a system of social relations and the second version of AF2, 'The true subjects of the practices of social production are the relations of production. Men are never anything more than the bearers/supports/ effects of these relations'? One might say that this restricted sense is, as it stands, a way of locating the site of important theoretical and philosophical problems. It is not a theory. It is not a solution to these problems. But it does help to indicate something of the content that concepts in such a theory would have to have. It indicates that we need to understand the efficacy of structures of social relations and of classes, and it indicates that our understanding of what it is to be a human individual, a subject, will be dependent on, and not prior to, this understanding of classes (whereas in most philosophy, this order of things is reversed). As I understand it, AF2 is a formula which is based on an attempt to provide at least the outlines of such a theory and of such solutions. There are many criticisms that could be made of this formula. But if I am right about its theoretical origins, at least one kind of criticism will be quite wrong: that is, any criticism based upon identification of the view that men are the supports/effects of social relations with the view that 'the masses are the total objects of their circumstances'. Here we have arrived at the second of Geras's comments with which I am slowly dealing in this discussion. My reply to this second comment is that, regardless of other criticisms of AF2 one may wish to make, it is completely to miss the point of AF2 to criticize it on the basis of its identification with another formula, which it is in fact designed to replace; or to interpret it in terms of a problematic with which it is meant to mark a break.

The concepts supports/social relations are specifically designed to *replace*, not to be translations of, the concepts men/circumstances. They do this by attempting to theorize a relation in which 'men' and 'structures of social relations' are internally related and mutually determining, rather than externally related and causally co-mingling. The trouble with the Geras comment, then, is that it is so wrong that it makes any criticism or discussion of AF2 impossible. This is equally true of his remark in the *NLR* article in which he sums up his exposition of AF2 by saying: 'Thus, the human subject is definitively abolished.' It would, of course, take more than intellectual operations in Althusser's head, however byzantine, to abolish human subjects. An attempt has been made to *explain* human subjectivity, to *identify* human agents as effects of social relations, to *deny* that human subjects are the subjects of the social processes we call history. Is this to abolish them? It is rather as if a philosopher who defended the 'identity thesis' were criticized on the grounds that he had *abolished* human pains. It is the kind of remark that merely cuts off discussion.

However, at this point I want to deal separately with two distinct problems. (1) There may be involved in Geras's rejection of Althusser's AF2 certain implicit general assumptions about the question 'Who makes history?' with which I would agree. What is at stake here is this. What kinds of abstraction and what concepts do we need in order to understand social formations, political practice and history? Can we formulate some very general criteria of what would count as mistaken answers to these questions? This is a very risky enterprise because the possibility of rigour is very limited. But we can try. (2) The second problem I'll try to deal with is that of the interpretation of AF2. Geras relies on an interpretation which I think is incorrect. What is the correct one?

In answer to the first question here, a number of possibilities should be treated with caution. (1) Whatever might be meant by saying that men are 'ensembles of social relations' in Marx's formulation, or 'supports/effects' of social relations in the Althusserian 'improvement', such a formula must not be given an interpretation which is incompatible with the fact that human social relations are only possible because they involve (whatever that means) *men* and not, say, rocks or dogs. There is an intelligible and important problem here how, by virtue of what, is it possible for there to be human social relations? Such a question does not necessarily involve the assumption that we need a 'science of man', but it does involve the assumption that there must be sciences other than the science of social formations, sciences such as linguistics, psychoanalytic theory, anthropology. Inasmuch as the phrase 'never anything more than . . .' in AF2 is a denial of this, then it is a mistake. What Althusser is, correctly, keen to emphasize is that such sciences cannot be subsumed under a general heading, 'the study of human nature', where this is given the interpretation it was given by all philosophical and proto-scientific enquiries concerning man before Marx (and by and large since Marx also). Thus is he concerned to emphasize that one cannot *first* study 'human nature' and *then*, on that basis, study human social relations. What he has neglected to emphasize (although he has never denied it and clearly believes it to be true) is that the science of social formations does not exhaust the scientific knowledge of human life.

(2) A connected point: if Althusser has not abolished the human subject, has he perhaps sought to abolish the *concept* of 'the human subject', or the concepts 'man' and 'men'? I said earlier that HF and

AF1 are conceptually incompatible. I take this to mean not that there is *no* admissible concept of 'men' or 'subject', but that any such concept could not be the same concept as that of 'men' (and 'subject') as they exist within *either* the pre-Marxian problematic *or* the ideological discourse of everyday life. That this is, in part, what Althusser means, and that he is not in the absurd position of having asserted that men do not exist, is clear for example in *For Marx* (pp. 229, 243): 'It is impossible to *know* anything about *men* except on the absolute precondition that the *philosophical (theoretical)* myth of man is reduced to ashes . . . Once the scientific analysis of this real object has been undertaken, we discover that a knowledge of *concrete (real) men*, that is a knowledge of that ensemble of the social relations is only possible on the condition that we do completely without the *theoretical services* of the concept of man (in the sense in which it existed in its theoretical claims even before the displacement).' But I would certainly agree that such statements are not so rigorous that one could guarantee that they could not have undesirable effects in politics and science.

(3) Geras may be relying on the criterion that any view would be incorrect (and would have undesirable effects in politics) if that view had the implication that human subjectivity and human agency are only epiphenomenal to the process of historical change; that is, that they are not implicated in the causal mechanisms which produce that change. I agree with this. The question of whether Althusser has views which do have this implication is a difficult one. Certainly he would not admit to holding such views. They would not only contradict other views that he clearly does hold (e.g. about political practice), but would amount to a version of reductivist materialist determinism that so much of his work on the dialectic and on over-determination has sought to refute. However, Geras is right in the *NLR* article when he insists on the Althusserian view that 'the rigour of a text counts for more than the intentions of its subject-author'.

The Concepts of the Second Anti-Humanist Formula

Now for the problem of the interpretation of AF2. I do not want to minimize the difficulties — these are in part certainly caused by the fact that Althusser has made no attempt to give to AF2 the extended exposition that it requires. The off-hand way in which this formula is sometimes dropped into the argument without detailed exposition is bound to have, as Althusser would put it, undesirable effects in science and politics.

As I understand it, the concept 'support' (*Träger*) as used by

Althusser has two quite distinct origins. The first is in structural linguistics and related areas of research such as structuralist literary analysis and psychoanalytic theory. In the sections of *Reading Capital* in which Althusser discusses (theoretical and ideological) discourse, symptomatic reading, and so on he is, without ever discussing the problems involved, leaning heavily on the methods and concepts of these 'structuralist' sciences, in particular on Lacan's psychoanalytic theory (hence the appearance of the concept of 'the unconscious of a text'). Now, I do not want to attempt here any discussion or assessment of this aspect of Althusser's work, except to say that the concept of 'subject' is very much in the nature of a *problem* for *all* the structuralist-influenced theoretical enquiries. Inasmuch as Althusser gives the impression in these sections of *Reading Capital* that he is relying on some body of accomplished philosophical research, he is guilty of at least evasion. For all the back-pedalling in the 'Forward' ('we believe that despite the terminological ambiguity the profound tendency of our texts was not attached to the "structuralist ideology" '), he can be accused of having allowed some attachment to give his work a false sense of rigour.

Notice however, that I am not saying that this attachment to a structuralist terminology and method, as applied to the analysis of texts, is *wrong*. The particular form of abstraction involved in this approach raises serious questions. One practises an abstraction that produces, as an object of analysis, a text. For the purposes of analysis one severs the links which existed between the production of the (real, concrete) text and (a) the activity of a subject-author and (b) a social formation. (On the latter aspect of the abstraction see Geras's useful discussion in the *NLR* article.) Althusser practises this abstraction but does not discuss *how it is possible*, nor demonstrate its limits. I agree with Geras that this lack of discussion leads Althusser (and this is even truer of Rancière) to adopt positions which are idealist.

Träger in Capital

The second source of the concept 'Träger' is its use by Marx in *Capital*. Let us be quite clear about this. The concept is *not* just one which was invented by Althusser in order to give a modish structuralist flavours to his work. It is Marx's concept; it occurs regularly throughout *Capital*. If we need a philosophical exposition of it, this is not because there is any a priori obligation on us to defend Althusser. It is because we need to understand Marx.

In Marx's use the concept is once again produced by abstraction, in this case with the production of the concept 'men only in so far as they are bearers/effects of the economic social relations of production of the capitalist mode of production (CMP)'. The question is, what is it that makes this abstraction possible? I can't provide here the detailed analysis of *Capital* that would be required to answer that question properly. But the concept *Träger* does seem to be an important aspect of the scientific achievement of *Capital*. It is important to study it and understand it, and on *that* basis to decide whether or not the use made of it by Althusser is correct.

Here are three points about Marx's use of *Träger* and its variants in *Capital*. Each of them is related to the inadequacy of the concepts 'men' and 'circumstances' in the analysis of the CMP.

(1) In *Capital* the capitalist is said to be 'personified capital'. In his actions he is 'the effect of a social mechanism in which he is merely a cog. Moreover, the development of capitalist production makes it necessary constantly to increase the amount of capital laid out in an industrial undertaking, and competition subordinates every individual capitalist to the immanent laws of capitalist production, as external and coercive laws.'[7]

One of the points of the concept 'effect/support' is then to get at the way in which each individual capitalist (or worker) is related to the necessity which derives from the laws of operation of the system as a whole. There are only a certain number of 'places' in this system which an individual can occupy (schematically, capitalist of the industrial, landlord, merchant varieties, productive and unproductive labour etc) and these places are continually reproduced and continually develop in what 'they' demand of their occupants. Certain laws operate in the process of reproduction of these places and relations; competition between individual capitals, exploitation of wage-labour by the appropriation of surplus value, and so on.

(2) 'As the conscious bearer (*Träger*) of this movement, the possessor of money becomes a capitalist. His person, or rather his pocket, is the point from which the money starts, and to which it returns. The objective content of the circulation we have been discussing — the valorization of value — is his subjective purpose, and it is only insofar as the appropriation of ever more wealth in the abstract is the sole driving force behind his operations that he functions as a capitalist, i.e. as capital personified and endowed with consciousness and a will.'[8]

---

7. *Capital* Volume One, Harmondsworth 1976, p. 739.
8. Ibid., p. 254.

The point here is to do with the way in which occupying a 'place' in the structure of the social relations of production is related to the subjectivity of the individual 'bearer', to his consciousness and his will. This seems to be the area of discussion that Althusser has in mind when he talks of the problem of the 'historical forms of the existence of individuality'. (*Reading Capital* p. 112). But these human subjects, although they are subjects active within the process of social production, are not given as the subjects *of that process*, nor as the *objects* of that process (these are Geras's concepts — he says that men are *both* of these). Insofar as he occupies a place (is a capitalist, for example), it is because the objective basis of circulation (valorization of value) becomes his subjective aim (ownership of wealth in the abstract, money).

(3) On the other hand, it is only insofar as men personify economic social relations of production that they enter into the analysis of the CMP. 'As we proceed to develop our investigation, we shall find, in general, that the characters who appear on the economic stage are merely personifications of economic relations; it is as the bearers of these economic relations that they come into contact with each other.'[9] This is, of course, the fundamental point about Marx's analysis on which Balibar relies in his exposition of the '*Träger*' concept in *Reading Capital*. It is essential that we investigate the significance of this fact, that Marx demonstrates the structure of the social process of the capitalist production, its reproduction and the laws of its development without having to discuss men (as subjects, as individuals with consciousness and will) except insofar as they 'personify' or are 'effects of' the social relations of production. And let us not underestimate the scope of Marx's discoveries about the CMP made on this basis. Not just the reproduction of capitalist relations of production. But also the laws of development; the concentration of capital, the socialization of productive forces (development of forms of organization and cooperation), the extension of capitalist social relations to all branches of production and the formation of a world market, the constitution of an industrial reserve army, and the decline in the average rate of profit. (This list is an approximation of that given by Balibar in *Reading Capital* p. 284.) As far as this analysis is concerned, Marx nowhere relies on the notion that 'men make history', and it is surely correct that this notion would in fact have constituted an obstacle to the production of this scientific knowledge. (The one reference Geras gives to *Capital* as a source for this formula

9. Ibid., p. 179.

is actually a quote from Vico.)

The Limits of the 'Träger' Concept

What are the limits of the knowledge given in *Capital?* The absence of 'men' in *Capital* is determined by the limits of the object of the theory given in that text. That object is the economic instance of the CMP. I shall raise two issues about the extent to which concepts found in *Capital* might not be sufficient for the production of knowledge of other objects. Is the conceptual restriction, whereby men enter only in so far as they are supports/effects of social relations of production, possible when it is a matter of knowledge of periods in which the *political* class struggle is dominant, for example of periods of transition between modes of production? And secondly, is this restriction possible when it is a matter of knowledge of a conjuncture?

The mechanisms of the structures of the economic social relations of the CMP as described in *Capital* only operate on the assumption of the dominance of the economic instance, and of the successful articulation of this instance with the operations of the structures of the political and ideological instances. One might ask what is involved in that assumption. Whatever the answer to that question, outside the limits of this assumption the laws of the capitalist economic structures break down (or have yet to be established). This is clearly seen in *Capital* in its treatment of the transition from feudalism to capitalism, and marginally in its few remarks about the dissolution of capitalism. In those parts of *Capital* in which Marx is discussing periods such as these, when political class struggle is dominant, his analysis no longer operates within the same conceptual limits. In relation to the transition from feudalism to capitalism Marx says that once the CMP is established, the reproduction of the social classes can be left to the 'natural laws of production'. That is, 'it is possible to rely on the worker's dependence on capital, which springs from the conditions of production themselves, and is guaranteed in perpetuity by them. It is otherwise during the historical genesis of capitalist production.'[10] In this genesis capitalist social relations were established by force and by the use of the State, in short by political and ideological class struggle.

As Balibar puts it in *Reading Capital:* 'Instead of an intervention governed by the limits of the mode of production, primitive accumulation shows us an intervention of political practice, in its different

10. Ibid., p. 899.

forms, whose result is to *transform* and *fix* the limits of the mode of production . . . In a transition period there is a "non-correspondence" (between the different levels) because the mode of intervention of political practice, instead of conserving the limits and producing its effects within their determination, displaces them and transforms them.'[11] Are there laws of development of such a process which could be analysed in the same way that the laws of the development of capitalism are analysed in *Capital?* Balibar's discussion of the possibilities of analysis here is as follows: 'But the analysis of this struggle and of the political social relations which it implies is not part of the study of the structure of production. The analysis of the transformation of the limits therefore requires a theory of the different times of the economic structure and of the class struggle, and of their articulation in the social structure. To understand how they can be joined together in the unity of a *conjuncture* (e.g. how, if other conditions are fulfilled, the crisis can be the occasion for a — revolutionary — transformation of the structure of production) depends on this, as Althusser has shown in an earlier study ('Contradiction and Over-determination')'.[12] Indeed everything depends on this. What kind of knowledge is knowledge of a conjuncture? What forms of abstraction and of conceptual restriction are possible here? *What* has Althusser shown, in his famous essay, about conjunctural analysis?

Althusser cites Lenin's statement: 'The soul of Marxism is the concrete analysis of a concrete situation.' *Capital* does not, by itself, provide such a concrete analysis; it develops some of the concepts for such analyses. Althusser's insistence on the formula 'the masses make history; the class struggle is the motor of history' is related to his investigation of what is involved in the concrete analysis of a concrete situation. In these discussions, which he conducts in terms of the concepts 'primary and secondary contradictions', 'uneven development', 'the complex whole with the unity of a structure articulated in dominance' etc., Althusser does not rely on a doctrine that, in a knowledge of a conjuncture, men would only appear insofar as they were the 'effects/supports' of the places distributed by the social relations of production. What he does rely on is what I called above 'the restricted sense' of this concept that men enter always as members of classes, or of fractions of classes, and as engaged in class struggles and operating with class ideologies. But there is all the difference in the world between talking about bourgeois ideology and

11. *Reading Capital*, pp. 306ff.
12. Ibid., p. 293.

talking about 'supports of the ideological relations of production' or 'personification of political social relations' or whatever. The stronger sense, that involved in AF2, would suggest that the structure of class relations, and its development and transformation, could be known 'with the precision of natural science', and would be experienced as external necessities beyond men's control. And yet the whole point of revolutionary political practice is to know how to act so as to shift the basic balance of forces in a concrete situation, and ultimately to produce a 'ruptural unity' in which the decisive transformation can come about.

Theory and Politics

The problem of knowledge of the conjuncture brings me, at last, to the third of Norman Geras's comments on Althusser which I wish to discuss. The problem here is theory and its relation to politics. Even less than with the above problems is it possible for me to do justice here to the complex issues involved.

Geras says that it follows from Althusser's AF2 that men can only transform social relations 'by the power of a knowledge (Theoretical Practice) brought to them from elsewhere'. This is taken by Geras as following from the doctrine that men are nothing more than the supports/effects of social relations. It does not in fact so follow. On the incorrect interpretation of this doctrine given in his essay (which equates the doctrine with the view that 'the masses are the total objects of their circumstances'), it would not follow because there would be no *elsewhere* for theoretical practice to come from. This is so because the doctrine that men are supports of social relations, whatever interpretation it is given, is a doctrine about *all* men and not just about the masses. So there would be no possibility of *some* men, e.g. intellectuals, being different from the masses in this respect and hence being the 'elsewhere' from which the power to transform social relations by theoretical practice could come. If, however, we take instead the interpretation of the 'supports/effects' doctrine that is implicit, in Geras's *NLR* article we find the following. The concepts 'supports/effects' are given content by their place in the more general theory that men function as occupants of places in systems of social practices (economic, political, ideological, scientific). These practices are 'mechanisms' whereby various kinds of production occur by work performed on different kinds of objects. Now, Althusser explicitly identifies *political* practice as the practice which transforms social relations by work performed on the object 'the present conjuncture'.

We have the problem of what it means to say that within these practices men are 'supports/effects', and the question of whether this whole conceptual construction is in any case based on a generalization of concepts which in Marx perform a much more restricted role. But whatever the answers to these questions, it is quite clear that to the extent that men are not the subjects of the processes performed by political practice, they are to exactly the same extent not the subjects of processes which come about as a result of theoretical practice. Theoretical practice could not therefore be brought from anywhere at all to save men from the consequences of not being the subjects of social processes. It is also clear that, in any case, it is political practice, and not theoretical practice, which transforms social relations.

So it is quite impossible to find room within this theory for the view that theoretical practice transforms social relations, or that theoretical practice is achieved by some group within society but elsewhere than with the masses e.g. by intellectuals or philosophers. There is thus no basis in any of this for Geras's charge that for Althusser 'the relation between Marxist theory and the working class is a unilateral and purely pedagogic one: the intellectuals "give" the class the knowledge it needs. This is only the final consequence of every idealism: elitism. When knowledge celebrates its autonomy, the philosophers celebrate their dominance.'[13] It is certainly true that Althusser has not produced a satisfactory account of the 'mechanisms' which produce knowledge, nor of the relationship between theory and politics. Althusser has himself pointed this out. But it is equally clear that the abstract thought-objects 'Theoretical Practice' and 'Political Practice' do not designate real objects which are to be found distributed respectively to the social groups known as 'the intellectuals' and 'the masses'.

On a connected point, it is also perfectly clear that the concepts 'science' and 'ideology' do not refer to realities (systems of representations) which can be located in the heads of, respectively, intellectuals (or philosophers) on the one hand and the masses on the other. If the masses live ideologically, according to Althusser this is not because they are the masses but because they are men, and this goes for intellectuals too. Whether the ideology is mystificatory or 'depends on science — which has never been the case before',[14] depends not on the bearer of that ideology being an intellectual or a worker but on that ideology being produced within bourgeois or socialist society.

13. 'Althusser's Marxism', op. cit., p. 84.
14. *Reading Capital*, p. 131.

These points about Althusser are important not just because it is important to defend him against a charge of being an elitist, but because it is important to emphazise what we can learn from him about the relation between theory and politics. Two themes run through his work which are not only direct refutations of the charge that he is an elitist but important truths which it is important for us to understand and assimilate. The first of these is the centrality in Marxist theory and practice of the knowledge of conjunctures. Revolutionary political practice is guided not by Marxist science in the abstract, but by the application of Marxist science within the political class struggle to concrete situations. Put like this one can see the absurdity of supposing that the task of producing the knowledge required in political practice and for political practice should fall on the shoulders of that thoroughly unrevolutionary bourgeois group 'the intellectuals'. And this is the second theme: the intellectuals. Here one should study the following texts by Althusser: 'Interview on Philosophy' and 'Preface to *Capital*';[15] and Althusser's contributions to Macciocchi's *Letters from Inside the Italian Communist Party to Louis Althusser*. But also read Macciocchi's own contributions to this important and exciting book. Althusser on intellectuals: 'It is extremely difficult for specialists and other bourgeois and petty-bourgeois "intellectuals" (including students). For a mere *education* of their consciousness is not enough, nor a mere reading of *Capital*. They must also make a real *rupture*, a real *revolution* in their consciousness, in order to move from their necessarily bourgeois or petty-bourgeois class instinct to proletarian class positions. It is extremely difficult, but not absolutely impossible . . . A proletarian *class position* is more than a mere proletarian "class instinct". It is the consciousness and practice which conform with the *objective* reality of the proletarian class struggle. Class instinct is subjective and spontaneous. Class position is objective and rational. To arrive at proletarian class positions, the class instinct of proletarians only needs to be *educated;* the class instinct of the petty-bourgeoisie, and hence of intellectuals, has, on the contrary, to be *revolutionized.* This education and this revolution are, in the last analysis, determined by proletarian class struggle conducted on the basis of the principles of Marxist-Leninist theory.'[16] Of one thing we can be sure. It is not the intellectuals, not even the philosophers, who make history.

Reprinted from *RP* 6

15. Ibid., Both in *Lenin and Philosophy*, NLB, London 1971.
16. Ibid.

Reason as Dialectic:
Science, Social Science, and Socialist Science

Roy Edgley

The Current Crisis, Social and Intellectual

The current crisis in world affairs, in particular the economic and social crisis in those countries that dominate world affairs, the advanced industrial states of Europe and America, is reflected in an intellectual crisis, especially in those countries. As they move into the so-called 'post-industrial' phase, into 'technological society', their dominant form of theoretical knowledge, scientific knowledge, increasingly becomes a crucial economic resource, a factor of production; and the intellectual crisis reveals itself as a radical uncertainty about the nature and status of science. Europe invented modern science, and just as, during the centuries of European imperialism, Europe sought to dominate the rest of the world, so Europe's dominant form of knowledge, science, has been involved in the imperial conquest of other cultures. Thus the conflict between the advanced industrial states and the Third World, a conflict that is an essential component of the current world crisis, is reflected intellectually in a conflict between science and other forms of thought — for example, between European *medical* science and such apparently unscientific forms of medicine as acupuncture.

As social institutions designed for the production and distribution of theoretical knowledge, the universities are of course deeply involved in the crisis, and it is not surprising that they have been centres of ferment in the last decade or so. They are the social points at which the intellectual aspect of the crisis has its most explicit theoretical expression. Anthropologists have become hypersensitive about applying their own concepts of science and rationality to what used to be called 'primitive' cultures and belief systems. Psychologists and psychiatrists discuss and re-draw the distinction between sanity and madness. And at the most abstract level, philosophers — well, many English-speaking philosophers, I suppose, continue to do logic, philosophy of logic, and epistemology as if they inhabited the ivory tower of timeless Platonic forms, the Third World of Popper rather than of Che. But even ivory towers cannot be completely insulated, and the general philosophical preoccupation with the distinction between reason and unreason has taken specific forms that relate more explicitly to the social situation. In particular, in English philosophy two new sub-disciplines, not distinguished and named before, have emerged as growing points within and between the old philosophical specialisms, and both in that historical fact and in their own content have reflected intellectually the general social crisis. I am referring to the philosophy of science within the general field of epistemology, and to the philosophy of the social sciences which has developed between the philosophy of science and the old sub-discipline of political philosophy. The chief preoccupation of these two new sub-disciplines has become the distinction between science and ideology.

In both fields one can trace in the analytical tradition a more or less gradual relaxation of the constraints thought to be implicit in the idea of science and reason. In the philosophy of science Popper sought to replace inductivism and verificationism with the less stringent requirement of falsificationism; Kuhn argued that even that was too stringent for revolutionary science; and Feyerabend has argued that all science is or ought to be revolutionary science, and in his article and book *Against Method,* as the title indicates, claims that the only rule of method in the acquisition of knowledge is 'Anything Goes'. In a rather different way, the philosophy of the social sciences has similarly helped to soften up the idea of rationality: as a practising social scientist with an unusual degree of philosophical self-understanding, Chomsky has attacked behaviourist constraints imposed in the cause of scientificity; and Popper's doctrine of the unity of science, implying that in methodology and logical structure the social sciences are indistinguishable from the natural sciences, has been opposed by the idea that the social sciences have their own special logic and methodology. In some writers — Winch, for instance — this methodology involves the claim that societies under investigation may legitimately employ canons of rationality quite different from, but not inferior to, its own. We seem to be presented with a choice between equally unacceptable alternatives: on the one hand, an empiricism that is unable to account for much of the historical phenomenon of science; and on the other hand, a relativism that makes radical rational criticism impossible, and in doing so seems to be self-refuting.

Marxism as Scientific Socialism

The place of Marxism in this discussion is distinctive and instructive. Its failure to fit the dominant empiricist model in the philosophy of science is even more striking than the failure of other, more generally accepted, theories and phases of modern science: within the European conception of science it is a genuine peculiarity. Yet Winch's relativism does not obviously save it, even as relativistically rational. Marxism is, after all, a European product, conceived explicitly as heir to the great tradition of natural science that Europe invented: it is not a form of thought characteristic of a foreign society, defining a conception of rationality necessarily alien to our language and culture, and therefore apparently uncriticizable from our European point of view. On the contrary, to the extent that Marxism characterizes other cultures, it does so as one of those cultural exports that Europe's imperial capitalism did not, so to speak, bargain for, and which it now faces as an alien threat.

Endogenous to Europe, then, Marxism has been typically criticized by European intellectuals within the analytical tradition, especially philosophers of science and of social science, as unscientific, as muddled about the nature of science and its own relation to it: those with an explicit demarcation criterion, such as Popper, have put it firmly in its place as pseudo-science. But this general difficulty of appreciating Marxism's claim to be a science is not peculiar to analytical philosophers and those scientists whose understanding of science has been articulated and shaped by analytical philosophy. It is not even peculiar to non-Marxists in general. Within Marxism itself, many have deeply felt and wrestled with it. There is in fact one specific form of the problem that is common to Marxist and non-Marxist discussions — a form posed by Marxism's self-description as 'scientific socialism'. Marxism presents itself as both social science and political movement, as both scientific theory and revolutionary practice: as something concerned not only to understand the world but also to change it. Discussions within Marxism about whether the socialism is distinguishable from the science, and if so how these two elements are related, reveal that certain conceptions of science and reason are deeply entrenched as common property on both sides of the divide between Marxists and non-Marxists.

These common conceptions involve a family of shared ideas about the distinctions between fact and value, theory and practice, description and prescription, science and morality. Contemporary English-speaking discussion of these ideas has a characteristic parochialism, and seems to suggest that apart from anticipations by Hume ('is' and 'ought') and perhaps Mill (science as indicative and art as imperative), their history belongs to 20th-century analytical philosophy, from Moore's 'naturalistic fallacy' through the emotivism of Ayer and Stevenson to Hare. But it is clear that the European mainland shared much of this thinking and made its own contribution to the history of the distinctions as they developed under the impact of science and capitalism from the 17th-century onwards. Kant, Comte, Weber and Poincaré, as well as Mach and the Vienna Circle, all struggled to digest philosophically the phenomenon of science, and in the process distinguished it logically and epistemologically from value, or practice, or morality. Here, for instance, is Poincaré making the point in a way familiar to contemporary English philosophers:

> It is not possible to have a scientific ethic, but it is no more possible to have an immoral science. And the reason is simple; it is, how shall I put it? for purely grammatical reasons. If the premises of a syllogism are both in the indicative, the conclusion will equally be in the indicative. In order for the conclusion to be put in the imperative, it would be necessary for at least one of the premises to be in the imperative. Now, the principles of science, the postulates of geometry, are and can only be in the indicative; experimental truths are also in this same mode, and at the foundations of science there is not, cannot be, anything else. Moreover the most subtle dialectician can juggle with these principles as he wishes, combine them, pile them up one on the other; all that he can derive from them will be in the indicative. He will never obtain a proposition which says: do this, or do not do that; that is to say a proposition which confirms or contradicts ethics. ('Morality and science', 1913)

Given such a general climate of opinion, Marxism seems to be faced with some difficult choices: as social science it cannot be socialism, and as socialism it cannot be social science; the two elements might be conjoined, but not logically connected or unified. 'Value-free' science can, of course, have a practical application as technology, but technology can only specify means to ends and must therefore be supplemented with a choice of ends or objectives that cannot be settled scientifically. This is roughly the view of the Austro-Marxist Rudolf Hilferding, in his book *Finance Capital*, and of most of the orthodox Marxism of the Second International. In his neo-Kantian version of Marxism in his lecture on 'Kant and Marx' (1904), Karl Vorlander identifies the values of Marxism as ethical: 'Socialism cannot free itself from ethics historically or logically, neither on the theoretical level nor in fact.' But *ethical* socialism is Utopian, and in practice reformist rather than revolutionary, liberal and social-democratic rather than Marxist; and it is well known that Marx himself was contemptuous of morality and treated it theoretically as essentially ideological. Under these constraints *scientific* socialism came to be represented, predominantly in the Third International and in Stalinism, as a theory specifying laws of inevitable social change. Between this and the alternative of ethical socialism, Marxism as a programme of revolutionary action was effectively squeezed out of the picture of coherent possibilities.

This ideological emasculation no doubt reveals the almost inexhaustible capacity of the status quo to protect itself under threat. But is that emasculation avoidable from a rational point of view? I want to make some suggestions to that end: suggestions that are both fairly simple and very general because they re-theorize (by developing arguments originally put forward in my *Reason in Theory and Practice,* London 1969) the overall structural relations between the relevant basic and very general categories. From this perspective the conception of science from which the emasculation results is itself ideological, in fact a crucial part of the European ideology out of which Marxism developed as a radical innovation and critique. As ideology, this conception reflects important, but relatively superficial, aspects of science, aspects that mask and contradict its deeper nature and potential. Historically speaking, it is this embryonic reality within the womb of European science that Hegel and Marx, heirs and critics of the Enlightenment, develop and deliver as social science. As such, the Marxist conception of science is both continuous with, and radically different from, the prevailing conception. The question of the scientificity or otherwise of Marxism cannot therefore be answered by noting its failure to conform to Enlightenment standards of science articulated by Hume and Kant and developed by their modern followers. On the contrary, the question is whether Marxism embodies a different conception that supersedes its rivals.

Science and Reason as Dialectic

The conception of science and reason that Marxism explicitly offers in distinguishing itself from the Enlightenment is: dialectic. It is this Hegelian inheritance that is contrasted with the 'metaphysical' conception of science shaped in 'the mechanical philosophy'. Mechanistic science is allowed to have both a necessary historical role and a continuing validity in certain areas of investigation. But dialectic, it is claimed, is essential for the 'historical' sciences. Moreover, to focus on the present topic, Marxists have frequently claimed that this conception of science as dialectic is required to solve the problems set by the idea of scientific socialism. The deformations of both ethical socialism and Stalinism involve mechanistic conceptions of science.

It is this view that I want to explore and give support to. But first it should be noted that there is an easy way out which in fact settles nothing. A dialectical conception, it might be said, is a view that conceives of opposites as in unity: scientific socialism is such a unity, since it unites fact and value, theory and practice, science and political revolution. That, of course, only sets the problem. It doesn't solve it. The problem precisely is how to conceive of science in such a way that value and practice can be seen as involved in it.

I shall now try to outline a solution of this problem in terms of the idea of contradiction, which is central to dialectic. The idea of contradiction is also, of course, central to analytical philosophy. But on this matter the two traditions face each other with blank incomprehension. For both, contradiction is a concept, or rather a category, of logic; and it is in the philosophy of logic of each tradition that the differing conceptions of science have their roots.

Roughly and briefly, the Hegelian view is that reality is in a constant process of change, and that this temporal, historical process is due to the contradictions within the essence of things. These contradictions oppose each other, and change is the resolution of that opposition and the replacement of those contradictions by others on a higher plane, so that change through resolution continues. Now Hegel was, of course, an idealist, and though analytical philosophers claim to see some truth in the claim that *ideas* can be contradictory, the Marxist dialectic is materialist, not idealist, and from the analytical point of view the doctrine that there are contradictions in material reality seems nothing short of outrageous. In such a context, the concept of contradiction, it seems, must lose its specifically logical content and cease to be a category of logic: it can only mean something like 'conflict' or 'opposition between forces'. Marx himself sometimes speaks of 'collisions' rather than 'contradictions'; and many Marxist writers, when discussing dialectic, seem satisfied with this evacuation of the specifically logical content of the idea of contradiction, or at least fail to take up the point seriously, as if they have no understanding of the basic position from which the objection is made.

The Analytical View: Dialectic not Logic

We can see the analytical side of this lack of comprehension starkly represented in Popper's critique of the idea of dialectical logic in his 'What is Dialectic?'[1] Popper claims that dialectic is most plausible as an empirical theory about the temporal or historical development of thought. But under that interpretation, it precisely cannot be logic, and this for three general reasons that can be identified in Popper's argument and its background of modern philosophy of logic:

(1) There are no contradictions in reality. Popper approvingly quotes the words of the mathematical logician Hilbert: 'The thought that facts or events might mutually contradict each other appears to me as the very paradigm of thoughtlessness.' Now, it might be supposed that this doctrine is true of material reality and thus undermines the Marxist dialectic, dialectical materialism. But, it might be argued, it could be taken to be true of the whole of reality only if the common philosophical contrast between thought and reality misled us into believing that thought itself is not a part of reality; but, of course, thought is a part of reality, and in that part there can be contradictions. However, to the extent that it is admitted that there can be contradictions in thought, the concession is heavily qualified. For the argument that there can be no contradictions in reality seems to apply in some sense to any part of reality, thought included. The argument is that if the proposition 'p' contradicts the proposition 'q', the proposition 'p' & 'q' must be false, i.e. nothing in reality can correspond to it. In other words, if the proposition 'p' contradicts the proposition 'q', it is logically impossible that both p and q: there can be no state of affairs corresponding to a contradiction.

(2) As this argument presupposes, logical relations are truth-value relations between propositions. In the paper 'What is Dialectic?' Popper speaks of sentences, but whatever the word used they are denizens of what Popper now refers to as the Third World.

(3) Logical relations are atemporal, not chronological relations. Logic, unlike dialectic, is not concerned with temporal or historical change, with processes. In particular it is not concerned with the origins of processes or with genetic or causal explanations of them. It is not developmental (or any other kind of) psychology, or history, or sociology.

These three doctrines are the basis of the philosophy of logic characteristic of twentieth-century analytical philosophy, and consti-

1. *Mind*, 1940; reprinted in *Conjectures and Refutations*, London 1963.

tute a central part of the self-reflective theorizing involved in the development of the special discipline of modern logic, and with it the logic and methodology of science, between Frege and Popper.

An Analytical Mode of Science

With this in mind, I want now to reconstruct a simple but influential model of science incorporating these ideas, and show how it relates both to our original question of science, values and action, and to the connected question of dialectic. The relevant aspects of the model are articulated in Wittgenstein's *Tractatus*. The logic and methodology of science represents science as a body of propositions between which hold certain truth-relations (including, perhaps, probability-relations). The basic notion of truth is essentially concerned with the relation of a proposition to the reality it is about, the relation of a proposition to its subject-matter — to what, in view of the tradition, we had better call its object. It is often said that the aims of science are to describe, explain, and predict. In the philosophy of science these aims are represented in the claim that scientific theories are descriptive, explanatory and predictive. But it is essential to ask: descriptive, explanatory and preductive *of what*? The answer is that these categories of description, explanation and prediction characterize ways in which scientific theories relate to their object; or perhaps better, as in Popper's account (with description replaced by testing) these three characterize aspects of the single way in which scientific theories relate to their object. At any event, scientific theories are propositions that describe, explain and predict the reality they are about. Guided by the central importance of this distinction and relation between theory and reality, or what a different tradition would have called subject and object, we realize that if a theory is self-contradictory it is logically impossible for reality to be truthfully described by it. There can be no contradictions in reality.

Science as Practical: Technology

It seems to be a consequence of the structure of this model that in being descriptive, explanatory and predictive of reality, scientific theories cannot be evaluative or practical, cannot have any evaluative or practical implications. Yet is this really the case? One vitally important kind of evaluative and practical implication is commonly attributed to science conceived in this way — namely technological implications. Indeed, it might be said that once science is conceived in this way, technology is its only possible evaluative and practical role, so that as a paradigm of rationality in theory, science constitutes for practice the paradigm of technological rationality. For example, Ohm's Law in theory of electricity says that in any electrical circuit the voltage, current and resistance stand in a constant relationship, that is, with a given voltage and a higher resistance the current flow will be lower. From this there seems to follow a technological implication that can be characterized in a variety of such general ways as that it tells us: what to do in order to do something else; or, how to do a certain thing; or, by what means or in what way we can do something. In this example, Ohm's Law seems to imply that in order to lower the current flow in a circuit with a constant voltage, we must or may or ought to increase the resistance. It is this piece of technological know-how that is embodied in the electrical device known as a rheostat, a variable resistance that can be wired into a circuit, e.g. in a wireless receiver, to enable us to control the current flow in the instrument. In general, it is by virtue of this sort of implication that scientific knowledge, in Bacon's aphorism, is power; that science gives us mastery or control over nature, making us, in Descartes's words, 'masters and possessors of nature'. This is certainly at least a part of what was in Marx's mind when he urged the crucial role of science in man's relation to Nature and society: at present they dominate and master us, but with the knowledge science gives us, we enter a cosmic struggle in which we can ultimately realize the ancient Faustian dream without its awful penalty; we can turn the tables on Nature and society, liberate ourselves by mastering them, and so move from the realm of necessity to that of freedom, in which at last we make our own history.

These dramatic possibilities, long dreamed of by the great visionaries of the scientific revolution, seem at this very moment to be starting their conversion into reality. As advanced industrial societies move into the so-called post-industrial stage, into technological society, their essential structure is changing to bring about this unity of theory and practice, the systematic application of scientific knowledge to the problems of production through technology. That being so, it is of some interest to note that philosophers, especially analytical philosophers, have devoted so little time and effort to investigating and clarifying the concept of technology, by which scientific theory seems to come into such close logical relation to practice. It is this idea, of course, that Hume is seeking to characterize in his famous aphorism 'Reason is and ought only to be the slave of the passions'; Kant considered it in his account of 'hypothetical imperatives';

Sidgwick says some things to the point in *The Methods of Ethics;* and in *The Language of Morals* Hare developed a theory that has since been sporadically examined and criticized by others. Significantly, all these contributions have been made by ethics; though this is clearly an area of important overlap between ethics and the philosophy of science, the latter has on the whole steadfastly ignored the problems of technology, apparently conceiving itself, perhaps with unconscious but understandable elitism, as the philosophy of 'pure' science rather than the philosophy of science both 'pure' and 'applied'. As far as our present topic is concerned, the chief problem in this area of technology is precisely whether, and if so how, scientific theory, or more generally factual, empirical or descriptive propositions, can have evaluative and practical implications: for instance, how, if at all, Ohm's Law can imply a technical imperative or value judgment containing the word 'ought' or one of its family, e.g. that in order to increase the current in a circuit with a constant voltage, one must or may or ought to lower the resistance.

I shall not pursue this problem here,[2] but simply record my view that technological statements, though not moral judgments, are genuinely prescriptive, practical, or evaluative, and really do follow from empirical statements of fact and scientific theories; and therefore, that technology represents a crucial breach, from within science itself so to speak, of the supposed logical barrier between fact and value, between theory and practice. But what kind of practice is legitimated by the idea of technological rationality? The first thing to note is that technology is not simply the use of knowledge for some practical purpose, as if knowledge were here just a means to some practical end: the idea of technology is not just the idea that knowledge is practically useful. For instance, the knowledge that a diplomat is homosexual may be used to blackmail him. In this sense, the knowledge is a means to an end external to its content; whereas in technology it is the content of the knowledge that represents theoretically the real relation of those state of affairs that a practical point of view represents as means to ends. As we have seen, among the categories involved in this idea are those of power, control and domination; and just as it is essential in characterizing science as descriptive, explanatory and predictive to ask 'Descriptive, explanative and predictive *of what?*', so it is essential here to ask 'Power, control and domination *over what?*' The answer is, of course, the same in both cases. What a scientific theory, as technology, gives us power,

2. See my 'Reason in Theory and Practice', op. cit., chap. 4.11.

control or domination over is what it is descriptive, explanatory or predictive of: that reality, or part of it, that constitutes its subject-matter or object. As a theory of or about electricity, Ohm's Law in its technological applications enables us to control electrical phenomena. We could say that in technology the power relation has the same object as the theory whose application it is. More generally, if we can talk of scientific knowledge as a relation between subject and object, between a knowing subject and what he has knowledge about, we can say that the power relation has the same terms as the knowledge relation: the subject with the knowledge also has the power, and the object he has knowledge about is what his knowledge gives him power or control over. This is one of the main reasons why the *human* sciences, if conceived according to the doctrine of the unity of science on the model of the natural sciences, can seem to be oppressive rather than liberating in their practical applications. Unlike the natural sciences, which as technology give power to human subjects over non-human nature, the object of the human sciences is or essentially involves people, and it is over people that these sciences as technology give power. If in these sciences subject and object were identical, this technology would constitute (one kind of) self-control. When subject and object in the human sciences are different, or thought of as different, as in our society or the technocratic society some sociologists foresee for the post-industrial phase, the human sciences as technology constitute the power of some people over others: in B. F. Skinner's honest but menacing designation, the behavioural sciences, for instance, yield a 'technology of behaviour control'.

Science as Critical Practice

Even if it is the case, then, that the idea of technology helps to bring fact and value, theory and practice, into some kind of unity, it is far from obvious that this is the kind of unity envisaged by Marx's conception of science as dialectical. Indeed, this kind of unity, characteristic of technocratic society, seems to be involved in an essentially non-dialectical conception of scientific theory as purely descriptive explanatory and predictive of its object. It is because the relation of theory to object is conceived as purely descriptive, explanatory and predictive that the practical relation of subject to that object is a relation of power, the object of the theory being conceived in that theory's practical implications as under the control of the subject.

One important thing missing from this model of scientific theory — if it is compared with Marx's conception of social science — is the idea of *criticism*. Marx's social science is socialist science by being, as science, a critique of its object, capitalist society.

Now, the simple model of science already outlined contains not only the embryonic idea of technology but also the implicit notion of criticism. The notion is implicit rather than explicit because the model represents only the relation of a single scientific theory to reality, its object. But if we enrich the model with a second theory about the same object, and consider the relation not of theory to object but of theory to theory, the possibility arises of a relation between the two theories that is a relation at once of contradiction and of criticism. Given two theories about the same subject-matter, one can contradict the other and implicitly criticize it as wrong, as mistaken. This notion of wrongness or mistakenness, whether of action or theory, is evaluative, as criticism or appraisal in general is evaluative. It is not technologically evaluative. Nor is it *morally* evaluative. The familiar and widespread tendency to identify values with *moral* values, and to regard reason as value-free, is simply a fundamental part of the prevailing ideology of science.

Popper himself sees criticism, as well as description, explanation and prediction, as crucial to science; and he therefore sees science as in some sense essentially evaluative. But at vital points in his account he reveals how his Third World conception of logic, specifically his anti-psychologism in the philosophy of logic, misleads him. One central part of Popper's argument in 'What is Dialectic?' concerns 'the dialectical saying that the thesis "produces" its antithesis'. Actually, he objects, 'it is only our critical attitude which produces the antithesis, and where such an attitude is lacking — which often enough is the case — no antithesis will be produced. Similarly, we have to be careful not to think that it is the "struggle" between a thesis and its antithesis which "produces" a synthesis. The struggle is one of minds.' And later: 'The only "force" which propels the dialectic development is, therefore, our determination not to accept, or to put up with, the contradiction between the thesis and the antithesis. It is not a mysterious force inside these two ideas, not a mysterious tension between them which promotes development — it is purely our decision, our resolution, not to admit contradictions.' What is at least strongly suggested here is that the notion of contradiction, in being a category of logic, is not itself evaluative or critical, and does not imply criticism. To characterize something as contradictory, Popper seems to say, is one thing, a logical thing; to criticize it is another, logically independent, thing, a matter of psychological attitude and decision rather than of logic.

I have argued elsewhere that the connection here is, on the contrary, internal and conceptual; that to characterize something as a contradiction, where that concept is a category of logic, *is*, at least by implication, to criticize it; and moreover that to criticize a theory is to criticize the actual or possible acceptance of that theory by some actual or possible subject. It is in fact difficult to make much sense of Popper's notion of criticism, given his view that what one criticizes are *theories*, and his Third World doctrine of knowledge without a knowing subject, i.e. of theory without a theorizing subject. What would be the *point* of criticizing a theory, if not to criticize its actual or possible *acceptance*? Contrary to the Platonic conception of logic that has characterized the subject from Frege to Popper, logical categories are themselves implicitly critical; and in their use as characterizations of theories or propositions, they criticize or appraise those theories by criticizing or appraising their acceptance by actual or possible subjects. The connection between logic and the faculty of reason cannot be just contingent.

It follows from this — or is perhaps a presupposition of it, but in any case is true — that people, as well as propositions, can contradict themselves, i.e. that people can hold contradictory views. The critical point of characterising a theory in terms of the logical category of contradiction therefore implies or presupposes that in this sense there can be contradictions in reality. To say 'Smith contradicted himself' is to make a statement about Smith that is itself non-contradictory and at once empirical, logical and evaluative, i.e. critical; it could not be critical if there could not in this sense be contradictions in reality. The contradictory thing said by Smith does, of course, putatively describe something that is logically impossible; but his asserting and believing it is logically possible, though logically impermissible.

In this way, science in general must be critical and evaluative. But as has already been suggested, the evaluative nature of scientific theories in relation to other theories and views cannot be understood Platonically, simply in terms of logical implications between descriptive propositions and value-judgements. Just as, in construing these value-judgements as criticism, we imply that (in the sense outlined) *what* is criticized, e.g. a contradiction, can have a real existence in some subject's thoughts and attitudes, so the criticism itself is empirically instantiated as: opposition — opposition to what is being criticized. Indeed, criticism is an activity or practice, the activity or practice of opposing, and without that activity there could be no such thing as science. Science understood philosophically, i.e. Platonically, as a logical structure of theories would be impossible and unintelligible without the idea of scientific activity, theoretical practice, including the practice of criticism; and with it the understanding of an argument not abstractly, as a set of propositions distinguishable into premises and conclusion — with some logical relation between them — but concretely as the activity of arguing. Science essentially involves arguing against people's theories and views, that is, critically opposing them: or, as we sometimes say, *attacking* them. The representation of science simply as an attempt to understand the world forgets that its point in so doing is also to change that part of it which consists of misunderstanding. 'The real is partly irrational: change it': that is the imperative of science.

Social Science as Criticism of Its Object

Now, however true all this might be, it will no doubt be objected that it is irrelevant. For all these claims about the critical nature of scientific activity fail to come to grips with the essential feature of the Marxist conception of science as dialectic. Of course, it will be said, science involves criticism, but the object of that criticism, *what* is criticized, is always some other theory: the critical relation is always between theories; it is horizontal, so to speak, never vertical, never a relation between a theory and *its* object, the reality it is about. In relation to its *object,* a scientific theory is always descriptive, explanatory and predictive, never critical. For example, the cosmological theory that the universe is expanding may by implication be critical of the theory that the universe is stable, but it is not critical of its object, i.e. of the universe itself and of its size from one moment to another.

I am willing to concede this, as a point about *natural* science; provided that the criticism of theories is understood as having, even in natural science, a *social* target in the acceptance of those theories by possible subjects, including social institutions (e.g. the Church as a target of Copernican criticism). But Marx's theory of capitalism is *social* science, and although it is sometimes held by Marxists that all science is or should be dialectical, it seems indubitable that in Marxism dialectic is primarily and essentially intended to characterize *social* science. If we claim that all science, including natural science, is or should be dialectical, we must also recognize some crucial differences in what we might call degree of dialecticity between natural and social sciences. If we hold that the natural sciences are dialectical, this means: (a) that the reality investigated by natural science has an underlying core ('essence') that differs radically from (conflicts with) its phenomenal appearance; (b) that this underlying core is constituted essentially by conflicting forces; and (c) that the natural sciences develop historically through theory-change centrally involving determinate contradiction between theories, such that new theories both negate and preserve the old.

But in the social sciences there are further vital dimensions to the dialectic, involving the logical category of contradiction both at the level of the object and in the relation, the interaction, between theory and object. For the object of social science is or essentially involves people in society; people are peculiar as objects of science in being also subjects with their own theories, views and ideas, scientific and otherwise, about their activities, about their social practices and institutions. These theories, views and ideas stand in much closer logical relation to those social practices and institutions than do theories, views and ideas about the natural world to their object; and in particular, the logical relation of contradiction, at least in its form as inconsistency, can be instantiated not only between people's thoughts but also between their actions and practices. Marx says that people's ideas about their social practices and institutions *reflect* the society in which they live. Society is itself a human product, and its production and reproduction have to be seen partly in terms of the ideas that constitute the self-understanding of the members of that society. More specifically, these ideas reflect and are instantiated in the surface features of the social structure, and thus form an ideology that obscures the underlying realities of that structure. Scientific critique of this ideology reveals that its appearance as consistent contradicts its own deeper nature; under examination it is revealed as confused and self-contradictory, and even in that it 'reflects', though it does not assert, the confused and self-contradictory nature of the underlying social reality. In this way social science, in criticizing other, ideological social theories and ideas as deeply contradictory, and so contradicting them, at the same time criticizes as contradictory, and so contradicts, the society in whose structure those inconsistent and conceptually muddled theories and ideas are realized. Marx's critique of what he calls 'the system of bourgeois economy' attacks at one and the same time both the theories and concepts of political economy and capitalism itself.

It may be thought that this brief account fails to recognize that the Marxist dialectic is materialist, not idealist. My reply is that as a theory of society, Marx's materialism asserts that what is basic in society is the economy — that part of the structure concerned essentially with the production of material goods and thus the satisfaction of material needs. That this 'material base' of social activities is inseparably interwoven with ideas is evident from the section of *Capital* on 'The Fetishism of Commodities'.

Thus the critical practice constituting Marxist social science involves practical opposition to the basic self-contradictions of capitalist society, its aim (and thus prediction) being the supersession of those contradictions. In two crucial ways, Marx's critique is not a moral or ethical critique, and its practice is not moral practice, at least as those notions have often been understood. First, its criticism is not of personal immoralities but of society's structural irrationalities. Second, it is not doctrinaire in supposing that the changes required can necessarily be effected by ideas alone, i.e. by the theoretical practice of reasoning with and exhorting people. Whatever morality is, in both ways Marxism is not morality *as distinct from* science: its central values are (and need only to be) those of reason, i.e. dialectic.

To include self-reflectively: if that is the role of science, what place is left for philosophy? Coupled with the descriptivist conception of science has been a view of philosophy as itself analytical and descriptive: philosophy can (in the end) only describe the structure of (scientific and other) language, and must leave everything as it is. But in this paper I have been doing philosophy: my aim has been also to show by example that just as science in general can and must be critical, and at an epistemologically basic level critical of existing concepts, and just as social science in particular can and must be critical of its object, society, so philosophy can and must be part of that same general project of social criticism, distinguished if at all only by the fundamentality of its target, the basic categories instantiated in society, in terms of which reality, including the social reality of science itself, is currently understood and shaped. I have criticized a dominant conception of science, and therefore a powerful tendency in the current social practice of science and the emerging technological society in which that conception and practice have a central role.

Reprinted from *RP* 15

Realism and Social Science
Some Comments on Roy Bhaskar's 'The Possibility of Naturalism'

Ted Benton

1. Introduction

An increasing body of philosophical work[1] is now available which (a) presents a 'realist' alternative to the hitherto predominant 'positivist' and 'conventionalist' currents in the philosophy of science and (b) attempts to use this realist account of science in the analysis of social-scientific practice. In general the objective of this analysis has been to transcend the polar opposition, which has always characterized debate in the philosophy of the social sciences, between positivism and 'humanist', 'hermeneutic' or 'neo-Kantian' dualisms. Commonly the outcome of this work has been to sustain the explanatory procedures of historical materialism, in one reading or another, as compatible with realist philosophy. Further, elements of a realist epistemology have also been attributed to Marx, Engels and other Marxists in their philosophical writings. What is remarkable, though, has been the great diversity of readings of Marxism — ranging from Critical Theory to Althusserian structuralism — which

1. This includes: Roy Bhaskar, *A Realist Theory of Science*, Leeds 1975, and Hassocks and New Jersey 1978; 'Feyerabend and Bachelard: Two Philosophies of Science', *New Left Review* 94 (1975); 'On the Possibility of Social Scientific Knowledge and the Limits of Naturalism', in Mepham and Ruben, eds., *Issues in Marxist Philosophy*, Vol. III, Hassocks 1979; and *The Possibility of Naturalism*, Brighton 1979; Russell N. Keat, 'Positivism, Naturalism and Anti-Naturalism in the Social Sciences', *Journal for the Theory of Social Behaviour*, I, pp. 3–17; Russell Keat and John Urry, *Social Theory as Science*, London 1975; T. Benton, *Philosophical Foundations of the Three Sociologies*, London 1977, and 'Natural Science and Cultural Struggle', in Mepham and Ruben, eds., *op. cit.*, Vol. II; Andrew Collier, 'In Defence of Epistemology', *Radical Philosophy* 20, Summer 1978; and David Thomas, *Naturalism and Social Science*, Cambridge 1979.

seem to be indifferently assimilable to the realist defence.

Since, however, the new 'transcendental' realism is concerned solely with the general conditions of possibility of a number of characteristic forms of scientific activity (experiment, scientific education, etc.), it is neither surprising nor worrying to discover that it is equally compatible with several different, even mutually incompatible, substantive attempts at explanation within a particular science. What might be more worrying is that it appears to be compatible with more than one of a number of conflicting philosophical reflections on those scientific traditions. In part, this difficulty derives from the reliance of the most influential realist account of the natural sciences on consideration of a narrow and inappropriate range of these sciences. The application of the resulting model of natural-scientific activity to the social sciences has been problematic in such a way as to reproduce some of the familiar characteristics of the positivist/dualist opposition.

The influential work in question is that by Roy Bhaskar. His first book, *A Realist Theory of Science* (RTS from now on), made an immense contribution in establishing and systematizing transcendental realism as a coherent and well-articulated alternative to the established traditions in the philosophy of science. These rival accounts of science, characterized as 'empirical realism' and 'transcendental idealism', were subjected to formidable critiques, but almost wholly in relation to their accounts of the natural sciences. In RTS the question of the possibility of naturalistic social and psychological sciences is posed, but not systematically dealt with. Roy Bhaskar's second book, *The Possibility of Naturalism* (hereafter PN), takes up this challenge, arguing for:

> a qualified anti-positivist naturalism, based on an essentially realist view of science. Such a naturalism holds that it is possible to give an account of science under which the proper and more-or-less specific methods of both the natural and social sciences can fall. But it does not deny that there are significant differences in these methods grounded in real differences in their subject matters and in the relationships in which their sciences stand to them.[2]

In these general terms, I am in broad sympathy with Roy Bhaskar's project, but on the nature of the differences which he identifies, and their significance, I shall take issue. In particular, the extent and significance of the natural science/social science asymmetries which

2. Roy Bhaskar, *The Possibility of Naturalism*, op.cit., p. 3.

Roy Bhaskar claims to identify would justify description of his position as a form of anti-naturalism, rather than as a 'qualified naturalism'. It would follow from this that his intended transcendence of the positivism/hermeneutics polarity is not entirely successful. The failure in this respect derives from the reproduction in Roy Bhaskar's work of the very dualist ontology of a natural/human opposition which is the basis of hermeneutic and neo-Kantian forms of anti-positivism. This ontology is, in turn, sustained by an unnecessarily restricted conception of the natural sciences. This excludes, or under-represents, the philosophical and methodological characteristics of a range of historical and life-sciences whose bearing on the social sciences, both philosophically and substantively, is direct and most pertinent to Roy Bhaskar's philosophical project.

2. The Argument of RTS

It will be remembered that RTS poses in relation to a number of characteristic natural scientific practices the transcendental question, 'what are the conditions of possibility (presuppositions) of these activities (or their rationality, or intelligibility)?' The practices investigated in this way include experimentation, the applications of scientific knowledge in 'open' systems, scientific perception, scientific education, and change and development in science. There are, unfortunately, some ambiguities in Roy Bhaskar's posing of these questions, however, which have implications for the status of the answers he gives. Some of these ambiguities, and possible sources of misunderstanding, are cleared up in Chapter 1 of PN, but some are persistent. Most significant are ambiguities surrounding the premises of the transcendental deductions.[3] Are we to take as a premise the *existence* of a scientific practice, such as experiment, or, rather, its intelligibility, or, yet again, its rationality (in the sense of 'rational justifiability')? It could well be argued, of course, that since experiment is a symbolically meaningful cognitive practice, it could hardly be said to exist unless it were intelligible. But there remains an important difference between accepting as a premise the intelligibility of scientific experiment and accepting it as rationally justifiable. It seems to me that the strong ontological conclusions of the transcendental deduction follow only from the latter version of the premise,

3. See, for example, RTS, pp. 30–36, where 'presuppositions' become 'conditions of possibility' on p. 36. We also see shifts from the 'intelligibility' to the 'rationality' and 'existence' of practices such as scientific perception, as if these were equivalent.

and not the former. In other words, it is legitimate to argue from the *intelligibility* of scientific experiment to the *presupposition* that the world has such-and-such characteristics (i.e. that scientists who conduct experiments are thereby *committed* to the existence of a world with these characteristics). But that the world *really does* possess those characteristics, follows only from the premise that experimentation is rationally justified. It is, however, my view that these difficulties of articulation can be resolved, and, in any case, they are not centrally involved in this paper's concern with the application of the transcendental realist model of science to the social sciences.

In RTS, then, transcendental arguments are adduced to demonstrate the general characteristics which must be possessed by the world if it is to be a possible object of scientific knowledge, and by society if knowledge, as a species of social practice, is to be sustained. These 'conditions of possibility' of science can be grouped as belonging to two 'dimensions': *'a transitive dimension,* in which the object is the material cause or antecedently established knowledge which is used to generate the new knowledge; and *an intransitive dimension,* in which the object is the real structure or mechanism which exists and acts quite independently of men and the conditions which allow men access to it.'[4]

In the intransitive dimension, transcendental deduction yields the conclusion that the world is both structured and differentiated: that is to say, that the world (unlike the world of *empirical* realist epistemology) has ontological depth. It is constituted by mechanisms whose tendencies and powers may or may not be exercised. When exercised, the powers of real mechanisms may not be 'realized', and even when realized, the resulting event-sequences may not be detected by 'man'. The world is differentiated in the sense that mechanisms may exist and operate either in closed systems, where 'constant-conjunction' event-sequences do occur, or in open systems where the outcomes of the operations of a multiplicity of mechanisms are such that constant conjunctions do not occur. Characteristically mechanisms in nature operate in open systems: usually, though not always, closure is artificial, the achievement of experimental practice. Laws are 'normic' statements concerning the tendencies or powers of things, which are manifested in the form of constant conjunctions under conditions of closure, but which must be supposed also to exist and be exercised in open systems, where no constant conjunction is manifest, because of co-determination of outcomes by other mechanisms.

4. RTS, p. 17.

In the transitive dimension, RTS concludes, society must be an 'ensemble of powers irreducible to, but present only in, the intentional actions of men'[5] who must, in turn, be causal agents, capable of intentionally acting on the world, monitoring this activity, and engaging in second-order monitoring of this. In the transitive dimension, the 'object' is antecedently established knowledge which is transformed to produce new knowledge.

Now, it follows directly from this that, since social and psychological mechanisms and structures clearly cannot exist and act 'quite independently of men', they are not possible intransitive objects of scientific knowledge. It may be that certain of their general characteristics may be derived by transcendental deductions of the conditions of possibility of *natural*-scientific practices, but here they figure as conditions, in the transitive dimension, of scientific knowledge of nature only, and as objects of *philosophical*, rather than scientific, knowledge.

Futhermore, since Roy Bhaskar's central arguments have been concerned with the implications of experimental activity, since experimental activity presupposes the possibility of closed systems, and since we are told that social and psychological mechanisms occur only in open systems, there follows a further epistemological obstacle to naturalistic social and psychological sciences: the absence of experimental practice.

Strictly speaking, then, Roy Bhaskar's position in RTS commits him to a radical dualism of the human and natural domains, which further commits him to an epistemological dualism with respect to the possibility of knowledge of these domains:

NATURAL	HUMAN
1. Person-independent mechanisms	1. Person-dependent mechanisms
2. Predictive science possible	2. Predictive science possible
3. Experimental practice sustained	3. No experimental practice
4. Intransitive objects of scientific knowledge	4. Transitive *condition* of scientific knowledge only

5. RTS, p. 20.

The outcome of the position adopted in RTS, then, seems to be a dualist anti-naturalism, so far as the human sciences are concerned.

But this is not a conclusion which Roy Bhaskar is readily prepared to accept. Though apparently ruled out by definitional fiat, the possibility of a naturalistic scientific knowledge of social and psychological mechanisms *is* discussed in RTS. Roy Bhaskar recognizes that so far his central argument has 'turned on the possibility of experimental activity',[6] so either some analogue of this in the human sciences must be found, or we must 'appreciate the great gulf that must separate them from the sciences of nature.'[7]

Throughout the discussion there appears to be an assumed correspondence of experimental sciences with natural sciences, on the one hand, and non-experimental with human, on the other, though this is neither explicitly stated nor defended.

Fortunately, there is an analogue of experimentation in the social sciences. It is that theories which become embodied in social practices may come to be seen by participant social actors themselves as incapable of non-ad-hoc explanation of significant phenomena (e.g., neo-classical economics and the 1930s depression). However, the characterization of this experiment-analogue in RTS is very brief and sketchy. It also seems to be rather unpromising for any proponent of a naturalistic approach in the social sciences. Society itself is to be understood as a colossal self-constructed and self-interpreted experiment. There seem to be no room for social science as a distinct cognitive practice, with distinctive methods and autonomous theory, as is the case with the natural sciences. The conception also is comparable in several respects to the Popperian notion of 'social engineering' as the social science analogue of experiment, and is susceptible to broadly similar objections.[8]

However, leaving aside the question of the adequacy of this proposed experiment-analogue, it is important to recognize that the very speculation which gives rise to it — that naturalistic social science might be possible — entails a revision in the definition of the transitive/intransitive boundary. If it is possible even to consider that there may be scientific knowledge of social and psychological mecha-

. RTS, p. 244.
. RTS, p. 245.
. See, for example, my *Philosophical Foundations*, op. cit., pp. 38ff.

nisms, then it follows that it must be possible to consider person-dependent mechanisms as potential intransitive objects of knowledge. Since this is ruled out by Roy Bhaskar's original definition of the intransitive dimension, then it follows that a revision of this definition is required if consistency is to be restored and the possibility of naturalism explored.

3. The Argument of PN and Some Criticisms

A necessary condition of Roy Bhaskar's project in PN, then, is some revision of the transitive/intransitive distinction, and consequent dispersal of the natural/human opposition. Without this, the impossibility of naturalism follows directly. The first revision of the distinction comes in Chapter 1, where the mark of intransitive objects of knowledge becomes that they 'exist and act independently of the knowledge of which they are the objects'.[9] This revision does allow for the possibility that social and psychological mechanisms, processes etc., at least under some characterizations of them, might be intransitive objects of knowledge. It does, however, seem to rule out the possibility in the case of one class of such mechanisms and processes: namely, those which *constitute* knowledge. This problem of the partial identity of subject and object of knowledge is, indeed, a general difficulty for the maintenance of the transitive/intransitive distinction in the human sciences, and Roy Bhaskar later[10] produces a further revision in the distinction to take account of it. We can distinguish between existential and causal independence: such social relationships are existentially independent of knowledge, but causally interdependent with it. For the social and human sciences, their intransitive objects are existentially but not causally independent of the processes by which they are known.

But of course, to remove one obstacle to the consideration of the possibility of naturalism is not the same thing as to establish its possibility. It is to Roy Bhaskar's attempt to argue this that I shall now turn, focusing on his argument as it affects specifically social, as distinct from psychological sciences. The main burden of the argument with which I shall be concerned is given in Chapter 2 of PN. Here, the argument is that there are fundamental differences between natural and social objects of knowledge, which constitute 'limits' to naturalism in the social sciences, but that these differences are them-

9. PN, p. 14.
10. PN, p. 60.

selves conditions of possibility of social-scientific knowledge, in the same *sense*, but not achieved in the same way, as natural-scientific knowledge.

It might seem that, in investigating the conditions of possibility of social-scientific knowledge, and the question of their satisfaction, the most obvious method for a transcendental realist would be to apply the procedures of RTS to this new domain. Social-scientific practices would be identified, and a transcendental deduction attempted of their conditions of possibility. But, as Roy Bhaskar rightly points out, what is at issue here is precisely whether there *are* any social-scientific practices, and, if so, *which* they are. The extension of the method of RTS would simply beg the question in favour of not just the possibility but the actuality of naturalism.

Now, the alternative method adopted in PN is not entirely clear. There are conflicting accounts of it, and the actual practice does not seem to be entirely consistent with any of them. My reconstruction of the argument is, therefore, rather tentative. It appears to have three main phases. First, the a priori deduction of certain general properties of societies (and persons). Second, a comparison of these with those general properties of natural objects by virtue of which they are possible objects of natural-scientific knowledge. This comparison yields a series of epistemologically significant ontological differences. Third, the attempted demonstration that scientific knowledge of social objects is possible, notwithstanding, or rather, because of, these differences.

I shall deal with each phase of the argument in turn. The first phase, the a priori demonstration of the relevant emergent properties of societies, is problematic in several respects. Sometimes the claim is that this demonstration consists in an analysis of the necessary conditions for any form of social life,[11] whereas elsewhere it is presented as a derivation from the analysis of a number of characteristic types of human activity ('saying', 'doing', 'making').[12] The principal argument, however, seems to be one which takes the existence of intentional activity as such as its premise.[13] On all three of these characterizations the argument is a transcendental one — what *must* be the case if 'a' (activity etc.) is possible. If we take Roy Bhaskar's argument that the pre-existence of social forms is necessary for intentional action, for example, this is clearly a transcendental argument.

11. PN, p. 18.
12. PN, p. 43.
13. PN, pp. 46, 65.

But there seems to be nothing, except, perhaps, its greater generality, to distinguish it from other uses of transcendental argument-forms in substantive social-scientific research.[14] Its status as a specifically *philosophical* argument is in doubt. Its content and plausibility rely on the acceptability of the 'transformational' model of human practice which is introduced along with it, and on a specific *characterization* of intentional action which is subject to controversy among the different sociological research traditions.

Now, the significance of this criticism is not simply that Roy Bhaskar fails to sustain a distinction between philosophical and substantive enquiry in the social sciences. I am not sure that I would wish to place too much weight on this distinction, in any case, though *ad hominem* the argument must have some force, since Roy himself devotes considerable space and ingenuity in the attempt to preserve the distinction.[15]

Rather, the significance of this criticism is that the procedure adopted in this first phase of the argument involves Roy Bhaskar, after all, in siding with certain substantive research traditions within the social sciences (specifically, Durkheimian, and Marxian, or, rather, some versions of these) against others, and not just in his conclusions, but in his very *premise*: the characterization of intentional action. In short, this procedure is question-begging just as much as would have been a direct application of the method of RTS. There are, indeed, systematic links between disputes over the proper characterization of intentional action and disputes over what is and what is not a properly 'scientific' approach to social-scientific investigation. Similar remarks could be made about Roy Bhaskar's use of Durkheim's conception of the 'coercive power' of society to demonstrate its *sui generis* reality.

The second phase of the argument — the comparison of the general properties of societies with those of the objects of the natural sciences, with a view to their epistemological significance — is no less problematic. Of course, strictly speaking, if the first phase of the argument fails, then so does the second, but I propose to treat the comparison of natural and social objects in abstraction from the methodological difficulties involved in independently establishing the epistemologically significant properties of social objects. This is partly because Roy Bhaskar's argument has a great deal of intrinsic interest, and partly because I am in broad sympathy with some of the

14. See PN, pp. 64ff.
15. See PN, pp. 64ff.

most important features of his characterization of social objects, despite my reservations both about his methods of demonstrating them and about his ways of representing those methods.

Having introduced a limited dispersal of the human/natural opposition (by means of the revision of the transitive/intransitive boundary) as a condition of even posing the question of the 'possibility of naturalism', Roy Bhaskar now proceeds to reconsolidate that opposition in the form of a series of ontological, epistemological and relational 'limits to naturalism'. The first ontological difference between natural and social structures, which constitutes a limit to the possibility of naturalism, is that social structures do not, whereas natural ones do, exist independently of 'the activity they govern'.[16] Now, this supposed dis-analogy is imprecisely expressed, and, moreover, does not appear to have been established in phase one of the argument. It is introduced, rather, as if self-evidently true. However, on the most obvious interpretation of 'activities they govern', it simply is not true that the existence of social structures depends on these activities. For example, the concept of a power-structure required in empirical sociological research must enable the investigator to identify power-relations where powers are not, in fact, exercised, though they continue to be possessed.[17] In such cases, the activities constituting the exercise of powers (= governed by the power-structure?) are not necessary to the existence of the power-structure (though other activities may well be). The full coercive power of the state, for example, may continue to be possessed without being exercised, though such activities as the raising of taxes, the recruiting, training and equipping of armed personnel may well be necessary to the maintenance of that structure of power-relations. This is entirely comparable with many natural mechanisms. An organism may, for example, never engage in reproductive activity, yet retain its reproductive system and powers. However, *some* activities of the organism (such as nutrition) would be necessary to the retention of these powers, but not the ones directly governed by the reproductive system itself.

Elsewhere, Roy Bhaskar offers, possibly as a general proposition including the above, the characterization of social structures as not existing independently of their effects: they (social structures) are present only in and through the activities of human agents.[18] It

16. PN, p. 48.
17. See, for example, Steven Lukes, *Power: A Radical View*, London 1976. My paper, 'Objective Interests and the Sociology of Power', *Sociology*, May 1982 presents this argument in greater depth.

follows from this, then, that in the social domain, all activities are activities of human agents. But, to sustain the *sui generis* character of social structures, it is necessary to distinguish between those activities of agents which are exercises of their own intrinsic powers, and those activities which are really exercises of powers which reside in social structures, but operate through the activities of human agents. Surely, though, if any person 'A' is the agent of an activity, 'a', then 'A' must be the possessor of the power of which 'a' is the exercise. If this is accepted, it follows that, at best, we can distinguish only between powers of agents possessed in virtue of their intrinsic natures, and powers of agents possessed in virtue of their relational properties. Roy's conception of social structures does not, after all, sustain them as autonomous possessors of causal powers, or, therefore, as *sui generis* realities. Roy Bhaskar is, it seems, committed to a variant form of individualism in social science.[19]

A second ontological limit to naturalism is that social structures do not, whereas natural structures do, exist independently of agents' conceptions of what they are doing. This thesis of the concept-dependence of social structures plays a large part in the argument of PN, as well as in other anti-naturalist works,[20] but is subject to varying interpretations which radically affect its epistemological significance. Is the thesis that, in general, social structures exist only if agents have *some* conception of what they are doing? Now, it seems hard to sustain the concept of an agent at all without the notion of conceptualization of activity, so that insofar as human agents are a necessary condition for the existence of social structures (and this is hardly disputable), then the thesis is sustained. But, as it stands, it seems to have little or no epistemological significance. Certainly it suggests that, once established, scientific conceptions may be in competition with agents' pre-existing conceptions of the same activities. A series of political consequences and problems flow from this, but no special epistemological ones, vis-à-vis the natural sciences, where similar disparities between science and 'common-sense' persist.

At the opposite extreme, the thesis of concept-dependence may be to the effect that the existence of social structures depends upon agents'

18. For example PN, p. 50.

19. I am now somewhat sceptical as to the power of this argument, but I retain it because it seems to me to have intrinsic interest. I suspect that to see where it goes wrong, assuming it does, would be illuminating.

20. Most well known of these is, perhaps, Peter Winch's *Idea of a Social Science*, London 1959.

having the particular conception they do have of what they are doing. Some relationships are, indeed, like this (e.g. friendship). If *each* party to the relationship changes his or her conception of what the relationship is, then the relationship *ipso facto* ceases to exist. But many, perhaps most, and certainly the most sociologically significant, social relationships are not like this at all. Where society surrounds and sustains a relationship with sanctions, including coercive powers, social relationships can be, and are, sustained across great diversity of, and through immense changes in, the actors' conceptions of what they are doing. (Employer/employee relationships, imperial domination, and marriage are three clear examples of such social structures.)

Alternatively, the thesis of concept-dependence may be taken as specifying a causal relationship between actors' conceptions and the character of social structures, such that changes in actors' conceptions of what they are doing are among the causes of structural change. Such changes may or may not be in line with the intentions of the actors whose conceptions change. Again, this thesis is not obviously wrong. On the other hand, it hardly counts as an a priori demonstrable truth about society as such. Questions as to the causal relationship between social structure of various types, and actors' conceptions of them are open questions, whose answers require empirical and theoretical research. There is no reason to suppose that any answer universalizable across all types of social structure will be forthcoming. Furthermore, on this version, too, there seem to be no serious epistemological difficulties for the possibility of a social science arising from the thesis of concept-dependence.

The third supposed ontological limitation on the possibility of naturalism is that 'social structures, unlike natural structures, may be only relatively enduring (so that the tendencies they ground may not be universal in the sense of space-time invariant)'.[21] It is, of course, true that social structures may be in fact instantiated for historically limited periods of time, and within geographically restricted areas, but this is quite consistent with their tendencies and powers being universal wherever the appropriate structures are instantiated. This *is* space-time invariance in the required sense — i.e. spatio-temporal locations are not in themselves causal factors. Oddly, Roy Bhaskar himself seems to recognize this when, later on, he says that social laws may be universal within their range, though restricted in their scope.[22] But precisely the same is true of the laws and structures of

21. PN, p. 49.
22. PN, p. 165.

the natural world. As Engels argued, the discovery of historicity in nature was a distinctively nineteenth-century achievement, culminating in Lyell's geology and Darwin's evolutionary biology.[23] Natural mechanisms, like social ones, are not eternal, but have definite conditions of existence which may or may not be present at any point in space or time. If we take into account Roy Bhaskar's later qualification of his position with respect to the space-time variance of social structure, then he is committed to a denial of historicity in nature. This would, indeed, constitute a limit to naturalism in the social sciences. Fortunately, we do not have to agree that natural mechanisms are not historical in character.

There is one respect, though, in which the historicity of the social presents dis-analogies with the historicity of natural mechanisms which might be held to have epistemological consequences. It is generally the case that the historical changes which require basic conceptual distinctions in their science (i.e. 'qualitative' changes, in some uses of this term), have a temporal periodicity which is very great in relation to the periodicity of conceptual change in science itself. In all cognitively relevant senses, then, it can be said that the world which is grasped through the categories of a science following a revolution in that science is *the same world* as was grasped, perhaps with less penetration, by the superseded categories of the science. No major new division of living organisms was, for example, emerging contemporaneously with the Darwin/Wallace production of the concept of natural selection and which itself rendered earlier theories obsolete. Now, scientific revolutions and cognitive advances generally are social processes. When they take social processes as their objects, too, their objects have a temporal periodicity of change which is of the same order as the periodicity of change in the knowledge-process itself. Now this certainly can give rise to methodological problems in the social sciences — particularly with respect to long-term historical prediction. But epistemologically speaking, the situation is quite comparable with the natural sciences. On the very much greater time-scale of biological, geological and cosmological change, the comparable long-term historical prediction is equally suspect. There would be a distinctive epistemological problem for the social sciences only if there were some mechanism which assured a necessary correspondence between cognitive and broader social change. Such a mechanism is, indeed, suggested in RTS and is a familiar feature of some historicist Marxisms. Such a necessary cor-

23. See my 'Natural Science and Cultural Struggle', op. cit.

respondence is, however, quite incompatible with a conception of science as a distinct and relatively autonomous cognitive social practice which Roy Bhaskar (most of the time) and myself, too, would wish to sustain.

Next, Roy Bhaskar presents, as an epistemological limit to naturalism, the argument, familiar from RTS, that social mechanisms exist only in open systems and that, therefore, controlled experiment, prediction and decisive tests of theory are impossible in the social sciences. In answer to this, it is first necessary to ask whether decisive tests of theory are possible in the natural sciences either. Even with an experimental closure of the classic kind, assumptions have to be made in practice about whether a closure has, in fact, been obtained (i.e. an assumption of the non-interference of undetected extrinsic influences on the instance of the mechanism under investigation). Theoretical assumptions also have to be made concerning the characterization of the mechanism and its activities, as well as the instrumentation employed. Of course, Roy Bhaskar is, in other contexts, well aware of this, but the sharp natural/social science contrast he draws can only be understood, I think, in terms of a residuum of the positivist conception of the experiment/prediction/testing relationship in his thinking.

Connectedly, it seems to be presupposed in Roy's argument that the constant conjunction of events associated with closure is necessary for prediction. Why should this be so? What is to rule out the calculation of the resultant effects of the joint operation of a plurality of mechanisms? Prediction is always, of course, prediction of something *under some description*. Where very complex systems of interacting mechanisms, operating under conditions and initial states which may be known only approximately, outcomes may only be predictable as falling within a certain range of possibilities. Of course, it might be argued that even assuming a wide sense of 'prediction', the outcomes of multi-mechanism ('open') systems are only predictable if it is possible first to isolate each constituent mechanism to examine its operation independently and its relations with others. This, of course, is a methodological problem of the social sciences but not an epistemological one. Durkheim, for example, in his classic work on suicide,[24] uses elementary statistical comparisons in an effort to demonstrate that a definite coefficient of preservation or aggravation is associated with each of several different religious ways of life. The purpose of the statistical comparison in each case is to rule out the

24. E. Durkheim, *Suicide*, London 1952.

possibility that a given outcome (in this case, suicide rate), or given contribution to such an outcome, really is the result of religious confession, rather than the operation of some other mechanism (minority status in a society, persecution etc). Of course, Durkheim's implementation is susceptible of criticism, but the principle is clear, and more sophisticated (though still, of course, problematic in various ways) statistical techniques have since been developed. In cases like this, the isolation of mechanisms is achieved theoretically and theory is corrected on the basis of statistical comparisons of differently constituted systems which nevertheless have one or more mechanisms in common.

Roy Bhaskar further seems to neglect a range of natural sciences in which experimental closure is not an available means of empirical control on theory. Historical natural sciences such as geology and evolutionary biology explain phenomena in terms of the interaction of pluralities of mechanisms in open systems. In each of these sciences techniques have been developed — many of them directly comparable to the uses of statistics in sociology — for including an element of empirical control in the production and correction of theory. The classic experimental closure is one technique (class of techniques) among many, which is available in some, but by no means all, natural sciences. Roy Bhaskar's critique of the empirical realist, 'constant conjunction', conception of causal laws is insufficiently radical in that it retains a certain paradigm of experimental closure and its role in the testing of theories in common with the 'constant-conjunction' account. Again, the result of this is an artificial and unnecessary natural/social contrast.

Finally, Roy Bhaskar thinks there is a 'relational' limit to naturalism. This derives from the familiar thesis of the partial identity of subject and object of social knowledge. Knowledge is itself a social practice, so that when it takes social practice as its object, maintenance of the distinction between transitive and intransitive objects of knowledge is problematic. As I have already indicated, though,[25] Roy Bhaskar distinguishes existential and causal independence of the intransitive objects of knowledge. In the social sciences, it is possible to sustain the existential independence of social structures, etc., whilst conceding that there is causal interaction between subject and object of knowledge. But the same is true, surely, of the natural sciences. Experiment, for example, as RTS well argues, presupposes causal interaction between natural systems and human agents. If

25. See p. 180 above.

these points are recognized, then continued commitment to a natural science/social science dualism on the basis of the 'partial identity' thesis must derive from some conception of the special or distinctive status of self-knowledge, such as would be sustained by a residual Cartesian conception of the subject. This is, for example, the metaphysical basis of Lukács's classic formulation of this natural/social science opposition.

The result of Roy Bhaskar's comparison of social and natural objects seems, then, to be a series of concessions to anti-naturalism, such that his position would be better described as a form of anti-naturalism, rather than as a naturalism, however qualified. Nevertheless, he remains committed to the possibility of a *scientific* social science, if not a naturalistic one. But the greatest obstacle to even this — the absence of prediction and experiment in the social sciences — remains to be removed. As in RTS, the search is for a social-science analogue of experimentation. This time, it is the epistemological significance of social crises which seems to offer promise of a solution. If it is supposed that during periods of social crisis, the underlying generative structures of society become visible to them, then one result of crisis will be a transformation of participant actors' conceptions of their activities. These new conceptualizations may now serve as raw materials in the production of new knowledge of the social form.[26]

There are, however, some serious difficulties which hinder such a process from providing even a partial analogue of scientific experiment. First, it appears to be a condition of production of new knowledge, rather than a means of empirical control or correction. Second, it seems to entail that social-scientific knowledge is possible only for societies characterized by periodic crises of the required sort (capitalist societies?), unless there are yet other experiment-analogues appropriate to other types of society. Third, Roy Bhaskar gives us no theoretical account of the visibility/invisibility of generative structures, and, surely, even if he could, this would beg the epistemological question. Finally, one universal feature of social crises which is difficult to reconcile with Roy Bhaskar's epistemological requirements is that they polarize populations ideologically and politically. If actors make sense of the newly visible generative structures in profoundly diverse and antagonistic ways, what sense is it still possible to make of metaphors of 'visibility', and how are we to solve the problem of *which* actors' conceptions are adequate raw

26. PN, pp. 61ff.

materials for scientific transformation?

It seems, then, that Roy Bhaskar, having minimally dispersed the natural/social opposition as a condition of posing the question of the possibility of naturalism, goes on to reconstitute that opposition. The resulting philosophy of the social sciences is anti-naturalistic, and seems incapable of sustaining the possibility of even a non-naturalistic social science. The ontological opposition of the natural and human domains continues to affect the epistemological argument throughout *The Possibility of Naturalism*, determining concessions to anti-naturalism which are quite unnecessary. The ontology of the natural/human opposition is itself sustained by the unduly restricted range of sciences (mainly, though not exclusively, physics and chemistry) and, therefore, of scientific practices, which are paradigmatic for the model of science constructed in RTS and presupposed in PN. This model of the natural sciences has in common with the logical empiricism which it so effectively refutes that it under-represents historicity and development as epistemologically significant characteristics of the objects of the natural sciences. Evolutionary biology, cosmology, geology, embryology are all natural sciences for which historicity and qualitative transformation pose epistemological and methodological problems in many respects directly comparable with those encountered in the sciences of human history, society and psychology.

It is also a characteristic of these historical natural sciences that the explanatory models they employ designate mechanisms which are not practically isolable in experimental closures. If the impossibility of closure is an epistemological obstacle to a scientific sociology, then it must also be so for this range of natural sciences. In fact, a great diversity of non-experimental means of empirical control and correction, as well as adaptations of experimental methods themselves, have been developed in these sciences. This is true just as much of the historical social as of the historical natural sciences. If we consider, for example, the range of empirical controls involved in the production and later correction of Darwin's evolutionary biology, it is easy to see that these by no means all fit the paradigm of the classic 'experiment'. An important raw material for Darwin, which both establishes the possibility of organic transformation, and sets definite limits to the range of possible mechanisms which might be supposed to bring it about, are rule-of-thumb generalizations derived from stock-breeders and gardeners. These are forms of reflection on non-experimental human interventions in nature, which rule out certain theoretical explanatory possibilities, and set definite target-requirements for theoretical reasoning.

Another important set of empirical controls was the range of theoretically informed observations of the geographical distribution of living forms, together with palaeontological evidence of their historical succession, and the geographical distribution of 'related' forms. Again these are evidences from a non-experimental source which tell against the idea of special creation, and for the notion of common descent by gradual transformation. As to the mechanism of natural selection itself, of course, no experimental demonstration of the formation of new species by its agency is available, but the subsequent development of such adjacent sciences as genetics and ecology has both sustained and modified Darwin's conception, whilst *elements* of the process are relatively isolable, and have been examined by means of adaptations of experimental technique. For example, numerous investigators have exposed different colour-varieties of insect larvae against various backgrounds in the vicinity of the nests of insectivorous birds to discover differential rates of predation on them. These 'experiments' can be combined with statistical 'thought-experiments' to determine the effects on the gene-pool of a population through successive generations of such differential predations.

Finally, on the 'human' side of Roy Bhaskar's natural/human opposition, there is an unwillingness to conceive of forms of historical causality as really distinct from individual human agency, *despite* the prominence of the argument for the *sui generis* reality of social structures. It is this remnant of what has been called 'the problematic of the subject' which further sustains the ontological and epistemological dualism of PN.

At the beginning of this paper, I quoted Roy Bhaskar as advocating an anti-positivist naturalism, according to which 'it is possible to give an account of science under which the proper and more-or-less specific methods of both the natural and social sciences can fall'.[27] It seems to me that the anti-naturalist conclusions of PN are part of a demonstration that RTS failed in this respect, and that the model of science produced in that work requires revision to take into account, in particular, epistemologically significant characteristics of historical, developmental and non-experimental natural *and* social sciences. This would involve a systematic attempt adequately to characterize and analyse the conditions of possibility of the non-

27. PN, p. 3.

experimental empirical controls which I have above sketched in relation to evolutionary biology and Durkheim's work on suicide. I remain convinced that the outcome of such investigations would be a confirmation of the broad outlines of Roy Bhaskar's realist model, if not of some of its more detailed articulation.

In case I should be misunderstood as advocating the kind of conception of a monolothic unified science which for so long characterized logical empiricist orthodoxy, it may be necessary to point out that my arguments against Roy Bhaskar's anti-naturalism are designed less to show that the social sciences are (or could be) more like the natural ones than he supposes, than to show that the natural sciences, or, at least, some of them, are more like the social than he supposes. More importantly, though, I remain committed, as he does, to the view that there are significant differences in the methods of the different sciences, which are grounded in real differences in the subject matters of those sciences and the relationships of those sciences to their subject-matters.[28] Where I differ from Roy Bhaskar and other anti-naturalists is that I think these differences to be almost always of a methodological rather than epistemological kind, and that I do not, whereas Roy Bhaskar does, align the whole range of methodological diversity along a single fault-plane, dividing the natural and the social. Methodologically, if not epistemologically, the sciences display a 'family resemblance', of cross-cutting and overlapping differences and similarities of method.

Reprinted from *RP* 27

28. PN. p. 3.

Truth and Practice

Andrew Collier

Peter Binns' paper 'The Marxist Theory of Truth' in *Radical Philosophy 4* exemplifies what seems to have become a new orthodoxy among Marxists, as well as many bourgeois philosophers, and social scientists: that truth is historically and socially relative, and that the decision between contesting theories (and the associated practices) must be made on grounds of practical utility.

My aim in this paper is to defend an objectivist view of truth and hence of Marxism as the science of social formations, and to show the practical importance of this view. As the view which I describe as objectivist is roughly that which Peter Binns (and also Kolakowski, in a paper I shall be considering) calls 'positivistic' Marxism, I shall start by pointing out that the latter term is misleading, and that many of the ideas attributed to objectivist Marxists on the basis of their alleged similarity to bourgeois positivists are not in fact held by them.

The objectivist position is: (a) that a thought is true if it corresponds to or adequately reflects reality, (b) that thought is a product of and dependent upon reality, but reality is independent of thought, and not at all its product (though a given reality may be the product of action which has involved thought); (c) insofar as it is scientific, theory is independent of its subject; one must ask not Whose theory is it? but Is it adequate to its object? (These points, I take it, are shared by structuralists and so-called 'positivist' Marxists; my own view differs from the structuralism of e.g. Louis Althusser in stressing the importance of a genetic account of knowledge in relation to its object.)

Bourgeois positivism is by no means exhaustively defined by these beliefs; of greater significance are its views: (1) that theoretical knowledge is a construction out of sensations, (2) that a reality is only understood scientifically when it is reduced to atomic components, related only mechanically and differing only quantitatively; (3) that practical or evaluative conclusions cannot be obtained from factual premises.

So far as I know, no Marxist (except perhaps the empirio-criticists) has held (1), and none has held (2). (3) was held by Hilferding, but not by the other objectivists — Engels, Plekhanov, Lenin etc. Goldmann, who is by no means an objectivist, shares this last positivist assumption, and criticizes the objectivists for their 'fallacy' in denying it.[1]

Hence the accusation that the objectivist Marxists must be purely contemplative and individualistic in their conception of science is simply false. They are in no way committed to methodological individualism or to theory without practical implications. As to the social and practical nature of scientific enquiry and experiment, this is common ground not only of all Marxist theories, but of intelligent bourgeois theories as well.

Of course it is certain that for Marxism there is a close relation of theory to social practice, and not merely to the practice of scientific enquiry — 'theoretical practice' — but to social production and the class struggle. A Marxist theory of knowledge must therefore articulate the relations of theory to practice in all their complexity; it will not suffice to notice that they are connected in various ways and with no more ado stew them up in the same pot until they are indiscriminable. The defect of the pragmatist/relativist account is that instead of effecting a fusion of theory and practice it effects a confusion of them.

Essential to Marxist materialism, as to any non-idealist philosophy, is the primacy of being over thought, the dependence of consciousness on material reality. This dependence is twofold: in the dependence of man's consciousness on his social existence, and in the character of thought as a more or less adequate reflection of reality.

The 'interventionist' concept of materialism proposed by Peter Binns radically rejects this relation of thought to reality: 'An idea is material not because it is about atoms and physicality, but because it becomes a material force in a really existent society . . . The materiality of an idea is thus its actual power to influence, change and control social behaviour absolutely irrespective of the content of that idea'.[2] This would make Berkeley, Kant and Hegel into materialists.

A conception of the relation of thought to reality which is more representative of pragmatist/relativist Marxism is that of Karl Korsch. Peter Binns, if I interpret him correctly, makes the distinction

---

1. See his paper 'Is There a Marxist Sociology?' *Radical Philosophy* 1.
2. Peter Binns, 'The Marxist Theory of Truth', p 7.

between thought and reality and recognizes a one-way relation of determination between them — ideas determine reality through practice. The origin and object of the ideas are left out of account, and they are judged by their results. Korsch on the other hand is already compelled to reject the correspondence theory of truth by his conception of the relation of consciousness and reality, which is essentially that they are inseparable (a view criticized by Lenin in *Materialism and Empirio-Criticism*). Korsch says: '. . . the coincidence of consciousness and reality characterizes every dialectic, including Marx's dialectical materialism'.[3]

If consciousness and reality already coincide it cannot be asked whether or not they correspond; moreover, a change of consciousness will be a change of reality. Knowledge and practice become indistinguishable.

This is a view often encountered in Marxist circles; it is defended as 'dialectical', while its opponents criticize it as insufficiently materialistic. But the truth is that it renders any dialectic impossible, by making the notion of contradictions 'in the very essence of objects' incomprehensible. Subject and object are merged in a 'night in which all cows are black', and all contradictions resolved by the bald assertion of the identity of opposites (cf. Lenin: 'The identity of social being with social consciousness is sheer nonsense and an absolutely reactionary theory'[4]).

The dualism of consciousness and reality, subject and object, as represented by classical bourgeois philosophy has of course to be overcome. But this should be done by asserting that every subject is also an object; there is no such thing as the subject in the Kantian/Sartrean sense of 'that which can never be an object'. This solution retains the possibilities of interaction between subject and object, including their conflict, and of 'false consciousness'; it asserts the independence of the object and hence the possibility of its recalcitrance. If the subject's cognition of the object could change the object, the *practical* resolution of contradictions would not be necessary.

Every subjectivization or relativization of truth removes content from the theories it treats of; it cuts away their objective reference. If Marxism thus loses its objective reference and becomes merely the systematic expression of the class consciousness of the proletariat, it is no more a science than is theology, which is the systematic expression

---

3. Karl Korsch, *Marxism and Philosophy*, NLB, London 1970, pp 77–78.
4. V.I. Lenin, *Materialism and Empirio-Criticism*, in *Collected Works* Vol. 14, p 313.

of the consciousness of a religious community.

We cannot understand a belief or a theory unless we understand it as laying claim to truth, and hence as having the possibilities of truth or falsehood. Every theory is also the expression of a certain consciousness, class and individual. We can tell something — not necessarily something admirable — about the societies which gave rise to Newtonian and Darwinian theories by examining their content. But our prime concern with these theories is with their truth (or falsity), and this is determined by reference to their objects. If we ignored the fact that a theory laid claim to truth we could not even assess it as an expression of the consciousness of its epoch.

The whole point about a theory, as opposed to a fantasy, is that it is about reality, hence its value depends on its truth, and can only be determined by comparing it with reality, not by examining it itself, or establishing its subjective or social origins, although this latter may be of importance both in assessing the prevalence of a belief as evidence for its truth, and in studying the individuals and societies holding the belief.

Every correspondence theory of truth has the essentially materialistic consequences that reality precedes and is independent of thought, that thought lays claim to reflect and correspond to reality, that the truth or falsity of a thought is determined by reference to the reality it claims to reflect, and that the meaning and identity of a thought are determined by the conditions which would make it true.

The only way in which reality is determined by thought is insofar as it is altered by action which is based on thought. This brings us to the crucial question for a Marxist theory of truth: the relation of objective knowledge to practice, as forms of the relation between thought and reality.

It is a commonplace that for Marxism objective knowledge is closely connected to practice, in that social practice is the source, the test and the aim of objective knowledge. It is an easy — though mistaken — step from this recognition to a pragmatist view of truth, which defines truth in terms of practical usefulness, and opens the possibility that some theory may be true for me but false for you, because useful to me and detrimental to you.

I shall discuss this in relation to Leszek Kolakowski's paper 'Karl Marx and the Classical Definition of Truth' as this seems to me to be an unusually lucid exposition of a version of the pragmatist/relativist view.[5] Kolakowski begins by distinguishing two practice-orientated

5. In Leszek Kolakowski, *Marxism and Beyond*, London

theories to truth, and goes on to propose a compromise and attribute it to Marx. The first theory (the one I wish to defend) he calls 'Marxism of a positivist orientation', the theory of Engels and Lenin. This 'invokes the *effectiveness* of human actions as a *criterion* with whose help it is possible and justifiable to *verify* the knowledge we need to undertake any sort of activity . . . treats truth as a relation between a judgement or a sentence and the reality to which it refers; at the same time this relation is independent of man's knowledge of it. Man's practical activity does not create it but merely ascertains its occurrence.'[6] The other theory is that of William James and the pragmatists generally, for which 'usefulness is seen not as a tool for establishing the truth of man's knowledge independent of him, but as what *creates* this truth.'

As an example, Kolakowski gives the sentence: 'Rational beings are alive elsewhere than on earth.' We do not know if this is true or false. But we know the meaning, i.e. we know what it would be for it to be true. The view of Engels and Lenin recognizes that as at any time human knowledge is incomplete, our best scientific theories are imperfect and will be improved upon, though we cannot of course use any other criteria of the truth of specific statements than those currently at our disposal. In stating that there is absolute truth this theory states only that the above sentence, for example, must be either true or false, that its truth or falsity does not depend on our consciousness, and that the question can only be resolved by an extension of our knowledge of objective reality by scientific practice.

The pragmatist view would no doubt be that at the present time it is neither true nor false that there are rational beings elsewhere than on earth. The extreme pragmatist might hold — and perhaps we can pin this one on William James's tail — that we can decide the question on grounds of usefulness: suppose belief in bug-eyed Martians would promote world peace, it might be considered useful and therefore true. This kind of pragmatism is, as Kolakowski admits, an idealist theory, making being dependent on consciousness.

Now we come to Kolakowski's 'Marxist' synthesis. Its Marxian credentials depend on placing a weight of theory on the epistemological passages in the *Economic and Philosophical Manuscripts* which they cannot take. I am of the opinion that there is much that is of profound interest in these manuscripts, but it is not in the scattered epistemological passages, which are badly thought out and contain some sheer howlers — for instance, the response to questions about

6. Ibid., p 59.

the origin of the world and man. On the other hand there is no doubt that Kolakowski is correct in placing both Engels and Lenin on the side of opposition to his own theory. See Engels: 'It was decided mercilessly to sacrifice every idealist crotchet which could not be brought into harmony with the facts on their own and not in a fantastic interconnection. And materialism means nothing more than this.' And Lenin: 'If truth is only an organizing form of human experience, then the teachings of, say, Catholicism are also true . . . (truth) exists independently of everybody.'[7]

Note that Engels and Lenin are rejecting precisely those moderate forms of the pragmatist/relativist position that claim to be materialist on the grounds that they do not deny the objectivity of facts but only of their interconnection, or that they take social and not individual practice as defining truth.

According to Kolakowski's theory, there is a natural substratum of 'reality' which is independent of us, and resistant to our activity. However this remains an unknowable 'thing in itself': 'Only "things for us" and not "things as they are in themselves", can have conceptual counterparts.' The objects of our knowledge are supposed to be constituted as the objects they are by human practical considerations. 'Marx rejects the antithesis between the world shaped into a human image and the world pre-existing 'in itself' that one seeks to grasp in a futile attempt to go beyond oneself as a man. Active contact with the resistance of nature creates knowing man and nature as his object at one and the same time.'[8]

Here again we see the merging of subject and object into a primal soup, rather than a theory which would allow self-critical cognition by making the subject the object of scientific enquiry, discovering what its objective needs and capacities are, and possibly revising the conclusions of previous cognition. For instance, Kolakowski's question:

> What justifies our belief that the visual world of a fly, made up of light and dark spots of neutral colours, is less 'authentic' or less 'true' than ours, except the fact that ours is better adapted to our needs?

seems to disregard the fact that we can study the fly's visual system and understand why it is what it is; and we can do the same for our

7. Lenin, op. cit., p 110.
8. Kolakowski, pp 74–75.

own visual system. Again, take this passage from Kolakowski: 'What is lasting in human nature is also the inviolable datum of all analysis and is the only state that can possibly be the absolute starting point. We cannot weigh the influence of this "absolute" on our vision of the world. We can examine only what can undergo change; otherwise we would have to be able to shed our own skin and observe ourselves from outside. This is possible for the individual thanks to the existence of other individuals, but it is not possible for the social subject as a whole.'[9]

This seems to forget that what is lasting in human nature is the object of human biology and related sciences; it is not an inviolable datum, i.e. a fact which determines the nature of our knowledge but is not itself a possible object of knowledge. All data can be violated.

Kolakowski's main anti-objectivist point is that there are many possible sets of concepts with which to describe reality, and what we know as reality is that set of concepts determined by our practical needs. 'No division, not even the most fantastic as compared with what we are accustomed to, is theoretically less justified or less "true" than the one we accept in actuality.' And further: 'the surrealist world seems more "strange" to us than the usual one only because we do not have names for its components and do not use it in technology.'[10]

This is an unfortunate example, for he is arguing that only language and practical needs make us accept our world rather than the surrealist one. Yet surrealist art is precisely the pictorial transcription of connections made by language and fantasy — connections themselves determined by unconscious needs — and it is refuted as a picture of reality by reference to the objective world *as contrasted with* language and fantasy. When a surrealist artist paints a picture of a woman's stomach as an oven door which opens revealing a bun cooking inside, this derives from a connection made by language — the colloquial expression 'a bun in the oven' for pregnancy — which is in turn no doubt determined by unconscious connections. One falsifies this as a picture of reality by 'social practice'.

I shall now quote a passage from Kolakowski on the relation of practical needs to cognition, and I hope to show why his theory does not follow from certain of his premises.

The assimilation of the external world, which is at first biological, subsequently social and therefore human, occurs as an organiza-

9. Ibid., p 71.
10. Ibid., p 69.

tion of the raw material of nature in an effort to satisfy needs; cognition, which is a factor in the assimilation, cannot evade this universal determinism. To ask how the world would be seen by an observer whose essence was pure thinking and whose consciousness was defined exclusively by a disinterested cognitive effort, is to ask a barren question, for all consciousness is actually born of practical needs, and the act of cognition itself is a tool designed to satisfy these needs.[11]

'Cognition cannot evade this universal determinism': that is to say, our beliefs, like all other phenomena, have their causes, and these are to be found in the interaction of human activity. But this does not itself say anything about the truth or falsity of these beliefs. True beliefs have their causes, and so do false ones. I may believe that the sun is shining because I see that it is, and a causal account can be given of that perception. Because I am paranoid, I may believe I am being pursued by the police; and I may just happen actually to be pursued by the police; this would be a true belief, but not knowledge. Lastly, I may believe that a woman still loves me, when she does not, because it would be too painful to admit the truth to myself.

The identity of a belief is determined by its object, by what is believed, not by its causal origin. The truth of a belief is determined by its relation to the relevant facts, i.e. the reality of its object. The status of a true belief as knowledge is something to do with the causal relations of the holding of the belief with the fact by virtue of which it is true.

Hence (1) the fact that all cognitive processes are governed by causal laws by no means obliterates the distinction between truth and falsity; (2) the fact that false beliefs are as much accounted for by practical needs as are true ones, and indeed more obviously and directly accounted for by them (for where our interest is not involved we have less motive for self-deception or repression), calls into question the determination of *truth* by these ends.

Yet it can perfectly well be accepted that the function of consciousness is to serve practical needs. This is quite compatible with objectivism. Take for example Freud's account in 'The Two Principles of Mental Functioning'.[12] According to this, mental processes are originally under the sway of the pleasure-principle. 'These processes strive towards gaining pleasure; from any operation which might arouse

11. Ibid., pp 64–65.
12. *Collected Papers* Vol. 4.

unpleasantness ("pain") mental activity draws back (repression).'
The pleasure-principle therefore at first takes the line of least resistance and hallucinates satisfaction of its wants.

> This attempt at satisfaction by means of hallucination was aban-
> doned only in consequence of the absence of the expected gratifi-
> cation, because of the disappointment experienced. Instead the
> mental apparatus had to decide to form a conception of the real
> circumstances in the outer world and exert itself to alter them. A
> new principle of mental functioning was thus introduced; what
> was conceived of was no longer that which was pleasant, but that
> which was real, even if it should be unpleasant. This institution of
> the *reality-principle* proved a momentous step.

> In place of repression, which excluded from cathexis as productive
> of 'pain' some of the emerging ideas, there developed an impartial
> *passing of judgement*, which had to decide whether a particular idea
> was true or false, that is, was in agreement with reality or not . . .

> A new function was now imported to motor discharge . . . it was
> now employed in the appropriate alteration of reality. It was
> converted into action.

Freud here asserts the primacy of the pleasure-principle — i.e. of
human needs — explaining all knowledge of the world in terms of it.
Yet precisely to serve those needs, consciousness of the world must
cease to be determined by them. Only on the basis of this consciousness is their real satisfaction by practice possible. (Cf. Lenin: 'If the
sensations of time and space can give man a biologically purposive
orientation, this can only be so on condition that these sensations
reflect an objective reality outside man'.[13] What Lenin says here of
time and space applies *a fortiori* to other aspects of reality.)
    Practice itself both requires a knowledge the content of which is not
determined by practical considerations, and provides access to such
knowledge. One knows the world, not in pure contemplation, but in
acting upon it; that is true. But it is the opposite of pragmatism. It is
not that what reality is, is a construction made by us for practical
considerations; it is that the practice of transforming reality shows the
resistance of that reality to our ends, and forces us to acknowledge it
as an *independent* reality, which cannot be moulded by our conscious-

13. Lenin, p 166.

ness, but only by strenuous practical effort guided by painstakingly objective knowledge.

Not that the pragmatist wants to substitute fantasy for practice — far from it. The needs which according to his theory determine what is reality are practical needs, not the primary processes of which Freud is speaking. But at this more developed level of interaction of man and the world, the pragmatist's subjectivization of the concept of reality serves the same function of robbing the transformation of the world, including here the current modes of social practice, of its urgency.

Let me summarize my case against Kolakowski: he claims that we cannot know whether our concepts of reality are true of 'reality in itself', because:

(a) we have no reason to suppose that the categories imposed on reality by our needs have any basis in reality considered aside from our needs;

(b) we cannot 'jump out of our skin' to the extent that we could see how the needs which we actually have would affect our conception of reality;

(c) as all our beliefs are causally determined by a process in which our needs are determinants, we cannot judge their truth or falsity in abstraction from their function in relation to our needs.

I am claiming that (a), (b) and (c) are all false. (c), because precisely in order to serve our needs, cognition must attain a certain independence of them; (b), because we can study human needs objectively, and revise our account of 'external' reality insofar as it was in the first place distorted by their influence; and (a), because if reality were not *in itself* cognitively digestible, there could no more have evolved rational beings than living beings could have evolved in the absence of alimentarily digestible reality. It is not a coincidence that we need to divide the world into objects, classify objects into kinds, and isolate causal laws governing their behaviour; and that there really are discrete objects, natural kinds, causal laws. It is no more puzzling than that cats have slits in their skin at just those points where their eyes are.

The controversy about truth, between the objectivist and the pragmatic/relativist views, seems in relation to Marxism to be a meta-theoretical controversy, a debate about the status of Marxist theory which would leave the content of that theory untouched. Yet it should be obvious that neither side believes that the dispute is without implication for Marxist theory and practice. I shall try to show its relevance for two issues: (1) the relation of facts to values, and (2) the relation of freedom to necessity.

(1) Facts and Values

Like the 'neutral science' conception of Marxism held by Hilferding, pragmatist Marxism inherits the worn-out dogma of bourgeois philosophy and social science that one cannot reach conclusions in the imperative from premises in the indicative. Whereas this dogma leads Hilferding to divide Marxism into two distinct parts, a neutral science and an ethics, it leads the pragmatist to insist that Marxist science has premises in the imperative. Clearly this has the same tendency to deprive the imperatives of their ground in science. The question then arises: If you can't get practical conclusions from facts, where on earth can you get them from? And if we examine the roots of this dogma in bourgeois thought we can only conclude, Nowhere *on earth*. It derives from Kant's attempt to render morality independent of anything in man's empirical being, and ground it in a transcendent 'Reason'; it can be found in Kierkegaard's insistence that morality has 'no finite teleology' (or in plain English, no earthly use), and in Liberal Protestant theology's claim to base its speculative dogmas on its moral imperatives, justifying this in terms of the 'primacy of practical reason'.

It seems to me perfectly obvious that from certain kinds of facts — facts about human needs and wants and the practice necessary for their satisfaction, facts about the irrationalities and contradictions in existing modes of social practice — practical conclusions follow. Goldmann (in his paper referred to), which criticizing the objectivists, appears to admit that they can base a 'social technology' which equals socialist politics on their objective science of Marxism. But what more is required? One can only assume that this practice of 'social technology' is rejected because *it is not a moral practice*. But what place can a moral practice have in Marxism? Vorlander — himself a fact/value dichotomist — mentioned that he had been told by someone who knew Marx personally that Marx burst out laughing every time anyone spoke to him of morality (quoted by Goldmann, op. cit.). Are we to take that as merely a personal quirk of Marx's? Is it not rather to do with something about the form of every moral theory, properly so called?

The formal characteristic of every moral theory is that it issues imperatives which every individual is responsible to carry out (in appropriate circumstances), and may be blamed for not doing so. This can be summarized in three words — universal individual responsibility. (The theories of ethics of Aristotle, Spinoza and Nietzsche do not fit this model; but then they are in an important sense not moral theories; which is why they are of such value in developing a socialist theory of practical reason.)

Now the content of a morality may be rational — i.e. it may aim at the maximum happiness or satisfaction of human needs; or it may be irrational — i.e. it may enjoin the pursuit of aims not grounded in these, and potentially antagonistic to them. The history of moral philosophy has largely been the history of the dispute between these two types of morality. The latter type (e.g. Kant, Fichte, Kierkegaard) claim that morality has nothing to do with happiness or the satisfaction of human needs. I shall not dispute this, as though there were already some agreed content to morality, of which we could determine the relation to happiness. I shall simply say that if it is so, then morality is just another obstacle to happiness which we must seek to abolish, along with disease, ignorance, poverty, chastity and obedience.[14]

This sort of morality can be traced, as Marx did in the 1844 Manuscripts, to the need of capitalist society at a certain stage of its development to inculcate the virtues of thrift, hard work and sobriety in all classes.

The naturalistic morality which escapes this criticism (e.g. Utilitarianism, though this has the additional defect of conceiving happiness on the model of commodity-exchange) may be characterized as rational in content. But to the extent that it is so, the rational content comes into contradiction with the moral form — i.e. the fact that it addresses itself to universal individual responsibility. The contradiction consists in the fact that its rational ends cannot be achieved by moral means, for the following reasons.

(1) Individual practice can only to a very limited extent secure these ends. Individual practice should therefore be directed towards the collective effort to secure these ends. This collective practice is, from the collective point of view, self-interested and hence amoral; and under conditions of class struggle it may be highly immoral from the individual point of view. (Cf. Engels: 'It is precisely the wicked passions of man — greed and lust for power — which, since the emergence of class antagonisms, serve as levers of historical development.' Presumably the proletarian revolution is not exempt from this motivation.)

(2) The attempt to carry out a moral practice, on the part of the

14. Cf. Nietzsche: 'Insofar as morality condemns as morality, and not with regard to the aims and objects of life, it is a specific error with which we should show no sympathy.' *Twilight of the Idols*, Harmondsworth 1967, p. 46.

individual (even of all individuals), is actually antagonistic to the rational ends. Its tendency is to lead the individual to pursue that change which can be pursued in isolation — the change of himself, i.e. his adaptation to existing conditions, which is beneficial neither from the standpoint of his own possibilities of happiness nor from that of the rational collective practice (the struggle for socialism).

(3) While class rule remains with us, the universalism of morality has no basis in reality and can only be a mystification.

There may indeed be 'moral virtues' which have a provisional rationality within an irrational society — prudential virtues as long as there is material insecurity, qualities which are of value in the class struggle, even 'disinterested altruism', but it is best not to make virtues out of these necessities (cf. Oscar Wilde: 'The great advantage of socialism is that it relieves one of the sordid necessity of living for others' — *The Soul of Man under Socialism*). Marxists should recognize — as did the great Soviet philosopher of law, Pashukanis — that morality is destined to wither away, along with the state and law. The sort of 'virtues' which one might hope would flourish in a socialist society — sincerity and generosity in personal relations, devotion to the pursuit of truth, creativity, as well as mere abstention from anti-social acts — cannot be made the object of effective moral imperatives anyway; they can only be the product of a satisfying existence. (Cf. Nietzsche: 'A well-constituted human being, a "happy one", *must* perform certain actions and instinctively shrinks from other actions . . . In a formula: his virtue is the *consequence* of his happiness.'[15])

Though I believe there is generally a moralistic conception of Marxism in the background of attempts to make commitment prior to science and therefore arbitrary, it is often defended without explicit reference to morality, on grounds of class-relativism. The point of Marxism, it is said, is to serve working-class interests, that of bourgeois science to serve those of the bourgeoisie. This last statement of course is true, but it does not settle the question of the truth of these theories, which is a separate question from their social origin. Arguments have been put forward by Marxists as to why it is no accident that the proletarian theory should also be the true one (e.g. by Bukharin in *Historical Materialism*, by Goldmann in *The Human*

15. Nietzsche, p 48.

Sciences and Philosophy.) These arguments are a necessary part of Marxism as a self-critical theory. An extreme class-relativist would have no place for such arguments, as he is wholly concerned with the class nature and not at all with the truth of Marxism. (There is also a moderate class-relativism which concerns only the determination by class interest of the selection of certain facts as important. This is Goldmann's view in *The Human Sciences and Philosophy*, and that of E. H. Carr in *What is History?* It is quite acceptable with these qualifications: (a) the criteria for selecting certain facts as important can also be objectively valid or invalid; (b) Marxism can accommodate any fact unearthed by bourgeois social 'sciences', whereas the latter are unable to accommodate many Marxian discoveries, notably the existence of objective, internal, antagonistic contradictions in bourgeois society.)

One might ask the class-relativist: Why should certain individuals from other classes get involved in the workers' struggle? If there is to be a rational ground, and morality is ruled out, it must be conviction of the truth of the Marxist analysis. However a more important problem of the class-relativist position is that it assumes an already clearsightedly revolutionary proletariat; yet why should the proletariat be revolutionary? If bourgeois theories were correct, it would be rational for the workers to collaborate with the bourgeoisie to increase the GNP. The Marxist analysis of classes makes it clear why socialist revolution is really in the workers' interest; this is the case only given that it is true. Of course there are also good reasons why the workers should be receptive to Marxist theory, especially in times of capitalist crisis; they do not have the barriers that the bourgeoisie do to the understanding of the contradictions of capitalism, because they bear the marks of those contradictions in their own flesh.

But rational as it may be for the workers to be revolutionary, it is nevertheless the case that the majority are not. If Marxism is to serve the objective interests of the workers, it must come into conflict with their current beliefs about their interests. The workers like any other class are subject to false consciousness, and there have been theories which have been systematic expressions of proletarian consciousness, and yet highly reactionary. (Cf. Nietzsche's account of Master and Slave morality in *The Genealogy of Morals*.) One can easily see how the consciousness of an oppressed class could make it receptive to ideologies of renunciation in this life and punishment of the worldly and successful in the next.

Religion in its ascetic, other-wordly and vindictive aspects can be just as much an expression of the consciousness of an oppressed class as can a revolutionary theory. Of course it is not in the *interest* of the oppressed class to adhere to the former, but an objective analysis is necessary to show this.

Moreover, recent history has shown that the proletariat can often adopt fascist and sectarian politics which are even more regressive than those of the bourgeoisie. It is no use for the class-relativist to appeal to the concept of potential as against actual class consciousness, for Marxist theory is already needed in order to give an objective content to that concept; potential consciousness is by definition not a given which Marxism could 'express'.

There is not, as is so often assumed, anything elitist about the view that I am putting forward. The accusation that there is, is constantly reiterated; but it itself is based on the elitist belief that the 'intelligentsia' has the monopoly of science and the proletariat the monopoly of ideology. The issue is not intellectuals versus proletarians but science versus ideology. Prescientific consciousness is essentially ideological and if a workers' movement bases itself on this consciousness and not on Marxist science, it will be nothing but an instrument of mystification. Any attempt to make science relative to its class subject must inevitably lead to this. It involves a mistaken view of the relation of science to ideology in that science becomes expressive rather than destructive of ideology. But ideology is error: 'Establishment of Truth depends on destruction of Falsehood continually, On Circumcision, not on Virginity, O Reasoners of Albion!'[16]

Finally, one can see in practice how failure to recognize the objectivity of theory has led to its subordination to short-term practical and propaganda needs in the life of the workers' movement; the resultant errors have been far-reaching. Examples: (i) the concept of 'strict party discipline', so necessary to the period of revolution and civil war, which became so fetishized that it prevented Stalin's opponents within the party from appealing to the class over the heads of the party leadership until it was too late to do so; (ii) the rejection of Freudian theory by certain elements on the left as allegedly politically inconvenient, with their subsequent lapse into idealist psychology of consciousness on the one hand and Pavlovian crudities on the other.

(2) Freedom and Necessity

The cluster of views (pragmatist, relativist, subjectivist, interven-

16. William Blake, 'Jerusalem', *Complete Works*, p. 687.

tionist) which I have been criticizing also seems to involve a regression to a pre-Marxist conception of the relation of freedom to necessity, both in the sense of the relation of conscious human activity to the causal laws governing the historical process, and of the relation of the 'realm of freedom' to the 'realm of necessity'.

Already in the writings of Plekhanov — whose Marxism is infinitely more subtle and applicable to complex historical realities than that of most who dismiss him as a 'vulgar Marxist' — there is a definitive reply to those who see a paradox in the fact that Marxism stresses human activity and the role of theory, and also sees the historical process as governed by causal laws (see his *Fundamental Problems of Marxism* and *The Role of the Individual in History*.) It is simply a vulgar mistake to suppose that a Marxist will be any less of an activist for the knowledge that his revolutionary activity and the theory which guides it are themselves products of the historical process. The conception of freedom as the knowledge and use of causal laws, including reflective knowledge of the laws governing one's own knowledge and activity, is in no way paradoxical unless one already presupposes subject-object dualism; and it is integral to Marxism (though not unique to it; it is shared by the theories of Spinoza and Freud). Yet it continues to be a stumbling block to many would-be Marxists, and even to Marxist theoreticians. This can only be put down to a mystique of the subject in the prevalent ideology, a mystique which manifests itself in Peter Binns' paper: 'If knowledge of man is restricted to him *qua* known object rather than knowing object, then to the extent that we can obtain such truths about him, he is that much less able to subject himself to conscious self-modification.'[17]

But insofar as man is known, he is by definition known as 'known object'; this in no way precludes the identity of that known object with a knowing and acting subject. One is reminded of Marx's jibe against the Young Hegelians: 'Consciousness or self-consciousness is regarded as the only human quality. Love, for instance, is rejected, because the loved one is only an "object". Down with the object!'[18]

In connection with this subject-object dualism the term 'interventionism' is itself suspect. Intervention by whom into what? The human subject into objective causal processes? It is already part of them. The individual into history? He is already part of it. The party into the struggles of the class? Need I say more?

This picture of someone originally outside of the historical process

17. Binns, p. 9.
18. Letter to Feuerbach, 11 August 1844, in *Marx-Engels Collected Works* vol. 3, London 1975, p. 356.

stepping into it in order to know and act on it may have a superficial biographical justification in the case of us petty-bourgeois intellectuals. But the more correct picture is of someone who is already part and parcel of the historical process, whose whole being and consciousness is a product of that process, stepping back in order to obtain objective knowledge of that process, including his own being and consciousness, in order to demystify himself and act more effectively within that process. (Of course this stepping back is also part of the historical process.)

The dualist mystique of the subject is more consistently used in the attacks on Marxism of the non-Marxist left. I shall criticize this in relation to the following passage from Paul Cardan:

> What appears to us as questionable in *Capital* is its methodology. Marx's theory of wages and its corollary, the theory of the increasing rate of exploitation, begin from a postulate: that the worker is completely 'reified' (reduced to an object) by capitalism. Marx's theory of crises starts from a basically analogous postulate: that men and classes (in this case the capitalist class) can do nothing about the functioning of the economy.

> Both these postulates are false. But both have a deeper significance. Both are necessary for political economy to become a 'science' governed by 'laws' similar to those of genetics or astronomy. But for this to be achieved, the things to be studied must be objects. It is as objects that both workers and capitalists appear in the pages of *Capital*. If political economy is to study the mechanism of society, it must deal with phenomena ruled by objective laws, i.e. laws not constantly modified by the actions of men and classes. (*Modern Capitalism and Revolution*, p.33.)

Leaving aside verbal matters such as the misuse of the term 'reification' (which should be reserved for the appearance of social relations and human activities as objects, not of people as objects, which is a philistine cliché), it can be observed that Cardan is conflating two possible criticisms here: (1) that Marx, in formulating the laws governing the *economy* under capitalism, has abstracted from the politics of capitalist society, i.e. the class struggle. Insofar as this is true, however, it is a necessary abstraction, as one must know how classes are constituted by capitalist production before one can understand their struggle. Because political action is a relatively conscious activity as compared with economic activity, this is confused with (2) the methodological criticism that human activities, including purely economic ones, cannot be studied scientifically. In order to be objects of science, Cardan is claiming, men must be 'reduced' to objects. If 'object' here simply *means* object of science, object as opposed to subject, it is unclear where the 'reduction' comes in. More likely, what is meant is 'ruled by objective laws'. But unless human activities are to be separated off from the whole of material reality, in an idealist or dualist fashion, it must be admitted that they are ruled by objective laws; that fact does not make them passive, as Cardan seems to think. Some of these laws cannot be modified by the actions of men, but they *govern* the actions of men, they do not *preclude* them. Some of the laws governing the actions of men are also subject to change by those actions. But these changes themselves are governed by objective laws.

The metaphysical assumption behind Cardan's theory seems to be that men as subjects cannot also be objects; that as subjects they are active and this activity is not according to objective laws; from this he infers that treating men as objects is somehow 'reducing' and morally repugnant; that it is nevertheless a necessary condition of studying them scientifically, which is therefore also objectionable; that the motivation of such study must be the desire to make men the passive objects of bureaucratic manipulation, and hence that objective science is out of place in the workers' movement.

This subject-object dichotomy is probably derived from Sartre's earlier thought. Sartre did not work out his theory in relation to economics, but he did in relation to psychology. According to Sartre, subjectivity, human consciousness, can never be made the object of knowledge or activity; subjectness and objectness are seen as mutually exclusive. This leads to the granting of only a very precarious existence to the science of psychology. The objective laws governing the psyche, indeed its objective being, are said to be a product of the belief in those laws and that being, a belief which is in 'bad faith'. Hence the object of psychology is seen as having fictional existence only: laws only govern human behaviour because men, on the basis of a form of false consciousness, act as if there were laws governing human behaviour. Cardan has simply extended this theory from psychology to economics. It is easy to see the idealist implications of all this; the practical message of idealism has always been 'Don't bother changing the world, the source of your problems is in your own mind; change your attitude and all those nasty psychological and economic laws will go away.' The trouble with this idea of freedom is that it not only leaves everything unchanged, it incapacitates one for changing anything; for the freedom that can change things involves knowing and operating with causal laws.

No doubt Sartre and Cardan want to fill the vacuum created by the dethronement of science with a theory which will be an expression of the consciousness of the subject; but we have already seen what is wrong with this: it takes what is a product and symptom of the social reality of a given social formation, as a true reflection of that social reality. Hence it confirms everyday consciousness in the mystifications from which science could have liberated it. Yet the proletariat needs a theory, not to satisfy a desire for a systematic expression of its consciousness, but to understand and act upon social reality.

In this view of Sartre and Cardan we have an admittedly non-Marxist philosophy claiming that consciousness is independent of causal laws, and its description independent of science. It is clear how an adherent of this philosophy could deny the possibility of unbreakable laws in social science.

But it is worth pointing out that Marxism, in rejecting the autonomy of consciousness, rejects also the only possible basis for the doctrine that there are no immutable laws in social science. See for instance Marx's letter to Kugelmann about the concept of value in *Capital*: 'That this necessity of the distribution of social labour in definite proportions cannot possibly be done away with by a particular form of social production but can only change the mode of its appearance is self-evident. No natural laws can be done away with.'[19]

This brings me to my final point — the relation between the realm of necessity and the realm of freedom. In *Capital* (vol. III, pp. 799–800), Marx tells us: '. . . the realm of freedom actually begins where labour which is determined by necessity and mundane considerations ceases . . . With man's development this realm of physical necessity expands as a result of his wants; but, at the same time, the forces of production which satisfy these wants also increase . . . Beyond (the realm of necessity) begins that development of human energy which is an end in itself, the true realm of freedom, which, however, can blossom forth only with this realm of necessity as its basis. The shortening of the working day is its basic prerequisite.'

Marx, while recognizing a degree of flexibility and development in the concept of a need, clearly did not see the expansion of human needs as limitless, otherwise the conquest of the realm of necessity could never take place. If human needs are capable of indefinite expansion, and are thus totally socially relative, the absolute abundance which is the necessary condition of communism (i.e. of the realization of the principle: 'from each according to his ability, to each according to his needs'), and of the withering away of the state, is in principle unrealizable; scarcity and conflict about the distribution of material wealth must then be permanent features of human life. Precisely the attempt to treat everything as mutable leads to the conclusion that these features of all hitherto existing (primitive or class-divided) societies, are ineliminable.

Yet the constant concomitant of the pragmatist/relativist view of Marxism, with its Faustian conception of the autonomy of the subject and the omnipotence of practice, is that man is characterized by unlimited self-malleability as a species, and that the needs of the individual are totally socially relative.

This view of man, though it would render impossible communism and the disappearance of the state, would I admit by no means remove workers' power and the expropriation of the bourgeoisie from the agenda (though no doubt it would remove some of the subjective motivation for them). But the same can be said of ethology, yet socialists have generally felt obliged to marshal the arguments against this ideology (and rightly so; though it goes without saying that the case against ethology should be argued on the strictly scientific level, not that of utopian moralism).

Unfortunately the slogan — literally meaningless outside the context of idealism — that 'there is no such thing as human nature' has been repeated so often that it has acquired the force of a truism in Marxist circles, absolving Marxists from scientific investigation of just what needs, dispositions, laws and structures are invariant elements of human social existence, and under what conditions specific modifications of human motivation, consciousness and behaviour will occur.

The ideological possibilities of this doctrine of the limitless malleability of man should be obvious: (i) liberal utilitarianism, of the most inegalitarian variety. This is after all where the doctrine originated. Here it is used to defend the rejection of any concept of priorities of certain social needs over others; wants arising out of fancy or emulation are equated with those arising from the stomach (a conclusion sometimes erroneously drawn from the first page of *Capital*).[20] (ii) The apologetics of bureaucratic manipulation. If man is infinitely malleable, the road is open for bureaucratic politicans and educationalists to force people into whatever mould they consider desirable.

20. For a criticism of the use of this view by modern apologists of capitalism, see MacPherson's paper 'Post-liberal Democracy?' in Robin Blackburn, ed., *Ideology in Social Science*, London 1972.

Where this manipulation has socialist pretensions, it is often expressed as a reliance on moral conditioning rather than material conditions as the cement of socialist society (e.g. Che Guevara's essay on man and socialism in Cuba). But this amounts to the complete abandonment of Marxism.

Reprinted from *RP* 5

3. Morality and Politics

Mental Illness as a Moral Concept
The Relevance of Freud

Sean Sayers

The concept of mental illness has been the subject of heated controversy in recent years; and this debate has caught the attention of a wide public. The reason for this is not simply that the debate has sometimes been conducted in heated terms; but, more importantly, because it has raised central moral and social issues which are of fundamental concern. And it is in this respect — as an aspect of contemporary moral and social thought — that I wish to look at this controversy in this paper.

Even this intention requires some justification, however, since moral philosophers have tended to ignore it or simply to parrot what psychiatrists have to say about it; while most psychiatrists would dispute that their ideas on mental illness have any *moral* significance. Thus it is common for psychiatrists to regard their work as a kind of technology, which is seen as a means for producing a certain objectively definable result (mental health). And it is often argued that just because the goal of therapy is 'objectively definable', the only relevant criterion of the success of therapy is its *efficiency* in achieving this 'objectively-defined' goal, and therefore that moral considerations do not play any part. According to this view, then, which I shall call the 'psychiatric account', a judgement of illness is not a value-judgement, but an objective and factual one; and psychiatric theory is a scientific theory which neither raises nor answers any moral questions.

Broadly speaking, two sorts of criteria have been suggested in the attempt to define such an 'objective' concept of mental illness: statistical and clinical.[1]

According to the statistical approach, mental illness is to be defined in relation to statistical norms. The main advantage claimed for this

1. These terms are taken from F. Redlich and D. Freedman, *The Theory and Practice of Psychiatry*, New York 1966.

sort of definition is that it involves precise, empirical criteria. Thus Jaspers writes:

> The only thing in common (to the various states thought of as 'illness') is that a value-judgement is expressed. In some sense, but not always the same sense, 'sick' implies something harmful, unwanted and of an inferior character. If we want to get away from value-concepts and value-judgements of this sort, we have to look for an empirical concept of what sickness is. The *concept of the average* affords us such a concept . . . The concept of the average is an empirical concept of what concretely is.[2]

So Jaspers proposes to define illness as deviation from the average and imagines that by so doing he has produced a non-evaluative concept of illness. He is assuming that any concept with objectively specifiable criteria is a non-evaluative one, but this is a crass error about the nature of value-judgements which even our contemporary moral philosophers have avoided.[3] Just because precise and objective criteria can be specified for being Jewish, it does not follow that anti-Semitism involves no value-judgements.

Health and illness are *practical* concepts, and the need for them arises in the practical context of therapy. A purely theoretical science does not require them, but in the practical, medical sciences they are necessary to specify the goal and object of therapy. And so long as health continues to specify the goals of therapy, and illness continues to specify what is to be eradicated through therapy, these concepts will be evaluative ones, regardless of whether the goals are precisely defined in empirical terms. These remarks apply to the concepts of health and illness in general. In the specific case of mental health and illness, the value-judgements concern a person's actions and rationality and his relationship with others. There are good grounds, therefore, for regarding mental illness as a moral concept.[4] In the light of this, the statistical approach is clearly unsatisfactory: it seems to put an arbitrary value upon 'the average' and to claim a mysterious objectivity for itself in doing so.

The virtue of objectivity is also claimed for the clinical approach, which involves the altogether more sophisticated assumption that illness is *improper* or *abnormal* functioning. This view is best explained in terms of a frequently used analogy between curing an illness and

2. K. Jaspers, *General Psychopathology*, Manchester, pp. 780–81.
3. Cf. R. Hare, *Freedom and Reason*, Oxford 1963; P. Foot, 'Moral Beliefs', *Proceedings of the Aristotelian Society*, Vol. 59, 1958–59, for a discussion of words like 'rude' and 'nigger'.
4. See also J. Margolis, *Psychotherapy and Morality*, New York 1966, esp. chapter one.

repairing a machine. The doctor (either in general medicine or in psychiatry) is like a mechanic repairing a car. Just as the mechanic restores the car to its *normal* or *proper* functioning, so the doctor in his treatment is supposed to restore a person to his normal functioning and to right the abnormalities in his performance. The success of this analogy depends upon the applicability of the notion of function in both cases. There is little problem in talking of the function of a car, since a car is a human product and is produced *as* something with a function, as a means of transport. Furthermore, it is not difficult to see how the practice of physical medicine may be viewed in terms of this analogy. Although the body is not a human product and its function is not, in that sense, man-given, it often seems an uncontroversial matter to specify the basic functions which the body should fulfil and to decide whether it is functioning properly according to these standards.[5]

The problems of extending this mechanical analogy to the field of psychiatry are, however, much greater; for we must now consider the function, not just of the body, but of the *person*. Interpreted most widely, this poses the classical question of moral philosophy: What is the end of life? What is human fulfilment? I shall try to show how later. However, those psychiatrists who have adopted what I call the 'clinical approach' have typically interpreted the matter in the narrowest fashion. Thus, at the most basic level, it seems possible to say that a person is given a function by virtue of his particular role as a member of society, and that his function is to fulfil this role. Any person who cannot maintain a social role fails according to these minimal standards, and becomes a dysfunctional social unit, a 'deviant'. Clearly *idealism* is not one of the virtues of this account of the function of a person; however, a certain basic *realism* is. To live in a society, one must function in a certain fashion. Most people have large demands made upon them by their social lives — they must have the ability to feed, house, clothe and protect themselves and so on, with whatever help is available to them.[6]

From this line of thought arises the idea that mental illness is a failure *in a society;* and illness thus defined, as a form of social deviation, is a socially relative concept. The society and the individual's role within it are assumed to be normal (that is to say,

5. However, this can provide only the most minimal concept of physical health and illness.
6. The point is made at length by Peter Alexander, 'Normality', *Philosophy*, Vol. 48, No. 184, April 1973, pp. 137–51; however, he fails to see the *ideals* involved in the concepts of mental health and illness, the significance of psychoanalytic work, and so on.

'healthy': 'normality' is a common synonym for 'health' in psychiatry as in other areas of medicine). Indeed, the prevailing social environment is made the very criterion of normality, and the individual is judged ill insofar as he or she fails to 'adjust' to it.[7]

This clinical account claims to be objective because mental illness and health are defined in terms of a person's function, and this appears to be a matter of objective fact. A part, at least, of a person's function — his social role — seems to be objectively given to him by the very fact of his social life. The social demands upon the individual are real ones, which he must be able to meet for his social survival. If he is unable to do so, he becomes socially incapacitated and either he will seek 'help' or 'help' will be sought for him, at first probably from his family and friends, and ultimately perhaps from a psychiatrist. In this way, the psychiatrist's task appears to be given to him objectively by the society in which he and his patient live.

I have tried to present this argument with sympathy — indeed, I recognize the importance of the considerations it raises, as will become apparent. However, the argument clearly fails in its purpose of securely founding, upon a basis of objective fact, the value-judgements implicit in the concept of mental illness. Just because the individual *is* a part of society, and just because this society *does* make real demands upon him, it does not follow that these demands are to be valued as 'healthy'. What happens in the clinical account is that the prevailing social conditions are taken as fixed and given, and made the criterion of value upon which the account of health and illness is founded. What is valued is equated with what exists. However, this does not found these values on a factual basis; rather, it places a value upon things as they in fact are. Such an attempt to base the value-judgement implicit in the concepts of health and illness upon the foundation of 'what exists' (to use Jaspers's phrase) is in fact a way of endorsing conventional values.

This relative account of mental illness is the orthodox psychiatric view in its essentials, and the symptoms listed in psychiatric textbooks are abnormalities, in the sense I have just sketched, of a more or less socially disabling kind. I have argued that such an account of mental illness implies a value-judgement. However, precisely because the psychiatrist imagines his account to be an 'objective' one,

7. Of course those who think of mental illness in this way do not suggest that *all* deviations from social norms are mental illnesses. For example, the factor of suffering is often mentioned to distinguish illness from other forms of deviance; and the characteristic of *mental* illness is said to be changes of mental functioning which have no known physical cause. See, e.g., F. Kraupl-Taylor, *Psychopathology*, London 1966, chapter one. Needless to say, these lines of demarcation are at best extremely imprecise.

he is unaware of this value-judgement. In a formal sense, therefore, a value-judgement is made; but in a more substantial sense, no moral *judgement* is exercised — that is to say no moral *thought* is exercised in arriving at this account of mental illness. It is notable in this context that the psychiatric account of mental illness refers only to gross and immediately observable behaviour and is not framed in theoretical terms. That is to say, it assumes that mental pathology is immediately apparent and given as obvious fact. The values implied by the psychiatric account are unconscious and unthought.

We have already seen that health and illness are practical concepts, necessitated by the project of therapy. When the psychiatric account of these concepts is viewed in relation to its practical context of therapy, then the features to which I have pointed — its relativism, its endorsing of the prevailing social environment, and its idea of 'value-free' objectivity — become comprehensible. For this way of *thinking* about mental illness is in fact closely related to the *practice* of the individual therapist.[8] People usually (though not always) come to, or are brought to, treatment because they are unable to fulfil their social role. The individual therapist sees the patient only, abstracted from his social context. The therapist, *as* therapist, can act directly on him alone: the social environment from which the patient comes and to which he must return cannot be altered; it must be accepted as a given fact whose demands are (in this sense) 'objectively' and unalterably present. From the practical point of view of individual therapy, the environment is assumed to be 'normal' and illness is considered as individual conditions of abnormality against this background.

The psychiatric account, then, is a purely relative one; it is not based on a psychological or any other theory of human activity, but presents 'mental illness' as a purely individual condition, obvious and immediately apparent against the background of a social environment which is presumed (often unconsciously) to be 'normal'. For all these reasons the psychiatric account has little to offer anyone seriously concerned about the human condition, and it is increasingly being revealed as the rationalization and justification for present social and institutional means of dealing with the problem of 'mental illness'.

An awareness of these points has led to a widespread general scepticism about the concept of mental illness, which has been voiced

8. I am using this word widely to include medical psychiatrists, although I am aware that their 'therapy' often consists in nothing more than the administration of sedatives and tranquilizers and barely deserves the name.

by philosophers, psychologists and sociologists.[9] Thus R.D. Laing writes: 'The "cause" of "schizophrenia" is to be found by the examination, not of the prospective diagnosis alone, but of the whole social context in which the psychiatric ceremonial is being conducted.'[10]

On the basis of such an investigation, Laing concludes:

> There is no such 'condition' as 'schizophrenia', but the label is a social fact and the social fact a *political event*. This political event, occurring in the civic order of society, imposes definitions and consequences on the labelled person. It is a social prescription that rationalizes a set of social actions whereby the labelled person is annexed by others, who are legally sanctioned, medically empowered, and morally obliged, to become responsible for the person labelled. The person labelled is inaugurated not only into a role, but into a career of patient.[11]

Laing thus argues that mental illness is, in Szasz's words, a 'myth'.

The basis for this scepticism is that very relativism, the narrowly practical, technological perspective and covert conservatism in the psychiatric identification of 'illness' with lack of adjustment to the prevailing social environment. This scepticism leads to total rejection of the concept of mental illness as useful to psychology. Sociologists like Goffman and Scheff[12] in particular, have attempted to show that the behaviour of mental patients can be understood solely in relation to the social institutions in which they exist, without any reference to individual psychological considerations; and Laing, too, has often written as if he accepted this view.

Such scepticism has been polemically aimed at current psychiatric practice, and it has been valuable and illuminating as such. It has led to much critical and important work concerning psychiatric procedures, and it has enabled people to break from the psychiatric attitude — and such a break is nothing less than an essential precondition for a critical and scientific approach to psychology and the practical problem of 'mental illness'.

This scepticism has been valuable, then, but its significance is ultimately only *negative*. For in rejecting the concept of mental illness

---

9. For example, T.S. Szasz, R.D. Laing and his co-workers, E. Goffman and T.J. Scheff. See also Sartre's implicit critique in *Being and Nothingness*, part one, chapter two, 'Bad Faith'.

10. R. Laing, *The Politics of Experience*, Harmondsworth 1967, p. 86.

11. Ibid., p. 100.

12. E. Goffman, *Asylums*, Harmondsworth 1968; and T. Scheff, *Being Mentally Ill*, London 1966. See also the dramatic work by D.L. Rosenhan, 'On Being Sane in Insane Places', *Science*, Vol. 179, 19 January 1973, pp. 250–58.

altogether, it implicitly denies the existence of the practical problems of the therapist. To see this, it is again necessary to remember that psychiatry is a practical activity as well as a theory, and that the concepts of mental health and illness are *essentially* practical concepts that define the object and goals of psychiatric practice. The implications of the sceptical rejection of the concept of mental illness are, therefore, that the practical problems tackled by therapy are unreal ones and that the project of therapy should be abandoned.

To this, the psychiatrist will reply[13], surely with justification, that *there is* suffering of a non-physical kind which the concept of mental illness is supposed to describe and which is *real* suffering that cannot be ignored for philosophical niceties. The sceptical approach simply rejects orthodox psychiatric thought and practice; but in doing so, it entirely forgets the *practical need* for psychiatry: the real suffering and misery to which psychiatry is intended to be a response. In tackling the *practical problems* which this suffering presents, the therapist is, or at least ought to be, helped and guided by a theory. And for the theory to fulfil this practical task, it must portray such suffering as illness, over against health as a value.

The values of health and illness are the embodiment of the ideals of therapy, which are those of medicine: the relief of suffering, the healing of sickness. None of the arguments of the scepticism I have been discussing actually disputes these ideals. What this scepticism *does* argue is that such suffering has been conceived wrongly by psychiatric theory, and that orthodox psychiatric therapy does little or nothing to relieve and heal it. But because this scepticism is merely negative towards the concept of mental illness, it ends up denying these ideals altogether, without giving any argument.

Whereas the psychiatric account asserts these ideals blindly in an uncritical and mystified form, this scepticism denies them equally blindly. Both represent a failure to think through the practical problem in critical and theoretical terms; and that is to say, both represent a failure of serious moral and psychological thought.

In the remainder of this paper my main purpose will be to argue that psychoanalytic thought offers the basis for an alternative account of the phenomenon of 'mental illness' which is (at least potentially) critical of the psychiatric account[14] yet not totally sceptical, and in

13. See, e.g., H.J. Eysenck's reply to Laing, 'The Ethics of Psychotherapy', *Question 3*, January 1970, esp. p. 3.
14. The qualification is important. The psychoanalytic movement has reached a *modus vivendi* with psychiatry, a division of labour in this area. The effect at the *theoretical* level has been that psychoanalysts have tended not to develop the implications of their

terms of which the practical (i.e. moral and social) problems of 'mental illness' may be more adequately seen and discussed.

* * *

The significance of the contribution of psychoanalysis to the understanding of mental illness and mental health, and its significance for moral and social thought, are not well understood in this country, particularly among moral philosophers. This is partly because the positivist tenor of so much recent British philosophy has systematically blinded it to what might be of value, not only in psychoanalysis, but in all social and moral thought. It is hardly an exaggeration to say that the dominant tradition of moral philosophy in Britain has made no concrete contribution to moral thought — and, what is even worse, it has not attempted to do so, but has abdicated the task of substantial and *conscious* moral thought. (It is, of course, a substantial moral ideology, but it is so *un*consciously.)

Thus it is not surprising that even where the moral significance of psychoanalysis has been discussed by these philosophers, it has been misunderstood and misdescribed. For example, it is often thought that psychoanalytic theory is a theory only about 'pathological' or 'abnormal' behaviour, and that its moral significance is confined to the redefinition of our attitude to such behaviour. This is only a fragment, and a relatively minor one, of the truth.

An understanding of psychoanalytic thought does, of course, alter one's attitude towards the 'pathological'; but in so doing, it has profound and far-reaching implications for one's concept of 'the normal'. And it is in its relations about 'normal' everyday life that psychoanalysis has its major moral significance. Laing is particularly clear on this: 'The relevance of Freud to our time is largely his insight and, to a very considerable extent, his *demonstration* that the *ordinary* person is a shrivelled, desiccated fragment of what a person can be.'[15] Nevertheless, Freud did arrive at his psychological conclusions through his investigation of mental illness, and it was implicit in the theoretical understanding of mental pathology which he evolved. A very brief review of the history of Freud's discoveries will help to make this clear, and also to emphasize that Freud did not arrive at

theory which are critical of orthodox medical psychiatry.
15. R. Laing, op. cit., p 22.

this sort of conclusion speculatively or by any form of merely abstract reasoning.

Freud was trained as a doctor, and he accepted from this training the psychiatric and relative view of mental illness which I described earlier. His first patients were hysterics: that is to say, patients with *physical* complaints, gross and obvious symptoms which more or less incapacitated them in their everyday lives. At the very outset of his psychiatric career, Freud proceeded in the psychiatric manner, to attempt to *eradicate* these symptoms. Freud used hypnosis for this purpose, and (in the initial cases reported in his first major psychological work, *Studies on Hysteria*) he describes how he would command the disappearance of the patient's symptoms while the patient was hypnotized. This method of treatment — literally ordering the symptoms to disappear — is still used by some psychiatrists today. However, Freud was not satisfied with this procedure; his objections to it were both theoretical and practical. Such a purely symptomatic treatment offended against his very clear vision of proper scientific procedure in medicine; it was a purely pragmatic treatment which lacked a basis of theoretical understanding and justification. Furthermore, judged by pragmatic criteria, it was ultimately ineffective, as he learned from the case of Miss Lucy R. 'What had happened was precisely what is always brought up against purely symptomatic treatment: I had removed one symptom only for its place to be taken by another.'[16]

What set Freud on the path to psychoanalysis was his hearing about a case treated by his colleague and friend, Breuer — the case of Anna O. Breuer had found that when she remembered and communicated certain events associated in her mind with her symptoms, an alleviation of her symptoms ensued. Freud became interested in this case and tried applying its method in his own work. He was not a good hypnotist and quickly abandoned the use of it when he discovered that he could get his patients to recall the relevant material without its help.

These memories and associations, however, were not immediately present in his patients' consciousness; they had to be extracted against the *resistance* of the patient. The observation of resistance on the patient's part led Freud to the view that such *unconscious* ideas (which were highly charged emotionally) were actually kept out of consciousness by a force, which he called *repression*. Freud also observed that when he asked the patient what he remembered in connection with the

16. S. Freud, *Studies on Hysteria*, Standard Edition, Vol. 2, p. 119.

first onset of his symptom, the patient would sometimes say he could remember nothing and that nothing occurred to him. However, after some pressing, it would transpire that something *had* passed through the patient's mind, but that he had deemed it irrelevant and had not mentioned it. As a result of his investigations, Freud came to the conclusion that such apparently irrelevant ideas ('free associations') in fact occurred for a reason; and that by trying to discover this reason he was in fact pursuing his investigation of the nature of the symptom; and that he could get the patient to recognize, and possibly even reconcile himself with, the repressed and unconscious ideas and desires which were at the root of the symptom (its hidden nature, its 'latent content').[17] Furthermore, Freud discovered that these repressed ideas and desires were commonly sexual, often of the most tabooed form, and had a continuous history stretching back to earliest infancy.

In this way, and gradually over a long period of time, Freud came to a theoretical understanding of the nature of neurotic symptoms. According to this theory, neurotic symptoms arise from a conflict between a person's libidinal and pre-social instincts and opposing repressive forces within the personality, particularly the dictates of morality and conscience. Although the idea of a conflict between desire and morality was a common one before Freud, what he showed was that if this conflict became too intense and anxiety-provoking, the desire, the instinct, was repressed — put out of mind and inhibited from active expression. This was not the end of the story, however, for the repression of the instinct did not abolish it. It continued, as Freud put it, 'to press for satisfaction', which it achieved (in a compromise form) in *thought* in the form of fantasy, and in *action* in the form of (neurotic) symptoms.

This theory of neurosis not only altered Freud's understanding of, and therefore approach to, 'mental illness'; it also changed his attitude to normality. For the explanation which Freud had developed of the psychiatric symptoms of hysteria applied equally to a very extensive range of absolutely normal behaviour. What Freud discovered was that a great deal of 'normal' behaviour in fact had exactly the same structure as did neurotic symptoms. Again he discovered this through his analytic practice. For example, he noticed that his patients frequently and spontaneously recounted their dreams to him for no apparent reason, as 'free associations'. Instead

17. Freud describes his initial discovery of these facts in his account of 'The Case of Elizabeth von R.', in *Studies on Hysteria*.

of brushing these aside as irrelevant to the treatment, Freud investigated them, and this investigation led to his richest work, *The Interpretation of Dreams.*

Freud's theory of dreams portrays them as having *exactly* the same structure of repression and compromise and wish-fulfilment as do neurotic symptoms. And in addition to dreams, Freud argued that many other absolutely 'normal' phenomena, like symptomatic errors and slips of the tongue, certain very common patterns of relationship which he called 'transference', and also traits of character, compulsive moralizing and 'the fear of God', had the structure of neurotic symptoms.

Although, as we shall see, Freud did not follow the implications of this theory through to the end, this psychoanalytic account of neurotic symptoms ultimately implies an approach to the problems of mental illness which is distinct from, and in contradiction to, the orthodox psychiatric account. On the basis of this psychoanalytic theory, it seems that what is characteristically *pathological* about a mental symptom (i.e. what makes behaviour symptomatic) is that it involves *repression.*[18] Mental pathology is thus thought of as *division* within the personality, and health is conceived as the unity, integrity or wholeness of the person and the absence of wasteful, energy-consuming self-division and self-alienation. The goal of psychoanalytic practice is then (in theory at least) to *heal* the mind and person, in the original sense of 'to heal' which is 'to make-whole, to make-one'. Some of Freud's own formulations emphasise this healing function of psychoanalysis. For example, he writes: 'The aim of our efforts may be expressed in various formulas — making conscious the unconscious, removing the repressions, filling in the gaps in memory, they all amount to the same thing.'[19]

It is clear that this represents a way of thinking about the concept of mental illness that is very different from the orthodox psychiatric account. First, the concepts of mental health and illness are now absolute and not socially relative concepts. Mental illness is thought of as an individual condition, the distinguishing criteria of which refer not to the prevailing social environment, but only to psychological processes within the individual. This absolute account of mental illness does not therefore make the prevailing environment

---

18. More accurately, a symptom according to Freud involves 'the return of the repressed' desire. But the repressed wish always 'returns' and gains expression, if only in dream and fantasy. These assertions need further discussion which cannot be given here.

19. Freud, *Introductory Lectures on Psychoanalysis*, 2nd edn, London 1929, p. 363.

into the criterion of normality and health.

We have seen how the psychiatric account maintains that the function of a person is to fulfil his basic role as a member of society. By contrast, the absolute account considers the function of a person abstractly in-itself, and not in relation to his particular social role. The function of a person is thus thought of in terms of self-realization an an integral person, lack of alienation and wasteful self-repression, satisfaction of his basic human nature (i.e. instincts), happiness, and so on. Freud was aware of the conflict between these two accounts. In present conditions at least the social environment requires the individual to repress many of his desires. And so, the sort of absolute definition of mental illness which is suggested by psychoanalytic theory, so far from making the social environment the criterion of health, tends to be critical of prevailing social conditions in the name of health. Repression, and therefore neurosis, are absolutely normal and universal features of our present lives. As Freud says: 'It is impossible to overlook the extent to which civilization is built up upon a renunciation of instinct; how much it presupposes precisely the non-satisfaction (by suppression, repression or some other means?) of powerful instincts. This "cultural frustration" dominates the large field of social relationships between human beings.'[20]

The state of 'normality', which is the assumed standard of health in the psychiatric account, is revealed by this view as one of unconsciousness, alienation and neurosis. Laing puts this view forcefully when he writes: 'As adults, we have forgotten most of our childhood, not only its content but its flavour; as men of the world we hardly know of the existence of the inner world; we barely remember our dreams, and make little sense of them when we do; as for our bodies, we retain just sufficient proprioceptive sensations to coordinate our movements and ensure the minimal requirements for biosocial survival — to register fatigue, signals for food, sex, defaecation, sleep; beyond that, little or nothing . . . The condition of alienation, of being asleep, of being unconscious, of being out of one's mind, is the condition of the normal man.'[21]

The standards of health and illness are here applied according to criteria which transcend the particular social environment of the individual and appeal to absolute values. These criteria are not the result of direct and immediate observation. They are the product of the

20. Freud, *Civilization and its Discontents*, London 1963, p. 34.
21. R. Laing, op, cit., pp. 22–3.

attempt to comprehend the phenomenon of normal and abnormal behaviour theoretically. Furthermore, because they suggest that everyone is 'ill', their practical implications for therapy are idealistic.

Freud himself, however, never endorsed the absolute account I have just outlined (even though it is implicit in his theory), nor did he ultimately acknowledge the ideals of health of the absolute account or its practical implications. This is not to say that the practical implications of psychoanalytic theory were entirely ignored in Freud's therapeutic work. In fact, this did change considerably in character with the development of his theoretical understanding. As Reiff observes 'in the beginning . . . through the patients Freud treated did disclose doubts about what to do with their lives . . . there were always tangible symptoms — a paralysed leg, a handwashing compulsion, impotence — by the resolution of which one could certify the cure . . . [but later] all experience is sympatomatic . . . People seek treatment because they sleep poorly, or have headaches, or feel apathetic towards loved ones, or because they are dissatisfied with their lives.'[22]

Nevertheless, as I have argued already, psychoanalytic theory implies that a vastly more extensive range of phenomena than this are pathological. However, in practice, patients do not come wishing to be cured of such 'normal' neuroses, unless they are causing them impairment in their everyday lives.

Freud is ultimately unwilling to divorce the concepts of health and illness from the context of therapy, and it is for purely *practical* reasons, connected with therapy, that Freud is reluctant to abandon the psychiatric and relative account of mental illness, no matter how much it conflicts with his psychoanalytic theory. Thus he says: 'The healthy man . . . is virtually a neurotic, but the only symptom he *seems* capable of developing is a dream. To be sure, when you subject his waking life to a critical investigation, you discover something that contradicts this specious conclusion; for this apparently healthy life is pervaded by innumerable trivial and practically unimportant symptom-formations. The difference between nervous health and nervous illness (neurosis) is narrowed down therefore to a practical distinction, and is determined by the practical result — how far the person concerned remains capable of a sufficient degree of capacity for enjoyment and active achievement.'[23]

22. P. Reiff, *Freud: The Mind of the Moralist,* London 1965, p. 304.
23. *Introductory Lectures,* p. 382.

In other words, according to psychoanalytic theory everyone has neurotic *symptoms*, but it does not follow that everyone is *neurotic*, because the concept of illness (unlike that of symptom) is a practical and not a theoretical one. What Freud means by 'practical' here is shown in the following passage, where he considers the question of whether everyone might be neurotic. 'May we not be justified in reaching the diagnosis that, under the influence of cultural forces, some civilizations, or some epochs of civilization — possibly the whole of mankind — have become "neurotic"? . . . As regards the therapeutic application of our knowledge, what would be the use of the most correct analysis of social neurosis, since no one possesses authority to impose such a therapy upon the group?'[24]

What Freud is saying here is that from the point of view of individual therapy, the absolute account of mental illness and health is an impractical and utopian one. And it is for this reason that he retains the psychiatric and relative account as well.

Freud thus tries to hold on to both the psychiatric account and the psychoanalytic theory of neurosis at the same time — but these two are in contradiction. Freud never properly appreciated this contradiction in his thought, and he tended to ignore the implications of psychoanalytic theory and to dismiss them on the narrowly practical grounds of the possibility of individual therapy when they came to his attention.[25] Freud's account of mental health and illness is contradictory, therefore, since it contains (implicitly at least) both the accounts of these concepts which I have outlined: the relative and the absolute.

In conclusion, I want to argue that this contradiction in Freud's thought has an important significance, and that we can learn from it; and that it should not simply be dismissed as a sign of mere confusion, as many contemporary British philosophers are inclined to do when they come upon contradictions. For there are *reasons* for Freud's thought being contradictory on this matter, there are *reasons* for asserting both of these contradictory accounts.

Earlier I argued that there is a real basis to the psychiatric account in the real problems that confront the psychiatrist in his practice; and I have also tried to show that the account of mental illness given by psychoanalytic theory is a well founded one. Both of these conclusions

24. *Civilization and its Discontents*, p. 81.
25. He also had more sophisticated, though purely speculative, ways of dealing with this contradiction; for example, his talk of 'qualities of psychic energy bound in repression'. However, to discuss this matter adequately would take me too far from my central purpose.

need to be incorporated in an adequate account of mental illness, and yet they seem to be opposed. For the struggle between the social values of conformity embodied in the psychiatric account and the apparently individual values of fulfilment expressed through psychoanalytic theory is a real one.[26]

Freud, when he did not just ignore it, thought that this was an eternal conflict, and in the nature of things. His pessimism is notorious: he did not believe that the individual can achieve fulfilment; neurosis, and the frustration it involves, were for Freud, inevitable. And he saw no alternative to a familiar and very real dilemma: either you are spontaneously free and unrepressed, in which case your society will suppress you; or you repress yourself and comply with the demands society makes upon you.

But these are not the exclusive alternatives; and the belief that they are, it seems to me, derives from the fact that ultimately Freud adopted the individualistic perspective of the therapist — the psychiatric account of mental illness, which accepts the social environment as fixed and given. However, Freud's theory suggests that the social environment may itself be pathological. The practical implication which Freud drew from this was that a therapist is needed with the authority to treat society as a whole. This is hardly practical, but surely a more realistic conclusion would be that social and not merely individual change is necessary if the therapeutic project of eliminating illness and promoting health is to be achieved. What psychoanalysis reveals is the social and ultimately political content in the concepts of mental health and illness.

The problem of mental illness, then, is a social and a political problem, but it is not *just* a social or political problem. It is also an immediate individual problem, and this is stressed by the psychiatric account and must not be forgotten either. The problem of mental illness does not initially and immediately arise as a social one. Immediately and initially it confronts the practising psychiatrist as an individual problem, in the shape of individual patients who are suffering and need help. This immediate problem is a real one, and people need the kind of help which psychiatry is supposed to provide, but too seldom does. *Simply* to say: the problem is really a political one and will be solved only when a revolutionary social change has abolished the family, exploitative work and the other alienating

26. I have used Freud's dichotomy between social and individual, but it must be critically re-examined (along with other aspects of Freud's thinking on human nature and society) if the contradiction in Freud's thought that I am discussing is to be resolved satisfactorily.

features of our society — to say just this is to ignore the immediate practical problem which confronts the psychiatrist.

The immediate problem requires action, and it is only through the attempt to deal with this immediate problem, both practically and theoretically, that its social and political dimension is revealed. In other words, the problem is *both* individual and social; and each of the accounts I have described in some way ignores this.

Psychiatry must be a twofold activity which acts at an individual and at a social level. The psychiatrist must help the individual as he can, and also fight those alienating and repressive social and psychiatric institutions which frustrate this work. The concepts of mental health and illness (or their equivalents), critically and theoretically developed, are valuable in guiding this task; and it is possible to reject the blinkered conservatism of psychiatry without ending in a total scepticism which has the effect of ignoring the real problems. Perhaps the concept of mental illness is too tainted by its psychiatric use to be anything but misleading for these purposes. The concept of alienation is a natural alternative,[27] but unfortunately it has lost almost all precise meaning through over-use in recent years. Despite this, however, the concept of alienation has the advantage of suggesting a *social* aspect to the condition it describes; and in addition to this it has close historical associations with the concept of mental illness in the 19th century ('alienism' was a common word for psychiatry). But most importantly, the term 'alienation' has evaluative implications, and the use of it involves the recognition that such states, no matter how 'normal', are states of suffering and ought to be a cause for concern.

The concepts of mental illness and alienation are moral concepts. Indeed, they are among the most important categories of contemporary moral thought; but not in the sense of 'morality' in which many contemporary British philosophers, to judge from their examples ('He ought to do x', 'y is right', 'z is good' etc.) appear to understand the term. 'Mental illness', as I have tried to show, is not a *merely evaluative* concept: it is always embedded in a 'theory' — a more or less systematically organized point of view — by means of which people and their activities are understood and assessed. The discussion of this concept by recent British philosophers has, however, often quite deliberately excluded any critical consideration of psychology, social theory etc., etc., with the result that it has tended uncritically to endorse conventional attitudes by reporting 'ordinary usage'. This is a sure recipe for producing ignorant apologetics.

27. See Laing, op. cit., and J. Gabel, *La fausse conscience*, Paris 1962.

Anyone with a faith in the possibility of philosophy being used as a weapon of criticism (i.e. a radical philosophy) will see the need to expose such ideological philosophy and replace it. For this, a concern with psychology and social theory is essential. This is not something 'in addition' to moral philosophy but rather one of its essential aspects.

Reprinted from *RP* 5

Moral Philosophy without Morality?

Richard Norman

Of the traditional areas of philosophy, moral philosophy is one in which the inadequacy of recent work has been most obvious. The writings of people like R.M. Hare can readily be seen as representing in an extreme degree the barrenness of so much contemporary philosophy. A common response to their work has consequently been to say something like this: that recent moral philosophy has been so arid and sterile because philosophers have turned away from substantive moral questions and have occupied themselves solely with 'the language of morals', with the analysis of moral concepts. This diagnosis might seem to be confirmed by their own pronouncements about what they are doing. Although it is perhaps unfair to do so, I cannot resist quoting, as an example, the write-up on the back cover of Nowell-Smith's *Ethics:*

> 'What ought I to do, here and now?' This is a question which each of us frequently has to answer. More rarely, in a reflective moment or when faced with a difficult moral problem, we ask such questions as: 'What ought I to do in general?' 'To what moral code ought I to adhere?', 'Why should I adhere to any moral code at all?'. These are the perennial questions of moral philosophy. It is not, however, the aim of this book to answer these questions.

There is indeed a certain truth in the above explanation of why recent moral philosophy has been so boring. As it stands, however, it accepts these philosophers' own characterization of their work at face value. There are two main respects in which the explanation is inadequate:

(a) Modern moral philosophy has *not* in fact been morally neutral. It has been done from a specific moral standpoint. This has become quite explicit in some of the more recent work; G.J. Warnock, for example, in *The Object of Morality*, is concerned to argue that morality has a specific content, and to justify its having such a content. But one can also identify a particular morality (and, significantly, it is more or less the same morality) which is implicitly presupposed, though unacknowledged, in the work of writers like Hare who take moral philosophy to be concerned solely with the *form* of moral discourse.

(b) What is really significant about the method employed by modern moral philosophers is not the fact that it consists in conceptual analysis, but rather their particular view of what 'conceptual analysis' actually is. This view is epitomized in the following quotation: '(Contemporary philosophers) would say . . . that philosophy is the study of the concepts that we employ, and not of the facts, phenomena, cases, or events to which those concepts might be or are applied. To investigate the latter is to raise political or moral or religious, but not philosophical, problems or questions.'[1]

What we have here is essentially a Platonic view of concepts. It is supposed that concepts on the one hand, and facts, phenomena and events on the other, belong in two different realms, and that they can therefore be investigated quite separately. What is usually then implied is that the investigation and analysis of concepts is a purely a priori study, whereas knowledge of things in the world and of facts about the world is obtained entirely by empirical investigation.

Now, put like that, as a kind of Platonic dualism, the thesis is obviously untenable, and I doubt whether any contemporary philosopher would subscribe to it. Nevertheless, some such view does in fact underlie the practice of recent moral philosophy. In opposition to such a view I would claim that although philosophy certainly does involve the analysis of concepts, and although this could even be regarded as distinctive of philosophical enquiry, still, the analysis of concepts is not a self-contained activity. How we analyse concepts will affect our view of facts about the world. (For example, if we accept a Humean analysis of the concept of causality, we are committed to a certain belief about events in the world, namely that they are not linked by any necessary connections.) And, perhaps even more importantly, our factual beliefs affect the concepts we employ. If our knowledge of empirical facts about the world changes radically, this will require a corresponding revision of our concepts.

Applied, specifically to moral philosophy, this means that, most obviously, our empirical knowledge of social and psychological facts will be relevant to the analysis of moral concepts. Depending on what

1. G.J. Warnock *English Philosophy Since 1900* (Oxford, 1958), p. 167. The quotation is actually taken from Sean Sayers's article 'Towards a Radical Philosophy', which appeared in the *Cambridge Review* (20 Oct. 1972). The ideas in that article have stimulated much of what I have to say here.

one takes to be the nature of contemporary society and the nature of human behaviour, particular moral concepts will have to be regarded as more or less appropriate, and will need to be interpreted in different ways. The most important general indictment of recent moral philosophy is that it has studiously ignored relevant empirical facts of this kind. Consequently, it has taken moral concepts to be essentially uncontroversial. Moral concepts have been accepted as ready-made, as if their status and viability, their appropriateness to human activity, were not in question, and as if they could be analysed in purely a priori fashion.

The exception proves the rule. Warnock, in his recent book, thinks it important to ground the concept of morality on a general view of what he calls 'the human predicament'. But he demonstrates how out of practice philosophers are at this game, both by the obvious embarrassment with which he sets about his task, and by the banal half-truths he comes up with. Whenever he uses the term 'the human predicament', he apologises for talking 'pompously' or 'in archaic style'. As for what I have referred to as the 'banal half-truths', the following is typical: 'It seems reasonable, and in the present context is highly relevant, to say, without necessarily going quite as far as Hobbes did, that the human predicament is inherently such that things are liable to go badly.'[2]

*   *   *

I shall now attempt to substantiate these two points — that moral philosophers have been committed, even without acknowledging it, to a substantive morality, and that they have dealt in a purely a priori fashion with concepts whose status is called in question by empirical considerations — by looking at some of the basic assumptions which have been most influential in recent moral philosophy.

(a) The first of these is the primary role which has been given to the concepts of wants, desires, interests, etc. Moral beliefs have been widely thought to be reducible to statements about these. It has been assumed by many philosophers that at least the most basic and most important wants and desires are simply given; that with regard to those things which are desired for their own sake, rather than for the sake of any further end, such desires are immune to further assess-

2. *The Object of Morality*, p. 17.

ment. They may indeed conflict with one another, and if they do so, one of them may have to be sacrificed to another. But in themselves, it is thought, they are immune to criticism.

What is significant is that this view has been maintained in the face of so much evidence of how, in our society, people's wants are manipulated, are artificially stimulated and created. People can be said to have 'false wants' both insofar as they are deliberately manipulated, by techniques of persuasion such as advertising, and also insofar as they unconsciously adapt their wants to the kinds of satisfaction attainable within the limits of the existing social structure. Certain kinds of 'false' wants are built into the operation of the economy, for example, and are thus adopted unconsciously by people as their own. I cannot elaborate on this here, but it should be obvious that I am thinking particularly of Marcuse's writing, such as his *One-Dimensional Man*. Thus if people appear to want, for their own sake, such things as social status or superfluous material luxuries, we cannot simply stop at that fact. Such wants are *not* just 'given'. The concept of 'wants' and 'desires' therefore cannot be treated as philosophically unproblematic, nor can it play the kind of role widely assigned to it in practical reasoning. From a philosophical point of view what is needed, in the light of these empirical considerations, is an examination of the distinction between true and false wants, true and false needs.

(b) A second typical feature of recent moral philosophy has been the fundamental importance attached to the concept of altruism and to the egoism/altruism distinction. The notion of altruism, when added to the notion of desires, has regularly been taken to be the defining feature of morality. It has very often been suggested that practical reasoning falls into two clear categories: reasoning concerned with the satisfaction of one's desires is prudential, and reasoning which takes equal account of everyone's desires, others' as well as one's own, constitutes *moral* reasoning. Moreover, philosophers have thought that it can be proved entirely a priori that one ought to be altruistic. The notion of 'universalizability' is usually invoked as the means of proving that anyone who doesn't give equal weight to other people's desires, when these will be affected by his actions, is being irrational. Now, if it were not for universalizability, I would be inclined to say that this is just *obviously* false. It seems to be simply obvious that egoism is not irrational. The idea that the arguments of someone like Nietzsche, for example, could be countered by a simply logical appeal to 'universalizability' is surely intrinsically implausible. Of course egoism makes sense. Of course it is not irrational.

It may even be right.

More important, however, are those psychological considerations which call in question the egoism/altruism dichotomy altogether. I have in mind, in particular, what might be called 'the ambiguity of altruism'. Supposedly altruistic behaviour can in fact have a psychological character of widely differing kinds. To take the most basic opposition: altruistic behaviour may be masochistic behaviour, the product of frustrated aggressions which are turned inward against oneself and thus produce an attitude of self-negation and self-denial; or, at the other extreme, it may be the genuine, spontaneous generosity and sympathy and humanity of someone who can afford to give freely of himself, who is able to recognize others as independent beings with needs and interests of their own, because he is secure in his own identity. I think it would be fair to regard only the latter as genuine altruism. Now, this point is sometimes formulated by saying that 'one cannot love others unless one also loves oneself'.[3] This locution, however, is misleading. By linking concern for oneself and concern for others *instrumentally*, it preserves the conceptual dichotomy between the two. It invites the response: 'This is simply a contingent connection which you are pointing out; you are telling us that the most effective means of being altruistic is to love oneself equally; but though this may be true empirically, the fact remains that there is a conceptual distinction between egoism and altruism and that the latter concept is definitive of morality.' The point, however, is precisely that the contingent empirical facts have conceptual implications. They require us to revise our conceptual categories. They point to the need for some basic ethical concept which is prior to both egoism and altruism — perhaps something like 'health' or 'harmony' or 'integrity' or 'fulfilment'. And altruism would have then to be seen simply as one particular natural manifestation of such a state.

(c) The third idea which I want to mention is less widespread, but equally significant. In the last few years some philosophers, apparently still impressed with the idea that morality comes into play when one extends one's behaviour from a concern for one's own interests to a concern for the interests of others, have tried to base this extension on the concept of a 'contract'.[4] The idea has a long history

3. Cf. Erich Fromm: *Man For Himself*, ch.IV section 1. Despite its limitations, Fromm's discussion, and the book as a whole, are a useful application of psychological ideas to philosophical ethics, and far more valuable than most recent moral philosophy in th analytical tradition.
4. I have in mind such works as G.R. Grice's *The Grounds of Moral Judgement*, D.A.

we could trace it back to Hobbes, for example (for whom, of course, the connection between morality and the contract is mediated through the notion of political authority), and, further back, to what is perhaps its classic statement in Book II of Plato's *Republic,* where it is put into the mouth of Glaucon. The idea is this: given the basic postulate that individuals are concerned to satisfy their own interests, and given the fact that these interests conflict, it is in people's interest to enter into a contract whereby they undertake to respect one another's basic interests. It is such a contract which creates moral obligations; having entered into it, men have obligations towards one another in respect of these basic interests.

Now, there is a familiar and insuperable objection to the traditional 'contract' theory — namely, that no such general contract has ever been entered into. Contemporary attempts to revive the 'contract' idea have therefore been formed not in terms of any actual contract, but in terms of a purely hypothetical one. The suggestion is that, where it would be in our interests for such a contract to exist, we ought to act *as though* we had contracted with others to respect certain interests of theirs in return for their respecting our interests. Our obligations towards others are thus supposed to derive from this hypothetical — that is, non-existent — contract.

The objection to this is obvious: Why on earth should I be bound by a contract which I have never made? If the contract is purely hypothetical, it cannot generate any actual obligations. The whole point about a contract is that it provides some kind of guarantee of how other people are going to behave. Given the guarantee that others are likely to respect my interests, it is worth my while to limit my own actions in accordance with the contract. But if the contract is only hypothetical, there is no such guarantee. The supposed reason for acting in accordance with the contract therefore disappears.

The issue here is not just an academic one. Professional politicians and ideologues often talk as though social and economic relations could be seen as some kind of implicit contract. The constant appeal to 'the national interest' invokes an idea of the economy as a joint enterprise in which all, workers and capitalists alike, pool their resources and abilities, and make certain sacrifices in return for mutual benefits. It is then suggested that the workers ought to limit their wage claims, and in general ought to moderate their concern for

---

Richards' *A Theory of Reasons for Action,* and J. Rawls' *A Theory of Justice.* Though these are, in varying degrees, more impressive than anything in the 'Language of Morals' vein, I still feel that they are open to my general criticisms of the tradition.

their own interests, because this is their side of the bargain. The same idea is in fact extended to the whole field of social relations — one is asked to forego one's own interests in return for the same restraint on the part of everybody else. Here again therefore we must emphasize that no such contract exists. As a matter of empirical fact, social relations within our society are simply not like that. Power and wealth are unequally shared, and those who have an abundance of both have not been restrained in the acquisition of them by any contract. Consequently those who are deprived of power and wealth are under no corresponding obligation to forego their own interests. On the contrary, the appropriate response to their situation is for them to assert their own interests and to aim at the satisfaction of them. In this context, and in relation to the whole question of altruism, we can fittingly quote what Marx and Engels say in the *German Ideology:* 'The communists do not preach *morality* at all . . . They do not put to people the moral demand: love one another, do not be egoists, etc.; on the contrary, they are very well aware that egoism, just as much as self-sacrifice, *is* in definite circumstances a necessary form of the self-assertion of individuals.'[5]

So far, in discussing these three ideas, I have been concerned to emphasize the apriorism of recent moral philosophy, and to indicate how empirical considerations actually call in question the role which this philosophy ascribes to the concepts it analyses. My other intention has been to show that this philosophy is not morally neutral, and this will, I hope, be fairly obvious by now. The idea that individuals are entirely autonomous in the wants and needs which they aim to satisfy and the goals which they pursue, that these are entirely personal and that there is no room for external criticism of them; the idea of morality as a device which supervenes upon this private activity and prevents people from getting in one another's way when they pursue these ends, by requiring them to take account of one another's interests; the idea of one's relations to other people as essentially contractual — what is all this but the morality of liberalism?

This liberalism is specifically apparent in the frequent distinction, found in a number of contemporary moral philosophers, between, on the one hand, the private and personal ideals which each person pursues within his own individual life, and, on the other hand, a social

5. Marx and Engels: *The German Ideology*, Lawrence & Wishart, p. 267.

morality whose function is to arbitrate between competing interests. That this division is characteristic of the liberal tradition will, I think, be obvious. It is epitomized in the view which Mill ascribes to Bentham: 'Bentham's idea of the world is that of a collection of persons pursuing each his separate interest or pleasure, and the prevention of whom from jostling one another more than is avoidable, may be attempted by hopes and fears derived from three sources — the law, religion, and public opinion.'[6]

Mill intends these to be rather scathing remarks, yet he never succeeds in freeing himself from these same limitations; his essay *On Liberty*, for example is dominated by the same conception. What is significant for the purposes of this paper, then, is that we find the same division, between private ideals and socially negotiated interests, prominent in recent moral philosophers. It plays a large role in Hare's *Freedom and Reason*, for example. It occurs in Warnock's *The Object of Morality* when he asserts that morality does not tell us 'how one should live' or what could constitute 'the good life'. That, he says, is a matter for individual life-styles, and one may, according to one's individual personality, regard the good life as that of the man of action, or the dedicated artist, or the religious recluse, or the professional golfer.[7] What morality does is to produce the appropriate conditions *within which* various kinds of individual lives may be lived. Perhaps the most explicit statement of the morality of liberalism is in Strawson's paper 'Social Morality and Individual Ideal' (*Philosophy*, 1961). He talks there of the diversity of individual ideas as a sort of picture-gallery of possibilities; he then goes on to suggest that the observance of a recognized social code of morality is necessary as a pre-condition for the pursuit of these ideals, and that a liberal society is one in which the pursuit of a variety of conflicting ideals of life is possible.

If it were my main concern here to criticize this latter-day liberalism, I would try to show how, on the one hand, the quality of one's life as an individual is conditioned by the nature of the social relations and social patterns of behaviour in which one is implicated (think, for example, of how any discussion of alienation would require the abandonment of the liberal dichotomy), and how, on the other hand, one's conception of the general nature and purpose of human activity — one's 'ideals', to use the liberal word — will determine one's view of what men's interests consist in, and will affect one's

6. J.S. Mill: *Essays on Bentham and Coleridge*, Chatto & Windus.
7. These revealing examples occur on page 90 of *The Object of Morality*.

attitude towards social conflicts of interest and towards the ways in which these can or cannot be resolved, whether by a 'social morality' or by some other means. However, I cannot go into this now. What I want to stress is that recent moral philosophy has tended to presuppose a specific morality, that this morality is contestable, and that if philosophers had been less anxious to limit themselves to a priori analysis and more inclined to look at what human societies and human behaviour are actually like, they might have been led to question the moral concepts which they have been content to analyse.

*　　*　　*

If we are to take this critical function of moral philosophy more seriously, then the very first concept to look at critically might be the concept of morality itself. There are certain standard objections to the use of the concept of 'morality', and in particular to the use of the epithet 'immoral' as applied to men and their actions. These objections are formidable ones. Whether they are entirely valid, I'm not sure. But they certainly need to be taken seriously by moral philosophers, and I therefore want to put them forward now.

(a) We can approach the first objection by taking up my earlier point about altruism. If it is indeed the case that the basic value-concepts to apply to people's lives are concepts such as health and harmony and balance, fulfilment, self-realization, and so on, then I think we could reasonably add that these are not specifically moral concepts. It would be out of place to assert that people *ought* to aim at these. Not only would the 'ought' be essentially redundant; it would miss the point as to why men fail to achieve such ends. The answer to that question would need to be in terms of factors which are not primarily individual but social. If we take seriously the question 'What is it that screws up people's lives?', then, ultimately, the answer must be: not individual failings and weaknesses, but corrupt and oppressive institutions.

(b) The second objection focuses on the particular kind of motivation which moral behaviour seems to involve. If, as I think we should, we try to attach a fairly definite meaning to the notion of 'morality', so that moral considerations are not just equated with practical considerations in general but are a particular subset of the latter, then one way of pinning the term down is by noting that it is ready associated with the notion of 'conscience'. Morally motivated behaviour is typically equated with actions performed in obedience to conscience. And conscience, in turn, is characteristically seen as something which imposes itself from without. It is essentially an external kind of motivation. This feature of morality is brought out most clearly by Kant, with his emphasis on the opposition between inclination and duty. Think of Kant's contrast between practical love and pathological love. Morality requires that I show concern for another not because I love him in any normal sense, or because he is my friend or my comrade or stands in any other spontaneous human relationship to me, or even because his situation as another human being evokes my sympathy or pity; I must show concern for him simply and solely because that is what morality commands. We may well wonder how this abstract concern, produced by command, can be genuine or can have any real human value. Kant's picture is at least true to the concept of 'morality' and 'moral duty' and 'moral conscience'. But we are also led to ask how this kind of motivation can be possible. How can moral actions be called forth by this abstract sense of duty? And here the most plausible explanation is the familiar Freudian account of the super-ego. What it implies is that such motivation is, as I indicated, essentially external. Though conscience is regarded as being in some sense internal, it is nevertheless the internalization of an external authority. Initially the appropriate actions are produced in response to an authority, just because they are what the authority commands; and the role of this external authority is then taken over by an internalized version of it. In short, morally motivated behaviour is compulsive behaviour.

(c) The third kind of objection which I have in mind tends often to be put in terms of an opposition between *determinism* and morality — misleadingly so, I shall suggest. It is supposed that the standpoint of determinism rules out that of morality, that once an action has been causally explained and thereby shown to be inevitable, the agent can no longer be regarded as morally responsible and it therefore becomes inappropriate to assess the action in moral terms. This case tends to be argued largely by appeal to examples, and especially to examples from the law courts. A typical one which comes to mind is of a young boy who, a few months ago, was given a massive sentence after being convicted of 'mugging'; people then pointed to the area where he lived, to the depressed environment in which he had grown up, the high level of unemployment, the absence of any meaningful opportunities for a worthwhile life; and they were then inclined to say: 'How could he help it? He was bound to act as he did, he didn't have a chance, you can't really blame him.' Examples of this kind do seem very forceful, and yet the reference to determinism obscures what is really significant about them. The problem — that of the inappropriateness of moral vocabulary in such situations — arises regardless of whether or not we suppose the action to be 'inevitable'. It arises, rather, because once we *understand why* the individual acted as he did, there is no longer the same inclination to condemn him as 'immoral'. The real opposition is between, on the one hand, an *understanding* of the action, as an intelligible response to a situation, and, on the other hand, a characteristically *moral* view of it. The latter in fact cuts short all understanding. It simply categorizes and labels the agent with some such assertion as 'He is immoral', 'He is guilty'. The moral point of view seems to involve a particular view of responsibility, one which sees 'evil' as some kind of quality residing wholly in the person and, as it were, making up his whole identity. It would be fair to characterize this as a 'judicial' mentality, concerned not with why the agent did what he did, but solely with the question 'innocent or guilty?' It is the mentality which is concerned with passing sentence. I would suggest that we should be more struck by the use of the phrase 'moral judgements'. As this is used, it is not just analogous to 'factual judgements' or 'scientific judgements'. People regularly talk, even within moral philosophy, about '*passing* moral judgements', and this brings out very dramatically the judicial connotations of the phrase. This aspect of morality is one of the main grounds for Nietzsche's attack on the concept. Nietzsche, of course, linked the moral point of view closely with Christianity. In *The Twilight of the Idols* he has a fine phrase: 'Christianity is the metaphysics of the hangman.' I would say there is a good deal of truth in that.

It is important to notice what concepts are being called in question by these considerations. It is not just a matter of the concept 'moral'. As I have intimated above, the objections also apply to the concept 'ought', at least in its characteristically moral sense, which has occupied the attention of philosophers. Of course there are other senses of 'ought'. The 'ought' of advice, as in 'You ought to see the film at the Odeon this week' or 'You ought to see a doctor' is obviously indispensable. But the moral 'ought', which, as Hare rightly says, has the force of an imperative, stands or falls with the concept 'moral', for reasons which I have already indicated.

It is remarkable how philosophers, having accepted that the language of moral oughts belongs with the language of imperatives, have seen nothing questionable about the use of such language. They have apparently given no thought to the question how one can be in a position to issue imperatives to other people. In the case of most uses of imperatives the answer will be obvious and uninteresting. But in the case of moral commands and moral 'oughts', their use seems to carry with it an assumption of moral superiority which, to say the least, needs examining.

What this shows, then, is that even the most general concepts, so general that philosophers have thought them morally uncontentious, actually have a specific moral content. In analysing the terms 'good' and 'right' and 'ought', philosophers have thought they were on safe neutral ground. I would say they were mistaken.

Another concept which we should seriously consider jettisoning is that of 'the virtues'. The most recent attempt to revive this concept, by G.J. Warnock, is open to objection on both the first two counts. Warnock thinks that the most important reason why 'things tend to go badly' is the fact of limited human sympathies — roughly speaking, the fact that men are too selfish. He gives no attention at all to the idea that things might 'go badly' because of the kind of society in which men have to live and the kinds of institution within which they have to act. Secondly, there is the question of moral motivation. Warnock says that, because men have limited sympathies, morality seeks to counteract these limitations.[8] What is this supposed to mean? He can't mean literally that 'morality' does this. It must be understood as, in some way or other, a claim about what *human beings* seek to do. But it is difficult to see how *men* can provide the required countervailing tendency, since, according to Warnock, the human predicament consists precisely in the fact that men are not sympathetic. Warnock seems to imply that morality manages to impose itself by some kind of sleight of hand — men are, in themselves, selfish, but thanks to morality they can turn out to be more sympathetic than they really are. As it stands, this is logically incoherent. What makes it plausible is the psychological fact I mentioned earlier — that moral motivation does characteristically impose itself as something external, as the internalization of external authority.

*   *   *

It is not clear whether these are decisive objections to traditional moral concepts, but they are certainly important. Two reservations, in particular, need to be made.

8. *The Object of Morality*, p. 26.

(a) I do not simply want to say that everything is political. The first of my three objections above might be thought to lead to the conclusion that all talk about the desirability of one kind of life rather than another is political discourse, requiring a political solution. Well, it does require a political solution, but that does not mean that the necessity for personal decisions disappears. Whatever beliefs one has about the necessity for political action, one's own commitment to the political cause requires a decision — a personal decision, moreover, which depends not just on an abstract calculation that the world after the revolution will be better than it is now, but on showing that an engagement in political activity makes sense in terms of one's own life. Furthermore, I would not go along with the mentality which postpones everything worthwhile until 'after the revolution'. The fact is that one has to live in the existing world, and one has to make one's own life tolerable and meaningful within the existing situation. This split in one's consciousness, between the personal and the political, is an undeniable fact of experience. The appropriate response is not to pretend that the personal can be somehow swallowed up in the political, but to find forms of activity which link the two in a meaningful way. Women's Liberation is a movement which has to some extent succeeded in doing this, though the tensions are apparent even there.

(b) My second reservation is this: given that moral motivation can be characterized as external and compulsive, it does not follow that the alternative is one of sheer immediacy. One writer who sometimes seems to suggest this is Wilhelm Reich. Consider for example the following passage, where he is talking about patients who have undergone his character-analytic treatment:

> If one represses one's own sexuality one develops all kinds of moralistic and aesthetic defences. When the patients regain contact with their own sexual needs, these neurotic differentiations disappear ... Previously, the insoluble conflict between instinctual need and moral inhibition forced the patient to act, in every respect, according to some law outside and above him ... When the patient, in the process of acquiring a different structure, realizes the indispensability of genital gratification, he loses this moralistic straitjacket and with it the damming up of his instinctual needs ... Moral regulation becomes unnecessary. The previously indispensable mechanism of self-control is no longer needed. This is so because the energy is being withdrawn from the anti-social impulses; there is little left which needs to be kept under control. The healthy individual has no compulsive morality because he has no impulses which call for moral inhibition. What anti-social impulses may be left are easily controlled, provided the basic genital needs are satisfied ... The organism is capable

of *self-regulation.*[9]

Much of this passage is clearly reminiscent of what we've said previously — 'the healthy individual has no compulsive morality', and
so on. But if this is taken to imply that the healthy individual acts
entirely on impulses, entirely in accordance with his most immediate
inclinations, this hardly seems either plausible or satisfactory. I do
not think it either possible or desirable to eliminate the notions of
internal conflict and struggle, and to reduce one's activity to this sort
of one-dimensional level. In order to talk realistically of acting spontaneously, without external and compulsive moral inhibitions, one
has to pose the idea of acting in response to a higher self which makes
demands upon one, but which one accepts just because one recognizes it to be one's true self. I regard the proper elucidation of these
ideas of a true and a false self as one of the most pressing tasks of
philosophy.

*   *   *

In view of all these points, there does remain a need for something
like moral philosophy — perhaps it should be called 'ethical philosophy', to indicate that within it the status of 'morality' is an open
question. The task of this ethical philosophy would be to articulate a
workable set of ethical concepts in terms of which one could direct
one's life and activity. In a sense, then, we are brought back to a
notion of conceptual analysis. However, it would be not just an
analytical but also a critical activity — it would not simply accept
unquestioningly those ethical concepts which are in current use, but
would involve judgements as to which of these are acceptable and
which ought to be jettisoned. Thus it would not purport to be a purely
neutral activity — it would be quite explicitly *for* some ethical ideas
and *against* others. And it would no longer be a purely a priori
activity — it would embody the recognition that ethical concepts
have to be assessed in the light of psychological and sociological facts,
perhaps very general but nevertheless empirical facts. Again, it would
be primarily concerned with what have been misleadingly called the
secondary evaluative concepts — not ones like 'good' and 'right' so
much as ones like 'self-realization', 'health', 'authenticity', 'conscience', 'the true self', as well as more frequently discussed ones like

9. *The Sexual Revolution*, pp. 6–7.

'freedom' and 'justice'.

There remains one other vital difference. What I would stress is the necessity to articulate a *system* of concepts. Concepts of the sort to which I have referred have to some extent been discussed by analytical philosophers. But they have been discussed piecemeal — and this fact largely accounts for the lack of critical thrust in such philosophy. Taken in isolation, a concept like 'conscience', for example, can be analysed and various different senses can be assigned to it. But the crucial question is: can it form one element in a coherent ethical perspective alongside the other concepts we want to employ? Can it cohabit with concepts like 'authenticity' or 'self-realization'? This demand that one's ethical concepts constitute a coherent system corresponds to the necessity that one's life as a whole should have an overall meaningfulness and coherence. Academic philosophers tend to sneer at the suggestion that philosophy has anything to do with questions about the meaning of life. I think it is time that they stopped sneering.

Reprinted from *RP* 6

'The Economist' on Allende's Chile:
A Case Study in Ideological Struggle

John Krige

In political, philosophical and ideological struggle, the words are also weapons and explosives or tranquillizers and poisons.

Louis Althusser[1]

This paper[2] explores some of the ways in which the ideological discourse associated with liberal democratic theory masks our cognitive access to social reality, and isolates for special consideration one form that that discourse takes (the so-called technocratic ideology). It also discusses the way that material conditions underpin an ideological system of thought. It arose as a direct response to the brutality recently unleashed in Chile by the military junta which ousted Allende's government, and the material which will be analysed relates to events which occurred in that narrow slice of Chilean history occupied by the Allende regime.

The election by bourgeois democratic procedures of a Marxist president, who formed a government composed predominantly of Socialist and Communists, posed acute problems for the proponents of liberal democratic theory once that government began to implement socialist policies. These problems were generated in part by the assumptions which that theory makes regarding the relationship between the political and the economic spheres of society. Crudely put, liberal democratic theory insists that parliamentary democracy guarantees that power lies in the hands of the 'people', who 'govern' through their elected representatives; but it also demands that state interference in the economy be consistent with the aims of capital,

1. L. Althusser, *Lenin and Philosophy and Other Essays*, NLB, London 1971, p. 21.
2. I am grateful to Roy Edgley and John Mepham for extensive criticism of an earlier draft of this paper.

thereby imposing a limit to popular control of the area most crucial to the overall well-being of the population. It justifies this exclusion on the grounds that the maintenance of the capitalist system is in the 'general interest' anyway, so that the limits posed to the domain of popular control precisely serve to block, rather than to encourage, the emergence of narrow, sectional interests. On this view, the health of the body politic as a whole demands that a wedge be driven between the economic and political realms of society. What then is to be its response when a democratically elected parliamentary party which supposedly represents the will of the people, strikes at the very basis of the capitalist system — private ownership of the means of production? At one extreme it can claim that the interests of capital must prevail, as the genuine 'general interest' — in which case the limits it places on the 'sovereignty of parliament' are clearly exposed. At the other extreme, it can cling to the latter, even if it involves accepting the dismantling of the capitalist economic base, and the concession that that base is not necessarily consistent with the general interest. Either way the theory stands to lose, being forced to pose questions about precisely who *does* govern and control the functioning of a liberal democratic system, and whose interests are served thereby. Rather than face up to these dilemmas, however, the ideological discourse we shall analyse below develops mechanisms for alleviating the intellectual tensions.

Most of the raw material for this discussion is provided by reports which appeared in the *Economist* between 1970 and 1973. Ever alert to the changing balance of forces in Chile, this newspaper always carefully considered the interaction between the economic and the political within the framework of liberal democratic theory. Aligning itself uncompromisingly with the interests of capital, which it takes to be the general interest, its reports provide a valuable insight into how ideological discourse can 'tranquillize and poison' a confused mind, providing rationalizations when pressures other than those of reason gain the upper hand.

In what follows, the *Economist*'s treatment of three specific events in Chile are discussed in some detail: the mid-term elections in 1973, the departure of certain key technicians in the copper industry soon after Allende's election late in 1970, and the attempts made by the International Telephone and Telegraph Company (ITT) to subvert that election. The first example thus involves reports on a political event, the second on an event in the economic sphere; while in the third, which was prompted by the publication of a series of ITT internal memoranda by Jack Anderson of the *Washington Post* in March 1972, the political and the economic clearly confront each other. There is, however, a more significant difference between this third case and the other two, for here it is the organizations and institutions of capitalist society, and not of Allende's Chile, that are under scrutiny. This demanded a completely different kind of analysis from the *Economist*. For whereas in the first two cases the desirability of the liberal wedge between the political and the economic could be taken for granted, and was used to discredit Allende's socialist programme, in the case of ITT the existence of the wedge had to be argued for — that is to say, it had to be shown precisely how the alleged gap between the political and the economic levels in the capitalist society was maintained. As we shall see, to do this the *Economist* structured its analysis of the ITT affair through a technocratic ideology itself resting upon a conception of reason from which liberalism draws its strength.

In each case considered preliminary steps are taken towards unravelling the conditions which make adherence to an ideological scheme of thought possible: in other words, an attempt is made to explain how such schemes can persist in the face of facts so obviously at variance with them. Although no attempt is made to develop a systematic theory of the tenacity of ideological discourse, in the analysis I have constantly kept in mind Engels's discussion in *The German Ideology*, and Mepham's[3] and Althusser's[4] treatment of ideology. To anyone familiar with them, the influence of a book and a recent paper by Edgley will be manifest.[5]

The Political Struggle

In several Latin American countries, a marked trend to the 'left' occurred in the 1960s. The precise form was determined by the prevailing balance of forces in each social formation; in Chile the politicization and mobilization of the masses during this period resulted in a majority vote at the polls for Salvador Allende in the Presidential election held on 4 September 1970. Allende was leader of the Popular Unity (PU) coalition of Socialist, Communist and Radical parties, which was committed to the expropriation of foreign and private capital and to an effective programme of land redistri-

3. J. Mepham, 'The Theory of Ideology in *Capital*', *Radical Philosophy* 2, Summer 1972, pp. 12–19.
4. Althusser, pp. 127–186.
5. R. Edgley, *Reason in Theory and Practice*, London 1969; 'Freedom of Speech and Academic Freedom', in John Mepham, ed., *Ideology, Social Science, Freedom of Speech*, Harvester Press, 1974.

bution within the overall framework of socialist policies.

Allende's majority was a narrow one, and reflected the disillusionment which both the 'left' and the 'right' felt with the reformist policies of his predecessor, Christian Democrat President Frei. Allende gained 36.3 per cent of the vote, just beating Alessandri of the right-wing Nationalist party (35 per cent) but well ahead of Tomic, the Christian Democrat (CD) candidate, who gained only 27.8 per cent. Furthermore, Allende's coalition of parties was in a minority in the 200-seat Congress, so that his ratification as President was not assured. To gain the necessary majority in Congress the support of about 25 CD members was required. Despite intense efforts to swing the CD behind Alessandri, or to provoke military intervention, both to be discussed in more detail below, Tomic carried the party with him behind Allende, who was nominated President by an overwhelming majority of Congress on 25 October, and inaugurated on 3 November 1970.

The precise details of what happened in Chile during the next two years are not relevant here. Let it suffice to say that in the edition of 24 February 1973, the *Economist* claimed that the state controlled 80 per cent of industrial production, and that three-quarters of the cultivated land had been brought into the reformed sector. As pointed out above, the penetration of the state into this level of the economic fabric of society puts acute pressure on the assumptions of liberal democratic ideology, and if they are not to be questioned, mechanisms for dissipating this pressure must be evolved. The ones we shall explore in this section represent attempts made by the *Economist* to save the theory by accepting the sovereignty of parliament, only to deny that the measures which Congress approved while Allende was in power could be in accord with the will of the people.

Of course the crudest way of doing this is to point out that the party in power does not command a majority of the votes cast in the election. Thus in the above article the *Economist*, discussing the forthcoming mid-term elections in Chile, emphasized that a 'majority vote for the opposition parties would show those who still remain to be convinced that Dr Allende's regime is not the people's government that it claims to be'. And again, after the election, in which the PU coalition gained 43.3 per cent of the vote — an increase of 7.1 per cent over the figure for the 1970 election — it remarked that 'Sunday's election in Chile underlined the basic fact about his (Allende's) government: a clear majority of Chileans are opposed to it' (10 March 1973, p. 18).

This kind of criticism, unless directed against the adequacy of the electoral process as such as a mechanism for expressing the will of the majority, simply cannot stand up to scrutiny. Heath formed a government in Britain in 1970 although the Conservatives won only 46 per cent of the popular vote; and even more obviously, Wilson was asked to form a government in 1974 although his party not only won a mere 37 per cent of the popular vote but actually polled fewer votes than the Conservatives did. Nixon's 'mandate' from the 'silent majority' to govern, given in 'a landslide victory of historic dimensions' in the US Presidential elections in 1972, although representing 61 per cent of the popular vote, in fact represented only 32 per cent of the eligible electorate, almost half of whom simply did not bother to go to the polls.

Perhaps it was the subterranean pressures exerted by considerations like these that led the *Economist* to present a different set of arguments to show that Chile's elected government was not a 'people's government'. Here is a quote in which one such argument is presented:

> The advances made by the marxist parties can give the misleading impression that they gained more ground than they actually did, since the real comparison is with the last parliamentary election in 1969, before Dr Allende came to power. By comparison with the latest nationwide elections — the municipal poll of 1971 — the Popular Unity vote actually dropped by about 6 per cent. Even so, the Communists gained one more deputy and two more senators and the Socialists jumped from 14 to 27 deputies and from three to five senators. The government coalition as a whole now has 63 deputies and 19 senators (against 57 and 16 before); the opposition alliance has 87 and 30 compared with 93 and 32 before. (10 March 1973, p. 38).

This is utter gibberish. Having claimed that the real comparison is with a parliamentary election held in 1969, the *Economist* goes on to compare the results of the mid-term Congressional elections in March 1973 with those of the municipal poll held in 1971! Be that as it may, these comparisons have the effect of making the reader move mentally from the idea that the results are misleading, to the idea that Allende's popularity has actually dropped, and on to the crucial accusation that 'even so' the PU coalition has increased its number of seats in both houses. This accusation is consistent with the campaign waged from the very beginning of PU rule to the effect that Allende's government would institute a one-party system. One of the *Economist*'s articles on 12 September 1970 (p. 40), written immediately after Allende's success at the polls, was headed 'But can they vote him out again?';

and in another (p. 19) it claimed that Allende's promise of elections in 1976 did not inspire confidence since he had hinted at legal and constitutional changes, and would probably sink his scruples and introduce a one-party state. After all, it pointed out in the pre-election article of 24 February 1973 (p. 14), Allende's 'Socialist party have been telling their followers not to worry about the results of what they claim to be merely a "routine democratic exercise" — one more move in a game whose rules they never really believed in.' It is hard to know what elections are if not a 'routine democratic exercise', or why a party which fears a reversal at the polls should not try to dispel its supporters' fears. And if Thorpe says that the present British electoral system is a 'travesty of democracy', is he not expressing disgust with the rules of the game as presently constituted? Is he not permitted to try to change those rules with the power at his disposal? However, the *Economist*'s purpose here is clearly not to provide a balanced analysis of the political manoeuvring of the Allende government — an analysis which would, for example, have exposed the fact that many aspects of its programme had the support of sections of the Christian Democrats who are lumped with the 'opposition alliance'. Remarks such as these rather serve to prepare the ground for justifying the removal by non-electoral procedures of the Allende government.

That this in fact is the case is apparent from the changing form of the allegations of electoral malpractice which were used to detract from Allende's success in the mid-term elections. On 10 March 1973 (p. 18) the *Economist* wrote that: 'There have been accusations of fraud, and several bags of stolen ballot papers have already been found. The process of cross-checking makes it unlikely that systematic fraud could have accounted for more than 1 per cent of the government's vote, but if it happened *on anything like that scale* the fact will *soon be known*.' (Emphases added). By 18 August (p. 34) suitable facts were ferreted out as the campaign to smash Allende's government gained momentum; it was reported that the Law Faculty at the Catholic University had found that 'up to 200,000 (about 5 per cent) pro-government votes may have been fictitious. Even if these charges prove exaggerated, the government has a case to answer, and the evidence tabled so far does not encourage optimism about its democratic intentions.' This concession to its previous claim that malpractices of the order of 1 per cent would be readily detected evaporated as the *Economist* desperately tried to justify the brutality of the military coup. In the article written partially to discredit the 'campaign of organized hostility in the West' against the junta (13 October 1973, p. 43), it claimed that the voting lists needed to be cleaned up since they had been 'padded out with false names before the legislative elections in March. Dr Allende's defenders rarely mention the fact that this may have accounted for as much as 5 per cent of the votes that his supporters received on that occasion.'

As a postcript to this sorry affair, here is a quote from an article in the *Times Higher Education Supplement* of 9 November 1973, written by a number of Chilean academics and professional men who fled the country. It suggests that the facts concerning allegations of fraud were indeed soon known, although the *Economist* did not report them, and they would have enabled it to maintain internal consistency in its own articles. The authors speak of a report 'prepared by the Faculty of Law in the Catholic University in May, just after the Allende regime had increased its percentage of votes from 36 per cent to 44 per cent. The lawyers concluded that the ballot had been falsified. This was proved two weeks later to have no basis. The principal author of this report, Jaime Guzmán, has now been asked by the junta to rewrite the Chilean Constitution.'

What these examples show is that, rather than admit that parliament is sovereign only as long as it does not threaten the interests of capital, the *Economist* attempted to discredit that institution's legitimacy during the latter part of the Allende regime by implying that it was not truly representative of the will of the Chilean people. To do this, it not only resorted to crude and mystifying arguments, but went as far as to redescribe events in ways which were inconsistent with its earlier descriptions. Its uncritical use of these devices to distort events in Chile can, in the first instance, be explained in terms of its bias. This bias springs from too close an identification with the interests of capital, and makes it possible for the *Economist* to resort spontaneously to these devices, which protect its liberal democratic ideology from assault. Although implicit much of the time, this bias emerges into full view as the need predominates to protect those interests against a 'campaign of organized hostility', sweeping away any vestiges of impartiality and swamping the pressures exerted by reason. Its presence makes the *Economist*'s (sincere) claim to be 'an independent newspaper' which helps one to 'find out what's going on' sound rather hollow; its progressive elimination, along with that of ideological thought, requires nothing less than the removal of the economic base on which class society is founded and the ongoing democratization of the ensuing politico-economic system.

The Copper Industry

Copper accounts for 80 per cent of Chile's foreign exchange. Until the 1960s the industry was almost wholly controlled by Anaconda and Kennecott, two United States based companies. Norman Girvan[6] has remarked that 'the Chilean mines proved highly profitable to both companies over the bulk of the life of these operations. From 1915 through 1968 (excluding Kennecott after 1964) the companies earned a total of $2,011 million in net profits and depreciation from Chile, of which $738 million only was used for reinvestment.' To assure some measure of Chilean control over these companies, Allende's predecessor, President Frei, initiated steps to nationalize the mines. The deals which he negotiated with Anaconda and Kennecott involved the immediate takeover by the State of a 51 per cent share of the industry, with compensation guaranteed, to be followed by the gradual, phased transfer of full ownership to the Chilean government.

Once the PU coalition came into power, a bill was presented to Congress which proposed the immediate expropriation of the companies concerned. This was passed unanimously on 11 July 1971. A long and bitter struggle[7] ensued between the companies and Allende's government over the issue of adequate compensation, which culminated when Kennecott gained a court order in Paris that 1½ million tons of copper bound for Le Havre should be seized. The dispute has apparently now been settled. On 15 December 1973 (p. 102) the *Economist* reported that the company had a good chance of getting $300m in compensation from the Chilean junta.

The specific issue I wish to use to expose the *Economist*'s ideological discourse concerns the way in which it reported on the loss of skilled and senior personnel in the copper industry during the first six months after Allende came to power. On 20 March 1971 (p. 87), discussing difficulties at Chile's second biggest copper mine El Teniente, it said that 'The smelting furnaces broke down after a *walk-out* by 300 mine managers opposed to President Allende's policies.' A report two months later made it clear that this was no ordinary walk-out. On 22 May 1971 (p. 48) the *Economist* pointed out that Chile's economic strategist, Vuskovic, 'will still have to work out how to replace the copper technicians who have been *streaming abroad*

6. N. Girvan, *Copper in Chile*, Institute of Social and Economic Research, University of the West Indies, 1972, p. 60.
7. This is discussed in more detail in my 'Copper: The Chilean Experience', of which I have a few copies available.

since the PU coalition took office last November.' On 19 June 1971 (p. 85) the *Economist* wrote of the '*withdrawal* of *American* technicians', thus beginning to shift the responsibility for their departure off their own shoulders. By the end of the year (25 December 1971, p. 78), it remarked that a new copper company in Iran, was to 'be manned partly by up to 200 Western copper men, many recruited among Anaconda's copper technicians *laid off* by the nationalized mines in Chile.' By early 1972, as the opposition's attempts to limit the scope of state intervention in the economy were constantly thwarted the *Economist* lost all semblance of impartiality. On 11 March 1972 (p. 25), in an article purporting to explain the alleged drop in production from the expropriated mines during the first nine months of 1971, it claimed that 'systematically government agents have worked *to expel* managers and technicians regarded as politically "unreliable". The result has been the loss of scores of trained men with many years of experience.' On 14 October 1972 (p. 50) it bemoaned the 'administrative chaos' which occurred when 'trained managers were *pushed out* in favour of "politically reliable" supervisors' during the first six months of 1971. Three months before the military coup the newspaper became quite hysterical: production in the mines, it said on 23 June 1973 (p. 88), 'has fallen steadily since the American management was *kicked out.*' (My emphases throughout this paragraph.)

Here then we have travelled all the way from a walk-out by management and other senior personnel to their being kicked out. If we are to explain this somersault, given the wedge which liberal democratic theory drives between the political and the economic, we must first ask what kinds of reasons, consistent with the framework of that ideology, highly skilled and qualified personnel could have for 'walking out' of a production process. One kind of reason which is excluded is that they were politically motivated; as a result the PU coalition's attempts to replace them with 'politically reliable' men is construed as being unreasonable. What is implied, however, is that their reasons for doing so were purely technical ones, which in turn suggests that the American managers 'walked out' because (unspecified) perturbations to the smooth and efficient running of the industry were proving intolerable. That granted, we see that what is merely insinuated in the early reports becomes progressively more explicit. The use of the term 'kicked out' by the *Economist* suggests that it was precisely state interference in the copper industry which led to losses in production, and which made unbearable the lives of key personnel committed to efficiency.

Obviously this entire edifice rests on the claim that production losses occurred in the Chilean copper industry which could be attributed to the expulsion of skilled and managerial personnel. There is strong evidence to suggest that this was not the case. The United Nations *Monthly Bulletin of Statistics* of April and November 1972 shows that the monthly average of copper ore and refined copper produced in Chile between January and September 1971 was roughly the same as the monthly average for the previous year. In fact there was a massive increase in September 1971 as mines abandoned by the American companies as unprofitable were reopened by the government. Admittedly production may have fallen short of estimates based on earlier plans for expansion, but that is an entirely different matter. There were undoubtedly difficulties in the Chilean copper industry while Allende was in power, and political activity in the mines was probably one factor which contributed to them. But it is only one aspect of a complex situation, in which, for example, the depressed copper prices which persisted until early 1973 and Kennecott's ability to block purchases of the metal also played an important part.

The shifting character of these accounts in the *Economist* reveals the tremendous flexibility of ideological discourse, as opposed to the rigour of scientific discourse. Precisely why a sequence showing this particular trend was used can be explained, again only in the first instance, by attributing it to bias. In the early days of the Allende regime, when the precise form of its intervention in the economy had not yet crystallized, pressures springing from the need to defend the interests of capital were counterbalanced by those arising from an acceptance of the legitimacy of parliamentary democratic procedures, which were relatively deeply embedded in Chilean history. But as the PU coalition extended its socialist policies over more and more sectors of the economy, the former pressures intensified, and the latter were deflected by 'showing' that Allende's coalition of parties was simply using parliament as a means to further its own sectional interest, and was not a 'people's government'. Its alleged willingness to disrupt the copper industry to serve its political objectives revealed that it was prepared to sacrifice the lifeblood of the nation on the altar of Marxist ideology. With nothing to check the passion to defend the interests of capital, the *Economist*'s bias burst to the surface. That it was always there is most clearly shown by the newspaper's willingness to discredit the political process, without ever asking whether the capitalist economic base is, in fact, consistent with the general interest.

The Case of ITT

In the earlier brief survey of the events surrounding the election of Allende on 4 September 1970, it was pointed out that the support of the Christian Democrats was essential if he was to be ratified as president on 25 October. This time delay provided Allende's opponents with an opportunity to thwart his bid for the presidency, and they pinned their hopes on the creation of suitable conditions. The so-called 'Alessandri formula' was promoted. This rested on one of two lines of attack. Either Frei was to persuade his followers to back Alessandri rather than Allende on 25 October, in which event the former would be elected president; or the military were to be persuaded to intervene, deposing Frei (who was apparently not averse to a military coup) and then calling for new elections. If Frei was successful, Alessandri would immediately resign the presidency, Frei would again be eligible for re-election for a further 6 years, and it was felt certain that in a straight Frei-Allende fight the former would easily win. If the military intervened, Alessandri would again not participate in the new elections; the problem here, though, was that Chile was almost unique among Latin American countries in its record of military non-intervention, and only a very serious threat to the country's stability could provoke them to act.

It was realized by Alessandri's camp that the alignment of the Christian Democrats behind the right, or military intervention, depended on the threat that economic chaos and possibly bloodshed would ensue if Allende were victorious. This was the atmosphere which they tried to create during the key fifty days between the elections and the nomination of Allende; and the Anderson papers provide a valuable insight into the co-operation which they received from several United States based organizations. The ones discussed below cover the period from 14 September to 18 November 1970.[8] It is necessary to analyse these in some detail before discussing the *Economist*'s part in them.

It is clear from the Anderson papers that Allende's enemies in the United States realized that outsiders like themselves would have to work through the existing Chilean political system to achieve their objectives. Furthermore, they realized that in 1970 any American action had to be taken in the light of growing anti-US sentiment in

8. *Subversion in Chile: A Case Study in US Corporate Intrigue in the Third World*, Spokesman Books, Nottingham 1972. Figures in brackets in the text refer to page numbers in this selection from the Anderson papers.

Chile. If their involvement was too blatant, the Chilean people would swing decisively against the right, and unite solidly behind Allende on an anti-imperialist platform. Then the deep split in the electorate would temporarily recede into the background, and the spaces in which the opposition could move to overthrow Allende would contract accordingly. This probably explains why Berrellez, an ITT employee based in Buenos Aires, emphasized that 'every care should be exercised to insure that we are not — repeat not — identified openly with any anti-Allende move' (p. 43). He also spelt out the conditions which would have to be met if the 'Alessandri formula' was to work: 'Chances of thwarting Allende's assumption of power now are pegged mainly to an economic collapse which is being encouraged by some sectors in the business and political community and by President Frei himself . . . Undercover efforts are being made to bring about the bankruptcy of one or two major savings and loan associations. This is expected to trigger a run on the banks and the closure of some factories resulting in more unemployment' (p. 42). It was hoped that the economic chaos would convince the Christian Democrats that the business community had no faith in Allende's policies, so that they would side with Alessandri, or that 'massive unemployment and unrest might produce enough violence to force the military to move' (p. 43). Yet they were not optimistic about the latter. Berrellez and a colleague, Hendrix, reported: 'The Marxists will not be provoked. "You can spit in their face in the street," Matte (Alessandri's brother-in-law) said, "and they'll say thank you." This means that the far left is aware of and taking every precaution to neutralize provocation' (p. 32).

Let us now look separately at the roles played by the State Department, the CIA and ITT in this deliberate attempt to provoke unemployment and violence in the name of defending freedom and democracy.

The State Department

The State Department's agent in Chile was Korry, the US Ambassador in Santiago. His 'gutsy final effort to block Allende, so unusual in our diplomats' (p. 105) was praised by Berrellez. Yet it is clear that he acted more or less independently of State for much of the time, taking a far harder line than Assistant Secretary Meyer or his deputy Crimmons would have liked. Long before receiving any official authorization, Korry had been putting pressure on Frei to unite the party behind him and against Allende. Admittedly, about 10 days after the September election 'Korry finally received a message from State Department giving him the green light to move in the name of President Nixon. The message gave him maximum authority to do all possible — short of a Dominican Republic-type action — to keep Allende from taking power' (p. 29). Nevertheless, it was only with difficulty that Korry persuaded Washington to reduce by as much as possible the $30m of aid already in the pipeline for Chile, and to block existing letters of credit. ITT official Neal reported: 'This "cut-off" will be denied by State, who will say, as it has in the past, "there has been no shut down of aid to Chile; the programme is under review" ' (p. 57).

The CIA

The political and economic initiatives taken by the CIA were of a rather different kind. On 9 October Merriam, the ITT president in Washington, informed McCone, a former CIA director, and then an ITT Board member, that the CIA had continued to make approaches 'to select members of the Armed Forces in an attempt to have them lead some sort of uprising — no success to date' (p. 52). A week later Hendrix reported that, at about that time, Washington had in fact discouraged Roberto Viaux, a brigadier-general in the Chilean army, from staging a coup. It was felt that he did not have sufficient support for such a move, and that if it failed it would be counter-productive. 'As part of the persuasion to delay,' Hendrix added, 'Viaux was given oral assurances that he would receive material assistance and support from the US and others for a later manoeuvre' (p. 60).

On the economic front CIA Director Broe approached ITT Vice-President Gerrity late in September, 'looking for additional help aimed at producing economic collapse' (p. 40). He presented a five-point plan to Gerrity involving the application of pressure by both financial insitutions like banks, savings and loan companies, and businesses like ITT. It was suggested that the latter 'should drag their feet in sending money, in making deliveries, in shipping spare parts, etc.,' and 'should withdraw all technical help and should not promise any technical assistance in the future. Companies in a position to do so should close their doors' (p. 40).

ITT

Probably the most sensational aspect of ITT's involvement in Chile was its offer to Broe of the CIA of a million dollars for use in any plan to defeat Allende. Less frequently spoken of is the offer made by Company President Geneen to the State Department's Latin American adviser to Kissinger to 'assist financially in sums up to seven figures' to protect its Chilean interests. As Neal pointed out on this occasion: 'All along we have feared the Allende victory and have been trying unsuccessfully to get other American companies aroused over the fate of their investments, and join us in pre-election efforts' (p. 28).

It is clear that ITT's senior personnel regarded intervention of this kind to be a logical extension of US policy in Chile as it had developed in the 1960s. Neal, complaining bitterly about the State Department's hesitancy in dealing with the new Chilean situation, analysed figures for US economic assistance to the country during this period and concluded that 'the US realized the danger of Marxism in Chile; so fought it with grants and loans but did not have the extra forethought to follow its intuition by taking a more active part during the pre-election period to assure the defeat of Allende. Why should the US try to be so pious and sanctimonious in September and October 1970,' he added, 'when over the past few years it has been pouring the tax-payers' money into Chile, admittedly to defeat Marxism' (p. 47). Hendrix echoed these judgements: 'The United States failed even to head off in 1970 that which it so successfully and energetically aided Chileans to avoid in 1964 — the emergence of a Marxist president. Meyer and Crimmons jointly led the effort to make certain that the US this time did nothing with respect to the Chilean election' (p. 91). Even though these analyses crudely ignore the changes which had taken place in Chile during Frei's presidency, changes which precisely made possible the election of Allende, they are particularly revealing about the aims of the United States AID programme, and the actions which ITT personnel took to be 'normal' practice.

The pre-election difficulties which ITT had had to persuade other US business interests to support their attempt to block Allende probably accounts for Gerrity's lack of enthusiasm for Broe's plan for economic subversion discussed above. He noted that there was a growing economic crisis anyway, and also established that Hobbing, another CIA agent, had been told by an Alessandri representative to 'keep cool, don't rock the boat, we are making progress . . . This is in direct contrast to what Broe recommended' (p. 45). Nevertheless, apparently to appease Broe, ITT 'made repeated calls to firms such as GM, Ford and banks in California and New York' (p. 51), but without success. As Merriam reported to McCone: 'Practically no progress had been made in trying to get American business to co-operate in some way so as to bring on economic chaos' (p. 52). GM and Ford claimed that they had too much inventory on hand in Chile, and, despite assurances to the contrary, the Bank of America did not close its doors in Santiago.

These activities by ITT on the home front were complemented by direct action in Chile and elsewhere, much of which reflected its importance as a communications company. Hendrix and Berrellez identified Frei and the Mercurio newspapers that were outspoken in their condemnation of Allende — and under severe pressure from Allende aides immediately after the election in September — as two crucial supporters in the campaign to stop Allende taking power in November. Korry applied pressure to Frei, telling him 'to put his pants on' (p. 31) and ITT offered financial help to the Alessandri group, as well as pumping advertising into Mercurio. Hendrix and Berrellez also suggested that 'we help with getting some propagandists working again on radio and television', that the Washington office of the United States Information Service (USIS) be approached and asked to distribute Mercurio editorials around Latin America and in Europe, and that ITT's contacts in the key European press be urged to 'get the story of what disaster would fall on Chile if Allende & Co. win this country' (p. 34). They also proposed that the company assist financially to relocate in Argentina, for a month to six weeks, the families of certain central figures involved in the fight against Allende.

By the middle of October it was clear to ITT management that Frei could not carry the Christian Democrats with him, and that a military coup was most unlikely. Assuming that Allende would be inaugurated in November, they drew up a detailed set of recommendations pertaining to US action on Chile. These were to be put to the State Department and to Kissinger in the White House, and demanded the diplomatic and economic isolation of Chile if adequate compensation was not paid for expropriated properties. It was also recommended that US representatives on international banks be told to block the extension of credit to the Allende regime (which did in fact happen). Furthermore, in an attempt to discourage 'leftist nationalism', in other countries in Latin America, threats to sever their lines of credit were also proposed. At this time an appropriation of $2.9 billion to the US-government sponsored Inter-American Development Bank was awaiting final ratification by the Senate. Merriam reported that 'we are planning . . . to approach Senators Scott and Mansfield to see if they will just "forget" to take up the bill. We could prepare statements from them which would get a message to the other

Latin American countries that Chile's action is affecting them too, albeit indirectly' (p. 72).

The overall picture which emerges from the Anderson papers is that three United States based organizations applied pressure at those points at which each thought it could be most effective in bringing about economic chaos, unemployment, violence and bloodshed in Chile. With the possible exception of the State Department, which was committed to a 'low-profile' policy in Latin America, neither ITT, the CIA nor Korry had any compunction about generating the conditions in which a military coup would be possible, and bloodshed inevitable, in order to thwart Allende's bid for the presidency. As far as they were concerned, it was essential to stop him before it was too late, for if he succeeded, 'Whatever the trappings, there is unlikely ever to be another truly free election in Chile' (p. 84) — truly free, that is, for the US 'successfully and energetically' to intervene to stop the emergence of a Marxist president. 'The repression of the human spirit which the doctrinaire Marxist always imposes' was to be countered by setting in train a series of events in the hope of precipitating violence, which is somehow supposed to expand and enrich the 'human spirit'. Writing to Kissinger, ITT Vice-President Merriam said: 'Our company knows the peoples of the Americas deserve a better way of life, and we believe we have a substantial interest in diminishing their problems. The countries themselves are unable to furnish necessary development funds, the US taxpayers cannot, and US private enterprise can provide only that part which a proper climate affords' (p. 95). And, of course, as far as he was concerned, if the 'proper climate' did not prevail, it was up to organizations in the United States to create it, and then to maintain it at all costs by all possible means. 'The peoples of the Americas' deserved nothing less.

The Limits Set by Technocratic Ideology

It is clear that activities like those we have just discussed, in which a business concern unambiguously aligned itself with one side rather than another in a political conflict, and attempted to subvert the democratic political process to serve its own interests, can present problems to the adherent of liberal democratic ideology. It does not necessarily produce such problems because, for example, in this case the involvement occurred in a so-called 'under-developed country', characterized by a low GNP and per capita income, a lack of health and educational facilities, and a high incidence of poverty and misery.

To solve these problems, a massive injection of foreign capital is allegedly required, so that the subversion of political moves which threaten the flow of 'development funds' is readily justified on the grounds that the unimpeded operation of capital is in the 'general interest'. As Merriam put it above, 'the peoples of the Americas deserve a better way of life'. And it is considerations like these which serve to deflect any pressures generated by a concern for the sovereignty of parliament, or for those people who may have been harmed if attempts to provoke violence and bloodshed had succeeded.

However, in the particular case of ITT involvement in Chile, wider issues were at stake which effectively blocked this loophole in the liberal scheme and questioned its most basic assumptions. For the Anderson papers provoked hearings by the US Senate Foreign Relations Committee on the influence which multinational firms had on the course of political events in the countries in which they operated; as the *Economist* put it (1 April 1972, p. 42): 'It is often said, and is being said of ITT, that the huge assets and omnipresence of the multi-national companies give them virtually the status and the power of governments.' Clearly if this allegation was shown to be true, the postulated symbiotic relationship between the political and economic spheres, with power residing in the former, would be placed under severe strain.

In an attempt to come to terms with this threat the *Economist*, in the article referred to above, analysed the Anderson papers within the framework of a technocratic ideology. Its treatment provides a valuable insight into how this ideology, which shares with liberal ideology certain general postulates about the domain of reason and the relationship between reason and action, limits one's thought about the problem under consideration.

Central to the technocratic conception of reason is that the term 'rational' be reserved for the means an agent uses to achieve certain ends; the question of the rationality of the ends themselves does not arise. These are non-rational; they serve to activate one's deliberation about means, which pre-suppose the intention on the part of the agent to achieve the end, but cannot themselves be the object of deliberation. Of course some ends (e.g. stopping Allende from taking power) are intermediate, means to a further end (i.e. staving off expropriation), and as such their rationality can be debated. But again they are only judged, not as ends, but as means to achieve that further end, where the most appropriate means is that which achieves the end with the greatest efficiency. 'Know-how' enables one to make this decision;

once equipped with it, the agent is in a position to select from the means at his disposal that which is most likely to assure the successful attainment of his objectives with the least possible input of the available resources. As such, it helps him to avoid behaving irrationally, and thereby to control his own destiny. Since it enables those who have acquired it to do things they would not otherwise be able to do, 'know-how' is the source of the power agents have to achieve the goals they set themselves. It is also the prerogative of experts in specialized disciplines, who have had the requisite training and are equipped with the skills necessary to decide on the most rational course of action in a particular situation.

This pattern of relationships permeates the *Economist*'s discussion of the Anderson Papers. It is realized that ITT could only achieve an economic objective (staving off appropriation) by achieving the intermediate political objective (stopping Allende from taking power). And the crucial question of whether or not the company had the 'status or the power' of a government is construed as the question of whether a business concern staffed by economic experts had personnel with adequate political know-how to achieve this political goal. The criterion for the rationality of the measures which ITT took to thwart Allende's bid for the presidency is the views of the political experts: Korry in Santiago, and the State Department in Washington. Measures which deviated from those deemed appropriate by these experts were judged to be irrational; that ITT entertained them at all indicates its lack of know-how, and suggests its corresponding inability to influence the course of Chilean political affairs.

Two examples from the report in question will show how the choice of certain words at key points in the description alludes to the technocratic ideology which structures it. The first concerns the offer of financial assistance made by ITT President Geneen to Kissinger's White House office, which is described in the following terms: 'Perhaps the weirdest fact to emerge from the ITT Chile papers is that one of the company's men, in a telephone conversation with a Latin-American specialist in the White House, actually offered to help with the cost of stopping Dr Allende "in sums of up to seven figures". Naturally the offer was not taken up, but the papers show no echo of any clear sharp Administration voice telling ITT that this is not the way government is conducted.'

The incredulity which this account expresses is without foundation. There was nothing 'weird' about the fact that ITT 'actually' offered money to the State Department. As I pointed out above, the Anderson papers themselves show that the US played an active role in promoting Frei's successful bid for the presidency in 1964, and continued to funnel money into Chile to block the emergence of a Marxist president thereafter, so ITT had good reason to think that it would do so again. An offer to provide $1m to protect interests in Chile which it valued at over $150m was quite reasonable, particularly since a precedent had already been set. This explains why ITT was not rebuked for being prepared to assist financially; on the contrary, Meyer of the State Department 'said he could understand Mr Geneen's concern and appreciated his offer to assist' (p. 28). Whether or not Meyer subsequently took up the offer is not clear from the papers; what is clear is that Broe of the CIA told ITT Vice-President Gerrity that 'money was no problem' (p. 40). There was thus nothing 'natural' about the fact that the offer were not taken up; it was turned down (and, as we saw, subsequently used by ITT for other purposes), because sufficient funds had already been made available, at least to the CIA.

Be that as it may, the *Economist*'s report has created the impression that ITT personnel came up with a 'weird' and 'unnatural' scheme to block Allende's bid for power. The 'natural' way of conducting government is that embodied in the methods favoured by Latin American experts in the State Department and the White House, who have the requisite know-how to deal with political affairs.

What is only implied in this description of the more sensational aspect of ITT activities is quite explicit in the reports account of the corporation's role in implementing the Alessandri formula to thwart Allende's bid for the presidency. It will be remembered that this required the creation of a climate of economic uncertainty and instability that would be sufficiently unsettling to swing the allegiance of the Christian Democrats away from Allende, or, failing that, to provoke military intervention. It is referred to on two separate, unrelated occasions in the article: 'A scheme was promoted which would have produced new elections, but nothing came of it. This was the outcome that Mr Korry predicted'; and 'Other memoranda in the file suggest that the ITT men buoyed up their fading hopes with thoughts of military intervention and of creating something they called "economic chaos" (a relative term in Chile) which might mysteriously cause Dr Allende to be excluded, or to fall, from power. They do not contain any evidence that the ambassador or the State Department entertained either of these ideas.'

Both of these quotations suggest that the Alessandri formula was something dreamed up by ITT employees, and both effectively discredit the political acumen of those personnel, suggesting that they lacked the know-how to pursue their objectives successfully and efficiently. It was presumably because of what the *Economist* called their 'unquenchable spirit' that they persisted with their ill-conceived plans, ignoring the rational advice of their political mentors. After all, Korry had 'predicted' that their scheme would fail; neither he nor the State Department 'entertained' any other possibility. (Although it is clear from the Anderson papers that it is the question of the formula's success that is at issue here, the second quote above is in fact so ambiguous that it might even be taken to mean that the proposed measures were so bizarre that they never even occurred to the political experts.) In the light of this it comes as no surprise to find that the report concludes that ITT, and, if it is at all representative, other multinational firms do not have 'the appropriate men or the corresponding knowledge' to achieve political ends.

The use of the word 'mysteriously' in the second quotation above is particularly significant. It is not merely that it leads the reader to think that ITT's proposals for stopping Allende were hopelessly inappropriate. It is rather that there was nothing 'mysterious' at all about how economic chaos would do so; in fact, one of the ways in which ITT men, and others, thought that this would happen is stated in the quotation itself, i.e. by creating a climate which would provoke the military to intervene. A careful reading of the Anderson papers leaves one in no doubt about this, since Barrellez unambiguously ties the two together: 'Chances of thwarting Allende's assumption of power now are pegged mainly to an economic collapse . . . massive unemployment and unrest might produce enough violence to force the military to move' (pp. 42–3).

This is a striking example of how ideological discourse structures an analysis, radically distorting the material at its disposal. In this instance the confusion arises in the following way. If the military had intervened, it would thereby have denied Allende the presidency. These are not two events, but one and the same event under two different descriptions. Economic chaos was the means thought most likely to achieve this single objective. Yet in the *Economist*'s report it is seen as a rival to military intervention; the experts are said not to have entertained '*either of* these ideas', which are constructed as alternative means to the same end.

It may seem remarkable that the central link in the chain of events leading from economic collapse through unemployment and unrest to military intervention could thus disappear from view. Its absence indicated pressures arising from another source: the liberal democratic wedge between the political and the economic, the influence of which explains how it was possible for the report to regard military intervention and the inducement of economic chaos as separate, rival means to thwart Allende. Their isolation from one another governs the statement that ITT 'thought of military intervention and *of creating*' economic chaos, which identifies the economic sphere as the domain of activity of a business concern. This wedge is consolidated by the remark in the report that ITT thought that an economic collapse 'might *mysteriously*' block Allende — which implies both that its personnel's specialized skills do not extend beyond business matters, and that there is an unbridgeable gap between the political and the economic. In this respect the use of the term 'mysteriously' serves the same purpose as that served by the term 'naturally' in the first example discussed above; there it was said that White House officials 'naturally' did not accept ITT's offer of financial assistance for a programme to stop Allende, because this is 'not the way government is conducted'. By thus dovetailing liberal democratic and technocratic ideologies, the report in question so structures its argument that the conclusion — that multinational companies do not have significant political know-how and therefore power — is already contained in the premises from which it is drawn.

As another instance of this dovetailing one can cite the exclusion of any discussion of the contacts between ITT and the CIA from the report in the *Economist* which we are analysing here. This is presumably because, as a clandestine intelligence organization, the CIA is supposedly not a political organ, and the links established with it are accordingly deemed irrelevant to an evaluation of ITT's ability to control political affairs. The inverse of this position is that adopted by many radical critics of American involvement in the Third World: namely, an exaggerated emphasis on the role of the CIA as an instrument of subversion, to the exclusion of an appraisal of the political leverage contained potentially in 'foreign aid' programmes, for example, which are administered by more 'respectable' organizations. By assuming that injections of foreign capital are politically neutral, so that the only external threat to the sovereignty of the government in a 'less developed' country comes from an underground organization like the CIA, these 'radical' critics are adopting a position consistent with the assumptions of liberal democratic ideology. They are not rejecting that mode of discourse; they are operating within its framework and contributing to its tenacity.

Another significant absence from the *Economist*'s report is an evaluation of ITT activities from a moral point of view. The additional misery which the already oppressed would have faced if the attempts to create unemployment had succeeded in sparking off unrest, violence and bloodshed is nowhere commented upon. This is a consequence of the alleged value-free and morally neutral character of technological statements which, identifying rationality with efficiency, relegate considerations about the harm done to others in achieving pursued ends to the 'irrational' and 'subjective' — domains which lie beyond the scope of cold, calculating technical reason. That granted, the *Economist*'s conclusion that 'in short, nothing terrible was done' cannot be countered with the argument that ITT's deliberate attempt to create an explosive and unstable situation in Chile was 'something terrible', and potentially harmful to the oppressed masses in that country. For the *Economist*'s position is clearly not a moral judgement, but one that reflects the tendency to reserve the notion of 'doing something' for actions which achieve some objective, as if trying to achieve a goal is not also something that an agent can be said to do. This, of course, is a consequence of looking at actions only from the point of view of their efficiency or success in attaining a pursued end; if they fail to achieve it, not only has the agent done 'nothing terrible', it is sometimes even said that he has done nothing at all.

The systematic exclusion of moral considerations by the discourse that constitutes technocratic ideology and in behaviour which is guided by it, is symptomatic of its manipulative character. Its adherents assimilate the social to the natural universe, treating human beings and the groups and classes which they form as objects only to be reasoned about, not as members of a rational species which can also be reasoned with. Control over them as individuals or groups is exercised by giving them reasons for pursuit of the goal that the technocrat chooses for them. From this vantage-point 'deviant' behaviour either is irrational or reveals that the agents have chosen to pursue a different objective which conflicts with the one preferred. These alternatives exact different responses from him. He can either argue that the agents in question are incapable of behaving rationally, and commit them to a mental institution; or he can escalate the pressures on the agents until the reasons they have for pursuing the set goal outweigh the reasons they have for pursuing a 'dysfunctional' objective of their own choosing. The rational thing for them to do will then be to bow to the will of the technocrat and to pursue the goal which he has set for them. In either case the influence of technocratic ideology and the institutions which embody it gradually permeate society, and existing patterns of dominance are reproduced on an ever-expanding scale.

If this seems unduly exaggerated and pessimistic, it is only because the account given here is one-sided. It is important to emphasize that the escalation referred to above arises in response to pressures within the body of society itself, and that the limits to which it can be pushed, and the success which it achieves, will themselves be subject to the prevailing balance of forces. On the other hand, it would be a mistake to think that social theories do not insinuate themselves into the very body of society, structuring the social system to fit their patterns of commitments. Consider, for example, how readily a theorist like Downs slips from a passive to a manipulative posture in his discussion of the meaning of economic rationality, which relies heavily on the technocratic conception of reason:

> Economic analysis thus consists of two major steps: discovery of the ends a decision-maker is pursuing, and analysis of which means of attaining them are most reasonable, i.e., require the least input of scarce resources. In carrying out the first step, theorists have generally tried to reduce the ends of each economic agent to a single goal, so that one most efficient way to attain it can be found. If multiple goals are allowed, means appropriate to one may block attainment of another; hence no unique course can be charted for a rational decision-maker to follow. To avoid this impasse, theorists posit that firms maximize profits and consumers maximize utility . . . Even though we cannot decide whether a decision-maker's ends are rational, we must know what they are before we can decide what behaviour is rational for him.[9]

On this view an economically rational society is one in which different groups of economic agents pursue a single goal uncompromisingly — the maximization of profits by the producer and the maximization of utility by the consumer. To ensure that limited resources are not used inefficiently, 'we' must not 'allow' other goals to 'block' the attainment of these objectives. If society can be structured in such a way that each economic agent is given reasons sufficiently strong to outweigh all those which might distract him from their pursuit, an 'impasse' can be 'avoided' and a 'unique course can be charted' by 'us' which, if followed, will guarantee that no irrational waste of resources occurs. Technical reason notwithstanding, we are here clearly confronted not with a value-neutral theory, but with one committed to the reproduction on an expanding and all-pervasive scale of the capitalist mode of production, the success of which demands engineered conformity.

9. A. Downs, *An Economic Theory of Democracy*, New York 1957, pp. 4–5, 6.

The 'we' of whom Downs speaks in the above quotation refers of course to the experts, the faceless theorists who have 'tried to reduce the ends of each economic agent to a single goal'. This elevation of the technocrat to the status of guardian of rationality is an integral feature of a mode of ideological discourse which assimilates the social to the natural world, with the manipulative consequences we have been examining. It arises because the relationship between expert and layman in the natural sciences is one which, by definition, excludes the socialization of most, if not all the former's knowledge beyond the confines of the scientific community of which he or she is a member. If an astronomer predicts that a comet will appear over Britain in January 1974, the fact that he or she, as an expert, thinks that this is so, is good reason that a layman can have for thinking that the comet will appear. As a layman, the reasons which the astronomer has for thinking this do not enter into the formation of his beliefs; those reasons are, rather, subject to criticism from fellow-members in the community of astronomers, who are sufficiently familiar with the theory on which the prediction was based. The natural scientist reasons about nature with scientific colleagues, and his or her conclusions constitute the rational grounds for many of the layman's beliefs about the natural world.

If the social world is reduced to the natural one, considerations like these come into play structuring the way in which a theorist like Downs thinks about his object of study. If one is to escape from the constraints imposed by a technocratic ideology, it is essential that one concede that, in respect of human societies, the object of study comprises groups of rational interacting human beings, who can be both reasoned about and reasoned with. This implies that the community of social scientists can, potentially at least, be expanded to embrace the members of society themselves; and that with this socialization and democratization of knowledge the distinction between layman and expert is progressively eroded. The opinion of the 'expert' then loses its sacrosanct character and no longer serves in itself as a rationally adequate ground for the layman's beliefs about society.

Considerations like these provide us with some idea of the sense in which an ideology may be said to 'reflect' a material base. For it is now clear that the technocratic mode of thought derives its plausibility from the fact that it is grounded in a social system which is characterized by a rigid division of labour, and by a corresponding fragmentation, specialization and hierarchization of knowledge, which is taken to be of the 'natural order' of things. As a consequence of these divisions, the utterances of those who wield power are set up as if they were not to be questioned by the masses, who are always confronted by jargon whenever they attempt to penetrate beyond the claims of those in authority. As such, the ideology not only 'reflects' a social system, it also legitimates and reinforces it, precisely by posing questions which presuppose its basic divisions rather than undermining them. What is more, a technocratic ideology serves as a basis for the reproduction and intensification of the divisions from which it springs, to the extent that it is embodied in institutions which so structure society that conflicts between 'multiple goals' are not 'allowed'.

Explanations of this kind do not exclude explanations for the tenacity of ideological discourse which appeal to bias. As was suggested in the earlier part of this paper, the occurrence of bias has itself to be explained in terms of a particular kind of social structure, and we have here tried to unravel some of the characteristics of that structure. What has emerged is that the cleavages which underpin liberal democratic ideology and the related technocratic ideology can be woven into the very framework of a social formation, shackling in the first instance the minds of the intellectuals who reflect upon it. Nothing short of a revolution in consciousness is required of them if they are to free themselves from the limits it imposes.

Reprinted from *RP*8

4. Philosophy and Gender

Feminism: History and Morality

Jean Grimshaw

Janet Radcliffe Richards's book *The Sceptical Feminist*[1] is an attempt to extricate feminism from ideological commitments which, in her view, are not essential to it and serve merely to confuse feminists themselves, and to alienate potential supporters. The image of the feminist movement, she says, is 'unattractive': it is understandable why people tend to dislike feminists so much, since some of them have gone out of their way to make themselves unattractive; what is more, they have tended to engage in polemics and dogma at the expense of careful reasoning. Instead they should learn to argue clearly and rationally with their opponents, separating out what is essential to feminism from what is inessential.

There can of course be no question that feminism, like any other movement, has bred its fair share of bad arguments, poor reasoning, and dogmatic and ill-considered pronouncements; and I have no wish to quarrel with the value of arguing soundly, although in some circumstances argument may be pointless and not the best strategy. Demonstrating incoherence in the arguments of those who oppose feminism, for example, can be a very useful thing to do, as opposed to simply accusing opponents of bias, or ill-will or indoctrination. (One reason for this is that the stereotype of female irrationality is still very powerful, and anything that will help to counteract it is worth pursuing.)

We need, however, to consider what conception of 'argument' we are operating with. If we look at many issues with which feminists are concerned, we find that they are often presented as a conflict about 'values' or 'morality'; and that these 'values' themselves tend to be presented as if they had no history and bore no relationship to social processes or structures. Thus, the debate about abortion is often

1. *The Sceptical Feminist*, Routledge and Kegan Paul, London 1980.

presented as if it simply involved philosophical or moral arguments about the 'right to life', or whether a foetus should be regarded as a person. This may sometimes serve to conceal the fact that other issues are involved in the debate, which have much more to do with questions of power and domination and a particular ideology of the family.

In her book, Radcliffe Richards aims to present feminism as just such a set of arguments about 'values', which can be divorced from questions about 'facts'. The consequence is that, despite the value of many of the specific arguments that she offers, her 'feminism' is ultimately an enfeebled and unviable thing, which capitulates at crucial points to some of the very things feminists should be fighting against.

The Essentials of Feminism

She argues that the essence of feminism should be seen as simply the belief that women suffer systematic social injustice because of their sex. She recognizes that this definition would be regarded as inadequate by many feminists themselves, and that it does not tally with many popular conceptions of what feminists do and believe in: 'Feminists are, at the very least, supposed to have committed themselves to such things as participation in consciousness-raising groups and non-hierarchical organization, to the forswearing of femininity of appearance and demeanour, and to belief in the oppressiveness of families, the inherent equality of the sexes (or the superiority of the female) and the enslavement of women as the root of all oppression' (p. 2).

Radcliffe Richards, on the other hand, wants to define feminism as a movement concerned with the elimination of sex-based injustice; it therefore turns out to be a movement which is neither specifically of women, nor for women, even though in practice most sex-based injustice is suffered by women.

Why does she want to redefine feminism in this way? There are, I think, two reasons. The first is expressed as follows: 'The conflation of the idea of feminism as a particular ideology with that of feminism as a concern with women's problems means that people who do not like what they see of the ideology (perhaps because they are keen on family life, or can't imagine a world without hierarchies, or just don't like unfeminine women) may *also* tend to brush aside, explain away, sneer at, or simply ignore all suggestions that women are seriously badly treated. Resistance to the feminist movement easily turns into a resistance to seeing that women have any problems at all' (p. 3). So the first reason is really a matter of strategy: feminism is losing supporters by its doctrinaire insistence on things other than a very general belief that women are treated badly by society.

The second reason is not just a matter of strategy, and it is brought out in statements such as the following: 'Feminism has come to be associated with particular theories about what kind of thing is wrong, and whose fault it is; how it came about and what should be done to put matters right' (p. 2).

This Radcliffe Richards believes to be wrong, and not just as a matter of feminist strategy, but as a matter of logic. Throughout the book she urges that it is possible to be a feminist — to have a general concern about the position of women and to believe that they are unjustly treated — without this necessarily implying any particular beliefs about why women are unjustly treated, or any particular political views. 'It is . . . very important,' she writes, 'to separate the question of whether anything is wrong with the situation of women from questions about whether there is any justification for particular ideas of ways to put matters right. Most people, including most feminists, take what conspicuous feminists say about political policy and social theory as integral to the whole cause. However, the question of whether anything is wrong is clearly separable from that of what to do about it' (p. 269). Similarly: 'The most important thing is that our ideals should not commit us to any details about the kinds of social arrangements which will be found in the ideal society. They should involve only general principles which provide criteria for deciding when one society is better than another; principles like, for example, "The ideal society is one where there is the maximum total happiness" ' (p. 33).

She does not merely hold that feminism involves no specific political commitments, or commitments to particular forms of social change. She also believes that it is compatible with any (or no) beliefs about the 'natures' of men and women, and with any (or no) beliefs about the particular causes of women's oppression. Thus she says: 'We need to know about the nature of the world we are dealing with, to as great an extent as possible, in order to proceed with our programme of change with any hope of success. Nevertheless the knowledge we have of the natures of things in no way dictates what use we should make of the raw material' (p. 64).

Feminism, she argues, does not depend on 'matters of fact'. 'Of course, if feminism really did depend on beliefs about matters of fact, and those turned out to be mistaken, we should simply have to accept that feminism should be abandoned. We must certainly take that attitude to any specific feminist demand whose justification depends on the truth of particular propositions' (p. 42).

Fortunately, however, she thinks that feminism is a question of values and of moral opinions about justice, and that it will therefore not fall hostage to facts, not even if the facts turn out to be not what we had hoped. Thus, when she is discussing the issue of (supposed) male dominance, she says: 'Feminism, as it happens, by no means stands or falls according to whether women are inferior to men, or equal to them, or superior to them, in any or all respects' (p. 43). Suppose, she suggests, that it *were* the case that men were in some sense naturally dominant. 'Even if men are naturally inclined to dominate, it does not follow that they ought to be allowed to run everything. Their being naturally dominant might be an excellent reason for imposing special restrictions to keep their nature under control . . . one of the functions of society is to protect its weaker members' (p. 44).

Now this begs the issue of what is meant here by 'natural', since in most theories of 'natural' male dominance (e.g. that put forward by Steven Goldberg in *The Inevitability of Patriarchy*, or by Tiger and Shepher in *Women in the Kibbutz*), it is held that men will *inevitably* end up dominant, since their dominance is firmly rooted in their biology, and the modifying effects of culture can at most be ephemeral. More generally though, the sort of separation that Radcliffe Richards envisages between 'feminism' as a question of values on the one hand, and explanatory theories or political proposals on the other, is fraught with problems.

Imagine for a moment an analogous theory about racism. If Radcliffe Richards had written a book about racism, or opposition to racism, that was like her book on feminism, she would have said something like this. If we want to attack racism, we have to concentrate on the moral question of what is fair and just in dealing between black and white people. This essential right in no way depends on the truth of any 'factual propositions'. Questions about whether or not blacks are really inferior to whites are irrelevant to the problem of social injustice. If they really are inferior, then that is all the more reason to ensure that they get fair shares by some policy of positive discrimination. And the fight for racial justice in no way depends on any particular analysis of things like colonialism and imperialism, or any understanding of, say, the history of British immigration policies. We can shelve, or be agnostic, about that, and still fight for racial justice. Those who hold radically different theories about why there were riots in St Pauls or in Brixton, and those who have no theories at all, can sink their differences and agree that the really important thing is fairness and justice.

Now, firstly it is very curious to suppose that the fight against racism does not intrinsically involve an attempt to understand the causes and psychology of racial oppression. Secondly, there are theories which argue that it is *impossible* to achieve social justice or harmony between different racial groups, since human nature, the biological makeup of human beings, will not allow it. There are political parties whose beliefs are incompatible with a belief in, or a fight for, racial justice.

As I have just pointed out, there are also theories — such as that of the biological inevitability of male dominance — which imply the impossibility of ever realizing many feminist demands, and these are ignored by Radcliffe Richards. She argues that the fight for 'sexual justice' does not imply, or depend upon, any particular understanding of the causes of sexual injustice or oppression; the goals of feminism are in no way dependent on 'facts'. Presumably therefore, *qua* feminists, our main concern should not be an understanding of the causes of sexual oppression, but the moral fight for 'sexual justice'.

Such a separation between moral goals or aims and attempts at understanding the causes of oppression seems to me to be quite untenable. For example, it has often been pointed out that it is not enough to challenge things like educational or job discrimination at the legislative level; women are oppressed by social institutions, by language, in their very psychology, in ways that legislation cannot touch. Radcliffe Richards herself recognizes this, and then promptly shelves the question. But such a recognition *depends* upon insight into, and understanding of, some of the causes of women's oppression; and its consequence will be that both the goals and the strategies of feminism will be changed. The importance, for example, of consciousness-raising groups in the women's movement has depended on insights into the psychology of oppression; it was not something that women just decided arbitrarily to try. The importance of the issue of child care is necessarily related to discussion of the nature and role of the family, and of women within the family. And so on.

It is perfectly true, of course, that feminists disagree about many aspects of the nature and causes of women's oppression; and at this point I imagine that Radcliffe Richards might object that feminism can survive the discovery that any particular theory about the causes of women's oppression is false. If, she suggests, it proved wrong that capitalism and the family were of crucial significance in women's oppression, and we either discovered that something else was the root cause or had no idea what this was, it would not stop us fighting for sexual justice, or asking whether it was fair that women should do all the childcare, and so forth.

Two things seem badly wrong with this argument. First, it implies a very curious view of social causation, and of theories about the causes of oppression. Radcliffe Richards writes as if we were faced with a list of discrete or separable causes of oppression, such as 'the family', and as if the task of theory were to try and eliminate them one by one, until we arrive at the real cause or causes. But it seems to me absurd to suppose that something like 'the family' can be isolated in this way, that one can answer yes or no to the question of whether it is responsible for oppressing women. The question is not *which* social institutions oppress women, but *how* and *in what ways* things that are oppressive to women permeate the whole social structure.

Secondly, Radcliffe Richards writes as if the fight for justice were a goal of feminism in relation to which everything else is simply a means; as if it were an open question whether the family, or traditional sex roles, or conventional feminity, or anything else under attack, could actually lead to justice. The implication is that if traditional sex roles, for instance, were discovered *not* to lead to injustice, then we would have to give up our attack on them. But this presupposes that we *first* have to know what we mean by 'justice', and *then* look at social institutions to see if they are just; so that the process of finding out what we mean by justice is simply one of armchair philosophical argument. But is it the case that there is a totally decontextualized and ahistorical conception of 'justice', whose validity has ultimately to depend upon the moral institutions of right-minded people who have done a sufficient amount of clear thinking? I do not believe that such a conception of justice is adequate, or that one can thus abstract from each other the task of saying what justice means or what it really is, and the task of looking at the history of injustice or oppression and the reasons why particular forms of these have predominated. The problem is that if you try to turn feminism into an abstract fight for an ahistorical 'justice' and 'fairness' — if you try to discuss feminity without any analysis of the history of the notion, or of the uses to which it has been put — then what you say will have an in-built tendency merely to recapitulate features and values of the current social order, and to lapse into an eclectic and uncritical common sense. This is precisely what happens in Radcliffe Richard's book; and I want to illustrate this from the chapter on sexual justice, and the chapter entitled 'The Unadorned Feminist', where she discusses the common feminist rejection of 'femininity' of appearance.

Sexual Justice

Radcliffe Richards relies heavily on John Rawls's theory of justice. She starts by saying that justice is about sharing out the good things of life. 'Having determined what the good things in life are, the next problem is to determine how they should be shared out' (p. 90). (She does not discuss the problem of how, except by abstract moral argument, we are to arrive at our conception of the good things in life; nor does she ask whether 'sharing them out' does not itself depend on an ideological conception of the good things in life as rather like a cake of which everyone should have fair shares.)

Like Rawls, she denies that justice is synonymous with equality, and she basically defends his 'difference principle' that social and economic inequalities are to be arranged so that they may reasonably be expected to be to everyone's advantage. 'The criterion of justice is not equality of well-being, but something like the difference principle; a just society is one in which the least well-off group is as well-off as possible' (p. 96).

Rawls said that the inequality between men and women would be justified if women were better off under the present arrangement than they would be under one of greater equality. Radcliffe Richards points out that this is highly tendentious, since it simply assumes that women are to be inferior to men in such an arrangement. Nevertheless, with this qualification she accepts what Rawls says.

Most of the rest of the chapter on justice is devoted to a discussion of selection discrimination, and of whether it is ever fair or just that women applicants for jobs and so forth should be discriminated against on grounds of their sex. Radcliffe Richards recognizes that, in the view of many feminists, women not only tend to lose out when they are competing with men for specific things like jobs, but are put at a disadvantage by the basic social structures. She states, however: 'It is extremely difficult to prove the truth of the vague proposition that the structure of society really does work against women' (p. 99), and says no more about the subject, but simply passes on to discuss the problem of selection discrimination. Her central point is: 'Discrimination on grounds of sex is counting sex as relevant in contexts where it is not, and leads to the rejection of suitable women. It is not discriminative on grounds of sex to reject women who are not suitable, even if their unsuitability is *caused* by their being women' (p. 99).

As it stands, this would make it appear open to anyone to reject any woman for anything, since it does not specify any constraints whatever on the grounds on which women might be regarded as 'unsuitable'. Radcliffe Richards does recognize this: and she goes on to offer arguments against certain interpretations. Thus, one cannot rationally defend the view that women are naturally weak and in need of protection, and that therefore jobs should go to men; or that women in general are inferior in ability, and that therefore men should have priority; or that it is in the best interests of society as a whole that women should stay at home and be mothers. She points out, correctly, that arguments about the *general* inferiority of women miss the point, unless they accept the implausible proposition that all women are inferior in ability to all men; since the point is whether the *particular* woman or women in question are more able than the particular man or men concerned. She also maintains that some 'reverse discrimination' can be legitimate — that is, the appointment of a less able or qualified woman, even if there are better men candidates around — if the aim of this policy is to improve the general position of women.

But her arguments do not go far enough. For, if one tries to arrive at a conception of 'the socially just way of going about things' (p. 104) without some form of analysis or critique of the social processes that have produced current 'injustices', one is almost bound to reify current notions like 'suitability', 'fair shares', 'equal competition', and so on, as if they provided a sort of moral package to which one can appeal in a completely unhistorical way to provide answers to tricky questions like those about justice, and as if the answers merely lay ultimately somewhere in our moral intuitions. In fact, however, notions such as 'fair shares' or 'suitability' simply do not have a universal clear meaning which we can settle once and for all; we cannot *first* define our terms, and *then* look at social reality to see if it measures up to our definitions. Rather, the definitions are themselves part of current social reality; they have a history; they are tied to sets of social practices and institutions; and they may sometimes be implicitly used to buttress these, or to prevent critical questions being asked. It is not that we should stop bothering about whether our arguments are sound, and simply look at their history; it is rather that unless we take this history into account, we are liable to fall into the trap of supposing that current 'common sense' dictates not merely the solutions of problems, but also the terms in which they are to be discussed. An essential task of feminism should be not simply to provide 'answers' to problems posed in commonsensical everyday language, but to look critically at that language itself, and to trace its relationships to the social and historical conditions that have led to its use. And this sort of criticism is not and cannot be politically neutral; or uncommitted to any attempt at explanation and analysis.

Feminism and Sexuality

I want finally to illustrate again the way in which Radcliffe Richards's dehistoricized approach to feminism leads her into an uncritical acceptance of common-sense categories by looking at the chapter entitled 'The Unadorned Feminist'.

Feminists, says Radcliffe Richards, have rightly criticized the amount of time, money and anxiety that women have been expected to put into their personal appearance. But, she goes on to argue, this does not account for the 'deliberately unfeminine' style of dress adopted by many feminists. They treat traditional feminine dress not as something to which one should simply devote less effort, but as inherently pernicious; because the idea of feminine dress is associated with the idea of trying to attract men, or being regarded as 'sex objects'. Some feminists, she says, even aim deliberately to be un-pleasing to men; either because they reject association with men as far as possible, or because they want to be loved 'for themselves', and not because of their beauty or attractiveness or the way they are 'improved' by their clothes.

This attitude of deliberately rejecting concern about one's personal appearance will, says Radcliffe Richards, get rid of men who have the '*wrong*' attitude to women. The trouble is, she thinks, that it may also get rid of those who have the '*right*' attitude; and this is a pity, unless it happens to be your aim to get rid of men altogether.

> Certainly it will get rid of the men who are interested in women only from the point of view of sensual pleasing, but it is bound to affect at the same time not only them, but also the ones with excellent senses of priority; the ones who value character, intelligence, kindness, sympathy and all the rest, far above mere sensual pleasing, but nevertheless would like that too if they could get it as well as all the other things . . . The best judging man alive, confronted with two women identical in all matters of the soul but not equal in beauty, could hardly help choosing the beautiful one . . . A man who would not change his woman for any other in the world might still know that she would please him even more if she looked like the centre fold from the latest *Playboy*. (p. 189).

So, she continues, if feminists persist in making themselves deliberately unattractive, 'they are not only keeping off the men who would value their more important qualities too little, but are also lessening their chances of attaching men who care about such things at all. If they think that is a good thing to do, they must be prepared to argue that it is positively bad to care about whether people are sensually pleasing or not; that if you do not care at all about people's beauty you are morally superior to someone else.' Beauty and the sensual enjoyment of sex may often be of low priority, but they are not actually *bad* things. So if sensual pleasing is important, why not be feminine and wear pretty clothes?

I find this cluster of arguments rather extraordinary. Firstly, I do not know of *any* feminist who has found anything inherently wrong in the sensual enjoyment of sex, or has even regarded sex as of 'low priority'. It is true that feminists have talked about celibacy as a viable option for women if they want; and they have rejected ideas about marital duty and so on. But most feminists have urged women to rediscover and explore and celebrate their sexuality in new ways, free from the old tyrannies of reproduction, marital duty, or the assumption that only heterosexuality is legitimate. If there is sometimes a streak of puritanism in some feminist attitudes or writings, this is not where it is to be found.

Secondly, note the way in which Radcliffe Richards writes. Men are said to be 'choosing women for their qualities'; a man 'would not change his woman for any other in the world' . . . this is the sort of language in which one might talk about cars or other commodities. The old banger may have a lot of dents and be a bit rusty, but it's been a good friend and its reliability outweighs the dents, just as character and intelligence may outweigh gap-teeth or being rather overweight. If you use language like this, women appear, not so much, in the hackneyed phrase, as 'sex objects', but as *commodities*, whose qualities you can list in relation to the function they are going to be expected to fulfil. Note furthermore, that Radcliffe Richards says that if feminists make themselves 'unattractive' they will not 'attach men'. It is this sort of *language* in which some women's magazines discuss the issue of 'how to get your man'; and it is precisely this sort of way of describing relationships between men and women which ought to be one of the targets of feminist attack.

Thirdly, note the way in which Radcliffe Richards tends to conflate terms like attractiveness, beauty, sex, sensual enjoyment, sensual pleasing. She displays minimal recognition that one might want to draw *distinctions* between, say, conventional 'femininity' of appearance, and the notion of sensual pleasing; that these are not necessarily the same thing. Nor does she seem to recognize that there may be *contradictions* between these notions in the way that they sometimes currently are socially used. Some aspects of conventional femininity of dress, for example, may militate *against* sensual enjoyment or sexual pleasure, particularly of women. (Think of women who feel compelled to get up early to make up their faces so that their husbands don't see them without makeup, or suffer agonies in case their hair style is being ruined.) Radcliffe Richards would presumably reply that this is an instance of *excessive* concern about one's personal appearance which should of course be rejected; the trouble is that this sort of eclectic commonsensical reasonableness is incapable of exploring the contradictions such as that mentioned above, of understanding the function and historical emergence of current ideas of femininity, or of articulating a coherent critique of them.

Fourthly, note the way in which she sees sex and sensual enjoyment as having a rather low priority compared with things like character and intelligence or the virtues of the soul. True, she is at pains to stress that she does not see sex or beauty as bad in themselves; nevertheless what we have here is simply a modified version of the old split between 'higher' and 'lower' pleasures, or between the sensual and the spiritual, which has been extremely influential historically in justifying the oppression of women. It underlies the 'double standard' for men and women; the view of women as divided into two categories, those who are 'pure' or 'virtuous', and those who are not (the ones you marry and the ones you don't). It underlies the constant reiteration in the press, during the reporting of the 'Ripper' killings, that there was *more* cause for concern and anger when he attacked 'respectable' women. Now, I am sure that Radcliffe Richards would not want to agree, say, with this distinction between the victims of the Ripper. But the point is that the sort of language she uses is precisely that which is used by those who *do* want to make the distinction; she accepts uncritically so much of the current language in which sexual relationships are described, and current conflations between sensuality or sexuality and conventional femininity of appearance, that her criticisms are vitiated or rendered weak and ineffectual from the start.

Radcliffe Richards's defence would be that it is just a (cosmically unfair) fact that some women are more beautiful than others, and that men will tend to prefer these women rather than the ugly ones; and that no amount of argument about different standards of beauty in different cultures can sensibly deny this. It is just a hard fact of life that if you are born deformed or ugly, you will have a harder time of it, and it is pointless expecting men all suddenly to become so idealistic and altruistic that they will cease to care whether women please them sensually or not. And there is nothing wrong in trying to improve yourself, including your appearance, if nature hasn't done a very good job to start with.

But this again misses the point, which is not whether we should expect men as individuals to be more or less altruistic. The point is rather that at no stage does Radcliffe Richards challenge current definitions of feminity and their connection with relationships between men and women, or suggest that they need to be challenged. She simply argues that, relative to other things, we should perhaps devote a bit less time and effort to the achievement of a feminine appearance. In fact, she argues that the question of how much effort one should or should not put into the cultivation of 'beauty' or of one's appearance is not really anything to do with feminism at all (p. 196). This is because feminism is, as we have seen, to be defined as essentially to do with sexual justice, so the proper feminist concern turns out to be only that women should have to put no more effort into working on their own personal appearance than men do, and that men should demand no more of women in this respect than they are willing to give themselves. Both sexes, she says, should be able to allow themselves 'the luxury of being able to choose a beautiful partner' (p. 196). After all, if we care about beauty in other aspects of our lives, there is no reason why we should not care about it in the personal appearance of other people, just so long as this affects men and women equally.

This, of course, offers no critique at all of current ideas of feminine beauty. But Radcliffe Richards sees the only alternative as a blank cultural relativism, which merely harps on the fact of differences between cultures. She offers no conception that a critique of femininity might involve more than an appeal to commonsense categories on the one hand, or an appeal simply to cultural differences on the other; that it might ned to involve a *historical* account of the emergence of the modern concept of femininity; that this might involve looking at the ways that women's roles and women's lives have changed under industrial capitalism, and at the role that the family plays in this. Shorn of this historical and critical dimension, feminism is so enfeebled that it is hardly worth the name.

In the last section of the same chapter, Radcliffe Richards does try to rehabilitate sexuality and to save it from the designation of being 'lower' or less worthy in itself than other activities. To this end, she suggests that there is nothing wrong in principle with selling sex, or with pornography or strip shows; it is merely that in the course of pursuing these activities, men do not treat women properly. She argues: 'What feminism really needs is . . . women who are very desirable to men, but who will have nothing to do with any man who does not treat them properly' (p. 204), and she suggests that really feminism has fallen into the old puritanical trap of saying that sex is wrong unless it is purified by the presence of other emotions and feelings. Why should this be so, she asks, and why should relationships based on anything other than sex not need this special purification?

Now, most feminists would not use such terms to express their objections to porn shops, strip shows, Miss World contests or the like; nor would they see sex as a special case in this sort of way. One does not have to believe that sex should be sanctified by finer feelings in order to object to porn shops and the sexual exploitation of women, or the predatory way in which many men think of sexual relationships. The point is not that sex is a special case, but that sexual relationships often provide an extreme and striking example of the *general* 'commodification', as one might call it, of the relationships between men and women, in which women are expected to play the role of servicing men, whether it be sexually, or as secretaries or sock-washers, with little regard to their own human needs. (It is also of course true that the denial of humanity in relationships and the reduction of relationships to that of mere functions affects men as well as women, in all sorts of ways; but the ways are not identical, and one of the main tasks of feminism is to point out and analyse this asymmetry, and to attempt to understand why the burden has fallen particularly heavily on women.)

The other problem is that if you put the matter in this way — if you suggest that the trouble is simply that men do not treat women properly and that women should insist that they *are* treated properly — it sounds as if it is simply a question of getting individual men to behave themselves. This leaves untouched the question of what 'proper' behaviour amounts to. (What, incidentally, would Radcliffe Richards think was the 'proper' way to behave in a porn shop or at a strip show?) It does not ask whether certain institutions or forms of social organization make it impossible, or extremely difficult, for people to behave towards each other in more human and non-exploitative ways. You cannot change relationships between people, including those between men and women, if you leave completely untouched the social structures within which these relationships take place. Radcliffe Richards dislikes moralizing about prostitution, and she is right to do so. But she makes two mistakes: firstly, that of supposing that moralizing is what feminists do, as if they were only a hair's breadth from Mary Whitehouse; and secondly, that of just substituting one form of moralizing for another. Instead of gunning for the prostitutes or the strippers, we are to go for the men who will not behave properly and lecture them until they do. But if it were that easy, there would hardly be a need for feminism; blank moralism is no substitute for critical analysis of the conditions which breed the very things to which this moralism is supposed to be a response.

*　　*　　*

I have taken these two chapters to illustrate the fundamental weakness of Radcliffe Richard's book: namely, her conceptionalization of feminism simply as a moral fight about abstract, decontextualized and dehistoricized issues such as 'sexual justice'. She tends merely to recapitulate current terms and categories, failing to recognize how often many of the things which feminism is fighting against are expressed in precisely those terms. This is why I think that ultimately Radcliffe Richard's 'feminism' is often scarcely worth the name, and rarely transcends everyday commonsense to ask why things have *become* commonsense. In a way, for all that it offers some useful ammunition to feminists at certain points, the book is another exemplification of the barrenness of an ahistorical moral philosophy or moralizing. The terms of moral debate do not exist in a remote philosopher's heaven, but underpin and are underpinned by social structures which may themselves have an interest in concealing this fact.

Reprinted from *RP* 30

Masters, Slaves and Others

Genevieve Lloyd

In *The Second Sex*, Simone de Beauvoir utilized some of the basic concepts of Sartre's *Being and Nothingness* — concepts such as 'immanence' and 'transcendence', 'being-for-self' and 'being-for-others', 'bad faith' and 'authenticity' — in a profound diagnosis of the condition of women. That she could thus use the framework of Sartrean existentialism is, as Michèle Le Doeuff has pointed out,[1] both surprising and impressive. The existentialist emphasis on radical freedom seems to leave little scope for the idea of oppression; and Sartre's notorious descriptions of the horrifying 'immanence' of the female body may well seem to make his book unpromising material for appropriation to the expression of feminist ideals. It cannot be denied that the apparently unpromising Sartrean framework, as used by de Beauvoir, has proved very fruitful for understanding the peculiarities of the situation of women, and the strange tensions they continue to experience between their gender and prevailing cultural ideals of what it is to be human. This philosophical framework, however, also underlies some of the limitations which can now be seen in de Beauvoir's diagnosis of the situation of women and some tensions in her articulation of feminist objectives.

The problems centre on the critical notion of 'otherness' which de Beauvoir presents as the basic trait of woman — the peculiar way in which a free autonomous being finds herself compelled to assume the status of the Other, stabilized as an object, doomed to 'immanence'. Woman's 'transcendence' is overshadowed and itself transcended by another ego which is 'essential and sovereign'. In *Force of Circumstance* (1963) de Beauvoir expressed some second thoughts about her formulation of this central theme of female 'otherness'. She did not, however, express any reservations about her articulation of feminism in

1. Michele le Doeuff, 'Operative Philosophy: Simone de Beauvoir and Existentialism', I & C, No. 6, Autumn 1979.

terms of the existentialist ideal that women should come to present themselves as 'the eye that looks, as subject, consciousness, freedom.'[2] The goal is a female attainment of Sartrean 'transcendence'. In this paper I want to explore some of the philosophical tensions in this ideal. De Beauvoir's concept of 'otherness' and the co-relative ideal of 'transcendence' have their origins in Hegel's version of the struggle of consciousnesses in the section on Lordship and Bondage in *The Phenomenology of Spirit*. To see the problems in de Beauvoir's application of them, we must take them back to their Hegelian origins and follow them through their adaptation by Sartre.

Hegel on Masters, Slaves and Women

Hegel's famous master-slave dialectic occurs in the context of his treatment of the emergence of sustained self-consciousness out of less advanced stages of consciousness — sense-certainty, perception, understanding.[3] Two points are crucial for our purposes: Hegel's understanding of the relationship between self-consciousness and Life, and his claim that sustained self-consciousness involves a struggle between consciousnesses. For Hegel, self-consciousness is one stage along the grand unfolding of Spirit from Nature and its eventual return to Nature. It is a moment in the series of negations and transformations through which Substance becomes determinate, a stage in the unfolding of Spirit in which consciousness 'presses forward to its true existence'. What is distinctive about the stage of self-consciousness is that it defines itself against Life as its opposite; its peculiar richness derives from what it has as its opposite pole. The stage of simple immediacy of consciousness — 'sense-certainty' — gives way to the stage of 'perception', in which determinate but static objects are set over against consciousness. This is in turn transformed into Understanding, the stage where objects of consciousness are construed as having inner natures operating in accordance with Forces. This is associated with a tenuous form of self-consciousness: in thus understanding the world, consciousness understands itself. However, Understanding, if it is to become full self-consciousness, must be transformed so that its objects are not enduring, static things following external laws, but rather organic, living things — the proper objects of desire. Consciousness now apprehends itself as confronted with Life — an 'infinite unity of differences' — and this

2. *Force of Circumstance*, trans. R. Howard, Harmondsworth 1968, pp. 202–03.
3. *Phenomenology of Spirit*, trans. A.V. Miller, Oxford 1977, pp. 104–119. All quotations and page references are from this edition.

emerging self-consciousness takes the form not of a bare awareness of an object, but rather desire for a living thing.

The transition to Desire sets the scene for Hegel's claim that self-consciousness involves an inevitable struggle between conscious-nesses. There can, he insists, be no self-consciousness without inter-subjective awareness; an isolated consciousness cannot sustain self-consciousness. A consciousness can be aware of itself only by having consciousness presented to it as an outer object; but because this stage of developing consciousness takes the form of desire, a contradiction arises. The emerging self realizes that the object of its desire is independent of itself. The object is an 'other' and its otherness must be overcome if the truth of self-certainty — the sustained grasp of self as there in the world — is to be achieved. Even the lower forms of life, Hegel quaintly observes, act in conformity with this need to super-sede the other by making it a part of themselves — they devour what they need from the world. However, for fully self-conscious beings the necessary incorporation of the other is a more complex matter than mere eating. Self-consciousness is certain of itself only by overcoming the other, cancelling its otherness. The satisfaction of desire over-comes this independent otherness. In destroying the independence of the other, a self objectifies its own self-consciousness as in the world. But this can now be seen as a self-defeating enterprise, for the very being of self-consciousness demands that there be an independent other to thus overcome. With the incorporation of the other, self-consciousness in which its own being will be mirrored back to it. Hegel's conclusion is that, if self-consciousness is to be sustained, the object set over against it must allow itself to be incorporated without thereby ceasing to exist: and the only way this can be achieved is through the recognition of one consciousness by another. 'Self-consciousness achieves its satisfaction only in another self-conscious-ness.' Consciousness here 'first finds its turning point, where it leaves behind it the colourful show of the sensuous here-and-now and the nightlike void of the supersensible beyond, and steps out into the spiritual daylight of the present' (pp. 110–11).

It is the necessity of recognition which makes sustained self-consciousness, for Hegel, inherently conflict-ridden. If self-conscious-ness is to be sustained it must be, as it were, confronted by itself in another; there can be no self-consciousness without consciousness of the Other. But this mutual need of the other's recognition — demanding, as it does, that each engage in its own negation in order to sustain the other's self-certainty — means that the two conscious-nesses must 'prove themselves and each other through a life-and-death struggle' (p. 114). The struggle may end in the actual death of one of the antagonists. The more interesting outcome, however, which makes possible a transition to richer forms of consciousness, is that whereby both survive but with one in a state of subjection to the other. Both have staked their lives, and by living through the fear of death they have attained to a kind of consciousness which transcends mere absorption in the immediacy of Life. They are now conscious of Life as something not exhausted by any of the particular determinate forms it takes. Hegelian self-certainty is grounded in this detached awareness; it stands above Life, rather than being absorbed in it as are the lesser forms of consciousness. The two consciousnesses in Hegel's story, however, are transformed in different ways by this fear of death they have each lived through. They survive as different kinds of self-consciousness: Lord and Bondsman.

It now turns out that, from the point of view of the Lord, the existence of the subjected consciousness no longer serves the purpose for which it was needed. Self-consciousness was to be sustained through the satisfied desire for recognition; but the outcome of the struggle is a recognition that is 'one-sided and unequal'. The object in which the Lord has achieved his mastery is not an independent consciousness but a servile one in which he cannot recognize himself; the required reflection of independent consciousness is distorted by the subjection which has been the condition of its attainment. Despite his 'victory', the Lord has found no external object in which his free, independent consciousness can be mirrored back to him and hence sustained. The kind of recognition he receives from the Bondsman is in fact detrimental to the project of sustaining awareness of self as free, independent consciousness; the self-certainty of the victor is once again under threat. Nor is this all there is to the souring of the Lord's victory. His relation to non-conscious things is now mediated through the bondsman's labour on them. He is thus deprived of what, for the bondsman, will prove the ultimately successful externalization of self — the capacity to labour on things and thus make them over in one's own form.

A correspondingly advantageous reversal is the lot of 'dependent' consciousness of the bondsman. Whereas the externalized truth of the Lord's self-consciousness is the servile consciousness of the bondsman, that of the bondsman is the free consciousness of the Lord — at any rate, for as long as that free consciousness can be sustained. The bondsman, moreover, is able through his enforced labour on things to transform his immediate relationship to the world into self-conscious awareness of it. Mere labouring on things, without having been through the life-and-death struggle, would leave consciousness immersed in the immediacy of lower forms of consciousness. But the consciousness of the bondsman has been through the fear of death, which has shaken everything stable in his world to its foundations; he is now aware of Life as something not exhausted by the immediate and particular vanishing moments of experience. Work, for this transformed consciousness, can now become a way of actually bringing about the 'dissolution of the stable', a reworking of natural existence in the worker's own form. It becomes 'desire held in check, fleetingness staved off'. Through forming and shaping things, the bondsman's consciousness acquires what eludes the Lord — an 'element of permanence'; he discovers himself in the forms his work imposes on objects (p. 118).

To see how all this bears on the question of women, we must see the master-slave dialectic in relation to the later sections of *The Phenomenology of Spirit* where Hegel explicitly discusses male-female relations.[4] His treatment of the theme arises in the context of a discussion of the ethical life and the contrasts between its self-conscious and its unreflective forms. In many ways, this reproduced the structure of Hegel's treatment of the relations between individual self-consciousness and the more immediate, unreflective forms of consciousness. The ethical life is an early stage in the unfolding of Spirit into social, cultural and political life — a relatively primitive stage which must go under in response to inner strains, passing over into the more advanced stages in Spirit's self-realization: law, culture and philosophy. The ethical life, in a typical Hegelian fission, splits into two forms: two 'ethical substances', identified with the 'human' and the 'divine' law. These are respectively associated with Society and the Family and also explicitly with the male-female distinction. Each side of the division is construed as a genuine 'moment' of the spiritual, ethical life. The Family, however, represents the 'unconscious' notion of the ethical order, as opposed to its self-conscious existence, embodied in the wider life of Society, where the ethical 'shapes and maintains itself by working for the universal' (p. 268).

We have seen that individual self-consciousness, for Hegel, demands an externalization of the self, so that it comes to find self, as it were, in the outer world. Without such objectification of selfhood, self-consciousness remains tenuous, liable to slip back into immersion in mere Life. The externalization of self makes possible a sustained self-consciousness; mere immersion in Life, in contrast, cannot

4. Ibid, pp. 267–290.

sustain a stable self-consciousness. This contrast is echoed in Hegel's treatment of human and divine law. Self-conscious ethical life demands an externalization into an outer realm beyond the particularities of Family Life; it is sustained through access to the wider life of Society, beyond the confines of the Family. And for Hegel, the crucial 'working for the universal' which goes on out there is explicitly the prerogative of the male individual. In the wider public arena, the male, on behalf of the Family, pursues the 'acquisition and maintenance of power and wealth' — a pursuit which for Hegel transcends its significance for the private gain of the individual and his family. The enterprise takes on a 'higher determination', which 'does not fall within the Family itself, but bears on what is truly universal, the community'. In relation to the Family, in fact, this external activity of the male has a negative role 'expelling the individual from the Family, subduing the natural aspect and separateness of his existence, and training him to be virtuous, to a life in and for the universal' (p. 269).

The Hegelian individual is 'actual and substantial' only through this richer dimension of universality, associated with life as a citizen, external to the Family. In so far as he is not a citizen but belongs to the Family, the individual is only an 'unreal, impotent shadow' (p. 270). The realm of the Family is the realm of 'divine law' — the realm of duties and affections towards blood relatives. All this Hegel sums up as the 'nether world'; and since women are not citizens it is also the realm of women. For them, there is no actual participation in the unfolding of Spirit into the advanced forms which go beyond family life. It should be stressed, again, that this is not for Hegel a matter of excluding women from the ethical order. Ethical life does occur within the Family; and despite their confinement to it women can be concerned with the 'universal' rather than with the particularity of 'natural' feelings. But because they lack access to that wider domain of fully self-conscious 'working for the universal', their ethical life involves a predicament which does not arise for men.

> In the ethical household, it is not a question of *this* particular husband, *this* particular child, but simply of husband and children generally; the relationships of the woman are based, not on feeling, but on the universal. The difference between the ethical life of the woman and that of the man consist just in this, that in her vocation as an individual and in her pleasure, her interest is centred on the universal and remains alien to the particularity of desire; whereas in the husband these two sides are separated; and since he possesses as a citizen the self-conscious power of universality, he

thereby acquires the right of desire and, at the same time, preserves his freedom in regard to it. Since, then, in this relationship of the wife there is an admixture of particularity, her ethical life is not pure; but in so far as it *is* ethical, the particularity is a matter of indifference, and the wife is without the moment of knowing herself as *this* particular self in the other partner. (pp. 274–75)

The point is that in so far as relations within the Family are 'particular' — focused on this particular husband or child — they are not also 'ethical'. Men, in contrast to women, have an additional, external sphere of activity, where they 'work for the universal'. A man can thus treat his family relationships as entirely 'particular', without sacrificing his ethical life. But a woman can have the ethical life only to the extent that she can transform the particularity of family relationships into ethical, 'universal' concerns — for husband and children as such, rather than for these particular people. So what for the male is 'particular' is for the woman 'universal' and ethical. And this gives rise, Hegel goes on to point out, to inevitable conflicts between male and female. From the male perspective, there are conflicts between the ethical and the merely particular. Family Life drags him back to the particular from the outer realm of universality. But for the female, as Hegel sees, the conflicts take the form of external encroachments on the ethical demands of the Family. The conflicts between the two spheres thus take the form of conflicts between *male* and *female* as different embodiments of the ethical stage of Spirit. Not just Family concerns but *womankind* itself becomes the enemy of the wider community.

Since the community only gets an existence through its interference with the happiness of the Family, and by dissolving (individual) self-consciousness into the universal, it creates for itself in what it suppresses and what is at the same time essential to it an internal enemy — womankind in general. Womankind — the everlasting irony (in the life) of the community — changes by intrigue the universal end of the government into a private end, transforms its universal activity into a work of some particular individual, and perverts the universal property of the state into a possession and ornament for the Family. (p. 288)

Under these strains, the ethical stage of Spirit goes under and Spirit advances on into its next stages — legal status and personality, which need not concern us. What is important is how, in the light of Hegel's treatment of male-female relations, we are to understand the implications of the earlier master-slave dialectic. The two struggles — master-slave and male–female — I want to suggest, should be taken in conjunction. They are, of course, not meant to be chronologically related. Rather they represent similar 'moments' in different versions of the story of Spirit's unfolding from Nature, told once as the story of the emergence of individual self-consciousness as a stage in human knowlege, and again as the emergence of fully self-conscious forms of social life. Each story illuminates the other, and what connects them is the theme of the conditions of sustained self-consciousness. Individual self-consciousness is associated with a breaking away — achieved through surviving the fear of death — from immersion in mere Life and its particular transient attachments. And self-conscious ethical life is likewise associated with a breaking away from the Family, which — at any rate from the male perspective — is also associated with particularity. In either case, it is by breaking away from the merely particular that true individuality is attained. The wider public domain outside the Family is the realm where the ethical life attains self-consciousness and is hence able to maintain itself in stable being without lapsing back into the particularity of merely natural feeling. From the male's perspective, the Family serves as a realm of containment of the particular: he must transcend it to reach self-conscious ethical life through 'working for the universal'. In thus breaking away from the realm of mere particularity, the male is breaking away from the domain and concerns of women. Women, if they are to be ethical beings, must do the best they can with the personal relationships that belong within Family Life. The brother-sister relation, Hegel thinks, has more potential for sustaining ethical self-consciousness than either husband–wife or parent–child relationships, holding some prospect of a free mutual recognition between selves, unmixed with struggles for independence or the sway of merely natural feeling (pp. 274–75). But the proper sphere of sustained selfhood is out there beyond the Family. Women are relegated to a different, private sphere, which is not primarily associated with sustained self-consciousness.

The point here is not that what awaits the male beyond the confines of Family Life is engagement in life-and-death struggles for recognition, issuing in relations of Lordship and Bondage. The two stories do not intersect in that way. The male, when he leaves the constraints of Family Life, engages in civilized activities associated with the acquisition and maintenance of power and wealth. The stories do nonetheless map one another. The master-slave story describes a recognition of a kind which will sustain self-certainty. And women, for Hegel, are outside the whole drama of the achievement of sustained self-consciousness. This is not to say that Hegel thinks that women do not actually have self-consciousness, or that they have no share in the more advanced stages of the unfolding of Spirit in human culture. The position is more complex. Spirit 'in its entirety' is supposed to be present at each of the advancing stages; but it is always a later stage that gives this presence of Spirit to a former. It is through its relation to human law that divine law can be seen as containing ethical Spirit, and this dependence is reflected in Hegel's corresponding remarks about the male/female relation. It is through their relation to men that women are part of the 'upward movement of the law of the nether world to the actuality of the light of day and to conscious existence': and it is through their relation to the Family and the feminine that men are involved in the corresponding 'downward movement' from actuality to unreality (p. 278). Women do have self-conscious existence and activity but only by virtue of their relation to men.

Hegel's master-slave dialectic is of course not formulated in ways that explicitly exclude women from engagement in life-and-death struggles for recognition. However, if we read these passages in the light of Hegel's subsequent explicit discussion of the male-female distinction it can be seen that the struggle which dramatizes Hegel's understanding of the preconditions of sustained self-consciousness is fundamentally a struggle between male consciousnesses. Women are outside the drama, although they are given a share in the spoils of victory. Hegel's struggle for self-consciousness is really a struggle between male selves and others. Women do not — at any rate, in their own right — fit into this dialectic as either masters or slaves. We should then expect some oddities in any attempt to apply the relations of recognition between Hegelian selves and others to understanding the condition of women. And some of the puzzling features of de Beauvoir's analysis of the condition of women, as we shall see later, do seem to derive from the underlying maleness of the original Hegelian confrontation of consciousnesses. However, de Beauvoir's application of the master-slave story is in fact taken not from the original Hegelian version but from Sartre's retelling of the story, which differs from Hegel's in some important and relevant respects.

The Sartrean Other

In the opening chapter of Part Three of *Being and Nothingness*,[5] Sarte hails Hegel's Master-Slave dialectic as a break-through in the philosophical understanding of self-consciousness. As Hegel sees, the appearance of the Other is indispensable to the very existence of self-consciousness. Self-consciousness cannot be attained simply by looking into one-self, as if one could perform some impossible intellectual contortion in which the subject becomes the object of its own gaze. Rather than trying somehow to derive our awareness of others out of our self-awareness, we must go the other way round. Sartre is deeply impressed, too, by Hegel's stress on negation and the element of conflict it introduces into the nature of self-consciousness. The Other is both the same as me, in being self, and not the same, in being another self. To be conscious of the Other is to be conscious of what is not me; and to be conscious of myself is to be conscious of what is not the Other. 'The Other is the one who excludes me by being himself, the one whom I exclude by being myself' (p. 236). Sartre elaborates Hegel's idea that there is an unavoidable power-struggle at the heart of self-consciousness into the claim that it is only in so far as each is opposed to the Other that they grasp themselves as selves, as having 'being-for-self'. Confronting the Other, each asserts his right of being an individual self.

Sartre's version of Hegel's master-slave story highlights this aspect of reciprocal recognition. The final stage of Hegel's story — the externalization of self through labour — drops out altogether in Sartre's version. Sartre, moreover, gives his own twist to Hegel's description of the struggle for recognition. The power-struggle becomes a struggle between competing 'Looks'. My very existence as a self-conscious being depends not just on the fact of the Other's recognition but on what kind of self the Other recognizes me as being. This creates a crucial dependence on the Other. 'As I appear to the Other, so I am' (p. 237). This mutual dependence on the content of the Other's perception gives a rather different role, in Sartre's version, to the contrast between the consciousness of the Master and that of the Slave. In Hegel's version, both consciousnesses live through the fear of death, and it is the freedom this brings that later enables the slave to externalize self in the world through labour. In Sartre's version, the benefits of having staked one's life and lived through the fear of death accrue entirely to the Master. 'The value of the Other's recognition of

5. *Being and Nothingness*, trans. H.E. Barnes, London 1958. All quotations and page references are from this edition.

me depends on the value of my recognition of the Other. In this sense, to the extent that the Other apprehends me as bound to a body and immersed in *life*, I am myself only *an Other*. In order to make myself recognised by the Other, I must risk my own life. To risk one's life, in fact, is to reveal oneself as not-bound to the objective form or to any determined existence — as not-bound to life' (p. 237).

Sartrean slave consciousness remains immersed in life as something too dear to lose; the consciousness of the Master, in contrast, through risking life breaks free to stand above it. Being prepared to die, he is no longer confined by the determinacies of his situation; he transcends all determination to any particular mode of existence. We can see emerging here Sartre's own existentialist preoccupation with absolute freedom as the achievement of a transcendence of all determinate situations. The Sartrean Master exults in having risked his life. On the other hand, 'the Other remains bound to external things in general; he appears to me and he appears to himself as *non-essential*. He is the *Slave* I am the *Master*; for him it is I who am essence' (p. 237).

Sartre himself makes explicit some other relevant aspects in which he departs from the Hegelian treatment of the role of the Other in self-consciousness. For Hegel, he complains, the problem of self-consciousness remains formulated in terms of knowledge, and this is falsely optimistic in two ways. Firstly, it is 'epistemologically optimistic'. Hegel thinks that selfhood, through the mediation of the Other, can be adequately presented to perception as an outer object. But, Sartre argues, this is impossible. Consciousness cannot be an object to consciousness without this fact modifying what it really is. To appear as an object to consciousness is no longer to be consciousness. I cannot be an object to myself, for the object is precisely 'what I make myself not-be' (p. 242). According to Hegel, the Other is an object and I apprehend my own selfhood in recognizing this external self. But the one of these affirmations, Sartre argues, must destroy the other. To be an object is precisely not-to-be-me. If the Other is to me an object, for that very reason it cannot reflect back to me my own selfhood. Between the 'Other-as-object' and 'Me-as-subject' there is no common measure (p. 243). Secondly, Hegel's position is 'ontologically optimistic'. In considering the problem of the Other, he places himself at the standpoint of the whole; and from this standpoint there is no real problem of particular consciousnesses. They can be considered as in genuine relations of recognition to one another; each is located in the unfolding, all-embracing Spirit. But from the standpoint of each consciousness this all-embracing perspective in which conflicts can be reconciled is not available. And this makes the struggles between consciousnesses of more consequence to each of them. 'No logical or epistemological optimism can cover the scandal of the plurality of consciousnesses' (p. 244). 'So long as consciousnesses exist, the separation and conflict of consciousnesses will remain . . .' (p. 244).

For Sartre, an adequate treatment of the relationship between self and other must start 'at the only possible standpoint' — that of a particular consciousness. It must nonetheless retain Hegel's 'brilliant intuition' that the self is dependent on the other in its very being. What this yields is the idea that we attain to self-consciousness not through an intellectual awareness of the Other as an outer object, but rather through emotion. Self-consciousness does not arise from intellectual awareness of objects but rather from the experience of such emotions as shame and pride; and at the heart of such emotions is the experience of finding within my own consciousness 'the Other himself as not being me'. The experience, and its bearing on self-consciousness and freedom, are described in the section on 'The Look' (pp. 252–302). As the points Sartre makes here are essential to understanding de Beauvoir's application of the Sartrean notion of the Other, I will focus on the section in some detail.

The experience of being looked at is the source of our apprehension in our own 'inmost depths' of the Sartrean Other. But the apprehension of another's look — a look directed at me — cannot, Sartre argues, be the apprehension of an object. The experience of being looked at is quite different from the apprehension of an object and excludes it. The point becomes clearer in Sartre's contrast between the experience of looking at someone who is not looking at me, and our experience of a look directed at ourselves. I am in a public park. Not far away there is a lawn and along the edge of that lawn there are benches. A man passes by those benches. Instead of a grouping towards me of the objects, there is now an orientation which 'flees' from me. I experience a 'reorganization of space'. This man, we suppose, sees the lawn. He may walk on the grass, and so on. I am aware of a spatiality that is not my spatiality. Among the objects of my universe, an element of disintegration has appeared. '. . . an object has appeared which has stolen the world from me'. There is a decentralization of the world which 'undermines the centralization which I, as perceiver, am simultaneously effecting'. '. . . it appears that the world has a kind of drain hole in the middle of its being and that it is perpetually flowing off through this hole' (p. 256). But all of this, so far, is contained within my centralization of the scene. This man who is effecting the 'internal hemorrhage' (p. 257) of my world is himself an object in my spatialization. The bleeding away of my world is controlled, localized. His look directed at other objects is itself contained in my world. The situation becomes quite different if he now looks at me; his look can no longer be contained as an object in a world centred around my own look.

The point Sartre extracts from all this is that we cannot at the same time perceive a look as an object and apprehend a look fastened on ourselves as object; it must be either one or the other. To apprehend a look directed at us is not to apprehend an object; it is consciousness of being *looked at*. It is this experience which yields the Other to us. The Other is in principle 'the One that looks at me' (p. 257). This Look need not be 'the convergence of two ocular globes in my direction'; it can be a rustling of branches, the sound of a footstep followed by silence, the opening of a shutter, the movement of a curtain. It is this sense of the Other's Look that is involved in shame. Listening behind a door out of jealousy, I hear footsteps behind me and experience shame, which involves awareness of myself as object to the Other (p. 259). The immediate effect of this awareness is a denial of my 'transcendence', so that I become fixed with a determinate nature. The Look of the Other fixes my possibilities. By thus denying my transcendence it denies my freedom. I am placed in danger — a danger which is no accident, but the permanent structure of my 'being-for-others' (p. 268). This is the state of the Sartrean 'slave consciousness'. Whereas the consciousness of the Master retains transcendence of all determinate situations, that of the Slave is immersed in determinacy.

The self that is given me through awareness of being looked at, then, is never the self as transcendent. What I am aware of through being looked at is not my self as a free subjective being, but rather an objectified self — the 'self-for-others'. For Sartre there is no possibility of reciprocal recognition between transcendent selves. The Look transforms its object from a transcendent being into a degraded consciousness. This objectification is a 'radical metamorphosis'. My being-for-others is a fall through absolute emptiness towards objectivity. There is, however, something intrinsically false, Sartre suggests, about this objectification. I cannot ultimately be deprived of my transcendence, for this would involve an alienation of my selfhood. The Other does not constitute me as an object for myself, but only for him. I take on, as it were, his alienating gaze; but I cannot really be alienated from myself. The objectifying force of the

Other's Look can in principle always be resisted. My absolute freedom as a subject cannot be denied. The resistance of the Other's objectifying Look is central to Sartre's version of Hegel's life-and-death struggle between rival consciousnesses. Each strives to be the one that retains freedom, turning the other into a mere object. It is impossible for both lookers to be reciprocally free, recognizing one another's 'being-for-self'. Thus the Sartrean antagonists struggle for the role of Looker. Each consciousness rejects the Other's objectifying Look, refusing to be limited to what it is perceived as being. Sartrean selfhood essentially involves this constant wrenching away from the Other's attempt to fix my possibilities by perceiving me as object; it involves a constant surpassing of fixed or 'dead' possibilities. The true Sartrean self is in this way a 'perpetual centre of infinite possibilities', which refuses to be known as an object. And it is this ideal of transcendence which de Beauvoir takes over in *The Second Sex*.[6]

De Beauvoir on Women as Other

De Beauvoir's idea of woman as 'other' is articulated in terms drawn from the Sartrean struggle for dominance between Lookers and Looked-at. There can at any one time be only one Sartrean Looker; the other must be looked-at. In appropriating this point to the analysis of the female condition, de Beauvoir introduces two variations to the Sartrean theme. The first is that, with respect to relations between the sexes, one sex is, as it were, permanently in the privileged role of Looker; the other is always the Looked-at. The second is that in her version of the struggle between hostile consciousnesses, one side connives in its defeat. Women are engaged in the struggle, but they are somehow not serious antagonists. Unlike the original master-slave struggle from which it all derives, the outcome here is not really a 'subjugation'. Women have themselves submitted to constitute a permanent Other. In the Sartrean struggle, two consciousnesses are locked in a combat of fierce, uncompromising Looks. The outcome is uncertain, although one must go under. In de Beauvoir's application of this model to the sexual division, woman connives at being the objectified Other. Women accept their own objectification, being well-pleased with the arrangement. 'To decline to be the Other, to refuse to be a party to the deal — this

---

6. *The Second Sex*, trans. H.M. Parshley, Harmondsworth 1972. All quotations and page references are from this edition.

would be for women to renounce all the advantages conferred on them by their alliance with the superior caste. Man-the-sovereign will provide woman-the-liege with material protection and will undertake the moral justification of her existence' (p. 21).

What makes this extraordinary arrangement appealing to women is elaborated in terms drawn from Sartre's treatment of the demands of freedom. The condition of being female comes out as, as it were, a permanent state of Sartrean 'bad faith', in which women connive at being turned into objects, denying their transcendence. The condition and its ideal alternative are expressed in terms of 'immanence' and 'transcendence'.

> Every subject plays his part as such specifically through exploits or projects that serve as a mode of transcendence; he achieves liberty only through a continual reaching out towards other liberties. There is no justification for present existence other than its expansion into an indefinitely open future. Every time transcendence falls back into immanence, stagnation, there is a degradation of existence into the *en-soi* — the brutish life of subjection to given conditions — and of liberty into constraint and contingence. This downfall represents a moral fault if the subject consents to it; if it is inflicted on him, it spells frustration and oppression. In both cases it is an absolute evil. Every individual concerned to justify his existence feels that his existence involves an undefined need to transcend himself, to engage in freely chosen projects. (pp. 28–29)

Many contemporary readers of *The Second Sex* will have reservations about Sartrean transcendence as a human ideal, even apart from what limitations it may have as a feminist one. Can any will really be as free as Sartre would have it? And should we really want to be transcendent selves, leaping about in triumphant assertions of will in defiance of all the apparent determinacies in our situations? The ideal of radical freedom and the associated idea of bad faith can be seen, too, as in some ways just adding an extra burden of self-recrimination on those — male or female — who find themselves caught in oppressive situations. However, the queries I want to raise here concern rather more specifically what becomes of the Hegelian and Sartrean treatments of self-consciousness in de Beauvoir's analysis of the predicament of women.

First, let me stress what I regard as a positive feature of de Beauvoir's use of the original Hegelian framework, as mediated by

Sartre. De Beauvoir is of course not explicitly addressing herself to Hegel's treatment of the condition of women. But her own account of the female predicament can nonetheless be seen as illuminating an inner tension in Hegel's position. Hegel did not regard women as lacking the status of spiritual subjects. It is true that he saw them as, in a sense, closer to Nature than men: the form of ethical life with which they are associated is a less advanced form of Spirit than that associated with men. It is nonetheless supposed to be genuinely ethical. Woman does share in the more advanced stages of Spirit; but, as we have seen, she does so in a curiously vicarious way, through her relations to man. For de Beauvoir, as for Sartre, the conditions of selfhood are in contrast quite uncompromising. Nothing short of actual engagement on 'projects' and 'exploits' will do. In the lack of that, human subjects are forced back into mere 'immanence'. There can be no vicarious selfhood; and it can be only through bad faith that women regard their relations to men as giving them a share in transcendence. The middle zone which Hegel sets aside for women — located between the merely 'natural' and full participation in the outer world of projects and exploits — must be seen as a delusion. If women are not out there engaging in their own projects and exploits, they are reduced to mere immanence or immersion in Life. There is no middle zone between transcendence and immanence, between 'being-for-self' and 'being-in-itself'.

In this way, we can see de Beauvoir's treatment of the Otherness of women as drawing out the inner inconsistencies in Hegel's treatment of woman's status as a spiritual subject. This repudiation of the Hegelian 'nether world' as nothing but the zone of bad faith, however, has some more negative consequences for de Beauvoir's account of the condition of being female. They come out especially in some of her remarks about female biology. In some passages, the female predicament is presented as a conflict between being an inalienable free subject, reaching out to transcendence, and being a body which drags this subject back to a merely 'natural' existence. It is as if the female body is an intrinsic obstacle to transcendence, making woman a 'prey of the species'. During menstruation, says de Beauvoir, a woman 'feels her body most painfully as an obscure, alien thing; it is, indeed, the prey of a stubborn and foreign life . . . Woman, like man, *is* her body; but her body is something other than herself' (p. 61). This apparently stark dualism between transcendence through the will and confinement to bodily 'immanence' is a disconcerting picture of the condition of being female. At this point the notion of woman as 'other' may well seem to have over-reached itself. How can objectification of consciousness make one's very body other to oneself? Why should a woman's direct experience of her own body be an experience of lack of transcendence, of 'immersion' in mere life? Why, at any rate, should this be so in any way that would not apply equally to the direct experience of a male body? Here it may well seem that de Beauvoir has appropriated, along with Sartrean ideas of transcendence, his notorious treatment of the female body as the epitome of immanence.[7] One need not endorse the more exultant celebrations of the personal and political potential of female biology and motherhood to think there is something unduly negative about de Beauvoir's depiction of female biology.

In partial defence of de Beauvoir here it can of course be said that the experience — however direct — of a female body which she is describing is the experience of a body which has been culturally objectified by centuries of exposure to the male Look. De Beauvoir warns in the Introduction to Book Two of *The Second Sex* that her use of the words *woman* or *feminine* are not intended to refer to any changeless essence; that the reader must understand the phrase 'in the present state of education and custom' after most of her statements. And there is certainly something correct about the suggestion that women experience even their own bodies in ways that reflect the conditioning effects of a male objectifying Look. It is not female biology itself, we may say, that poses the obstacle to a feminine 'transcendence', but rather what men, with the connivance of women, have made of female biology. And de Beauvoir does seem to have this distinction clearly in mind in the following passage:

> Men have presumed to create a feminine domain — the kingdom of life, or immanence — only in order to lock up women therein. But it is regardless of sex that the existent seeks self-justification through transcendence — the very submission of women is proof of that statement. What they demand today is to be recognized as existents by the same right as men and not to subordinate existence to life, the human being and its animality. (pp. 96–97)

But perhaps there is more to it than this. What makes the female body such a threat to Sartrean transcendence seems to be not just the result of its having been objectified by the male Look. Underlying de Beauvoir's descriptions of female biology is the original Hegelian opposition between the individuality of self-consciousness and the

7. *Being and Nothingness*, Part IV, Chapter 2, Section 3.

inchoate generality of mere Life. It is not just for straightforward practical reasons that woman's greater biological involvement in 'species life' poses obstacles to her attaining 'transcendence'. It is not just that, given the prevailing modes of social organization, woman's primary responsibility for child care or domestic labour sets limits to her involvement in 'projects and exploits'. There seem to be conceptual reasons, too, for her greater proneness to Sartrean 'immanence'. Sartrean transcendence, like its Hegelian predecessor, is precisely a transcendence of mere 'Life'. Man transcends species life; he 'creates values'. Thus the existentialist perspective, de Beauvoir claims, enables us

> to understand how the biological and economic condition of the primitive horde must have led to male supremacy. The female, to a greater extent than the male, is the prey of the species; and the human race has always sought to escape its specific destiny. The support of life became for man an activity and a project through the invention of the tool; but in maternity woman remained closely bound to her body, like an animal. It is because humanity calls itself in question in the matter of living — that is to say, values the reasons for living above mere life — that, confronting woman, man assumes mastery. Man's design is not to repeat himself in time: it is to take control of the instant and mould the future. It is male activity that in creating values has made of existence itself a value; this activity has prevailed over the confused forces of life; it has subdued Nature and Woman. (p. 97)

'Transcendence', in its origins, is a transcendence *of* the feminine. In its Hegelian version this is a matter of breaking away from the 'nether world' of women. In its Sartrean version it is associated with a repudiation of what is supposedly signified by the female body, the 'holes' and 'slime' which threaten to engulf free subjecthood.[8] It is as if, in the lack of a Hegelian 'nether world', all that is left for male subjecthood to 'transcend' is the female body itself. In both cases, of course, it is only from a male perspective that the feminine can be seen as what must be 'transcended'. But the male perspective has left its mark on the very concepts of 'transcendence' and 'immanence'. Perhaps it is not, after all, surprising that de Beauvoir should slip into those disconcerting passages where it seems that women must struggle not only with their own bad faith and male power but with their own

8. Ibid., pp. 609–14.

bodies, if they are to achieve true selfhood and freedom; as if they can achieve 'transcendence' only at the expense of alienation from their bodily being.

What I am suggesting here is that the ideal of 'transcendence' is — in a more fundamental way than de Beauvoir allows — a male ideal; that it feeds on the exclusion of the feminine. This is what makes the ideal of a feminine attainment of 'transcendence' puzzling. In Hegel's original version of the transcendence of mere Life, women were outside the drama, relegated to a 'nether world'. In de Beauvoir's application of the model, mediated through Sartre, women are slotted into the conflict of hostile consciousnesses; and her ideal is that they struggle to become Lookers rather than always the Looked-at. But can 'transcendence' be taken over in this way as if it were in principle a gender-neutral ideal? And what remains of it in the lack of that Hegelian middle zone which Sartre and de Beauvoir would have us repudiate as the zone of bad faith? Male transcendence, as Hegel himself partly saw, is something quite different from what female transcendence would have to be. It is a breaking away from a zone which for the male remains intact — from what is for him the realm of particularity and merely 'natural' feelings. There is for the female, in contrast, no such realm which she can both leave and leave intact. What would the distinction between 'transcendence' and 'immanence' amount to in a framework that entirely lacked that other more central and basically male-oriented distinction, between the 'private' realm of the Family and that 'outer' public domain into which free consciousnesses leap for the exhilarating pursuit of projects and exploits?

Reprinted from *RP* 34

Did Man Make Language?

Alison Assiter

'Males, as the dominant group, have produced language, thought and reality.' This sentence appears on page 143 of Dale Spender's book *Man Made Language*.[1] Spender believes that 'maleness' pervades language as a whole; and that the reality most of us inhabit most of the time is a male one because language (male language) creates reality. I shall argue that though Dale's examples are interesting, her major claims about language are sometimes unclear, and that where they are clear, they are positively *damaging* for women. I do not want to concede to the opposition, however, that there is no 'sexist' bias in the English language at all. I shall offer the outline of an alternative account of sexism in one area of language, the purportedly gender-neutral uses of the class noun 'man' and the pronoun 'he'.

Spender

In *Man Made Language*, Dale Spender argues two things: (i) that language determines the limits of our world and constructs our reality (e.g. p. 139); and (ii) that language is created by the males of the species and is still primarily under male control. She believes that there is a 'man's language' and a 'woman's language', men's and women's meanings: while the former are 'authoritative', 'serious', 'direct', the latter lack all of these qualities. It is not surprising, she further asserts, that men's and women's languages are seen to possess these various qualities — the one set, perfervid, strong, positive; the other weak, negative — because the very terms in which research projects have been set up, the rules governing them, the kinds of questions asked, reflect a male bias. This utter and total mastery over language, Spender contends, is one means by which males have

1. D. Spender, *Man Made Language*, Routledge and Kegan Paul, London 1980.

assured their primacy (p. 12). The English language is inclined toward males in both syntax and semantics. (Spender refers to English. Indeed, she argues that the supposed 'natural' gender in English — as opposed to the grammatical one in German, where a wife takes the neuter gender — reflects a *greater* degree of sexist bias.)

Spender presents a formidable array of examples in support of her thesis. She points out that the meaning of some words is different when applied to females and males. For instance: 'He's a professional'; 'she's a professional' (p. 19). Pairs of terms which appear to have approximately the same sense, the only difference being that the one is applied to males and the other to females, become non-equivalent, so that the female expression takes on derogatory significance. 'Lord', for instance, preserves its initial meaning, whereas 'Lady' has undergone a 'process of democratic levelling' and is no longer reserved for women of high rank (p. 17).

I believe, however, that Dale's main claims are often ambiguous and problematic. She does not explicitly characterize the theory of meaning upon which she relies, nor does she make reference to a number of distinctions drawn by linguists and philosophers of language. I shall refer briefly to some of these in order to bring to light some of the ambiguities and problems in her reasoning.

Some Difficulties in Spender's Reasoning

One distinction philosophers have seen fit to draw is that between the 'sense' (*Sinn*) of a sign, and its reference (*Bedeutung*). Frege described the former as the 'mode of presentation' of the sign and the latter as the object it picks out — its bearer.[2] He pointed to this difference as a way out of a puzzle about identity: the two expressions 'the morning star' and 'the evening star' are identical insofar as they pick out the same object (in reference), but they differ in sense. A philosopher from a different tradition has made a similar kind of point: Saussure's 'signified' is analogous to the Fregean 'sense'.[3]

Spender claims that language creates reality. She would presumably concur with Frege's view, therefore, that the 'sense' of an expression determines its reference.[4] The sense of the term 'table', for instance, determines which object it picks out. Since, moreover,

2. G. Frege, *On Sense and Nomination*, in H. Frege and W. Sellars, eds., *Readings in Philosophical Analysis*, New York 1949.
3. F. de Saussure, *Course in General Linguistics*, London 1966.
4. See M. Dummet, *Frege: Philosophy of Language*, London 1973.

Spender believes that language creates reality and that language is man-made, the senses of all expressions in language are determined by the males of the species. Hence, the references of every sign will have been decided upon by the males. Now, immediately, there is an ambiguity in Spender's case. In addition to the 'male' language, she believes that there is a 'women's language'. Is it her belief that the sense, and hence the reference, of the word 'table' was originally determined by the males of the species and that the females now use the expression in a male way? Or does she think that there is a 'masculine' and a 'feminine' sense for the expression? If the latter, are we to suppose that there are masculine and feminine referents for this term? Or do we conclude that the two referents coincide in this case? And, if they coincide here, why do they and what determines when they do not? The claim that the senses of all expressions were originally determined by males is much more plausible than the view that all terms now still have masculine and feminine senses. But it is a weaker thesis: it lends support to the view that 'reality' is male only in an attenuated sense. To draw an analogy: a house that is designed by an architect is, in a sense, the architect's — it is his or her creation. But it probably belongs to somebody else. On the present interpretation of Spender, language would be 'male' only in the sense that the house is the architect's. Perhaps an architect can make things difficult for the occupants of buildings he or she has designed. He or she might have created a house with a dining room far from a kitchen, and this would have made things awkward, indefinitely, for a housewife. Similarly, the male 'designers' of language may have created difficulties for females which last as long as the language survives. But this makes language male no more than it makes the house the architect's. Certainly the man's creation here, *ex hypothesi*, makes matters difficult for women. Just as the housewife may continue, for a long period of time, blaming the architect for his inconvenient design, so may the female language-user (if she were aware of the problem) criticize the men who 'produced' the language. But the housewife cannot blame subsequent architects for her architect's creation, nor could she (or would she) make out that any one architect owned the house. Similarly, female language-users would be wrong to blame all men — unless they consciously continued the tradition of the language creators — for their predecessors' folly. They would be mistaken too, if they to make out that any man 'owned' language as a result of his progenitors' act.

If we are to take the other way of interpreting Spender's claim that there is a male and female language: that there are *now* two sets of senses, we come up against another major problem. If language creates the world, if there is a man's language (a man's set of senses) and a woman's one, and if the two do not overlap, it follows that there is a man's world and a woman's world, and ne'er the twain shall meet. The wife inhabits one world, and her husband another.[5] So what? you may say. The point is important, however. If wife and husband live in different worlds, not only do they fail to communicate with each another (a well-known syndrome if the stories are to be believed), but they may be unable to understand each other. This cannot be put to rights through careful and painstaking effort by both parties; it is an unalterable state of affairs. Quine and Feyerabend describe this phenomenon as the 'incommensurability' of theories: if the corresponding terms in any two theories differ in sense, and sense determines reference, then the two terms pick out different objects. No two propositions — one from each theory — can contradict each other. They will simply be equivocal. I shall return to this point below.

I have mentioned certain problems that present themselves with Spender's thought if we point to one distinction philosophers and linguists have made. If we refer to a further set of distinctions, difficulties of another kind become apparent. Chomsky differentiated linguistic competence — the system of rules and norms of a language — from performance or actual speech behaviour.[6] Chomsky's pair corresponds roughly to Saussure's *'langue'* and *'parole'*. Inside the latter domain, another philosopher, J.L. Austin, has distinguished among types of acts.[7] First of all, there is the locutionary act — the act of uttering an expression with a definite sense and reference. Then there is the illocutionary act that I may perform in doing the locutionary act, — e.g., the promise I may make in uttering the words 'I promise'. Finally, there is the perlocutionary act I may succeed in performing by means of my illocutionary act — e.g. in saying 'the door is open', I may perform the perlocutionary act of getting you to shut it. Now, if we take Spender's claim as applying to linguistic performance, then her reasoning is ambiguous between these three types of act. At one point she suggests that the same linguistic behaviour may be found in members of each gender, but that the descriptions given of the behaviour are gender-specific. For

---

5. I put the point in this picturesque fashion for effect. It is, of course, intended to be generalizable beyond husbands and wives.

6. N. Chomsky, *Aspects of the Theory of Syntax*, Cambridge, Mass., 1965.

7. J.L. Austin, *How to Do Things with Words.*

instance, Spender criticizes Robin Lakoff for using a derogatory term like 'flowery' to characterize women's language. She suggests that some less denigratory term would have been applied to that very same behaviour in a male. However, if she admits that the behaviour could be the same, she may be conceding to her opponents that the language is the same. Witness the expression: 'I think that's a good idea.' Used by a male chairing a meeting, it could be interpreted as an authoritative, finalizing remark; whereas the same utterance issuing from the mouth of a female from the floor might well be interpreted as expressing hesitation, diffidence. The respective illocutionary acts here may well be very different. The male may have performed the act of closing the discussion; while the act of the female may have been that of agreeing with the previous speaker. Additionally, the relative perlocutionary acts may differ from one another: perhaps the male carried out the perlocutionary act of getting the meeting to move on to the next topic; maybe the female performed the act of getting the meeting to continue the discussion along the lines suggested by the previous speaker. However, the *locutionary* acts are the same in each case. Significantly, here, it is the relative illocutionary and perlocutionary acts which appear to exhibit the sexist bias; while it is the locutionary acts — what is said — which deal with reality. Where Spender takes for granted the existence of 'women's language', she is assuming its existence in the illocutionary and perlocutionary acts. But if she wishes to argue that 'male' language produces a male world, she must demonstrate that there is a gender-related difference in language-use specifically in the *locutionary* act, for it is here that reference to reality takes place.

Sense and reference; locutionary, illocutionary acts, etc., are two sorts of distinctions that philosophers and linguists have drawn. By making them we have brought to light some ambiguities in Spender's reasoning. A further area which might reveal difficulties is that of the speakers' intentions. On one theory of meaning,[8] the intentions of the speaker contribute to determining what the speaker meant by his or her utterance. But others disagree.[9] They would argue that what I intend to say when I use a form of words is often no good indication at all of what I have really said.

Spender argues that males intended to construct language in such a

8. See, for instance, H.P. Grice, 'Meaning', *Philosophical Review*, 1966.
9. For example, Keith Graham, in 'Illocution and Ideology', in *Issues in Marxist Philosophy*, Vol. IV, Harvester, 1981, argues that intentions are sometimes irrelevant in determining which illocutionary act has been performed. The speaker himself, he claims, may sometimes be unaware of the true import of his/her utterance.

way as to ensure their dominance. (See Chapter 5.) Thus she tells us that the use of the pronoun 'he' to cover both sexes was not just something that took on as custom and habit; it was deliberately enshrined in an Act of Parliament in 1850 (p. 150). As she points out, there were no female members of Parliament to vote against this Act. However, this does not of itself prove that the men passed the Act in order to ensure their dominance. That, in fact, would be a highly esoteric view of their intentions. In fact, the Act did not concern the use of the pronoun 'he' generally. It was passed in order to simplify the language used in Acts of Parliament. Its title is: 'An Act for shortening the Language used in Acts of Parliament'; and it says: 'Be it enacted, That in all Acts to be hereafter made Words importing the Masculine Gender shall be deemed and taken to include Females, and the singular to include the Plural . . . and the Word "Month" to mean Calendar Month . . . and "County" shall be held to mean also County of a Town or City . . .'[10] The intention of the man introducing the Bill was to shorten the language used in Acts of Parliament, not at all to ensure male dominance. The sentence about the masculine gender occurs in a passage containing several other proposals for the abbreviation of language, none of which conerns relations between the sexes.

Spender's way of presenting the evidence makes it look as though men have always worn dominance on their shirtsleeves, blatantly, for all, including themselves, to see. But they haven't. Though the effect of the use of 'he/man' language may be to subjugate the female sex, it is ludicrous to suppose that every man who has ever used such language intended to do that by his use of it. Many men may have had every intention of *not* doing women down, yet they may still have done so, precisely because their language has an effect that is not apparent to them.

I have mentioned some problems which arise in Spender's reasoning from her failure to distinguish features of language-use to which philosophers and linguists have drawn attention. But I want to argue, more strongly, that Spender's thesis about language is positively *damaging* for women. I believe this to be the case for four main reasons.

Spender's Thesis is Damaging for Women

First of all, on one interpretation of Spender, her thesis is just too bland to be of any value to women. Saying that all language is 'male' serves

10. *The Papers of the House of Commons*, 31 January — 15 August 1850, Bills, Papers 1.

to divert attention from those areas of language which really are sexist.

Secondly, there is the phenomenon to which I have already alluded: the fact that her thesis leads to incommensurability. This is damaging for women, I believe, for the following reason: if husband and wife can neither understand nor communicate with each other, then the wife cannot present criticism of the husband's use of language which he can come to accept. She and he will continue, whatever she says, to occupy their respective universes: he his, she hers. She cannot begin to enter his, nor he hers.

Now, whether or not women will agree that this is damaging for them may depend on their politics. Some feminists will draw the conclusion that this state of affairs is not deleterious to the feminist cause; rather, what it entails is that women should have nothing whatsoever to do with men. Men inhabit their patriarchal realm; women live in a different world — and women should do their level best to ensure that the two universes do not overlap in any sense. Whatever men do, they will be revealing their oppressive natures, so women should have nothing to do with them.

Notice that Spender's picture of language leads to this separatist position. If men and women inhabit different worlds as a result of their language use, then women are unable to communicate with men. They are consequently unable to change men, and they might as well start building their own world, independently of the male oppressor. This is not a positive reason for separatism: rather, separatism is an effect of a thesis about language.

A third reason why Spender's picture of language is damaging for women is that separatism — which is a consequence of Spender's view of language — is deleterious to women's cause. First of all, the separatist's characterization of men as oppressors will be self-confirming, because *any* behaviour on the part of a man will count as oppressive of women. The separatist's picture of males as oppressors may even be self-contradictory, since presumably the ascription of both of any pair of contradictory characteristics to an individual male will equally count as evidence of oppression. Thus a man may be seen to be oppressive if he either shouts at a woman or does not shout at a woman. But that makes the view about male oppression vacuous. Secondly, separatism leads to the view that men are *by nature* oppressors — perhaps biologically, or in virtue of some spiritual essence. What, then, are women by nature? Oppressed? Of course, no Revolutionary Feminist woman would argue that. Yet it seems to be the obvious option available to her.

The separatist may accept that communication has broken down, and suggest that only force can be effective. But force, on its own, unless supplemented by some account of why it may be justified in this case, cannot succeed in changing things for the better. An IRA member *may* (conceivably) get a point across by shooting a politician. But although such violence is nasty anyway, it would be cruel and pointless if there were no possibility of communicating a case. The separatist, similarly, who resorts to force after admitting the impossibility of arguing a point of view, acts both nastily and pointlessly.

Now, there is one option left for the separatist. She will argue for the elimination of all males. SCUM (The Society for Cutting up Men) proposes a particularly radical form of surgery. Perhaps the separatist who plumbs such depths has gone too far to be taken seriously. Without some males the species as a whole would probably die out (though SCUM believes otherwise). The possibility of nuclear war presents us with a very real threat of the Apocalypse. Perhaps historically, it is not accidental that the century which produces the technical means to destroy humanity should also give birth to a movement that believes in the elimination of half of the species.

There is something in Spender which relates to my final criticism of separatism, and which provides further evidence (my fourth reason) that her thesis is damaging to women. There is an ambiguity in Spender's use of the phrase 'women's meanings'. This ambiguity is obscured by her view that there are two worlds — that of the male and that of women. There are those women's meanings which are pejorative, derogatory, because according to her (or according to those whose research she is quoting) they are characterized in that way by males; and there are those new, exciting, different meanings which women begin to discover, as they talk to one another in consciousness-raising groups and suchlike. In these gatherings, according to her, women begin to grasp that there are male and female worlds; they begin to be critical of the dominant (male) world, and to fashion a new one.

Indiscriminate reference to 'women's meanings' — when Spender has these two, quite separate, senses of the expression — serves to gloss over the differences between them. According to her, 'women's language' is seen by men as 'flowery' (see Lakoff), irrational, imaginative, etc. Now, one possible response to this is to take the very same language but to view it positively — the women themselves may appropriate that 'language' and describe it in positive terms. Thus, to take an analogy, Hélène Cixous describes a Chinese story from Sun Tse's manual of strategy — a handbook for the warrior.[11] The story refers to a king who is reputed to have asked Sun Tse to train his one hundred and eighty wives in the art of war. But instead of learning the code, the wives began laughing and chattering and paying no attention to the lesson. To the men, here, these ladies had failed at the art of war. Cixous, however, describes the phenomenon as a divergence of 'two economies' — one masculine and the other feminine. The masculine economy is governed by order, by rules. The feminine one is quite different. The women's laughter and chatter is seen positively. It is part of their non-rule-governed nature. But to see their behaviour like this is simply to take women as we assume some men have wanted them to be, and to redescribe their behaviour. Women, therefore, will have a 'natural' way of being. Kristéva's work is an example of this same tendency. She speaks of 'feminine' discourses: poetry, irrationality, art, etc., which draw on areas repressed by the patriarchal culture.

It is not in women's interest, however, simply to remain as they have previously been characterized by males. Their 'natures' are not static. Women are not simply nurturant, passive, poetic and imaginative. They are not irrational. They are also active and rational creatures. Spender's picture of language — by leaving ambiguous the notion of 'women's meanings' — allows for the Kristéva reading of this expression. It allows 'women's language' to be the same as it is characterized by males, instead of being a new and exciting creation of women themselves.

Sexism and 'He/Man' Language

I believe, then, not only that there are problems with Dale Spender's thesis about language, but that her view is positively damaging for women. However, I do not wish to say that language never exhibits sexism. The use of the expressions 'he' and 'man', for instance, in their purportedly gender-neutral fashions, do reinforce power relations between the sexes. Let us look at some of Spender's examples.

She tells us that, in 1746, John Kirkby formulated his 'eighty-eight grammatical Rules'. One of these, she says, stated that the 'male gender was *more comprehensive* than the female' (p. 148). As she points out, in articulating this norm, Kirkby did not mean that there were

11. H. Cixous, 'Castration or Decapitation', *Signs*, Autumn 1981.

more males than females. What he must have been doing was reflecting the common belief, in society at the time, that males counted for more than females. Of course this common belief was actually *true*. It was the aristocracy and the gentry — males — who occupied the positions of power in England: they were the politicians and the doctors, and generally the educated. Women, as Rousseau said (and, of course, he meant upper-class women), were to be educated to be pleasing to men (i.e. males). And even in the working class, the man (the male) held power and authority in the family (though not in the work-place). So Kirkby's reasoning did indeed serve to reinforce a state of affairs that was already in existence: the domination of women by men.

Kirkby's Rule that the male gender is more comprehensive than the female makes no sense independently of these facts about 18th-century society. In a society where the roles of men and women were equal, no grammarian would propose that the male gender was 'more comprehensive' than the female. Kirkby did not need to justify his rule, since it was implicit in 'common sense' assumptions of the period. In fact, if allowed to stand on its own feet, independently of these assumptions which give it some sense, there are no grounds for accepting Kirkby's rule. By articulating these assumptions, and giving them the authority of a grammatical rule, Kirkby was surely reinforcing them. Subsequent usage of the pronoun 'he', in its supposedly gender-neutral manner, has continued this process.

With reference to the Act of Parliament mentioned earlier; although, as I have remarked, I disagree with Spender as regards the *intentions* of those proposing the Bill, I do believe that it had the effect, and even the function, of preserving male dominance. Once again, if it had not been for male dominance generally in society, there would have been no reason to propose that 'he' should encompass 'she' rather than the other way about. It did not have to be uppermost in the minds of those introducing the Bill that they wanted to ensure male dominance, because the phenomenon was already well entrenched at the time. After all, the proposal that 'she' should encompass 'he' would have fulfilled equally well their aim of simplifying the language. But they would not have been keen on this suggestion, because they would have seen it as leading in some way to the subordination of males. Some evidence that this would have been their reaction is provided by a recent parallel case, in which male nursery-school teachers objected to a proposal that 'she' should be a generic term for members of their occupation. They resented the suggestion because they believed it would have implied a lowering of their status.

This latter example suggests that 'he' is not at all functioning as a generally neutral term. 'One', unlike 'man', carries no non-neutral connotations. Old is sometimes used in neutral fashion, as in 'How old are you?', but it is invariably clear from the context that this is how it is intended. In the case of 'man' and 'he', however, the context does not always make it clear that the term is supposed to be being used in a neutral manner. Elaine Morgan provides an example of the prose used by evolutionists and ecologists: 'It is just as hard for man to break the habit of thinking of himself as central to the species as it was to think of himself as central to the universe. He sees himself quite unconsciously as the main line of evolution, with a female satellite revolving around him.'[12] The sense of the noun 'man' is *ambiguous*. It is not clear whether or not the expression is to be understood in a neutral manner. The ambiguity allows for the continued subjection of the female. Evolutionists began by thinking neutrally and then, tacitly, switched to thinking in terms only of the male. Employers who advertise for a 'man' can trade on the ambiguity (a) to dissuade women from applying for the job; and (b) to appoint a male.

Here the confusion generated by the continued use of 'he' and 'man' in their purportedly neutral senses, justifies the claim that continued use of such language serves to reinforce male oppression. So long as we can switch, unconsciously, from the neutral to the non-neutral senses, in one breath, we are silencing and excluding women.

There are two reasons, then, why 'he' language tends to reinforce unequal power relations between the sexes. First, the claim that there is a genuinely neutral sense of the term 'he' is, in fact, false; the introduction of such language presupposes unequal relations between the sexes; and its continual use reinforces oppression. Secondly, there are often tacit switches from the supposedly neutral to the non-neutral sense — slides which confirm that a greater degree of importance is often attached to the male in the neutral use of the expression.

Use of 'he/man' language, then, does seem to reinforce unequal power relations between the sexes. This conclusion, however, rather than indicating that such expressions are part of a male language reflecting a male reality, suggests that such discourse is *ideological* —it functions to disguise the power relations between the sexes. These relations are not presented clearly, for all to see; rather, it is because

12. Quoted in Spender, p. 152.

there is domination of one sex by the other that the expressions 'man' and 'he' can be used in their purportedly neutral senses. But, as we have seen, there is *really* no such thing as a neutral use.

To conclude: while I strongly disagree with the 'philosophical' strands in Dale Spender's book, she presents an array of examples from English, many of which do provide incontrovertible evidence of sexism in language. To recognize that 'he/man' language — as one case of such sexism — reinforces male supremacy is not at all to do away with that primacy. But it is a step in the right direction.

To say, as Spender does, that there are two realities — the male and the female — not only makes criticism of the male 'reality' impossible, but actually weakens the feminist case. For to suppose that the phenomenon is ubiquitous makes it more difficult to see where sexism in language really operates.[13]

Reprinted from *RP* 34

13. I should like to thank Jonathan Rée, Martin Barker and Keith Graham for commenting on an earlier draft of this, and Noel Parker for his assiduous commenting on several versions.

5. Confrontations

Discourse Fever
Post-Marxist Modes of Production

Tony Skillen

According to whoever wrote the editorial 'notes' for *Radical Philosophy* 17, 'The present upsurge of fundamental Marxist researches may indicate an exit route from the circle of philosophy's deaths and rebirths, via which the problem of the specificity of "the philosophical" might be both subverted and understood.' And according to Graham Burchell in *Radical Philosophy* 18, two books of Barry Hindess and Paul Q. Hirst 'may give some support to this hope.'

Are Hindess and Hirst the long-awaited intellectual hegemonogues of the British left? This is doubtful. Marxism needs, no doubt, to be transcended, but not, it seems to me, in favour of the phenomenalist relativism that pervades the writings of Hindess and Hirst and their co-thinkers. I want to discuss certain philosophical positions that have been advanced by them, especially in their writings in *Economy and Society* from 1974 to 1976 (including their letter of resignation from its editorial board and Hirst's 'Althusser and the Theory of Ideology') and Hirst's widely read Communist University of Cambridge lecture (*'Problems and Advances in the Theory of Ideology'*, hereafter PA, 1976). That these sources correspond to the doctrines of their books can be confirmed from Graham Burchell's précis (RP18), from Andrew Collier's article (RP20), from Tim Putnam's review in *Capital and Class* (Spring 1978) and from Rod Aya's review in *Monthly Review* (January 1978).

Hindess and Hirst deny the realist view that scientific theories are valid to the extent that they correspond with what is objectively the case. Rather they urge that theories can only be 'validated' within their own terms — none, therefore, is more 'valid' or 'invalid' than another. As this renders the very idea of intellectual validation redundant, Hindess and Hirst insist on a practical, *political* criterion of acceptability in terms of the capacity to 'provide strategic leadership for the political practice' (resignation letter).

So it is for 'history' and for 'ideology'. Historians have no independent object; their practices 'define the past'. Ideology is not, on the other hand, a misrepresentation of what science or history may truly represent: '. . . we do not have a truth/falsity, illusion/reality opposition here' (PA). Thus historians' work is the activity of 'social and political ideologies', and ideologies can be assessed only in terms of their *political* 'effects'.

I have stressed this common phenomenalist/pragmatist thread. But, as the arguments develop in specific ways according to the specific focus, I shall separate out four 'theses' for discussion purposes. I shall adopt what may be a tedious 'quotation' approach, at the risk of the radical and philistine unfairness that 'out of context' quoting achieves. I do this in order to display the sheer muddle of the work I am criticizing, a muddle that brief summary, were it possible, could only conceal. I shall comment on four strands of thought:

  A Discourse Phenomenalism
  B Ideology and Hirst's Steamroller
  C Historical Fordism ('history is bunk')
  D The Politicization of Analysis

Discourse Phenomenalism

Replying to a critical note of Ted Benton's (in *Economy and Society* 74–75), Hirst writes: 'My position is based on an attempt to break out of the circle of classical philosophy, to go beyond the opposition of idealism and materialism, to break the connection of epistemological theory with metaphysics . . . it is not committed to making ontological assumptions about the status of objects independently of the discourse in which they are designated.' Philosophical materialism, assuming 'that the real is ordered and knowable, that it is capable of giving rise to knowledge', 'necessary spiritualizes matter of materializes ideas'.

These doctrines are developed further in *Mode of Production and Social Formation*, (hereafter MPSF), extensively quoted and summarized by Graham Burchell in RP18, and, among many other writings, in *Marx's 'Capital' and Capitalism To-Day* (Hirst, Hindess, Cutler and Hussain, hereafter MCCT). In general, Hirst *et al.* argue, it is impossible to speak of objects existing independently of thought yet corresponding to thought in such a way that it can be said that the thought is true (or false) of such objects.

1. 'Objects of discourse are constituted in and through the discourse

which refer to them' (MCCT, p. 216).

2. 'What is specified in theoretical discourse cannot be specified extra-discursively: it can be conceived only through that discourse or a related, critical, or complementary one' (MCCT, p. 229).

3. This 'is not to deny forms of existence outside discourse but it is to deny that existence takes the form of objects representable in discourse' (MPSF, p. 21).

4. 'The rejection of epistemology implies that the relation between discourse and its objects cannot be conceived as an epistemological relation at all' (MPSF, p. 22).

Responses to 1–4 above

1. Hirst *et al.*'s claims here form *part* of a discourse. Hence the things they 'refer' to — other discourses (Marxism etc.) — are *ex hypothesi* constituted by the Hirst discourse. Hence they cannot claim to be telling us anything. They cannot be 'referring' at all. (Even a fiction pretends to be about people, etc.). Yet they certainly write as if they have something to tell us. It is important to note that the view under discussion lends as much intellectual legitimacy to Christian Science, scientology or astrology — each of which 'refers' to various 'objects' and 'processes' — as to botany, microbiology or linguistics. Removing epistemological 'tyranny' consecrates real tyranny. Come back Lysenko, all is forgotten.

2. It is tautological to say that you cannot 'specify' anything save through discourse. (Compare: 'you cannot perceive anything save through having perceptual experiences', the innocent truism with which Berkeley launches his position.) But that a thing cannot be discoursed about save through words, or conceived save through concepts, does not establish its linguistic or conceptual status. (Nor does the tautology that a 'speaker' is defined in terms of language establish that speakers are verbal entities.) It is a further question whether language is a condition of knowledge. As I think that animals know things, and that Hirst *et al.* fail to recognize the significance of our 'animal' faculties, it will be clear where I stand on that issue.

In this passage, Hirst *et al.* speak of 'related' or 'complementary discourses' as referring to 'a *common* discourse-object ("it")'. It is difficult to see how they can consistently speak in this way since object 'A'-in-discourse-D lacks criteria of identity (same at the level of homonymy) with object 'A₁'-in-discourse-D₁. I am assuming here that discourses can be (objectively) individuated, an assumption hard to reconcile with the doctrines in question.

3. If you say 'the ice won't break' and promply fall through it, it seems reasonable to say, once your teeth stop chattering, that the ice's 'form of existence' failed to correspond with your beliefs. And this remark seems to imply both a distinction between your 'discourse' and 'existence'; and the 'representability' of 'existence' in 'discourse' — a correspondence. Hirst *et al.* often speak of 'Discourse' and 'existence' ('reality' in scare quotes) as if one could, albeit to attack the idea, speak of a relation between 'discourse-in-general' and 'reality-in-general'. But, apart from anything else, it needs to be stressed that discourses are themselves as real as anything else and that, therefore, Hirst *et al.*'s ban ought to fall on the idea that *discourses* exist 'in a form representable in discourse'. Talk about discourses is not relevantly different in this respect from talk about ice — or about 'forms of existence outside discourse' for that matter.

4. Epistemology is the enquiry into the kinds of 'justifications', or lack of them, for different kinds of belief. It begins on the simple basis that claims are made, beliefs are held etc., *as* true. When, for example, Hirst *et al.* assert that 'the relation between discourse and its objects cannot be conceived as an epistemological relation', the question whether what they say is to be accepted is an 'epistemological' one. Similarly, if I am accused of *misrepresenting* their position, or of being *ignorant* of its historical background etc., an epistemic claim is being made. You can't bludgeon epistemology away.

I have been concerned to show the 'self-stultifying' character of the Hirst, Hindess, Cutler, Hussain type of position — to bring out its 'unspeakability'. As a reading even of Graham Burchell's summary brings home, their work is replete with claims about 'epistemology's' hunt for 'privileged access', 'the immediately given', 'absolute guarantees' etc. But it is a painful achievement of 'bourgeois' epistemology to have questioned these *el dorados* of philosophy and it seems to me a minor scandal that ancient slogans have been wheeled out in the guise of space-age semiology to condemn most 'hitherto existing' thought to the rubbish tip.

My response has been written from a broadly empiricist and realist standpoint — the one scoldingly ascribed to much of Marx by Hirst and his co-thinkers. I do not deny that there are big difficulties for such a position. What I do deny, however, is that the philosophical work of Hirst, Hindess *et al.* constitutes a serious challenge to that standpoint. Its a priori celebration of the impossibility of argument or discussion with the uninitiated functions, moreover, to ghettoize the left-intelligentsia even as it aims to liberate it from a fetishized

'Marxism', and to promote within it an almost paranoid irrationalism.

Ideology and Hirst's Steamroller

Marx did not invent the idea that people live their lives more or less befogged by illusion. What he did was to argue, against Enlightenment reformers' trust in verbal education presented by the educated, that these illusions were systematically bound up with people's 'real life conditions,' particularly with their economic conditions. Hirst well expresses Marx's view: 'Reality generates false recognitions of itself by subjecting subjects to circumstances in which their experience is distorted' (*Althussser and the Theory of Ideology*, hereafter ATI). What Hindess and Hirst try to do, however, largely following Althusser, is to refute, in one transcendental argument, both the Marxian orthodoxy and the more general idea of ideology as illusion or misrepresentation: 'The consequence of rejecting the concept of "representation" is to destroy the classic Marxist problem of ideology' (ibid.).

I shall address myself to the above article and to the 'more detailed' *Problems and Advances* pamphlet, bearing in mind that these articles advance their theses in critical co-operation with Althusserianism. (I think I omit explications of Althusser that Hirst himself rejects). Once again I quote:

1. 'Ideology is not a distorted representation of reality' (PA, p. 2); '. . . signification; the products of signifying practices, do not "represent" anything outside them, they cannot serve as a means of expression of class interests or of (functional) mis-recognition of social relations' (ATI).

    'The means of representation determine the represented. This obliterates the classical problem of "representation" ' (ATI); 'Knowledge is (*not*) formed through the consciousness or experience of human subjects', as maintained by 'Classical Empiricism' (PA, p. 2).

    'Althusser denies that knowledge through experience is possible and therefore that class positions automatically generate experience-effects' (ATI).

    'You can see here (in the "empiricist" view) that the reality or truth of ideology is outside it in the prior determination . . . of the system of places. It follows that reductionism is a legitimate mode of analysis' (PA, p. 4).

2. 'Ideology is not ideal or spiritual' (PA, p. 6). 'Ideas do not exist as

spiritual entities. Ideologies are social relations, they are as real as the economy' (PA, p. 7). 'For Althusser, ideas are real and not "ideal" because they are always inscribed in social practices and are expressed in objective social forms (languages, rituals etc.) As such they have definite effects' (PA, p. 7).

'Ideology is a set of social practices and social representations and rituals: it is a structure of social relationships' (PA, p. 6).

3. 'Ideology is not illusory for the reason we've given before; it is not illusion, it is not falsity, because how can something which has effects be false? . . . it would be like saying that a black pudding is false, or a steamroller is false' (PA, p. 14). 'The struggles involved are for the removal of real ideological obstacles; social practices, not illusions' (PA, p. 14).

Responses to 1–3 above

1. Empiricists traditionally present the paradigm of 'the knowledge relation' as an object causing (with the aid of other conditions) an experience of it (you *see* the apple because it affects your senses, etc.). Hence, as Hirst says, it focuses on origins (causes). Such a model, says Hirst, dominates traditional Marxism: the economy effects one's perception of *it*, but, depending on one's class vantage point, one's perception may be distorted. As Hirst mock-quotes: 'If one is a finance capitalist, one will see the world differently than if one is an artisan.' Hirst goes on to treat this 'vulgar Marxism' as an application of empiricist assumptions. But if you believe that ideologies 'represent' things as the case (illusorily) and that, however false they are, they nonetheless 'represent' (in another sense of that word — manifest, issue from) the 'actual life conditions' in which the relevant experiences have occurred, you are not compelled to embrace vulgar Marxism. Nor are you compelled to embrace 'reductionism', for any view of knowledge as a causal phenomenon would still need to distinguish causes which 'produce' knowledge from causes which do not. For example, the bright sunlight might cause you to recognize it. But some diseases or drugs might cause the same experience. Thus, when Marxists say 'you only think that *because* you are a petit-bourgeois', they need to show (a) the connection of consequence between the belief and the class position, and (b) how this position is *epistemically* relevant ('distorting'). Only by a pre-emptive insistence that economic conditions alone are *real* conditions would vulgar Marxism *identify* itself with empiricism (see certain passages in *The German Ideology*). Thus, as Hirst rightly suggests, the classical view of ideology

involves 'causal' and 'epistemic' dimensions. And, contrary to Hirst, we might go so far as to say that Marx did establish the importance of economic conditions in shaping human experience and human outlooks and that Hirst's arguments, despite their assimilation of the general conceptualization of 'ideology' to a vulgar economistic reductionism, do not refute this general view, but trade on the weakness of the specific vulgar theory which identifies 'reality' with the economy. As a corollary, the insistence on a pluralistic view of human social life does not require the abandonment of empiricism or realism.

2. There is a tendency in Marxism (much advertised in the writings of Acton, Plamenatz, et al.) to set up a dualism of thought (ideology) and reality (economy): as if the 'economic base' could even be abstractly conceptualized save as involving human goals, intentions or calculations. But then how can such things be 'superstructural'? And Hirst rightly notes a bad tendency to equate the 'economic' with the 'real' and the 'ideological' with the 'unreal' — hence their insistence on the reality of ideology: religious activity exists as much as does economic activity. (Whether their de-epistemologist vision allows them *any* such ontological claims is another matter.) But their abandonment of vulgar Marxism immerses them in other vulgarities.

If *anything* exists as a spiritual entity, it nonetheless exists and may have effects. It is a false antithesis to counterpose (in precisely the style of vulgar materialism) the *mental* to the *real*, albeit that Hirst's fallacy is concealed through a punning use of 'ideal' (= 'unreal'? = 'mental'?). This vulgar materialist assumption, I suggest, drives Hirst into *identifying* ideologies with their material and hence 'objective' embodiments, expressions or vehicles. Hence the shuffle between insisting (correctly) that ideologies are 'inscribed', 'expressed', 'represented', in rituals etc. and insisting that they *are* such practices. But a practice is only 'ideological' in virtue of its *significance* or *meaning*, insofar as it 'signifies'. Thus, while 'ideological struggle might consist in the destruction or suppression of monuments or rituals only dogmatism could blind us to the capacity of ideology to live on in people's brains. And only a dogmatic behaviourism would blind us to the distinction between the 'criticism of weapons and the weapons of criticism': between altered 'behaviour' and altered 'outlook'.

Human social practice 'communicates' a meaning: a ritual's *movements* signify what its words say about the order of the world; a businessman's suit and manner signify his busy, successful, probity. But that such 'signification' is general does not entail that 'signifying practices do not "represent" anything outside them'. In order to reverse the rhetorical effect of Hirst's spiritual/material contrast, consider the practices associated with physicalist ideologies of mental illness. Illnesses, depressions, etc. may 'present themselves' as simply happening for no good reason, and doctors may encourage this by prescribing pills and so forth. Yet, one who investigates such practice, such a 'mode of experiencing', may suggest that this ideology *misrepresents* what is *in fact* a *significant* process — an impotent, despairing protest, a response to abandonment or whatever. If this were the case, as it might be, it would involve an 'ideology representing something outside itself', even though what is represented (the illness) may itself be 'ideological'. One 'discourse' may misrepresent another; discourses can rely on 'meta-discourses' which misrepresent them. (Though they negotiate through echoes, blind people often speak of a 'sixth sense' or a 'cheek sensation' as guiding them.) Hirst denies that ideologies 'represent' — and hence 'misrepresent'. Sexist ideologies do not (distortedly) represent women as naturally inferior? Racist ideologies do not consign non-whites to perpetual savagery? Religious ideologies do not represent the world as the creation of gods? Capitalist ideologies do not represent human freedom and welfare as necessitating the private ownership of the means of production? The position may have earned its admirers through the sheer effrontery of its assertion.

3. Ideology, we are told, is not illusion, because ideology has effects (people actually go to work, to war, to Wembley etc.). Therefore it cannot be *false,* any more than a black pudding or steamroller can. Sufferers from delusions, nightmares, hallucinations, etc. will rejoice at this panacea. Their errors are, as a matter of logic, harmless and ineffectual. Not that Hirst even thinks that what has effects could be *true* either. Steamrollers cannot be that. Generally, though, we could retort, with the 'plain man' of bourgeois epistemology, that beliefs, outlooks, perspectives, assumptions, perceptions true *or* false, can and do have (real and determinate) effects. The argument is an invalid steamroller, a fallacious black pudding. Yet Hirst accords it a central place. And why one should think that a struggle against illusions is not a struggle against 'real obstacles' eludes me.

Historical Fordism: 'History is Bunk'

That history cannot be *a* science in the sense that physics or even political economy might be follows simply from the qualitative complexity of individual events, processes, things, people. This is not to rule out that historians can be 'scientific' in method and approach:

sifting evidence, comparing different situations to confirm or shake their hypotheses, and so on. But such banalities are swept away by the Hirst–Hindess broom. They attack historical research (they may except research into the history of their own thought) as (a) impossible and (b) irrelevant. The Resignation Letter is pertinent here. History, they say, is not 'a coherent and possible object of research'.

1. 'History is not a given object . . . since (by definition) it does not exist.'
2. 'These are only practices of writing and constituting definite histories. These practices define the past and transform artefacts (documents, bones, palaces, kitchen middens, etc.) into representations of the hitherto existing.'
3. 'It can be argued that, as the conditions of existence of social relations must be constantly re-produced in order for them to exist, no analysis of hitherto existing social relations has any relevance or epistemological privilege.'
4. 'Only teleology can ascribe an effectivity to the hitherto existing.'
5. 'Marxism is anti-historical because it is committed to history in another sense of the word, to the crucial struggle of our age.'
   [Althusser struggles laudably to] 'reconstitute a Marxism . . . capable . . . of providing strategic leadership for political practice.'

Response to 1–5 above

1. I do not know of anyone, even among those who believe there are 'given objects' at all, who think *'history* is a given object'. Knowledge of the past (like knowledge of the future) necessarily involves having *'presently* available evidence'. Hindess and Hirst, for example, claim to have 'consistently opposed' empiricism, including that of the *Economy and Society* editorial. The remaining editors reply that H & H helped write the editorial. Are we then to accept Hindess and Hirst's (historical) claim? We have *now* to investigate the evidence. Do Hindess and Hirst licence us regarding such things to think what accords with our 'ideological and political' practices? Are *these* 'the given'?

Hindess and Hirst are attacking what they argue to be an 'academicist' wallowing in the past that they see as characteristic of many 'Marxists'. In this attack they produce dangerous and self-destructive weapons — yet they go on writing as if they believe the world will go on 'reproducing' at least readers.

2. If there *are* 'definite' practices of writing history, then these

practices ('discourses'?) are *themselves* historical events. But *ex hypothesi* H & H cannot consistently speak of such things. (It is typical of theoretical phenomenalism to adopt a *realist* position towards theoretical endeavours, just as 'phenomenology' thinks it can at once 'bracket reality' and *quote* people's-real-*accounts* of 'reality'.) That historians can 'define' the past by 'constituting' the meaning of artefacts (bones?) in accordance with their own 'ideology', is a crass mockery of disciplined historical enquiry.

3. The 'need' for 'constant' 'reproduction' of 'conditions of existence' amounts, as far as I can see, simply to the 'need' for conditions to hold for the occurrence of whatever occurs — whether that be persistence or obliteration. How much this involves 're-production', in the sense of the bringing about of new *instances* of things or processes, is a further question. But that re-production occurs *over time* and is dependent on historically 'provided' materials and forms (which may or may not themselves be exhaustible) is obvious. And that historical research might assist enquiry into the capacity or likelihood of 'things' such as an amenable work-force being 're-produced' in certain conditions is obvious too. The necessity of continual re-production has no tendency to render history irrelevant.

4. Aristotle thought that efficient causes were coexistent with their effects. And, while Hume defined causes as *antecedent* to their effects, students of philosophy know that causality is a hellish problem. But those prone to accept Hindess and Hirst's a priori doctrine of impotence of antecedents should at least be concerned that it rules out the striking of a match as causally relevant to the later boiling of the kettle. That we are dealing here with a short-term sequence is irrelevant to the point of principle (ten minutes is a long time in philosophy). A hard doctrine! Hindess and Hirst speak here of 'teleology.' This seems mere paper-bag-bursting.

5. If Hindess and Hirst deny the 'effectivity' of the past on the present (has already gone out of 'existence' in their mortal phraseology). But, alas, the present precedes the future. Hence, by their own argument 'strategic' theory is as 'absurd' as poring over old documents to establish how things came to be as they are. For the present can have no 'effectivity' in the future. Plans, campaigns etc. (however short term!) are absurd — doomed to go out of existence before their goals come about!

The Politicization of Analysis

Hindess and Hirst abandon epistemic qustions (questions of truth, evidence, probability, etc.) in favour of a frankly 'political' criterion (continuing the 'theory in the interest of politics' line of their resignation letter). This view is developed, for example, in Hirst's *Althusser and the Theory of Ideology*.

1. 'Class analysis we may retain, not in the sense of sociological reduction but of political evaluation. Not a reference to origin but a consideration of effect.' 'To recognize ideological forms as "bourgeois" involves taking a political stand on what is and is not bourgeois' (ATI).
2. '. . . calculation of political consequences . . .' (ATI).
3. '. . . what the calculation of effect *is* depends upon one's political position . . . Consequences can be deduced from a definite political position . . .' (ATI). [Women's struggles] 'may be important in creating the basis on which an important section of the population is prepared to take socialist agitation seriously' (PA, p. 14).
4. 'The struggles involved are for the removal of real ideological obstacles, social practices, not illusions' (PA, p. 14).

Response to 1–4 above

1. Hindess and Hirst are right to stress the distinction between the origin and the political tendency of ideas and ideologies, and right to highlight the double talk that has tried to conceal this distinction in the name of preserving dogmatic versions of 'class analysis'. But they offer a pragmatist reductionism in place of a class-origin reductionism. Thus, in denying that 'bourgeois ideology' is 'bourgeois' in virtue of its origins, they rule out of account the possibility that some aspects of the bourgeoisie's class outlook might be progressive and even true. Or rather, they insist on their own doubletalk which would *deny* its bourgeois status, in virtue of its supposed serviceability to socialist revolution.

2. If I believed in the imminent collapse of capitalism from forces internal to the economy (falling rate of profit, etc.), then my *evaluation* of movements would be affected by this. But Hindess and Hirst, while pointing this out, insist that my calculation of *consequences* is itself a function of my political position (evaluation). So we are in a messy circle. Contrary to them, it might be thought vital for political activity that predictions be minimally contaminated by wishes ('pessimism of the intellect': Gramsci). Here again Hindess and Hirst's contempt for empirical reason lands them in gross subjectivism — a politics of wish-fulfilment.

3. In place of the dogmatic schoolteacher lecturing to the ignorant,

Hindess and Hirst offer us the manipulator backing movements on purely socialist-utilitarian lines. That the women's movement might have as much to *teach to*, as to learn from, male leftists is not on Hirst's cards. Rather, it is seen as a useful force to be backed, theoretically legitimated and *not* to be argued with or criticized (though its theories will no doubt be criticized for empiricism, 'humanism', etc.). Followers of the left will recognize the antiquity of this opportunist approach — and the shifts and reversals of 'analysis' that it entails.

4. I have pointed out already the fallacy of counterposing *illusions* to *real* forces. Illusions occur and have effects. Struggle against them is real struggle which consists in more than words. To counterpose politics to education (or to dis-illusionment) is fallacious as well as dangerous.

Generally speaking, a pragmatist reduction fails to avoid the epistemological issue. For the question always arises: will this line have these (desirable or undesirable) effects?[1] Moreover, a politics which not only downgrades questions of truth (Machiavellianism) but systematically seeks to extrude such issues from its frame of reference, must I suggest, be a politics of contempt — a *practical* anti-humanism. The extrusion can never be achieved. Always it will be a matter of hiding uncomfortable truths or promulgating useful fictions. It is handy, however, to think that, outside one's system, no justification need be sought for one's beliefs and one's practices.

Reprinted from *RP* 20

1. See my reply to Peter Binns in *RP*3; and Andrew Collier, 'Truth and Practice', *RP*5.

Marxist Modes

Jonathan Rée

Here is a tempting book[1] — a kind of teach-yourself the new semiotics, a simple primer about Barthes, Lacan and post-Althusserian Marxism. I came across it by accident, when I saw it peeping out of a friend's luggage. 'It's very good,' I was told: 'inspiring and clear.' I dipped into the book cautiously — attempting, as Virginia Woolf once advised, 'to get the hang of the sentences' and 'trying a sentence' or two on my tongue'. For a start: 'The emergence of mechanistic tendencies from structuralist analyses revealed its [structuralism's] complicity with the idealism of bourgeois ideology' (2–3). Something worried me about this one. It has a sharp flavour when you roll it round your mouth: 'complicity with idealism' sounds like the language of a state trial; and the menacing reference to 'mechanistic tendencies' reminds me of the righteous agents of Law, Order and Decency closing in on some furtive deviant. Over a few pages, I paused again: 'In spite of the radical potentiality of structuralist thought, therefore, there remains the danger of thinking of an immanent structure . . . ' (21). This has less of forensic acid, perhaps, but it evokes similar associations of smug authority; in fact it reminded me of school reports nervously delivered up to mother and father; 'in spite of Jonathan's undoubted potential, there remains a danger that . . . etc.'

Both these sentences struck me as having a strong flavour of manicheism: they are the sort of announcement made by people who live in a simple world of pure virtue and unrelieved vice, of god and the devil; they made me expect that the authors of *Language and Materialism* were going to try and set me on the true and only Path of Radical Potentiality, hurrying me past the enticing side tracks

1. Rosalind Coward and John Ellis, *Language and Materialism: Developments in Semiology and the Theory of the Subject*, Routledge and Kegan Paul, London 1977. My thanks to Wendy Hollway, Jean McCrindle, David Murray, Rip Bulkeley, Kate Soper, and especially Jim Hopkins.

leading to idealism, bourgeois ideology or immanent structures, where persons of mechanistic tendencies lie in wait.

But this is supposed to be a theoretical work, not an anthology of aphorisms. It is a guidebook to an intellectual synthesis advocated by some Parisian intellectuals (notably, Julia Kristeva and Philippe Sollers) over the last ten years. The *nouveau mélange* which it advertises has a variety of names: 'the new semiotics', 'neo-structuralism', 'discourse theory' and 'theory of the subject', amongst others. The purpose of *Language and Materialism* is to make out the claim that this mixture of ideas, taken from the psychology of Lacan, the literary theory of Barthes, and (with a pinch of salt) the social theory of Althusser, is the legitimate heir and successor not only to the dynasties of psychoanalysis, founded by Freud, and structuralism, founded by Saussure, but also to the dynasty of dialectical and historical materialism, founded by Marx. A settlement which united these houses would be momentous indeed. Let us see how it is proposed to arrange it.

One: Marxism and the Synthesis of Lacan and Barthes

The tradition to which the new semiotics stands closest is that of structuralism, whose origins are said to lie in Saussure's linguistics — especially in (a) the concept of *langue,* meaning a whole system of signs, whose entire structure of reciprocal ('diacritical') differentiation is necessary to confer meaning on any particular, token utterance (*parole*); and in (b) the concept of the doubleness of signs —with a visible or audible face (the signifier) and an inner meaning (the signified). (The signified in the sense represented by the signifier.) Some historians trace the whole history of 20th-century linguistics to these inventions of Saussure's; and many writers (notably Lévi-Strauss) have seen Saussurian linguistics as the model for the social sciences. The connection is made by seeing all human actions — non-linguistic as well as linguistic — as representing, in a sense, meanings, which presuppose a total structure of actual or possible actions, a kind of societal *langue*. In very general terms — in its dualism between a 'social world' of meanings and reasons, and a natural world of mechanisms and causes — this way of thinking has mingled with some of the softer elements of Anglo-American sociology; through the works of Sartre, Laing and Cooper it has entered many areas of English common sense and ordinary language; and, at another extreme, it connects both with phenomenology and with the anti-naturalistic philosophies of social science of, for instance, Winch and

MacIntyre. Roughly (*very* roughly, as you will see below, p. 344), this liaison was authorized by Saussure himself, who foresaw that his linguistics might one day be incorporated into a general science of signs in society — an unborn science for which he earmarked the name 'semiotics'.

The problem which (according to Coward and Ellis's version of history at least) obstructed the development of structuralist social science was that of 'the subject'. Traditional structuralism (they say) always presented structures as if they existed objectively, outside the individual. Individual subjectivity was placed beyond the pale of possible explanation, or even (with Althusserian ruthlessness) annihilated altogether. The new theory of the subject, according to Coward and Ellis, welcomes individual subjectivity back inside the portals of social science, not by abjuring structuralism, but by undertaking to explain subjectivity as an effect of structures. For Coward and Ellis, the pioneer of this revision of structuralism is Roland Barthes, especially in his commentary on Balzac's short story 'Sarrasine' (*S/Z*, 1970). In this book, Barthes tried to corrode the 'readerly' ideas that writing, especially fiction, is a matter of an author thinking up characters and writing a story about them which is to be passively ingested by a gormless reader. In truth, says Barthes, the effects of literature are produced by the reader rather than the author; the text originates not in the author but in the functioning of language as a transindividual structure; and the seeming naturalness of the characters and stories of realist fiction is an illusion. The realism of classical literature is thus, according to Barthes, a baroque subterfuge of inauthenticity: it claims to be the most natural, sincere and honest mode of writing, but is in fact the height of artifice; it practices an art that conceals the artificiality of human subjectivity — that of author, reader, and fictional character alike — by disguising the arbitrariness of language; and in this sense, it is a 'political' activity, and a reactionary one at that.

All of this, and Barthes's sentence-by-sentence commentary on Balzac's story, seems to me to be to a large degree substantial and intelligible. But Barthes himself does not offer any large, schematic generalities about the nature of 'readerly' writing. Coward and Ellis, however, following one or two scattered hints in Barthes, try to make good this deficiency: the distinctive feature of classical or realist writers, they say, is that they presuppose 'an identity between signifier and signified' (49). With this suggestion about the essential error of all realist writers, I find myself, I must admit, in dire difficulties.

But Coward and Ellis always try to be attentive guides, extending a helpful hand whenever they think I may be getting stuck. This is just such an occasion, and they offer a whole range of paraphrases to help me out. With realist writers, they explain, 'language is treated as though it stands in for . . . the real world'; or again, it is seen as 'identical with the real world'. 'The business of realist writing is,' they continue, 'to be the equivalent of reality, to imitate it'; and for the realist, finally, 'the world is identical to, the equivalent of, the real world' (47). How could I ask for more lifelines, and all of them compressed within the compass of a single paragraph? But surely — I soon notice — aren't they all tangled together, and pulling me in opposite direction? My initial difficulty was that I couldn't see how realist writers could be said to identify signifier and signified; and when the well-intentioned rescue party tells me that this means that realists confuse words with the world, and takes words and world to be 'identical', and 'equivalent', and on top of this that they see words as 'imitations' of the world, then I simply have to tell them to go away and leave me to my own devices. I asked for an explanation of a proposition about signifiers and signifieds, and I was given a set of obscure and probably incompatible formulations about words and the world — two relations which, whilst no doubt connected, are far from being identical. Can it be that our guides, in their scorn for the realist' supposed error of identifying signifier and signified, have themselves made the error of identifying 'signifier' with 'words' and 'signified' with 'the world'? (In the same way, perhaps, that they conflate *langue*, paradigm and synchrony, and *parole*, syntagm and diachrony in an extraordinary farrago on page 141).

Be that as it may, I find my guides worse than useless in rescuing me from the incomprehension in which their attempt to schematize Barthes on realism landed me. So I extricate myself unaided, and retrace my footsteps for a while; and as I do so, I distract my mind from gloomier thoughts by considering the tough question of why *Language and Materialism* — which is, after all, an attempt to tell me, as simply and briefly as possible, the basic facts about the achievements of Barthes and others — should not itself succumb to its authors' general disdain for realist writing.

The next task for Coward and Ellis is to introduce the second ingredient of the *nouveau mélange* — structuralist psychoanalysis. For some forty years, the French analyst Jacques Lacan has been trying to blend Saussure's terminology (especially the signifier–signified distinction) with Freudian psychology, on the one hand in the notion that the unconscious is 'structured like a language' (a notion rendered particularly obscure to me by Lacan's associated doctrine that the unconscious is, in effect, only half a language, in that it comprises signifiers, but not signifieds), and on the other hand in a theory about the relation between language-learning and the formation of the ego. It is on the latter that Coward and Ellis concentrate.

Freud's theory was that a child's ego is formed as a result of a series of narcissistic identificaitons, especially with parent-figures, in which what is at stake is always the child's sexuality, which in turn is organized around his possession (or her lack) of a seemingly unimportant appurtenance, a penis. Systematic psychic differences between men and women are ascribed by Freud to the Oedipal drama of ego-formation, since the process can never be properly completed, according to him, by normal women.

Lacan accepts this story, and elaborates it by distinguishing two turning points in the child's progress towards possession of an adult, male ego. The first initiates a 'mirror phase', when a rudimentary ego is formed on the basis of the child's perception of his own image: this takes place, says Lacan, at a private, inarticulable, non-universalizable, pre-rational, a-linguistic 'level' — that of imagination. The mirror-phase ego, however, is no sooner established than it is disrupted and transcended by the onset of the Oedipus complex, in which the child forms a much more sophisticated, but simultaneously more elusive, kind of ego — this time, through language. The Oedipal ego identifies itself (fallaciously of course, and, for that matter, phallaceously too) as the originator of the meanings of its words, including the word 'I'; it sees itself as a kind of horizon at which the parallel lines of signifier and signified appear to meet. It is on this basis that, as Lacan puts it, the child manages to make its way into the realm of the 'symbolic' (as distinct from the imaginary): the world of culture, reason, words and — ah yes — the phallus, the latter being, according to Lacan (though I don't know his reasons or evidence), the all-powerful signifier-in-chief. Thus Lacan lends his authority to the view that this item (or perhaps a phantasy representation of it) is a passport to the adult world. Bad news for little girls.

I am in no position to tell whether Lacan's elaborations are an improvement on Freud's original theory of the formation of the ego; nor do I know how they compare with rival post-Freudian accounts. I am told that most psychoanalysts are hostile to Lacan, but perhaps that should be put down to professional conservatism. It is possible to formulate some a priori doubts about his concepts, however — first, as to Lacan's presentation of the distinction and relation between the imaginary and symbolic realms (for instance, is a pre-symbolic imagination a coherent postulate?), and secondly as to the mono-causal obsession which leads Lacan to discount all non-linguistic factors in the formation of the Oedipal ego.[2]

But on the whole the question of Lacan ought to be settled by clinical practice rather than armchair speculation; and Coward and Ellis seem excessively charitable to Lacan in simply going along with his magisterial confidence in his own speculations, and with his habit of refusing to study alternative analytical theories.

Coward and Ellis now approach a more delicate stage in their work: the link-up between Lacan's account of the formation of the ego, and Barthes's account of classical realist fiction. Both of these coincide (so they seem to argue) in a 'theory of the subject' which defines subjec-tivity as the effect of some doomed-to-failure attempt to unite signifier and signified. Here, the difficulties for the Coward-and-Ellis synthesis begin to rain down ominously; and I believe that this is only the harbinger of a worse storm to come. Apart from assuming that the doctrines they find in Barthes and Lacan are beyond reasonable doubt, Coward and Ellis blithely neglect both the specificity of what each of their authorities writes and the particularity of the traditions to which they belong.

Lacan's speculations on the role of language and the Oedipus complex in the formation of the ego are not — whatever their merits — a universal account of 'subjectivity'. For subjectivity is not the same as the ego — as Lacan's own references to pre-Oedipal, prelinguistic forms of subjectivity testify. In psychoanalytic theory. the ego is not the only formation within the personality; and anyway, once a description of its general form has been given, the task remains of accounting for its particular contents in different groups and indivi-duals. Coward and Ellis ignore all this in order to forge ahead with their supersynthesis.

They behave similarly with Barthes's reflections on realism in classical French literature, telling us that realism, as analysed by Barthes, dominates the whole of 'traditional criticism' (43); indeed, it is 'the normal mode of writing'; it is the same as '*mimesis*' (47); they even allege, unless I have misunderstood, that it is co-extensive with '*Western thought*'; and then they sternly pronounce it to have been 'exposed in its complicity with forms of thought specific to Western

2. For an amusing cold douche on Lacan and Lacanianism, see Richard Wollheim's review article in *New York Review of Books* XXV, January 1979.

society' (33). (And if that be a crime who — by the way — shall then escape whipping?) By thus abstracting from Barthes's analysis of 'Sarrasine', Coward and Ellis satisfy themselves that they can herd all representations of subjectivity in Western literature into two manichean pens: 'realism' (Bad) and 'the *nouveau roman*' (A Good Thing). I can't help wondering how much light this can be expected to throw on poems, plays, myths or music-dramas.

With the positions of Barthes and Lacan thoroughly rinsed of particularity in this way — the theory of ego formation passed off as a theory of subjectivity in general, the theory of French classical literature as a theory of Western literature in general — Coward and Ellis attempt to link them together. The project seems unpromising. To my ears at any rate the crashing of machinery and ripping of gear teeth when they approach each other is agonizing, though not one of the four ears of Coward and Ellis seems to detect anything amiss. The effect is most noticeable when observed from the vantage point of geography and chronology. For mercilessly as they stretch Barthes's elasticated analysis of 'Sarrasine', it will never cover the same time or space as Lacan's analysis of the formation of the ego. Even supposing Barthes's ánalysis to have been successfully generalized to cover all the literatures of 'Western societies', that still leaves out peoples without written literatures, not to mention societies in 'the East', or for that matter, the South: all of which psychoanalysis, in its attempts to define the necessary conditions for the formation of human personality, claims to take into account. This, surely, indicates a rather serious gap betwen Lacan and Barthes.

Given a little more rope to play with, however, Coward and Ellis may, perhaps, be able to tie up their authors more firmly. Recall, first, that Lacan considers that the formation of the ego (if not of 'subjectivity') is based on language; notice, next, that the French literature dealt with by Barthes in his study of realism and subjectivity is also language; then, surely, you can see that Lacan approaches ego formation, as Barthes approaches subjectivity, from the point of view of language. What a coincidence! Surely, this gives Coward and Ellis the extra rope they need — in a word, *language*.

There are problems, however. In the first place, the language perceived by the pre-Oedipal child of Lacan's theory is presumably everyday speech, rather than the carefully wrought writing of French classical literature. Or do the infant subjects of Lacanian therapy have to read Balzac in order to induce the onset of an Oedipus complex? Actually, Coward and Ellis seem not to suppose so; instead, they attempt to reduce the literary arts, indeed art in general, to (spoken) language, as analysed by Saussure. They inform us, with a disarming air of stating the obvious, that 'Art is a practice of language' (35). Now, whilst there are important differences between understanding arts and understanding languages (for instance, you cannot translate from one art into another), there are also profound and fertile analogies.[3] Indeed, the existence of such analogies is implicit in Saussure's notion of semiotics. But there is an important difference: Saussure envisaged linguistics as a sub-discipline within a general science of signs, not as its foundation. He did not make the gratuitous and grotesque assumption that the conceptual apparatus of linguistics could be moved into non-linguistic domains (such as most of the arts) and applied there as if there were no difference. For Coward and Ellis, however, 'Art' (in general) simply 'is a practice of language'; and this — if it is to mean what they wish it to mean (that everything that needs to be said about art can be expressed in terms of linguistics) — will come as a surprise, and an offensive piece of petty-discipline-chauvinism, not only to creative writers but also to composers, choreographers, architects, designers, producers, photographers, instrumentalists, singers, dancers, directors, conductors, mimes, etc., and it certainly won't help them to identify something called 'bourgeois realism' in their own tradition. Perhaps it would be kinder not to give Coward and Ellis the extra rope after all.

Strange bedfellows, then, Lacan's theory of the formation of the Oedipal ego and Barthes's account of classical French literature; and it is hard not to admire the audacity with which our cheerful marriage-brokers cajole their third client, Marxism, into clambering in alongside the first two. This 'Marxism', however, is rather different from the character whom we may have associated with the name in the past; he is youthful, agile and broad-minded, not to say rakish: he has cast aside those rigid, puritanical dogmas of 'economic determinism' which used to make him such dreary company. Can it be the same 'Marxism' we used to know? And if so, what has wrought this marvellous change?

According to Coward and Ellis, it is the same Marxism; but his distressing economic-determinism complex has been completely cured. The cure has had two phases. First, under Dr Althusser, Marxism was brought round to the recognition that social formations have three eternally preformed 'levels' — the political, the economic, and the ideological — all interacting in easy-going reciprocity. There

3. For an acute discussion of art and language, see Nelson Goodman, *Languages of Art*, London 1976.

ensued a period when Marxism relished this new-found freedom, chirpily reciting the discovery that its 'levels' were 'relatively autonomous', though still harping on the idea that the economic was 'determining in the last instance'. But this healthy period was not destined to last, for before long Althusser's ban on 'the subject' began to cause unforeseen problems. So began the second stage of Marxism's cure: now under the care of cineaste and semiologist Christian Metz, Marxism was led to the liberating acceptance of a hitherto repressed fourth level within itself, a level to which Althusser's therapy had been blind. This was *the level of language*, of *'signifying practice'* — the very level at which, according to the new semiotics, subjectivity is made! From now on, surely all will be well with Marxism! How distant those anguished days of obsessive economic determinism seem now!

But let us check over the argument. Coward and Ellis tell us that language is neither base nor superstructure, and that it cannot be located at any of the three 'levels' of social reality. Next they point out that 'language is an active (and perhaps vital) constitutive part of social relations'; further, it has 'a reality of its own', and 'this reality is relations'; further, it has 'a reality of its own', and 'this reality is material'. Then they pull out their conclusion: 'It is for these reasons that it is necessary to propose the process of language as a fourth practice' (80).

That this argument is absurd can, I think, be easily seen. What could be more material, real and constitutive than sexual activity? Surely we must acknowledge a *fifth level!* Or eating? *A sixth!* Drinking and drugging? *A likely seventh!!!* And for good measure, singing and dancing, perhaps? *An eighth level!* Comrades may like to amuse themselves during meetings by seeing who can think of the most original new 'levels' of the social formation.

However many 'levels' Marxism may have — if indeed it is built on that design at all — it is, quite centrally, a theory about the place of capitalism in history, and was intended, in particular, to show that capitalism contains the seeds of socialism. It was on this basis that Marx and other 19th-century Marxists laid into fellow-socialists for being utopian, unhistorical, undialectical, idealistic, or unscientific. For Coward and Ellis, in contrast, Marxism is, above all, the opposite of 'bourgeois ideology' — a phenomenon to which, they believe, the new semiotics holds the keys. But as they discourse about it, a most disconcerting effect occurs: bourgeois ideology starts spreading like a great stain over acres and acres of the fabric of history; it engulfs all 'naturalistic' modes of thought, the whole of 'Western culture', the entirety of 'ideology' and even of 'common language'. It contaminates the whole of everyone's thought processes in Western society, regardless of class: all thought — sorry, 'Western thought' — capitalist and precapitalist, aristocratic, bourgeois, petty-bourgeois, peasant, artisan and proletarian, liberal, socialist and fascist, is embraced by this hospitable notion of 'bourgeois ideology'.

My present point is not to dispute that the new semiotics provides a theory of 'Western culture', or to deny to Coward and Ellis the right to set up shop in competition with the entirety of that imposing institution (though I know where I shall take my custom if forced to choose). My point is, rather, first to deplore the imprecision of referring to it all as 'bourgeois ideology', and secondly, to express wonder that, having done so, they should then enter the unedifying squabble for that not untarnished title, 'Marxism'. Why do they not abandon 'Marxism', with its three levels, four levels or no levels at all, along with the rest of 'Western thought' — with which it does, after all, have certain affiliations perhaps, even, as Coward and Ellis might put it, some 'complicity'?

The bridge to Coward and Ellis's interest in being considered 'Marxists' is the word 'radical', which, too, they define as the opposite of 'bourgeois ideology' and 'Western thought'. The horizons of French thought are scanned for signs of 'radical potentiality' as many as four times on a single page (123). The 'radical potentiality' of the new structuralism lies in its unmasking of the idea of individual subjectivity — the idea which has contaminated classical French literature, or rather Western thought, or rather ideology in general, or rather the necessary structure of the personality ever since language began: in short, what Coward and Ellis call 'bourgeois ideology'. Their 'politics' is 'radical' because it aims to *épater* this ubiquitous bourgeoisie. It is a 'politics', not of support for any movements stirring within existing society, but of antagonism to them all: it is a politics, perhaps, of situationism, or surrealism, or, better, of existentialism.

The 'radicalism' of Coward and Ellis is existentialist not just in the general sense that it is opposed to almost everything that exists, but also in its belief that if it can be demonstrated that the bourgeois personality is 'artificial', and in this sense a human creation, then one can draw the conclusion that it can be changed — which is surely the same solecism which disfigured the young Sartre's paeans to 'freedom'. Thus we are told that radical semiologists have demonstrated that 'what appears to be unchangeable is humanly created and can be recreated in certain directions' (32). This insipid equation of artificiality with alterability, and the refusal to recognize that what is humanly created might, for all that, be unchangeable, appears to be Coward and Ellis's chief claim to 'radicalism'. Surely, if the pessimistic patriarchs they claim to serve — Freud and Marx — were alive today, they would be turning in their graves.

Two: Philosophy and the Nouveau Mélange

So far, I have expressed some doubts about the first two ingredients of the *nouveau mélange* — structuralist literary theory and structuralist revisions of psychoanalysis. I have also argued that they don't fit together well, and suggested that their third ingredient, which they call 'Marxism', is — for better or for worse — not the genuine article. But my criticisms have been sporadic and ad hoc; they might, I suppose, turn out to be based on misunderstandings. So let us assume, for the sake of argument, that Coward and Ellis are right, and that the new semiotics really does furnish the basis for a merger between psychoanalysis, structuralism and historical and dialectical materialism. This leaves another question: is the new, synthetic theory actually *true*?

Most of the devices which Coward and Ellis employ to persuade us of the truth of their synthesis are, in a strict sense of the word, philosophical: they comprise, first of all, some arguments about dialectical materialism; then a philosophical criticism of Hegel; and then a philosophical disquisition on 'economic determinism'. Let us look at these devices.

Coward and Ellis begin with what are, technically, dogmatic philosophical arguments. Just like the authors of Stalinist textbooks of 'Marxist philosophy' in the 1930s and 1940s (and since), they frame their discussions in a traditional philosophical vocabulary, and specifically in terms of a dualism between 'metaphysics' and 'dialectics' and an intersecting dualism of 'materialism' and 'idealism'. Although this vocabulary is surely a main part of what Coward and Ellis dismiss elsewhere, with lofty disdain, as 'the language of Western metaphysics' (123), they embrace it here with a frank and wholehearted exuberance. Next they assume that Truth resides in Marxism, and that therefore its arbiter must be — as they put it — 'the philosophy of Marxism, whose lesson of dialectical materialism stresses precisely [precisely?] *process*' (4). Now listen to the deadening blows of the following credo: 'To analyse the structure without the subject can only be a form of metaphysical materialism; to analyse language without its object can only be idealism: and to analyse ideology without language will only ever be mechanical materialism' (92).

This method of argument seems to me to have nothing to recommend it; at least not without some explanation why we should go on listening to the 'lessons' of that frightful old pedagogue, self-styled 'the philosophy of Marxism'. We should surely inspect his credentials, and be suspicious about the fact that his lessons are always couched in pre-Marxist vocabulary, and that they have never changed in spite of decades of philosophical inquiry since he set up his school. But Coward and Ellis seem to trust him completely. This is particularly surprising in view of their strictures not only on 'Western metaphysics' but also on 'naturalistic' and 'realist' views of language. For it is a mistake, they tell us, to think that the relations of words to concepts (signifiers to signifieds) are ever a simple matter of one-to-one, once-for-all correspondence; on the contrary, they may 'slide' against each other. I suppose I agree. But what more crass example of such a mistake could there be than Coward and Ellis's supposition that every alternative to the new semiology can be consigned to oblivion as soon as it has had the words 'mechanical', 'metaphysical', or 'idealist' pinned to it? (Curious too, to find Coward and Ellis writing about 'materialist processes' (2, 86, 91), as though materialism were a property of the world rather than of world-views. Perhaps this is an example, if anything could be, of the confusion between word and world of which they accuse realist novelists!)

The gravest danger that Coward and Ellis see lurking about the groves of Philosophy is idealism: 'idealism, with its vision of things as isolated, static and unchangeable' (83); such idealist propositions, we are warned, 'underlie the fundamental assumption of bourgeois ideology, with its necessity/will to present society as consisting of "free" individuals, whose social determination results from their pre-given essences' (2). These are eccentric definitions of idealism, excluding as they do the systematic collectivism of Hegelianism — for which individuals depend for their identity entirely on the family, civil society, and the state. This exclusion, however, seems to be inadvertent, for Hegel is, to Coward and Ellis, the most notorious, unrepentant and died-in-the-wool idealist ever to have lain in wait for nice, normal materialists. Lacan's constant references to Hegel might give us pause, but Coward and Ellis are swift to reassure us that, in spite of appearances, Lacan's theory is 'grounded in materialism' (6);

and we are reminded, in a rather sharp tone, that 'the dialectic of desire as it appears in Lacan is in no way comparable to Hegelian idealism' (108); and also instructed, tetchily (and with a conspicuous lack of dialectical imagination), that Lacan's reading of Freud is 'in every way . . . opposed to idealism, and cannot therefore contribute to that idealism which serves existing society' (95).

It is impossible not to feel a prurient curiosity now as to what that respectable old professor actually got up to, and why the mere mention of his name should produce such a chorus of shocked tut-tutting amongst all right-thinking 'radicals'. The most explicit statement Coward and Ellis vouchsafe us is this: 'Hegel's idealist problematic proposed that the necessity of movement was engendered from an initial unresolvable gesture: the Idea. The process is then one of simple development or logical progression. . . . The dialectic is convergent on a defined conjuncture . . . and the subject is an entity whose identity of self is already completed. . . . The Hegelian dialectic is then purely logical, linear and hierarchical' (84).

Coward and Ellis use this description of Hegel's work as a foil to set off the 'philosophy' which they wish to recommend — a 'philosophy' which, in contrast to (what they take to be) Hegelianism, 'has no full stop, or centre' (20). The use of this metaphor of 'decentring' to criticize Hegel is, I believe, due to the influence of Althusser's well-known remarks about 'the Marxist dialectic'. It seems to me, however, that despite Althusser's authority, it remains a mere metaphor, with no theoretical bite — however menacingly and repetitively it may be chanted.

The reason is that 'dialectics' means — if it means anything — the attempt to explain changes in terms of the processes by which a system (whether natural, social, philosophical, or of any other kind) adjusts to internally generated conflicts, instabilities, or contradictions. A dialectical theory, in other words, must by definition specify some kind of conflict within a system and present the process with which it is concerned as an attempt to resolve it. And a moment's reflection should suffice to make it obvious that any dialectical theory will lend itself to expression in terms of a description of the system when the conflict is played out, stable equilibrium achieved, and the process in question, therefore, at an end. If the dialectical theory is about subject and object, then you can express it by describing the stasis of a subject–object unity; if it is about communal organization and private property, then you can express it by describing communism; if it is about bourgeoisie and proletariat, you can express it by describing a classless society. Of course, you may also think that the process you are describing will never come to an end — that it will constantly renew itself, or be interfered with by other processes. In that case, you will not believe that a state of equilibrium, unity or non-contradictoriness will actually be achieved, and you will regard descriptions of such states as — like many scientific statements — idealizations. Even so, the fact remains that, if you are proposing a dialectical theory, then you can express it by reference to what Coward and Ellis call 'a full stop, a centre'; and that this is a necessary property of any dialectical theory, regardless of whether it is to be characterized by the threadbare epithets of 'materialist' or 'idealist'. To talk of a dialectical theory which is 'decentred' is not to make any contribution to the theory of dialectics; at best, it is to make a bald, empirical, crackerbarrel statement about how complicated, inter-active, or interminable, the processes of this world are. That isn't philosophy; it's more like *cookery*.

Coward and Ellis are more cooks than philosophers in that they offer their precepts not on the basis of argument, but by offering assurances that their method somehow produces the best results. You tenderize your concepts of causality, slice your social formations into four sections, and plunge your Hegel-heads into boiling salt-water. Here is a typical tip from their book: 'To avoid idealism, the emphasis should be on one dividing into two rather than the logic of two fused into one — the latter being a logic which characterises and gives an idealist form to mechanical materialism' (88).

I am not sure how Coward and Ellis would argue with people who do not wish to avoid idealism, or with logicians who would say that their discipline does not deal in propositions of this kind. But one does not even have to venture into the realms of theory to see what a fatuity their advice is. 'The emphasis should be on one dividing into two', they say. But what if two do in fact fuse into one? What if water combines with sulphur dioxide or fat with flour? Where should the 'emphasis' be then? Does that refute Coward and Ellis's logic? Or vice-versa? But perhaps the principle is supposed to be practical rather than theoretical: in fact I believe it was first propounded by Mao as a way of claiming 'dialectical materialist' respectability for going against Stalin's advice and splitting with the Kuomintang. But what is the scope of the advice? Does it mean we should advocate streaming in schools, apartheid, division between boys and girls in education, and so on? Perhaps not. But so baldly presented, I don't see how it can fail to bear such constructions as well as any others.

Coward and Ellis make their most sustained attempt at philosophical argument in the pages where they take on 'economic determinism'. Their suggestion is that Marxists should put a larger measure of 'ideological practice' and a smaller measure of 'economic practice' into their historical materialism. They first tell us gravely of the days when 'ideological practice' was 'referred to as being merely a "system of ideas", "false consciousness" etc.' (68). But these, they continue, were 'crude ideas', owing to the extreme youth of Marx and Engels when they wrote *The German Ideology*. Next we are informed that 'the (dialectical materialist) idea that the production of representations necessarily entails the production of subjects for these representations has only been developed occasionally by such writers as Brecht, Mao and Althusser'. Let us take their word for it that this obscure proposition deserves a medal '*for dialectical materialism*' and that its ancestry can be traced to Mao and Brecht; still it is surely time Coward and Ellis gave us some argument for its truth. But what comes next? 'We assert that it is only psychoanalysis which has gone any way to analysing the formation of the subject.' Apart from the fact that, to be consistent with their last sentence but three, they will have to make the (surely difficult) case that Brecht was a psychoanalytic theorist and the (harder) case that Mao was one too, we asked for an argument, and they only gave us an assertion. But relax. Is this the argument coming along at last?

'The importance of understanding ideological practice in the way suggested by the articulation of Marxism and psychoanalysis is very great. The politics which flow from radical and Marxist thought can then be free from any economic determinism, that is, the idea that economic practice is more important than political or ideological processes in the social process. As long as Marxists still think of ideological practice as somehow subservient to the economy (as a 'super-structure' built on the economic 'base'), then their politics will always stress the economy as the principal determinant, and see economic crisis as the principal (or only) cause of social crisis' (69).

Practices, processes, importances, subserviences, principal determinants, only causes: what a motley collection of ill-defined categories! Constructing a theoretical argument from materials like this will be like trying to build a snowperson out of slush. An in any case, the discussion is going round in tedious circles. Coward and Ellis take the trouble to tell us that politicians who believe in economic determinism are likely to concentrate their work on 'economic practice'; but they seem to overlook the fact that, for all we have heard so far, these politicians may be right to do so. Next we hear that Engels himself was against economic determinism, but this can hardly carry much weight given that Engels has been unceremoniously dressed down for his 'crude ideas' earlier on the same page. And that is all.

Except, that is, for an illustration. The Chinese cultural revolution, we learn, shows the fallaciousness of 'economic determinism'. China, it appears, is a country where 'the outcome of ideology would determine the whole form of Chinese society. . . . The recognition of the determinacy of ideology . . . is the core of the difference between China and Russia' (70). Why don't Coward and Ellis discuss Lenin's Cultural Revolution? And why don't they enter into a debate with those historians (not all of them 'economic determinists', surely) who would attribute to different organizations of peasant land-holding, different soil and crops, different transport systems, or different levels and distributions of industry, some part in 'the core of the difference between China and Russia'? Such an analysis might not enable you to be immediately 'rid of any economic determinism', but might it not, for all that, be true?

Coward and Ellis come back to the question of China a couple of pages further on. 'In China, another revolution in ideology is taking place, overthrowing ideas of delegation, management, the handing over of power to 'representatives' or 'responsible individuals', ideas which are the keystone of capitalist production relations and bourgeois democracy. They are replaced with ideas of collective decision-making, of active thinking by all the people, summed up in the ideas of 'philosophy in the factory', 'philosophy is no mystery' etc.' (72).

There are of course still some historians who would wish to place exploitation, the wage relation, proletarianization, industrialization or abstract labour somewhere in the vicinity of the 'keystone' of capitalism; but Coward and Ellis seem to believe that they have left these poor scribbling hacks far behind. Might they not nevertheless consider the proposition that the 'idea' of collective decision-making, so widely publicized in China, may in fact *conceal* the true power relations? I am not asserting that this is so; merely wondering how their revamped 'dialectical materialism' can make them so sure that it is not.

Upon examination, Coward and Ellis's sophisticated philosophical argument against economic determinism turns out to be neither sophisticated nor philosophical; nor does it, so far as I can see, contain argument as opposed to blandishment. I am struck, however, by the fact that Coward and Ellis praise China for running philosophy courses in communes and factories where it is taught that 'philosophy is no mystery' (courses in which, incidentally, if my information is anything to go by, the students may not be able to make head or tail of what is being taught).[4] Now I must admit that, as a philosophy teacher myself, I may be liable to dramatize the mystery and glamorize the philosophy. But let me, on the other hand, make a ritual confession that, like any other academic discipline, philosophy is drenched in ideology — not fortuitously, but necessarily; not occasionally, but chronically; not locally, but ubiquitously. The fact remains, however, that it is an inheritor of certain traditions of theoretical work. I am not trying to proselytize, or to recruit students; in fact I believe that for many people, if not all, it may be best to ignore philosophy and get on with something else. However, those who, like Coward and Ellis, choose to defend themselves by philosophical means — and, I may add, by devices of an ancient, if not antiquated construction — ought to take some notice of their traditional uses.

Let us pass over their trusting use of the prestructuralist, pre-Marxist, and largely, pre-Hegelian vocabulary of 'materialism', 'idealism', 'dialectics' and 'metaphysics' and concentrate on their use of the word 'subject'. And let us forgive their confusion of 'subject' and 'ego' (see above, p. 342). And let us not grudge them the use of the word 'subject' to refer to an individual conscious being; or, following upon this, their punning way of referring to the individual's relation to the rest of the world as 'predication'. It is genial, perhaps, to speak of 'a subject different from and able to differentiate within a predicatable outside' (91), or of a subject 'able to predicate an outside' (94). But for their own safety they should have been warned that this has nothing to do with the relations of subject and predicate in logic and grammar, and therefore does not entitle them to bung logical and philosophical discussions of predication into their *mélange* along with everything else. This is what happens when they try to stir in a few remarks about Frege: 'He showed quite clearly that negative thought does not exist: he was starting out from the premise that the judging subject sustains all thought, and that this subject cannot therefore be negated. . . . Negation is simply a variation of the predicate, and is therefore impossible outside the syntactical relations of subject and predicate. . . . These observations confirm Frege's idea that negation belongs to the understanding, in that it is simply a variation of the act of predication' (138).

I do not enjoy behaving like an exasperated school-master, but I feel bound to explain that Coward and Ellis have not understood a single word of what Frege was about. The truth is that Frege was

4. See 'Philosophy in China', *Radical Philosophy* 14, Summer 1976.

utterly opposed to the idea that 'thought' depends on the 'judging subject'; he argued that thoughts existed objectively, independently of all thinkers. Of course he thought that 'the subject cannot be negated' — the subject, that is, as defined in grammar: this is a grammatical commonplace. However, none of this has anything to do with 'the subject' in the sense of 'the individual consciousness'. And besides that: Frege was impressed by the wide range of propositions which are not, from a grammarian's point of view, of subject-predicate form (identity statements, existential statements, relational statements); in addition, he argued (and many still agree) that the whole vocabulary of 'subject and predicate' should be scrapped, and replaced, for the purposes of logical theory, by the categories of 'argument' and 'function'. This is a technical matter, of course, and one of which most thinkers could safely remain in ignorance: but no one who chooses to drop Frege's name and use his authority to support some baffling statements about negation and the subject-predicate relation has the right to be so ignorant. Coward and Ellis invoke Frege on the basis of wholly spurious resemblances between psychological and logical theory, and attribute to Frege theses which are in fact opposed in every respect to the conclusions for which Frege painstakingly and scrupulously *argued*. Philosophy is no mystery, indeed!

Three: Arguments from Authority and the Fallacie., of Fashion

For reasons which are not at once apparent, Coward and Ellis make excited claims for the originality of the *nouveau mélange*. They assert that only — 'only' is a favourite word with them — *only* with the work of Barthes, Lacan and Althusser can we understand the ways in which 'bourgeois ideology' disguises the artificiality of human individuality. So, in praise of the new semiotics, all the remainder of existing science, culture and theory is blackened. An apocalyptic, manichean view of history stalks the pages, trying to point out a recent watershed after which a torrent of 'radical' truth, nouveaux romans and the Chinese cultural revolution has been thundering down the valleys, sweeping all before it; whereas formerly — with the exception of a few immaculately conceived ideas in the heads of Marx, Lenin, Brecht and Mao and perhaps also of Engels and Stalin — everything was Bad: economic determinism, realist fiction, and of course idealism, mechanism, metaphysics and the rest of 'Western thought'.

'Only the articulation of psychoanalysis and Marxism,' we are

told, 'can hope to give an account of such practices' (20). Freud and
Freudians other than Lacan are not given the chance to make out
their own claim to have given such an account; and we are hastened
on to the assertion, part of which I have already noticed, of a new
'philosophy', a philosophy which 'has no ultimate full stop, or centre,
to its process of structuring: it has no 'God', no 'human essence', no
'presence' as the transcendent term which makes the system possible
(20).

This is, of course, meant primarily as a swipe at Hegel, though at
this particular point Hegel is being represented by Lévi-Strauss. I
have already explained why this criticism of Hegel seems to me to be
entirely insubstantial. But there is another point about Hegel. Even if
you restrict yourself to one chapter of the *Phenomenology of Mind*, you
will find a beautifully composed, if somewhat elusive, description of
the varieties of contradictory ways in which personal identities are
formed for men and women, in Ancient Greece and Rome, in early
Christian communities, amongst monarchs and courtiers in pre-
revolutionary France, and so forth. Vague formulations about 'decentring' do not seem to me to be a very good reason for refusing — as
Coward and Ellis evidently have — to read or learn from Hegel's
after all very accomplished philosophical prose. And whilst I am on
the 'H' shelf of my bookcase, I wonder what Coward and Ellis would
make of the atheism of Holbach or Hobbes, or of Hume's attack on
ordinary notions of personal identity (surely there's some 'radical
potentiality' there!). Which reminds me, leaving 'H', that in Robert
Owen Coward and Ellis would find a militant socialist, and indeed
feminist, whose entire practice is based on a critique of the idea of
individual responsibility, which he — a harbinger, seemingly, of the
manichean Marxism of the new semiology — saw as the source of all
evil in 'the old, immoral world'. They would also find in Owen, if one
were needed, a refutation of their claim that 'unlike previous philosophies, Marxism has as its specific [specific?!] aim the transformation of the world' (82).

But setting aside classical writings, we also find 20th-century works
distorted and misrepresented to fit in with Coward and Ellis's view of
history. For instance Lukács and Goldmann are both reproved for
failing to envisage reality as 'a world which is produced by the whole
ensemble of social activities, including that of conceptualization in
language' (36). I do not see why Coward and Ellis find it necessary to
sneer at these not insubstantial theorists of literature; but I am
astonished that they should do so on the basis of an attribution which,
like this one, is 180 degrees off-target. (I feel the same uneasiness

when (3, 62) they claim as insights of structuralist linguistics propositions which are commonplaces of analytical philosophy; or (51), as
innovations of the new semiotics, positions that were at the heart of
the Cambridge English school in the 1930s!)

But these omissions and incriminations are insignificant compared with the next I shall mention. The claim which has got Coward
and Ellis excited is that the *nouveau mélange* successfully merges structuralism, Marxism and psychoanalysis. You would think therefore
that they would attempt to match and measure this claim against any
other body of work which might be taken to do exactly the same thing.
And whatever else may be said about it, it cannot be denied that
Sartre's work in the last twenty years, especially the *Critique of Dialectical Reason* (1960), tries to integrate structuralism (sociological as
well as linguistic), Marxism (historicist rather than structural) and
psychoanalysis (phenomenological rather than structuralist); moreover, Sartre's basic proposition — that the individual is produced by,
rather than simply presupposed to, social processes — is precisely
that for which Coward and Ellis wish us to thank the new semiotics.
And whilst it may not ultimately be successful, Sartre's synthesis is,
unlike the *nouveau mélange*, constructed in a systematic way, with
abundant historical illustration and a comparatively wide range of
reference to philosophical traditions. Coward and Ellis never once
mention any of Sartre's works or ideas: they seem to have excised him
from their manichean picture of the history of Marxism, no less
ruthlessly than Stalin obliterated Trotsky in the *History of the CPSU
(B)*. (Much the same could be said of their similar silence about
Marcuse.)

Their distorted view of the history of ideas may be only an incidental
feature of Coward and Ellis's presentation of the new semiotics. But
then again, it may be more: for it seems to be used as a kind of
argument, or argument-surrogate, to convince us of the truth of the
nouveau mélange. Again and again they present sequences of sentences,
beginning with statements which are simply attributive ('x says
so-and-so', 'radicals believe so-and-so') but ending with statements
saying that so-and-so is the case. Thus we are told that 'there is no
place in Marxist thought for the idea of a simple beginning' — which
sounds like a perfectly normal attempt at realist reporting of other
people's ideas. And a couple of sentences later, the 'conclusion' is
drawn: 'Reality, then, is an ever pre-given, complexly structured
totality' — which is no longer a statement in the historiography of
ideas, but a philosophical dogma. Need I point out that the slide from

the first kind of sentence to the second involves a fallacy?

The slide is greased, and the fallacy disguised, by Coward and Ellis's disingenuous habit of using idioms like 'sees that', 'notices that', 'recognizes that . . .' and so forth — phrases which are partly devices for ascribing beliefs to people and partly ways of endorsing the belief. Thus, when Coward and Ellis report that Marx 'rehabilitated the dialectic, the notions of struggle, contradiction and practice' (91), they are not only making a report on the history of ideas but also (by using the word 'rehabilitate'), informing us that Marx's attempt was successful. Readers, having accepted such a statement as a report on Marx's belief, suddenly find that they have swallowed a dubious philosophical thesis.

In a sense, all these fallacies are instances of the fallacious 'argument from authority' — arguments that something must be the case, because some authority says so. But in fact most of Coward and Ellis's fallacies are of a slightly different kind: they involve not so much referring to a particular authority, as watching the ways in which currents of opinion are flowing: a kind of punting on what future authorities will say, based on ideas of what can be 'seen', and seen 'only now'. Thus our tipsters tell us: 'It is no longer a matter of politics and ideology being superstructures which are supported/produced by the economic base. . . . It is rather a matter of seeing the articulation of the three practices' (69). (The fourth practice is not discovered for another few pages.) And then: 'The materialist dialectic must now be seen as the dialectic between history, language and ideology' (92).

Again: following a paraphrase of Barthes's position in *S/Z*, we are told: 'The political implications of this are clear: the domination of bourgeois ideology can no longer be seen as control of ideas by a class, it is a function of those positions established in relation to meaning' (7).

But wait: if 'it is no longer a matter' of base and superstructure, then surely it cannot ever have been? 'Must now'?' If this is a 'must' of logic, should it not apply then as well as now? And if it is only a 'must' of the moment, then surely its authority is only that of fashion, and so is liable to change again before one's ink is even dry. 'Can no longer be seen as control of ideas by a class'? Well, it may be so seen, and understandably, by, for example, victims of the *Berufsverbot*, defendants in the Official Secrets Trials, Italian *autonomisti*, and others. Barthes may not see it their way; but on the other hand, they may not see it his way; and the question is, who is right? Even if it were seen their way 'no longer', this might be because true beliefs were more widespread then than now; and besides, at a future time it might cease to be 'no longer' possible — 'no longer' no longer.

Perhaps the hidden premise of Coward and Ellis's arguments from fashion is an equation (surprising in such violent Hegel-bashers) between newness and epistemological superiority, an equation neatly wrapped up in their evolutionistic reverence for ideas which are 'advanced'. Time was, that the current theories of the literary and academic establishments would be automatically dismissed by Marxists as the latest siren-calls of the bourgeoisie. Terrible damage was done by this attitude — for example, in the conventional British Marxist contempt for 'Freudism' or 'the Bloomsbury group' in the 1930s. Coward and Ellis, however, seem to assume the exact reverse: they invite us to believe the 'most advanced' ideas not because they are true (which they may or may not be) but because it is 'no longer possible' not to. There is still something to be said, surely, for the identification of Marxism with a culture which strives to conquer subversive vantage points *against* the tides of fashion?

This is a weird and multiply contradictory book. It advocates a *mélange* of structuralism and psychoanalysis as the highest form of Marxism; but it repeatedly commits fallacies of fashion which distance it considerably from the oppositional, embattled and counter-hegemonic activities normally associated with the name of 'Marxism'; and it is all written in literary modes — realistic reportage, appeals to the obvious, and dogmatic assertion — that fit badly with the conclusions of structuralism and psychoanalysis. But the hostility it arouses in me makes me acutely uncomfortable. It causes an abominable figure of a huffy, complacent, conservative, xenophobic Oxford don to stir within me.

'Good God,' says the don, reading out sentences at random, 'they can't even write the bloody English language! They may pride themselves on their grasp of linguistic theory, but their linguistic practice certainly leaves a lot to be desired. . . . I suppose they call their book a 'text' because they want priests to make sermons from it, or examiners to 'set' it! . . . Their attitude to these Parisian chaps is one of pseudo-erotic infatuation — they have produced not a sober evaluation, but a pastiche, a child's guide to pseud's corner!'

There are two good reasons for barracking this complacent, chortling don. The first is that, if I am not mistaken, many of the propositions of structuralism, whether or not they are radical, or Marxist, or new, are in fact true, and offer ways of dismantling various obstacles to the formation of a critical and intelligent view of society.

The second reason for suppressing the reactionary don is that, as booksellers and publishers will tell you, Coward and Ellis, and others offering a similar commodity, seem to answer, if not satisfy, a real need. They have, strange to relate, the common touch. What is this need?

In parallel with *Language and Materialism,* I have been reading Edward Thompson's brilliant and blistering attack on Althusser and English Althusserianism in *The Poverty of Theory* (Merlin, 3.90). This essay is by turns skilful, inaccurate, devastating and banal. Thompson makes, amongst others, the following historical conjecture: that it became obvious to a generation of students about ten years ago that the academic disciplines into which they were being inducted were corrupted by a 'crass and abject empiricism'. Althusserianism seemed to make this criticism with verve; and their 'instant recognition' of the truth of the criticism, according to Thompson, provided 'the normal gate-of-entry for inexperienced readers, and. . . beckons them into the interior of his [Althusser's] absurd syllogistic world' (20).

I am encouraged by Thompson's essay to suggest a generalization about the historical conditions which have made the kinds of argument, or argument-surrogate, of *Language and Materialism,* possible. My conjecture is that they and their audience have been bored and irritated to distraction by the pomposities, idiocies and careerist gossip on board the ghost-ship of some claustrophobic academic discipline, condemned to sail the seven seas for ever, and never touching land. In this predicament, any tradition which is synthetic, interdisciplinary, critical and (at least in inspiration) politically engaged will seem worth trying. In the 1930s students would embrace the latest deliveries of dialectical materialism the moment they arrived from Russia, culminating in the translation of Stalin's *Dialectical and Historical Materialism* (1940); in the 1950s and 60s, they embraced Sartrian existentialism and Marxism, culminating in Laing and Cooper's *Reason and Violence* (1964), Marcuse's *One Dimensional Man* (1964) and the 'Dialectics of Liberation' Conference in July 1967; next, there was a phase of hard-line structuralist scientism, centring on the translation of Balibar and Althusser's *Reading Capital* in 1970, and going on into various essays in self-indulgence; and latterly, there has been an enthusiasm for the new semiology, represented in, among other things, *Language and Materialism.*

I can see lots of flaws in the generalization given above, but I cannot resist the temptation to press on with it. For — for all the differences and discontinuities which have to be taken into account — there are similarities between all these movements. Each of them has involved an importation which has been extremely ephemeral in its implantation in English culture; each of them has been introduced dogmatically, rather than through a proper critique of the available alternatives; each of them has, in one way or another, aggrandized itself by presenting a manichean-apocalyptic picture of its own place in the history of thought; each has exhibited, in some degree, both a considerable margin of conspicuous unintelligibility and an awe-inspiring habit of uttering preposterous falsehoods with imperturbable self-confidence; and so on. The doleful thought which assaults me as I squint out at a snowy New Year's Day, is that this book is just another episode in the same old comic drama: testifying to a real appetite for an alternative to bourgeois-academic organizations of knowledge, but incapable of permanently satisfying it. Perhaps, like *Dialectical and Historical Materialism*, or *Reason and Violence*, or *One Dimensional Man*, or *Reading Capital* it too will soon be abandoned, and, like them, wrapped in amnesia like an old childhood fetish.

Reprinted from *RP*23

The 'New Philosophers' and the End of Leftism

Peter Dews

Fashion moves fast in Parisian salons, and the taste for intellectual scandal demands the constant breaking of fresh taboos. In the spring of 1977 a group of young authors styling themselves the 'New Philosophers' moved rapidly to the centre of attention, making headlines not only in France but around the globe. The shocking novelty of the New Philosophers consisted in the fact that here was a group of young thinkers who were no longer prepared to dialogue with or work within the framework of Marxism, but who openly denounced Marxist thought as a philosophy of domination. After decades in which the vast majority of French intellectuals had instinctively placed them-selves on the left, this attitude marked an important departure. Indeed, the 'New Philosophy' opened the floodgates — from then on no theoretical or political position was too absurd or reactionary to merit attention. In dreadful confirmation of this, two years later the cultural pages of a weekly magazine with a circulation of 85,000, the Sunday supplement of *Le Figaro*, were taken over by a 'New Right' whose racist and elitist doctrines threw the anti-authoritarian and humanist character of the New Philosophers' critique of Marxism into sharp relief. In this respect the New Philosophers are already a faded page in the history of recent intellectual and political debate in France, their pamphleteering too flimsy — despite its original impact — to merit sustained attention as a theoretical contribution. Yet to affirm the ephemeral nature of the New Philosophers' work is not to deny the importance of the attitudes it expressed, or the significance of the moment of its emergence. For this emergence marked definitively what one recent chronicler of French philosophy can describe as Marxism's 'disappearance, perhaps temporary, from the field of discussion' in France.[1] In a country where Marxism, in one

1. V. Descombes, *Modern French Philosophy*, Cambridge 1980.

form or another, had provided a dominant frame of reference for work in philosophy and the 'human sciences' ever since the end of the Second World War, such a development clearly represented a major turning-point, and one which could not fail to find echoes in Britain. The following pages will hopefully make the underlying reasons clearer.

At the time of its first appearance the New Philosophy was surrounded by a good deal of confusion. Did its emergence signify, as the sympathetic response of *Le Nouvel Observateur,* France's leading left-wing weekly, seemed to suggest, the first serious attempt by thinkers on the left to deal squarely and without double-think with abuses of power by socialist states and the question of human rights? Or were the New Philosophers, as the approving reaction of certain commentators, and some of the company they kept, might lead to believe, the heralds of a swing to the right among intellectuals in the advanced capitalist countries? In part this uncertainty was due to the way in which the *Nouvelle Philosophie* was reported in a press always eager to relay the opinions of intellectuals 'disillusioned' with Marxism. The *Time* cover-story which immediately assimilated the ideas of the New Philosophers to those of such stalwarts as Arthur Koestler and Daniel Bell was a good example of this process, drawing some sarcastic feedback from *Le Nouvel Observateur,* which had originally given the new thinkers space to air their opinions. (At the other end of the political spectrum, an article in *Pravda* quoted opportunistically from a condemnation of the New Philosophers by Gilles Deleuze, a thinker with whom orthodox dialectical materialists could have little sympathy.) But the ill-defined image of the *Nouvelle Philosophie* cannot be attributed entirely to partisan reporting. The work of the New Philosophers *is* in fact an ill-considered *mélange* of theories, attitudes and reponses, in which positions inherited from the post-'68 far left mingle with themes which, under their veneer of novelty, can be seen to belong to the traditional repertoire of the Right.

This confusion and laying of false trails appeared clearly in the debate which occupied the literary magazines and weekly press in the year of the run-up to the legislative elections, and in which the established standard-bearers of the Left — Poulantzas, Debray, Castoriadis, Rancière — were aligned against the disruptive and voluble newcomers. In reply to those critics who suggested that a great deal of patient theoretical work would be required to back up the kind of generalizations which the New Philosophers were willing to make, Bernard-Henri Lévy, the publisher and *de facto* spokesman of the group, asserted that 'urgency today is a genre in itself', thereby justifying any intellectual shoddiness in the name of political 'relevance'. With the fervour of apostasy and revelation the New Philosophers denounced Reason itself, particularly in its Marxist and historicist form, as a kind of insidious balm, an ironing-out of the bloody irrationalities of history. Thus it was easy to reply to accusations of theoretical incoherenece with the suggestion that the critic was attempting to impose a 'totalitarian' rationality on the spontaneity and truth (for the New Philosophers the two terms are practically synonymous) of their protest, thereby betraying the implicit authoritarian designs of the Left in general. In portraying even social democracy as the thin end of a totalitarian wedge, the new Philosophy made its own a favourite delirium of the Right.

An alternative ploy was to suggest that the *Nouvelle Philosophie* was merely the construct of dogmatic imaginations: that there was only a disparate group of writers 'with nothing in common except the hazards of biography'. Here disingenuousness shaded into dishonesty. For it was Lévy who invented the name 'New Philosophers' as the title of a dossier which he edited for *les Nouvelles Litteraires* in the summer of 1976, and in which he undertook to 'introduce a few friends'. Furthermore, while Lévy was writing articles whose titles proclaimed that: 'La Nouvelle Philosophie n' existe pas'[2], *Grasset*, the publishing house for which he works as an editor, continued to print an advertisement in which it was boldly announced: 'The "New Philosophers" publish in the collections *Figures* and *Théoriciens* edited by B.-H. Lévy.' Admittedly there is a certain diversity in the output of the New Philosophers — but no more so than with any other group of thinkers who share certain common assumptions and emerge from a common context. On a cynical view, such as that of Gilles Deleuze, the 'varieties' of the *Nouvelle Philosophie* — Christian, leftist, liberal, Nietzschean — were simply different ways of dressing up the same reactionary message as to appeal to as many tastes as possible.[3] But even if the whole phenomenon had not been manipulated by the publicity-conscious Lévy in order to produce maximum impact, there would still be sufficient themes common to the New Philosophers, and these themes would be sufficiently rooted in a more general shift in the climate of opinion, to justify collective treatment.

On the question of political allegiance the New Philosophers betrayed further evidence of their evasiveness and bad faith. Most of

2. B. H. Lévy, 'La Nouvelle Philosophie n' existe pas', *La Nef* No. 66.
3. See G. Deleuze interview in *Minuit*, 5 June 1977.

them insisted that they were writers of the Left, addressing their appeals to the Left, yet their denunciations of 'totalitarianism' were focused almost exclusively on states where Marxism is the official ideology, predominantly the Soviet Union seen through the prism of the work of Solzhenitsyn. They equally exploited every opportunity of publicizing their views in the only-too-willing capitalist press and media, while depicting themselves as dissidents persecuted and censored by the rising 'red bourgeoisie'. If they were attacked by the Left as reactionaries, this could only be because they represented the true Left, despite the fact that they perceived little more than the shadow of the Gulag in Marx, and casually suggested the need for the abandonment of the 'entire socialist tradition'. In fact their self-location on the left was chiefly made possible by an insistence on the continuity between their writings and the spirit of the uprising of May '68: for the media the New Philosophers belonged to a 'lost genera-tion', disillusioned by the fading of the dreams and expectations of that time, yet continuing to bear witness to the 'inner truth' of the movement. In the similar terms of the 'minor' New Philosopher Michel le Bris: in May '68 a new experience of freedom had been born, but it had taken nearly a decade for 'consciousness to return into itself' and for the thought of that freedom to emerge.[4] However one interprets these claims, it cannot be maintained that the reference to May '68 is simply a publicity gimmick. On the biographical level most of the New Philosophers were active in the May events, and subsequently became militants in far-left organizations, the majority in the 'Maoist' *Gauche Prolétarienne*. Michel le Bris, for example, was jailed in 1970 for editing the GP's paper, *La Cause du Peuple*, as a result of which Sartre was invited — and accepted — to take over the posi-tion. Himself from a Breton peasant background, Le Bris was subsequently active in the Occitanian autonomist movement.

In repudiating Marxism, writers like Le Bris do not repudiate this past militancy. What has happened is that May '68 and its aftermath are now interpreted from a post-*gauchiste* perspective which assumes the redundancy of the Marxist categories which classified '68 as prelude to revolution, failing to recognize in the events a socio-political convulsion of a new kind. The libertarian aspect of May is prolonged in a critique of all official doctrines of revolution. (Le Bris' particular concern, for example, is with the positive values of the peasant way of life, condemned by Marxism as a result of its obsession with industrialization and the role of the proletariat.) It would there-

4. M. Le Bris, interview in J. Paugam, ed., *Génération Perdue*, Paris 1977.

fore be naive to portray the New Philosophers, as the Right attempted to do, as simply having woken up to the totalitarian dangers of Marxism. As E.H. Carr has recently pointed out, the volume of criticism of the Soviet Union in the West has never risen and fallen with the actual level of repression in that country — it has always rather been an index of changes of political climate in the country where it is voiced.[5] Accordingly, an understanding of the *Nouvelle Philosophie* must be genetic and contextual: it cannot be treated as a collection of statements to be assessed in abstraction in terms of truth or falsity.

How does one deal with an experience of exaltation, in which a radical transformation of human relations abruptly becomes a concrete possibility, when the moment of vision has faded and existence appears to have lapsed into a dreary normality? A useful way of looking at the diverse forms of the New Philosophy — and one which helps to explain the religious dimension of some of its productions — is to see them as different attempts to come to terms with this same fundamental problem. One immediate and evident response would be to strive to prolong or revive that experience, and this is precisely what most of the intellectuals who are now New Philosophers did. After May '68 most of them became militants in the *Gauche Prolétarienne*, a group which was formed from a fusion between the anti-authoritarian student movement, the *Mouvement du 22 Mars*, and the Maoist current of Althusserianism, the *Union de la Jeunesse Communiste* (*M.-L.*). Along with a number of other groups such as *Vive la Révolution*, which went even further in its rejection of Leninism, the GP attempted to keep alive the flame of the May revolt in anticipation of an eventual 'people's war' (the lack of a sense of reality is not something new in the New Philosophers). Although still organized on strict democratic-centralist lines, its message was populist and spontaneist. Mao had affirmed that 'the masses are always right', that all knowledge stems from and returns to the suffering people, and accordingly that the traditional roles of intellectual leadership and pedagogy had to be abandoned. The role of the party was no longer to form the vanguard and revolutionary elite, but to facilitate the expression of the desires of the masses, and to encourage their impulse towards rebellion by means of exemplary action. Yet no matter how far the GP went in this direction, it continued to work within a Marxist framework insofar as May '68 was read as a prelude to some greater insurrection, a sign that the proletariat was no longer willing to accept

5. E.H. Carr, 'The Russian Revolution and the West', *New Left Review* 111.

bourgeois rule unquestioningly, and that hegemony was being increasingly transformed into naked domination. With the rapid decay of French Maoism in the early '70s, and the reoccupation of the political terrain by the traditional parties of the Left, this confidence in the anticipatory meaning of May '68 for the class struggle began to fade. The new tendency was to accept May '68 'on its own terms', as a form of rebellion which could not be slotted into the Marxist schemas. A characteristic example of this interpretation can be found in Foucault's preface to the English translation of Deleuze and Guattari's *Anti-Oedipus*: 'Had the utopian project of the thirties been resumed, this time on the scale of historical practice? Or was there, on the contrary, a movement to the model that Marxist tradition had prescribed? Towards an experience and technology of desire that were no longer Freudian. It is true that the old banners were raised, but the combat shifted and spread into new zones.'[6] Despite the theoretical justifications of this reorientation, one should not overlook such 'banal' factors as the PCF's role in May '68. If the embodiment of the workers' movement could act as simply one more apparatus of repression, then the real struggle seemed to be no longer between worker and capitalist, but between institutionalized power and resistance. Progressively the idea of a 'critique of institutions' associated with the Events began to be detached from any reference to relations of production or the conflict of social classes.

The *Nouvelle Philosophie* 'transcendentalization' of this re-reading is perhaps most fully represented by Maurice Clavel, a novelist and philosophy teacher in whom Christian belief and sympathetic collaboration with the post-'68 Maoists combined to produce an avuncular enthusiasm for the new thinkers. In Clavel's interpretation May '68 was a prelude not to revolution in the political sense, but rather to a transformation of consciousness. It signified the opening of a 'cultural fracture' (a coinage intended to avoid the menacingly cyclic connotations of the term 'revolution'), a crumbling of the 'historico-cultural foundation which can be summarily termed "capitalo-communist"'.[7] Clavel is inevitably rather vague about what he understands by this, throwing off references to Berdyaev ('we are living the last days of the Renaissance') or lapsing into the Christian vocabulary of the 'liberation of the spirit'. But he is convinced that what happened after May '68 was an 'Indian summer' of Marxism in its anti-Communist Party forms. Because the radical novelty of the

6. M. Foucault, 'Preface' to *Anti-Oedipus*, New York 1977.
7. M. Clavel, 'Aujourd'hui la Révolution Culturelle', *Magazine Littéraire* Nos. 127–8.

'cultural revolution' would inevitably at first be misrecognized, its immediate participants were destined to continue trying to fit their experience into the outworn framework of Marxism. Yet the repercussions of the 'fracture' of May were bound eventually to result in a break with Marxist modes of thought.[8] Clavel claims to have foreseen that, after the debacle of Maoism, and after having passed through a period of despair, the true critics of Marx and harbingers of the coming spiritual/cultural transformation would emerge from the ranks of the former militants. Lardreau and Jambet, friends of Clavel and authors of *L'Ange,* one of the earliest successses of the *Nouvelle Philosophie,* take up some of the same ideas. During their time as activists in the GP they were both adamant Marxists and not Marxists at all, undergoing an experience which was at once political and spiritual, calling for the rehabilitation of Stalin and preaching a radical spontaneism. Like Clavel they now interpret their experience of 'the absolute certainty that the revolution was not only possible, but that we were in the process of making it'[9] in quasi-religious terms, in which the liberating break of revolution is opposed to the tyrannical continuity implied by the Marxist dialectic of historical progress.

Not all the writings of the New Philosophers have this overtly religious dimension, but in all some kind of celebration of the experience of rupture and rebellion is to be found. In André Glucksmann, for example, this experience is expressed in the secular form of a frantic anti-statism which has become an established part of the radical *doxa* in France, and whose potential for exploitation by the Right is all too evident. There are several features, however, which distinguish this anti-statism from the traditional doctrines of anarchism. Rather than being based on a faith in the innate goodness of

---

8. This interpretation is not the unique property of groups like the New Philosophers, but has more or less become the 'authorized version' of recent intellectual history in France. Vincent Descombes gives the following account: 'The recent orientation of the debate in France is a delayed effect of the experience of May '68, a month in which the French educated classes had the surprise of their lives. The revolution which had been spoken of for so long was triggered off without warning. Yet perhaps this revolution was not a revolution after all . . . For more than twenty years, intellectuals had made great efforts to instruct themselves in historical materialism, hoping to break away from the "petty-bourgeois ideology" of their origins. Now they discovered in this theory of history, in this political mode of thought, the obstacle that separated them from history at the very moment when history was knocking on the door.' *Modern French Philosophy,* p. 168.
9. G. Lardreau and C. Jambet, 'L'Ange, entre Mao et Jesus', *Magazine Littéraire* Nos. 112–13.

human nature, its backdrop is a kind of despair which, at its limit, depicts human society as permanently and inherently oppressive. Its inevitable outcome is the search for a 'provisional morality' and a 'politics of the least evil', the desire to be — in Camus's phrase — 'neither victims, nor torturers'. The *Nouvelle Philosophie* has no conception of historical advance or permanent transformation, but can only imagine brief fulgurations of rebellion which will inevitably fade back into the long night of oppression. In a further contrast with traditional anarchism, the *Nouvelle Philosophie*'s denunciations of totalitarianism, as has already been mentioned, are directed almost exclusively against left-wing regimes. The rationalizing, modernizing apparatus of state socialism appears as the dismal terminus of an increasing centralization of power. Typically Lardreau and Jambet can claim that: 'today, to think against the state is, to a large extent, to think against Marxism.[10]

Of course, other, very different accounts of the political trajectory of the New Philosophers are possible, perhaps the most incisive of which was produced by Règis Debray in a pamphlet published as a counter-blast to the wave of sentimental celebration which marked the tenth anniversary of May '68. Debray begins by debunking the idea that the Events marked a major revolutionary upsurge, a fundamental challenge to the structures of capitalism. He does not deny that in certain respects there was a violent confrontation with bourgeois order, but suggests that this was less because of the revolutionary temper of the proletariat than because the French bourgeoisie found itself 'politically and ideologically well behind the logic of its own economic development'.[11] Debray sees the central factor in the aetiology of the May movement in the far greater disjunction in France than elsewhere between the requirements of advanced capitalist technology and industry and cultural forms dominated by an extremely traditionalist, Catholic and rural-based bourgeois ideology. Whereas in other countries the transition to advanced consumer capitalism, and the corresponding transformation of attitudes to the family, sexuality, the forms and content of education took place comparatively smoothly, in France it required an abrupt convulsion to begin the process of bringing base and superstructure back into line. May '68

10. G. Lardreau and C. Jambet, 'Une dernière fois contre la "Nouvelle Philosophie" ' *La Nef* No. 66.
11. R. Debray, *Modeste contribution aux discours et cérémonies officielles du dixième anniversaire*, Paris 1978. Here quoted from the partial translation in *New Left Review* 115, May–June 1979, p. 48.

was therefore not a crisis of the capitalist system, but a crisis *in* the system, which — in contrast to a genuine revolutionary crisis — led, after the reimposition of order, to the installation of a regime very similar to that which had gone before, but now committed to the political and legislative assimilation of the innovations of the uprising. In the vagueness and self-proclaimed aimlessness of May 'the imaginary anticipated the real, and the law of the heart coincided with the law of efficiency'.[12]

Given this analysis, Debray can make clear, in a different way from the New Philosophers themselves, the connection between their present activity and their militant past. Cut off from the workers movement by the action of the Communist Party and the trades unions, the intellectuals have returned from 'politics' to theorize this isolation in anti-Marxist terms, and to exchange the quest for an alliance with the best traditions of the workers movement for an adoption of the better political and cultural traditions of the bourgeoisie (human rights, Albert Camus, the Centre Beaubourg). Only in France could the North-American commonplace of 'no necessary correspondence' between economic liberalism and social conservatism be experienced as a revelation. Whether one sees a genuine reflux from Marxism taking place, or whether, like Alain Touraine, one sees a confusion between libertarianism and Bolshevism which dates back to Sartre finally being cleared up, and an essentially liberal critique of state-power emerging from its ill-fitting Marxist-Leninist shell.[13] The fact is that the positions of the *Nouvelle Philosphie* (the state is the ultimate evil, 'to think is to dominate', the individual is sovereign) could merge almost imperceptibly into the doctrines of neo-liberalism, with its aggressive belief in private endeavour and the minimal state: 'What remains of 68 in 78, at the bottom of the retorts of social experimentation, and after the sieve of ten years of apprenticeships by trial and error, is the lowest common denominator: life can be changed without changing the State. (And if one cannot change other people's lives, at least one can improve one's own.) . . . The aberrant politicization of the private sphere (68) has been reversed into the aberrant privatization of the political sphere (78).'[14]

Debray clinches his argument with a reference to the recent proliferation of pirate radio stations in France. The nationalist and jacobin fraction of the bourgeoisie, Chirac's RPR, forced through a strict law

12. Ibid., p. 48.
13. See A. Touraine, 'Intellectuels d'en Haut et intellectuels d'en Bas', *L'Arc* No. 70.
14. Debray, p. 56.

against the 'free radios' in 1972, while other countries (Britain, Italy) were opening the way for a big expansion of private broadcasting. Thus in France it is left to the dissidents and autonomists of the airwaves to struggle against the now-outmoded idea of centralized state control of all broadcasting. Yet, despite appearances, they are merely blazing a trail towards the moment when advertising overload will force French legislation into conformity with the requirements of consumer capitalism. 'Anarchists' and 'capitalists' advance by opposed and yet converging paths.[15]

In a perceptive article Danielle and Jacques Rancière — who, like the New Philosophers, took the road from Althusser through Maoism, but who have gone on to uncover an important vein of historical enquiry — have similarly traced the itinerary of the intellectuals after May '68, this time with regard to their changing status, and to changing conceptions of their own role.[16] In the period immediately after '68 the attack on the hierarchies of the faculty became a kind of populism, in which the trickery and untruth of the discourse of the intellectuals was opposed to the authentic knowledge of the toiling and suffering masses. This was the time of *établissement*, the movement in which many militants abandoned courses and potential academic careers to work on the docks or in the big car factories,[17] and of Sartre's pronouncements on the coming end of the old-style intellectual cut off from the life of the people. The Rancières suggest that around 1972 disillusionment began to set in, due to the failure of the masses to manifest the kind of combativity which had been hoped for. (The lack of any significant working-class response after the shooting of Pierre Overney, a young Maoist worker, by a factory guard at Renault was a particularly bitter blow.) Consequently the intellectual began to reassume an autonomous function. This time, however, the idea was not that he or she take on the role of leader, representative, or universalizing spokesman, but that the task was to remove the institutional blocks which prevented the masses themselves from being heard. Thus Sartre described the

15. However, Henri Weber has offered a cogent critique of Debray's account, pointing out that the May uprising cannot be reduced to a simple functionalist 'ruse' of the mode of production, and that the genuinely anti-capitalist potential of May could only be deflected through a process of ideological class struggle. Unfortunately Weber's own account is vitiated by a return to the tired Trotskyist thesis of workers betrayed by a reformist leadership. See H. Weber, 'Post-May: Renewal and Recovery', *New Left Review* 115, May-June 1979.
16. J. Rancière, 'La Légende des philosophes', *Les Révoltes Logiques*, special issue, 1978.
17. For a first-person account of this movement see R. Linhart, *L'Etabli*, Paris 1978.

scandal for the bourgeoisie of *La Cause du Peuple,* the paper of the *Gauche Prolétarienne,* as consisting in the fact that — in contrast to papers which speak on behalf of the working class — it allowed the voice of the masses themselves to be heard. In this context a role for the intellectual appears, in which it is his or her *prestige* (as in the case of Sartre's editorship of *La Cause du Peuple*) which is put to use, rather than a capacity to provide a universalizing counterpoint to the concrete activity of the masses. But once this step has been taken, the way is open for the intellectual to reassume her/his traditional status, while masking this reassumption with a rhetoric in which universalizing discourse is denounced *in the name of* the masses. The *Nouvelle Philosophie* consists of a series of simplifications which betray the desire to 'have it both ways': the intellectual is restored to full rights as bearer of the banner of freedom against all forms of oppression and domination, but such domination is no longer conceived of in class terms. Rather it is theorized with convenient vagueness in a vocabulary of 'power', or in terms of a multiplicity of powers. At the same time the source of her/his authority is a past of militant activity and a direct appeal — in a reminiscence of Maoist populism — to the masses, to what is now termed the 'plebs'. Thus the inevitably complex and contradictory relation between the intellectual and popular movements, which Jacques Rancière and his team have recently been analysing in its historical detail, is transformed into a harmonious unity, in which the post-*gauchiste* intellectual employs the image of the plebs, of the suffering and downtrodden people, as the moral blackmail at the heart of an attack on the power-affiliations of learned discourse. The Rancières see the attack on Marxism as playing a central role in the elaboration of this elitist populism. By attacking the abuse of power by Marxist governments and parties, and attributing these abuses to the nature of Marxist theory itself, the New Philosophers can all the more efficiently avoid disconcerting questions about their own former role as militants. Furthermore, the attack on Marxism betrays a despair of the capacity of popular rebellion significantly to transform society, born out of the disappointments of their own experience. A blanket condemnation of Marxism spares one the trouble of analysing the nature and content of popular movements, since the Socialist Revolution can be explained away as an idea stuffed into the heads of the workers by the Master Thinkers in order to ensure their own universal domination. The rejection of Marxism, enthroned by their former teacher Althusser as the Theory of theories, becomes the only way for the New Philosophers to continue to affirm the plurality and gaiety of the revolts of May.

The New Philosophy, however, is not simply the terminus of a political itinerary which began in May '68; it is not just a collection of political attitudes, but also has a more specifically theoretical lineage, which can be deciphered in the debased forms of the theoretical 'underpinning' of its arguments. Since the mid-60s, with the crumbling of the orthodoxy of 'scientistic' structuralism, the avant-garde of French theory has placed an ever-increasing positive investment in the disruptive effects which plurality and singularity oppose to the efforts of theoretical system-builders. Whether this opposition is set up in terms of metaphysical closure and *différance,* as in Derrida, or of linguistic system and enunciating subject, as in *Tel Quel,* what has been valorized is the breaking-down and evasion of order. Given the close interaction between philosophical and political ideas in France, without parallel in the sealed world of analytical philosophy, it would have been naive not to expect, sooner or later, a political pay-off from this theoretical emphasis. Certain thinkers sought to delay this nemesis, in the case of Derrida by denying any definitive incompatibility between his ideas and Marxism, and in the case of *Tel Quel* by projecting their theories into the imaginary real of Maoist China. But with the *Nouvelle Philosophie* it finally took the stage in an eclectic and virulent form (and the modish *littérateurs* at *Tel Quel* were among the first to follow the new trend). However, the New Philosophers were not the first to attempt a marriage of the themes of difference and singularity with the more specific concerns of post-'68 *gauchisme.* The invasion by leftism of the theoretical terrain had begun several years earlier, perhaps most decisively marked by the publication in 1972 of Deleuze and Guattari's *Anti-Oedipus.*

Anti-Oedipus is not, and does not claim to be, a work of coherent theory. It is a celebration of the liberating force of what Deleuze and Guattari call 'desire', conceived of as free-flowing by nature, unrestricted in its choice of objects, and existing prior to any systematization. If only the level of this desire could be reached then all would be well, for 'desire is revolutionary in itself, and as if involuntarily, in wanting what it wants'. The universality of free affirmation would lead automatically not towards socialism (Deleuze and Guattari are convinced that socialization of the means of production can only increase the despotism of the state), but towards a vaguely-imagined utopia. The true revolutionaries are authors such as Nietzsche, Artaud, Henry Miller, the constant reference-points of the book, and not, in the words of fellow *désirant* Jean-François Lyotard, those 'paranoiacs who call themselves Marxist politicians'. Yet Deleuze and Guattari are also acutely aware that what they call 'true desire' is almost impossible to discover. True desire exists at the unconscious and pre-individual level, whilst all we are aware of is structures and social institutions which determine relations between 'whole persons'. These structures are the result of an ordering, which Deleuze and Guattari refer to as a 'territorialization' of desire, in which (since 'social production and desiring production are one and the same') desire turns against itself and begins to solidify into its own prison. Thus what begins as a celebration of untrammelled desire ends by being confronted with precisely the same problems as those of classical Freudianism, the difference being that Deleuze and Guatttari see the Oedipus complex not as the original 'tragedy' of desire, but as one further codification (the hermeneutic reduction of all libidinal relations to the sad, repetitive triangle of Daddy-Mommy-Me) imposed in the interests of preserving an increasingly unstable social order.

Three aspects of *Anti-Oedipus* are of primary significance for the form the *Nouvelle Philosophie* will take. The first is a radically undialectical view of the relation between individual and social formation: both are seen as constructed, in a way which remains unelucidated, by the activity of apersonal 'desiring machines'. All forms of order or codification are seen as oppressive, including the order of theory: 'It is not the sleep of reason which engenders monsters,' write Deleuze and Guattari, 'but a vigilant and insomniac rationality.'[18] By distinguishing between investments of desire at the unconscious level and pre-conscious investment of interest, *Anti-Oedipus* can suggest that apparently subversive organizations, and in the first place the revolutionary party, can in fact be reactionary and repressive from the point of view of desire. But by this time the concept of desire has become so extended as to have lost all meaning. It is no longer clear what Deleuze and Guattari are affirming. In a book devoted to its celebration, it is all but impossible to discover examples of liberated, non-oedipalized desire. Schizophrenic delirium seems to offer the closest approximation, but again Deleuze and Guattari claim that clinical schizophrenia represents a truncated and codified version of the true liberating experience. One is tempted to agree with René Girard when, in his perceptive critique of *Anti-Oedipus*, he writes: 'Do (Deleuze and Guattari) not limit themselves to placing beneath the Freudian edifice, shaken but intact, a new layer of the unconscious, far below or far above if you prefer, whose repercussions on our humble activities are about as concrete as would be the discovery of a

18. G. Deleuze and F. Guattari, *Anti-Oedipus*, New York 1977, p. 112.

new layer of gas in the atmosphere of Venus?'[19] *Anti-Oedipus*, and this is a prophetic trait, pays for the 'radicality' of its challenge to social institutions with an almost total vacuousness.

The second significant aspect of *Anti-Oedipus* is the way in which it takes up and elaborates a central theme of Wilhelm Reich's analysis of fascism. The libertarian impulse of May had encouraged analyses of the interplay between power (the institution) and desire (liberation), but *Anti-Oedipus* was perhaps the first work to emerge from this milieu to suggest that this interplay was more than a simple opposition. Just as in Reich's analysis of fascism a role is given to the pleasure derived from submission to power, so Deleuze and Guattari depict desire as capable of satisfaction through investment in authoritarian structures. Yet as good libidinal revolutionaries they feel obliged to disentangle this bad 'paranoiac' desire from liberating schizoid desire, a task which becomes increasingly difficult, and which in the end is tacitly abandoned. Even the much-maligned Oedipus complex returns to haunt Deleuze and Guattari, who are unable completely to conjure away the idea that Oedipus is based on something more than a psychoanalytical imposture: 'The oedipal practices of synthesis, oedipalization, triangulation, castration, all that refers back to forces which are a little more powerful, a little more subterranean than psychoanalysis, the fault, ideology, even taken together'.[20] Thus it is easy to see how the frantically affirmative *Lebensphilosophie* of *Anti-Oedipus* could rapidly flip over into a radical pessimism, since there seems to be no way of assuring the independence and priority of 'good' desire over 'bad' desire, the schizophrenic over the paranoiac, and the revolutionary over the fascist. Deleuze and Guattari lose themselves in a maze in their effort to deny the ultimate identity of these proliferating doubles. Their book is closest to schizophrenic delirium not in what it advocates, but in its own self-misrecognition and in its desperate attempts to escape conclusions ever more opposed to those which were intended.

Thirdly, *Anti-Oedipus* is important in the pre-history of the *Nouvelle Philosophie* as much for its tone and style as for its content. There is an element of random and peremptory affirmation in the book which neglects the patient work of argument in favour of the bludgeoning of repetition, and which even employs its own advocation of delirium as a counter to rational critique. In addition *Anti-Oedipus* represented one of the first appearances of a kind of throw-away philosophy. Neologisms and theoretical innovations abound; yet shortly after its

19. R. Girard, 'Système du délire', *Critique* No. 305, 1972, p. 961.
20. Cited in Girard, loc. cit.

publication Deleuze and Guattari announced that they had now abandoned the concept of 'desiring machines', the central organizing concept of the book, and one or two years later even initial enthusiasts had lost all interest in the new 'schizoanalysis'. Unargued affirmation and the built-in obsolescence of the affirmed seemed to go hand in hand.[21] This kind of 'theoretical practice' undoubtedly played an important role in the setting of the stage for the New Philosophy. This is not to say, however, that the New Philosophers are sympathetic to Deleuze's positions. Lardreau and Jambet express admiration for his scholarship (Deleuze published several widely-respected studies of classical philosophers before beginning the elaboration of his own ideas), but are severely critical of his affirmative conception of desire. Lévy goes even further, suggesting that the practical extension of Deleuze and Guattari's doctrines, in our imperfect world, would be an amoral individualism in which the pursuit of gratification would be set above any personal or social cost: *Anti-Oedipus* contains the seeds of a new fascism. Along with a number of other philosophers of his generation, Deleuze has replied in kind, denouncing the *Nouvelle Philosophie* for its flimsiness and commercialism. This antagonism is not universal, however. The New Philosophers do have their heroes and mentors among the previous generation of thinkers, but these are not the hard-nosed structuralists or philosophers of desire, rather the far more ambiguous Lacan and Foucault. The question of Foucault's influence on the *Nouvelle Philosophie* has been covered in detail elsewhere,[22] but the way in which the New Philosophers have taken up the ideas of Lacan deserves some consideration here.

It would be difficult to overestimate the influence of Lacan on recent French thought, not only through his writings, which were not published in collected form until 1966, but through his celebrated and long-running seminars. His work has been important for several generations of French intellectuals, its richness and ambiguity making it possible for diverse theoretical and political currents to discover a reflection of their own preoccupations: Merleau-Ponty, Jean Hyppolite and Louis Althusser are among those who have learned from Lacan's teaching. It was not until the late '60s, however, with the publication of the *Écrits*, that Lacan became a truly central figure; his work played an increasingly important role in the critique of structuralism which was then gaining momentum. This may at first

21. This account of the connections between *Anti-Oedipus* and the New Philosophy is indebted to D. Kambouchner, 'La Désorientation', *Autrement* No. 12, 1978.
22. See P. Dews, 'The *Nouvelle Philosophie* and Foucault', *Economy and Society*, vol. 8, no. 2.

appear surprising, since Lacan is often depicted as the originator of 'structuralist' psychoanalysis, but in fact right from the early '50s Lacan's use of ideas borrowed from Saussure or Lévi-Strauss entailed a simultaneous 'displacement' and critique. Throughout the period of high structuralism, with its asseverations of the theoretical redundancy of the subject ('the spoiled brat of philosophy', in Lévi-Strauss's phrase), Lacan persisted in theorizing the place of the subject in psychoanalysis. Thus it was predictable that, when the structuralist orthodoxy began to break down, Lacan would be at the centre of attempts to pose the question of the subject in a new way which would avoid the assimilation of the concept of 'subject' to that of 'consciousness', since his work is marked by a profound ambiguity, in which a structuralist emphasis on the determining role of symbolic systems is in interplay with the suggestion that there is always something which eludes and displaces such systems —the movement of desire. In terms of recent French philosophy, Lacan can be seen as playing Hegel to Deleuze's Schelling and Levi-Strauss's Kant, attempting to integrate the insights of romantic philosophy into the value of individuality and the subjective moment into a theoretical form which assumes the ultimate supremacy of the concept. The tensions of this position, midway between the seekers of immutable structures and the celebrants of *délire*, are given characteristically enigmatic formulation at the end of an interview dating from 1966: 'Psychoanalysis as a science will be structuralist, to the point of recognizing in science a refusal of the subject.'[23]

In a sense this ambiguity has been infused directly into the *Nouvelle Philosophie*, with its combination of an idealization of rebellion, and an ultimate passive pessimism or acquiescence in the status quo. The *Nouvelle Philosophie* may be seen as a rash politicization of the Lacanian thesis of an irrecuperable disjunction between the subject of enunciation and the 'grammatical' subject of the sentence. For Lacan the subject may be 'alienated in the signifier' — the entry into language entails the loss of a primary experience of unity — but at the same time the subject is irreducible to the signifier, so that its desire to articulate that lost unity continually destabilizes the pre-given system of meanings. Lacan opposed the 'truth' of this desire — which, like Heidegger's truth, is revealed only in the traces of its own concealment — to the truth of cognitive discourse. In this perspective what we refer to as science is seen as an attempt to 'suture' the faultlines continually opened up in representational discourse by the moment of

23. J. Lacan, 'Réponses aux étudiants . . . ', *Cahiers pour l'Analyse* No. 3, 1966, p. 13.

enunciation. Even in the discourse of science it is ultimately desire which speaks, although such discourse is constructed upon a systematic misrecognition of this fact. This identification of science by Lacan as an 'ideology of the suppression of the subject', which is not incompatible in his work with the capacity of science to reveal 'asymptotically' something of the real, has been inflated by the New Philosophers into an attack on the 'totalitarianism' implicit in the rigour of scientific method, complemented by a turn towards subjectivist and 'irrational' forms of expression. The tone of their own writings, poetic, oracular and avowedly 'metaphysical', confirms this order of priorities, in which madness or — in some cases — religious belief liberates, while rational discourse constructs a prison. Solzhenitsyn, the lone dissident and Christian believer pitted against the forces of a state ruled by 'Marxist science', becomes the central hero of this vision.

There is another aspect of Lacan's work, however, which is of equal importance for the New Philosophers. If the subject is irreducible *to* the signifier, it is at the same time dependent on the signifier, for there can be no subject beyond or outside language. The most that can be hoped for is that, through analysis, the subject can be brought to a tragic acceptance of its own alienation, and of the ultimate inaccessibility of truth. In contrast to Deleuze and Guattari, Lacan denies that the desire of the subject is a positive force restrained by the Law (the symbolic conventions of a society, particularly with regard to sexuality.) His reinterpretation of psychoanalytic doctrine in terms of the primacy of the signifier entails an erosion of the original Freudian energetics of libido, so that 'primary repression' is no longer the restraint of a pre-existing polymorphous sexuality, but the process whereby desire comes into being. Lacanian desire desires first of all the unnamable Other which is the place of the signifier, that is to say, in a certain sense, its own subjection to the Law. For without the Law it would cease to exist as desire. The possibility of an extension of this doctrine into a conservative politics is all too obvious, especially since Lacan has never attempted to conceal his own cultural pessimism (one of the authentically Freudian aspects of his work): 'In what way can one transcend the alienation of work? It is as if you should wish to transcend the alienation of discourse.'[24] Since the early '70s, with Lacan's development in his seminars of the theory of the 'discourse of the Master', according to which the very elusiveness of truth drives us to seek an authority to be its repository, these implications have

24. Ibid., p. 9.

become more explicit. Even before the *Nouvelle Philosophie* spelled them out, Elisabeth Roudinesco, a Marxist member of the *École Freudienne*, had noted: 'With the adoption [by Lacan] of Lévi-Strauss's myth/science division there is a strong risk of postulating, under the aegis of the discourse of the Master, a concept of history which conforms to the ideals of the eternal return: the slaves merely change their master, and the master is in charge of the Revolution.'[25] More recently Stephen Heath has indicated how the anchoring by Lacanian psychoanalysis of the symbolic of sexual difference in the — in its own terms — 'imaginary' vision of the phallus results in the evacuation from its domain of social formation and history.[26] These criticisms appear to be confirmed by the work of Pierre Legendre, a historian of institutions and Lacanian psychoanalyst who has produced a detailed study of medieval canon law. In his book Legendre attempts to show an essential continuity in the juridical science of western bureaucracies, which has centred on the devising of symbolic strategies which oblige subjects to desire their own submission to authority. Legendre's book, whose title — *L'Amour du Censeur* — speaks for itself, has been criticized for neglecting the moment of force in all domination. But it has been hailed by several of the New Philosophers as the first breakthrough to a 'Lacanian politics'. It appears to confirm their vision in which conflict is no longer a political conflict between social classes, but an ethical struggle within the individual between the 'desire for submission' and the 'love of freedom': in some sense we are all oppressors and we are all oppressed.

Perhaps the best way to explore the amalgam which these theoretical antecedents produce in the *Nouvelle Philosophie* itself is to look at the work of a particular representative author. Lévy is the obvious choice, since he has acted as the publisher and figurehead of the group. In addition his own book, which was probably the biggest success of all the *Nouvelle Philosophie*'s publications, is constructed to a large extent with ideas borrowed from his associates, so that it represents, despite its callowness and inconsistency, a useful compendium of *Nouvelle Philosophie* attitudes. A survey of *La Barbarie à Visage Humain* should give a good idea of the tone and content of the movement as a whole.

Lévy begins by presenting his biographical credentials, and this in itself is characteristic: the *Nouvelle Philosophie* has been marked not simply by the overshadowing of the work by its author, elevated to the

25. E. Roudinesco, 'Cogito et Science du Réel', *L'Arc* No. 58, 1974.
26. See S. Heath, 'Difference', *Screen*, vol. 19, no. 3.

status of a media 'personality', but by the irruption of the subject of enunciation into the text itself, an assertion of subjectivity against the blank uniformity of theory. The trick is once again due to Lacan, with his *ex cathedra 'je dis que . . .'*, but with the New Philosophers it takes on fresh significance. For the New Philosopher is equally, if not more, important for who he or she is and has been, than for what he or she actually says. It is a past of militancy and disillusionment which confers authority on current utterances. Lévy cannot himself claim a specifically 'Maoist' past, so a more general historical location has to suffice. His book opens with the following piece of self-dramatization: 'I am the bastard child of a diabolical couple, fascism and stalinism.'[27]

Lévy's first attack is against the theory of power of Marxism and of the Left in general, in which power is seen as maintained by varying combinations of ideological mystification and naked repression. In these theories Lévy perceives two apparently contrary but related mistakes. The first is a substantialization of power: power is seen as exercised through a specific range of mechanisms, as the possession of a dominant class. The second is the illusion that — since power is a delimited entity — it can be defeated or overthrown and that a 'liberation' from power can take place. Against this model Lévy deploys a vulgarized fusion of ideas drawn from Foucault and Lacan, in which power becomes both 'everything' and 'nothing'. It is nothing, since it cannot be located in specific mechanisms or institutions; rather than being imposed from above, it filters up from below, permeating every social relation; we are victims of 'the cop in our heads', of our own 'exteriorization of the law'. Against the Marxists, Lévy finds the most suitable metaphor for power in the Freudian concept of the phantasy. Like the phantasy, power is in some sense 'unreal', and yet it is inescapable in its effects, it is everywhere and 'everything'. With a little help from Legendre, Lévy attacks Deleuze and Guattari's idea of an autonomous and rebellious desire, or any concept of a 'freedom' anterior and counterposed to power: the final step is taken — and this is characteristic of the New Philosophy — towards the restoration of a concept of closure which the whole tendency of post-structuralist philosophy had been to undermine. Although condemned to a losing battle, in Foucault there are at least 'resistances' counterposed to power, and in Lacan 'la subversion du sujet' is a subversion *by* the subject, and not merely the subject being subverted. But with the *Nouvelle Philosophie* the idea of a difference or

27. B.-H. Lévy, *La Barbarie à visage humain*, Paris 1977, p. 9.

otherness opposed to the closure of the system (whether political or theoretical) becomes so aetherialized as to lose all effectivity. Since power and the real are now coextensive, and since — in a flattening-out of Lacan — 'to speak is (in all the senses of the term) to become subject',[28] 'otherness' can now only take the ultimate form of transcendence (as in the religious thinkers among the New Philosophers — Clavel, Nemo, Lardreau and Jambet) or disappear altogether as in the case of Lévy, for whom — at least during his blacker moments — 'desire is nothing but, and is entirely homogeneous with power'.[29] On this basis we can draw the conclusion that 'the Prince is the other name of the World', that the social bond is inherently oppressive (although some, i.e. liberal bourgeois societies, may be preferable to others), and that 'the idea of a good society is an absurd dream'.[30]

Having demonstrated *a priori* the impossibility of liberation, Lévy can go on to the next stage of his task, which is to show, following the *Nouvelle Philosophie* tradition of deducing historical reality from ideas, that socialism is merely an aggravated combination of capitalism and metaphysics. After all, the post-structuralists — Foucault, Derrida — have shown that teleological views of history are simply the last refuge of a doomed humanism, and the bourgeoisie at least seems to have learned the lesson. It no longer believes in an appointed mission, or pretends to the legitimacy of historical destiny. Capital's desacralization of all traditional beliefs and social practices has rebounded upon its owners, who are content opportunistically to manage an arbitrary system. (There is a hint in Lévy's book of the switchover already noted by Régis Debray, in which the kaleidoscopic, thrillingly aimless world of consumer capitalism begins to be seen as offering a kind of liberation which the struggle for political ideals cannot match.) The socialists, on the other hand, still believe in the rationality of history which, throughout all its reversals and detours, is slowly moving towards the realization of the Universal. Interestingly, Lévy does not suggest that such a realization is impossible, merely that it could only serve to increase our present misfortunes. The planned and ordered society of socialism is indeed being brought to maturity in the womb of capitalism, but not in the way that Marxists believe. Socialism is merely the capitalist ideal of technological rationality pushed to its ultimate conclusion. The 'trans-

28. Ibid., p. 51.
29. Ibid., p. 47.
30. Ibid., p. 38.

parent' society of the future is the society in which all social relations are visible and controllable from the central watchtower of the social scientists and the police. In fact Lévy begins to restore — one of many incoherences in the book — the teleology which he has just abolished. Capitalism is the destiny of the West, the ultimate stage of Platonism and the inevitable corollary of Descartes's mathematization of nature. The Russian Revolution did no more than speed up the tempo of this transformation of nature and human society into a system of calculable relations. Thus Marxism is merely the 20th-century form of this occidental destiny: 'the most formidable doctrine of Order that the West has ever invented',[31] allowing the discontent of the masses to be marshalled by politicians and parties, insisting on the demolition of traditional bastions of culture and belief, and paving the way for the installation of a socialism which can only be the 'barbarous modality of capitalism'.

It is not difficult to see this ill-considered jumble of attitudes as the *reductio ad absurdum* of a decade of French thought in which the concepts of reason, theory and history have been subjected to an incessant critique by theorists for whom Nietzsche and Freud have replaced Marx as the definitive *maîtres-à-penser*. The critique of dialectics elaborated by such thinkers as Derrida, Foucault and Deleuze has exacted a serious toll in the form of an inability to think in terms other than those of an all-or-nothing showdown, in which both the 'power' of the system and the 'dissidence' of its other become hypostatized contraries, while the rejection of the 'white terror of truth' (the phrase is again due to Jean-François Lyotard) has led to paradoxical attacks on science, and in particular on the human sciences, not because of the falsity of their discourse, but precisely because of its veracity. In Lévy's attack on Marxism, for example, his ultimate argument is not that Marxism is a false theory of society and of political action, but rather that it is an all-too-accurate account of the coming fate of the West. In Lévy's view we are enclosed within Marxism as Ptolomaic astronomers were enclosed within their cosmology, so that to reply to Marxist theory with a counter-theory would only result in a lapsing back into the 'discourse of the Master'. Thus the protest against Marxism can only take a moral form, and in this Solzhenitsyn, 'the Dante of our time', has shown the way.

Thus the *Nouvelle Philosophie* possesses a cover for its own extravagance and theoretical incoherence in the form of the assumption that

31. Ibid., p. 202.

the only reliable defences against the linked totalitarianisms of science and politics are aesthetic and ethical. The idea, of course, is not new; it can be found on the political right in Heidegger and in the long tradition of romanticizing reaction. The New Philosophers have taken up something of this tradition, in their exaltation of inherited beliefs and practices against 'planning', in Clavel or Nemo's nostalgia for the 'personal' bond between master and man in feudalism contrasted with the anonymity of commodity relations under capitalism,[32] and in a generalized hostility to the inheritance of the Enlightenment. (For Lévy the Gulag is simply 'the Enlightenment minus tolerance'. As Jean-Pierre Faye has pointed out, the New Philosophers, with their incapacity for historical dialectic, fail to appreciate that the concept of 'human rights' to which they are so attached is precisely one of the central acquisitions of the Enlightenment.[33]) But it can also be found on the left in thinkers such as Adorno and Marcuse, and the New Philosophers have something of their sense of an all-pervading one-dimensionality which has become so internalized as to be almost invisible. What may at first appear surprising is that such a combination of ideas should emerge again in Paris in the late 1970s.

There are a number of explanations of this phenomenon which do not simply remain at the level of the 'history of ideas'. First of all, the New Philosophy is not just the aberration of a handful of the high intelligentsia, but must be seen as mirroring a wide-spread mood of disorientation among the 'generation of '68' which ranges from — at its worst — a corrosive disullusionment and cynicism, to — at its best — a belief that smallscale cultural innovation and institutional reform are preferable to chasing the mirage of revolution. At another level, as Jean-Claude Guillebaud has suggested in his lively — if frequently facile — book *Les Années Orphelines,* the New Philosophy can be seen as a reaction to an increasing sense of ideological incoherence in a world in which Cuban columns march against Marxist partisans, while socialist states invade each other in South-East Asia. Guillebaud also rehearses the more cynical theory according to which, with the prospect of the Left coming to power through the ballot box in March '78, the obvious way for the intelligentsia to maintain the reassuring integrity of an oppositional stance was to make an anticipatory shift to the right. At the same time, however, recent developments in French theory cannot be viewed as simply a

32. See, for example, P. Nemo, *L'Homme Structurel,* Paris 1975.
33. See J.-P. Faye, 'Post Vocem', *Change* Nos. 32–3.

reflection of political developments: important texts by Derrida, Deleuze and Lacan which valorized alterity over identity and system had been published well before May '68, so that the turn against Marxism is more than a generational phenomenon. The intellectual autobiography recounted by François Châtelet, France's leading historian of philosophy, in his *Chronique des Idées Perdues*, is instructive in this regard. Beginning from an 'existential Marxist' position in the early '60s, Châtelet has shed more and more of what he sees as the Hegelian and historicist baggage of Marxism, welcoming the Althusserian intervention on the way, to arrive at a position which rejects the idea of sitting at 'the tribunal of Reason and History' in favour of a pluralist 'tracking-down of divinities of all kinds'. Similarly, Sartre stated in his last years that he would prefer the label 'existentialist' to that of 'Marxist',[34] and was said to be working on a new philosophy of freedom.

This revival of emphasis on the singular and the subjective (French periodicals in the late '70s announced the 'New Individualism' and the 'New Romanticism') is not entirely to be regretted, and can be seen as inevitable, given the 'anti-humanist' severity of structuralism and Althusser. It is arguable that there are dimensions of human experience which Marxism ignores at its peril, and which, if neglected, will sooner or later return to haunt its theoretical edifices in ambiguous forms. On the other side, however, the New Philosophers have at least rendered the service of making clear that the theorization of plurality and difference, already well established in France and beginning to appear in Britain in writings which reject *a priori* the idea of the social formation as an analysable totality, can only lead into a political cul-de-sac if taken as an ultimate. The emergence of regional, ecological and feminist struggles has taught the valuable lesson that not all sites of social conflict can be reduced to a unitary class contradiction, yet these struggles seem condemned to hopelessness in remaining localized, since what they contest is inevitably over-determined by the general process of capitalist development. In order to resolve this dilemma a 'principle of articulation' seems to be required which will not alienate these movements by reducing them to an *a priori* class determination, but is capable of hegemonizing and directing them towards common goals of democratization and social control. In the current theoretical confusion and loss of bearings on the Left — marked vividly by the New Philosophy and its aftermath in France, but starting to make itself felt no less here — this concep-

34. J.-P. Sartre, *Situations X*, Paris 1976.

tion seems to offer a possible direction for advance. We need to know how the unity of struggles, no longer pre-given by an inclusive primacy of class, can itself become a purpose of struggle.

Reprinted from *RP* 24

The 'Real' Meaning of Conservatism

Andrew Belsey

After the Affluent Fifties, the Swinging Sixties and the Doubting Seventies, what — the Authoritarian Eighties? Events around the world — in the Soviet Union, in the United States, in Thatcherite Britain, in South America, in Iran, Korea, Turkey and plenty of other places — suggest that aggressive, repressive, militaristic, nationalistic authoritarianism is increasing everywhere. Roger Scruton has spotted this trend and has decided to write a satire warning us against it, in some of its manifestations, at least.[1] Perhaps the biggest joke was to call this semi-fascism 'conservatism', for the True Conservative, as I shall call Scruton's anti-hero, has little sympathy for the British Conservative Party or its present government. In spite of their undoubted authoritarian tendencies, which Scruton does right to warn us against, they are still far too liberal for the True Conservative.

Scruton has indeed conceived an excellent political joke, though the delivery of it could have done with the services of a more skilled midwife. He has imagined a nation called 'England', whose citizens are entirely men — male people. By crystallizing the more fascist elements of Plato and Hegel, and adding touches of Machiavelli, Nietzsche and minor nineteenth-century fascists where necessary, he has invented for this imaginary state a constitution and a set of institutions of a suitably repellent kind. In the true spirit of satire he has presented his obnoxious content with an equivalent style, at once haughty, ugly and violent in its paratactic authoritarianism. Indeed, so successful is he in aping the disgusting crudities of the semi-intellectual fascist that it is difficult to sustain the realization that the whole thing is an elaborate joke. A clever idea, but perhaps too paradoxically convoluted for the average reader.

1. Roger Scruton, *The Meaning of Conservatism*, Harmondsworth, 1980. All page references in this article are to this book.

Nevertheless, the wants and beliefs of the True Conservative come across clearly. He (we have to get used to the idea that the True Conservative is always a 'he') is a patriot, believing in the history, culture, traditions, customs, ceremonies and rituals of his own nation, and relying on the prejudices that go with them. He also relies heavily on such terms as 'respect', 'loyalty' and 'discipline'. His world can in fact be seen as constructed solely from *tradition, authority* and *allegiance* (27). The True Conservative is a relativist, believing that there are many conservatisms within these abstract limits, each with its own 'national focus' (36).

His aversions too are just as clear. His 'principal enemy' is 'the philosophy of liberalism, with all its attendant trappings of individual autonomy and the "natural" rights of man' [16]. Freedom is an abstraction [16], democracy a contagion [53], as is egalitarianism [59]. Even equality of opportunity leaves him cold [156]. And such ideas as social justice [86] and progress [191] are just pathetic in their idiocy.

The True Conservative shows his colours most spectacularly in his attitude to the state. As we have just seen, the greatest threat to True Conservatism is not, as you might think, Communism (that is, the statist regimes of Eastern Europe), for any totalitarian system receives the natural sympathy of the True Conservative, but liberalism. Liberalism believes in the reality of individual autonomy, and therefore in the possibility and desirability of individual freedom in the political sense. The liberal — and this will include many who *call* themselves Liberals, Conservatives, Social Democrats, Socialists, Marxists, while the Anarchist merely takes liberalism to its logical conclusion — makes a strong separation in both theory and practice between *civil society* and the *state*, and approves of social links while deprecating and attempting to decrease the power and influence of the state.

The True Conservative, however, does not believe in any ultimate separability of state and society (27), and indeed prefers a term like 'nation' which neatly obscures the issue. The True Conservative believes that the state is an organism or even a person — it has will and personality to which the individual is 'subject', bound not by choice or consent but by a 'transcendent bond' which represents his determined acquiescence in the existing order (33). The True Conservative is therefore totalitarian in two senses. First, in believing that the real political unit is not the individual of liberal humanism but the total, the state. Second, in giving to the state absolute power. The individual, according to the True Conservative, does not even exist, but insofar as he comes into existence at all, is created by the state, within limits imposed by the state. It is only through allegiance to the greater whole that individuality and self-identity exist (34, 38). The state thus precedes the individual both ontologically and morally, and the idea of the individual asserting his 'rights' against the state is absurd. The state may grant *privileges*, but *rights* there are none.

'A society too has a will, and . . . a rational man must be open to its persuasion. This will lies, for the conservative, enshrined in history, tradition, culture and prejudice. England, far from being a savage society that would justify the imposition of overarching decrees, is founded in the maturest of national cultures, and contains within itself all the principles of social life. The true conservative has his ear attuned to those principles, and tries to live, as a result, in friendship with the nation to which he owes his being. His own will to live, and the nation's will to live, are simply one and the same' (24).

Therefore the power of the state is, and must be, unrestricted. The 'minimal state' is no part of conservative thinking (33), and the 'liberal' contortions of a Friedman or a Joseph in the dismal science of economics will be laughed out of court (97). The True Conservative will support capitalism mainly for pragmatic reasons (111), but knows the necessity of state discipline for both capital and labour (113). The True Conservative will believe in 'man's absolute and ineradicable need of private property' (99), but does not suppose that the free market is the obvious method of meeting this need. Indeed, the True Conservative would obviously regard the capture by *capital* a dynamic and progressive force (at least for a while), of *conservatism* as one of the more ironic triumphs of history. He prefers to quote Disraeli's remark that it is not feudalism that the conservative will advocate, but merely its 'main principle — that the tenure of property should be the fulfilment of duty' (115) — though with his tongue in cheek, no doubt. The True Conservative's ideal could well be called modern feudalism — a rigidly hierarchical society with an overwhelming state firmly in control at all levels.

There literally *cannot* be anything to restrict the state. The True Conservative, however, will recognize the need to dress this up a bit: '. . . his desire is to see power standing not naked in the forum of politics, but clothed in constitution, operated always through an adequate system of law, so that its movement seems (sic) never barbarous or oppressive, but always controlled and inevitable, an expression of the civilized vitality through which allegiance is inspired. The constitution, therefore, and the institutions which sustain it, will always lie at the heart of conservative thinking' (33).

Here we can see Scruton begin to twist his satirical knife, but delicately, just through the use of the word 'seems'. However, let us follow the True Conservative's line of thought on the constitution, this being defined as 'what guides, limits and authorizes power, and thus manifests itself primarily through law, through the "style" of law, and through the position of the citizen as defined by law' (52). The True Conservative thus puts much emphasis on law. Indeed, seeing the state as defined by its laws, he would sweep away any idea of the sovereignty of law (63). The True Conservative has little time for democratic Parliament, especially the House of Commons. The True Conservative is that rare figure, the unicameralist, though it is to the House of Lords, and especially the Law Lords, that he would entrust guidance of the ship of state (57).

So, in shaking his fist at democratic government, the True Conservative's delight in the law turns out to be somewhat hypocritical. Though he approves of the law, he has to find some reason to rule out much recently enacted law that he doesn't like; what he prefers is common law, equity and long-established statute. Though he cannot find a reason, he does find that the law comes to his, and its own, aid, and will manage to stymie the politician with the temerity to enact reform. Here the True Conservative makes a valuable point which radicals and reformers should certainly take note of.

The average politician, being a hot-headed careerist, does not understand the real nature of law. He enacts a statue, and sees it as self-contained, written down in black and white, its meaning clear to all. He forgets that before it can have any effect it has to be inserted into the English legal system, where it is subjected to the due processes of that system, to interpretation by tradition, to judicial precedent and death by a thousand qualifications. As a result it often turns out to have little or no effect at all, to the naive surprise of the politician, and to the delight of the True Conservative (63). In such a way does he look to the law to protect himself and his position from the madnesses involved in assaulting the constitution with new laws on equal opportunities, devolution, the Common Market, immigration and nationality. The politician may think of these as laws, but the True Conservative knows them to be 'inapplicable, perhaps even illegitimate' (69).

The cracks in the True Conservative's edifice are now becoming apparent, subtly exposed by Scruton's careful probing. By declaring parliament's enactments 'perhaps illegitimate' the True Conservative is devouring himself, flying in the face of the constitution he claims to uphold, and thereby proclaiming himself a social renegade.

'In England,' the True Conservative points out, 'there is a law which forbids the production and distribution of subversive material — the law of sedition' (17). So the True Conservative now finds himself in the same position as the Soviet dissident, whom he professes to despise!

Actually, the True Conservative's attitude to the Soviet dissident is well worth examination, bringing out as it does the full extent of his disgraceful and disgusting hypocrisy. Rejecting as fantasy any notion of universal human rights, the True Conservative has no sympathy for the 'seditious utterance' of the dissenter (49). Not surprisingly, the True Conservative has a Stalinist notion of freedom: it is 'comprehensible as a social goal only when subordinate to something else, to an organization or arrangement which defines the individual aim' (19). The citizen is 'subject' to the state (40), 'belongs' to it (47), whatever that state may be — provided only that it is true to its traditions, as the Soviet Union is. 'There can be no international charter for dissidents, and only one respectable (!) reason for one state to lend support to seditious utterance in another, which is the pursuit of power' (49). The full view of the True Conservative on this matter is worth quoting at some length:

> In every legal system . . . there must be provision against sedition, laws which enable the power of state to reassert itself against antagonists, and these laws may stand wholly outside the rule of natural justice, being determined by the principle of necessity alone. This truth is so evident that no political dogma can dispense with some soothing rhetoric that will serve to make it palatable. It is unquestionable that, if the power of the state is threatened, so too is its authority, and with it the structure of civil society. To sacrifice power for the sake of justice, is to make the exercise of justice impossible. It cannot, therefore, be an insuperable defect in a law of sedition that it provides for imprisonment without trial, a reduced judicial process, or summary execution. What matters is the extent to which such laws must be invoked. If this invocation constituted — as in Russia — a major portion of the judicial process, then clearly the power of state transcends the allegiance of the citizen. The whole arrangement stands on the brink of illegitimacy. (91)

Note the 'brink'. The True Conservative must regard the dissidents of the Soviet Union — or Argentina or South Africa — as rebels and traitors, deserving all they get. What they fail to realize is that dissent from the state is not merely a political inconvenience for the rulers, but a cosmic folly, the ultimate in idiotic hubris. All that is wrong in Russia is that the power of the state has outrun the allegiance of some of the citizens. The remedy, therefore, is not to reduce state power, but to *increase* it, and to obtain allegiance either through stronger repression, or through subtler ideological conditioning. This, then, is the reality behind the True Conservative's obeisance before 'order' (27).

The hypocrisy of the True Conservative can be further brought out by examining his views on power and authority. For the True Conservative power is all, yet paradoxically he knows the weakness of relying entirely on power. For since people (for reasons the True Conservative cannot explain) dislike bowing down before power, the True Conservative has the alchemic task of transforming power into authority, through legitimization. But the True Conservative is honest enough to recognize that *there is no such thing as authority;* or rather, that *authority is only accepted power.* The True Conservative's aim is 'power to command and coerce those who would otherwise reform or destroy, and its justification must be found within itself, in an idea of legitimacy or established right. The power which the statesman seeks must be, in other words, a power that is accepted. It must be regarded by the people as not just power, but authority' (25–26).

The True Conservative is thus a phenomenologist; he knows that it is how people *see* things (29), how power *seems* to them (33), that it is *appearances* that matter (36) — and all these can be manipulated. Of course, the True Conservative will say that 'people have the *idea* of legitimacy, and see the world as coloured in its terms; and it is how they *see* the world which determines how they act on it' (36) — as if these ideas and visions were *natural* and hence unquestionable, when in fact he knows that the individual subject is *cultural* rather than natural, and created in the state's own image. So authority, or legitimate power, is for the True Conservative simply power that can exercise a hegemony sufficient to prevent any challenge from the powerless. In other words, the passage from power to authority is guaranteed by nothing other than *ideology,* and it is a guarantee which turns out to be decidedly insubstantial. The True Conservative will refer to the necessity of myth (169), or will appeal to the 'natural charm of military ceremony, where power, through its transformation into symbol, acquires the aspect (sic) of authority' (167), or will be reduced to mouthing empty slogans such as that tradition 'makes history into reason' (40), but, having nothing more compelling with which to justify power, can hardly expect to be taken seriously.

So authority is nothing more than power having put on the symbolic order of rhetoric or ritual, with sufficient show of plausibility to pull the wool over the eyes of the subjected citizens. The True

Conservative will go on (and on and on) about 'tradition', 'history', 'culture', etc., in an effort to dress naked power in the robes of legitimacy, but it is a case of the Emperor's new clothes. But so confident, or cocksure, is he of the clothes' visibility that he will unabashedly produce the demolition of his own rickety structure in an unconscious homage to his Marxist opponent: 'Now the Marxist would see the dispute in quite other terms, seeking to demystify the ideal of "authority' and replace it with the realities of power. "Authority", for the Marxist, is merely the ideological representation of power — power imbued with the false aura of legitimacy, made absolute and unchangeable, translated from a historical reality into a sempiternal ideal' (19–20). '. . . For the Marxist, "authority", and the concept of "legitimacy" through which it dignifies itself, are merely parts of the ideology of class rule, concepts belonging to and inculcated by a ruling "hegemony" ' (28).

And the funny thing is that in his heart-of-hearts, the True Conservative knows that the Marxist is correct!

But the True Conservative is a hypocrite and a liar. He knows that the myths that pretend to legitimate class rule are merely modern versions of the Platonic 'noble lie' (139–40), and he will have no hesitation in murdering the history of a nation to produce them. The True Conservative believes in an inegalitarian, hierarchical society, recognizes that the stability of such a society requires acceptance by the unprivileged of their position, but reckons that such acceptance can be 'induced' (140). This again can be arranged via ideology, especially 'the attempt to represent the unpleasant fact of inequality as a form of natural order and legitimate bond' (141). Once again it will be the (rhetorical) 'representation' that veils ruling power and privilege.

So the foundation of the True Conservative's appeal to authority is nothing but a colourful display of flatulence, and Scruton brings this out nicely. But the fun gets even greater if we attempt to probe deeper into the basis of True Conservatism. For the True Conservative claims to be producing a work not of political philosophy but of dogmatics (9, 11). But it is this gap between philosophy and dogma that makes the hole through which True Conservatism finally swallows itself. The testament of the True Conservative becomes the ultimate self-consuming text, marvellous in its self-contradiction, hollow in its abysmal emptiness, full of lies and hypocrisies, and in the end unable to prevent itself from revealing itself truthfully to the world.

The dogmatics of the True Conservative is 'systematic and reasonable'; yet it cannot be presented as such because 'the essence' of conservatism 'is inarticulate' (11). To this contradiction is immediately added another: that in spite of its inarticulateness it is 'capable of expression' (11). Ah, but the contradictions resolve themselves at a higher level. Reading the True Conservative's testament, we find that he expresses himself mostly through allusions, images and examples, which allow a good deal of vagueness and imprecision into his discourse. Though 'it is of the nature of conservatism to avoid abstractions' (17), in fact it rarely descends from them, not even when offering an example, as it does not show how the example relates to the abstractions. We look for reason, we look for justification. All we find is a tottering tower of rhetoric, which collapses at the first gentle impact of the critical probe. Conservative dogmatics is a fine example of what can be called 'the higher mystification'.

It is certainly not reasonable. Intuition, that eternal enemy of human rationality, is all the True Conservative has to fall back on: 'Like any political being, a conservative is "for" certain things: he is for them, not because he has arguments in their favour, but because he knows them, lives with them, and finds his identity threatened (often he knows not how) by the attempt to interfere with their operation' (12–13).

But this is wool-pulling again. The True Conservative knows that it is not his identity but his power and his privilege that are threatened. But he cannot *say* this. Conservatism is literally *unspeakable*. And yet so ridiculous, almost pathetically so, is the True Conservative that he cannot stop himself giving the game away. He knows that the cupboard of justification is bare, but finds himself compelled (he knows not why) to open its door wide to the outside world: 'A political creed, insofar as it is formulated, is partly an exercise in rhetoric, to be revised and restated whenever the times demand that the ruling intuition be given its new dressing of necessity' (20).

Yet since the creed 'provides no answers' to the abstract questions of political philosophy (11), we can remove the superfluous word 'partly', and reveal the True Conservative naked and exposed, flashing his meagre endowments in a laughable attempt to appear the stormtrooping superman. But *admitting* that 'the pursuit of truth leads one to doubt the myths' (190), he *knows* that the myths of authority and allegiance are merely lies. So what next? Well, the 'reflective conservative' (a rare breed, no doubt) can only perform the ultimate act of self-immolation: '. . . the reasons he observes for sustaining the myths of society are reasons which he cannot propagate; to propagate his reasons is to instil the world with doubt. Having struggled for articulacy, he must recommend silence' (191).

Now, of course the testament of the True Conservative is here shown to be ridiculous. The True Conservative cannot give a true account of conservatism; this would be to give the game away, exposing it as a sham. Yet in admitting this, this is precisely what he has done! So the ridiculousness is for two reasons. The first is the obvious absurdity of gabbling through 190 pages of text to a conclusion recommending silence. But the second reason is even deeper. The 190 pages of text *are* silence; they say *nothing*; their value as any form or combination of speech-acts is *non-existent*. The text, representing the final testament of the True Conservative, has devoured itself. As a 'systematic and reasonable' account of conservatism it might just as well be replaced by 190 blank pages.

After this, anything further must be anti-climax. Yet the consummating act of self-abuse ripples throughout the text, so that we find similar contradictions everywhere. Take another of the True Conservative's attempts to provide some sort of reasoned support for conservatism. He will appeal to 'human nature' (66), 'natural prejudice' (68), 'normal feelings' (92), 'common intuition' (119), and will even pretend that the arrangements he recommends arise out of 'natural necessity' (31). But at the same time he knows that this is all fake; there are indeed prejudices, but these are not normal, natural, common or instinctive but are *constructed* by the very society that they are supposed to justify. As the True Conservative says quite clearly: 'It is basic to the conservative view of things . . . that the individual should seek and find his completion in society, and that he should find himself as part of an order that is greater than himself, in the sense of transcending anything that could have been brought about through his own enactment. He must see himself as the inheritor, not the creator, of the order in which he participates, so that he may derive from it (from the picture of its "objectivity") the conceptions and values which determine self-identity. He will see his extension in time from birth to death as taking on significance from civil stability: his world was not born with him, nor does he die when he departs from it' (66).

Again the True Conservative has to expose himself. There are no natural instincts in such a constructed creature. There is only ideology; a 'picture', and its objectivity is only 'objective', a simulacrum determined by myth, and true only to its own lying essence.

As if this were not enough, the True Conservative has the gall not only to ground *conservatism* in human nature, but also to *dissent* from the authoritarian diktats of the True Conservative (91). The True

Conservative's model of human nature is thus not the real essence but a plastic imitation, infinite in its possibilities, able to accommodate even contradictions, nugatory in its explanatory function. Then take the True Conservative's attempted demolition of the central idea of liberalism: that power becomes legitimate authority only through contract, deliberation, choice; in other words, consent by autonomous agents. The True Conservative has the cheek to call this a myth (29). But what is his real strategy? The True Conservative despises liberal consent: the free and genuine consent by responsible beings. Yet he is willing, nay, eager, to devote the power of the state to engineering its own acceptance through the creation of myths of authority and allegiance. Real consent is thus rejected, while manipulated consent replaces it. The True Conservative is thus in the pathetically absurd and contradictory position of scorning the genuine article while embracing and valuing the fake. Hardly a recipe for a successful journey through life, one might think.

Then there is the question of natural justice. The True Conservative is at first concerned lest he appear forced to support whatever power is established, however arbitrarily (84). Is there an independent criterion by which the exercise of power can be judged? Natural justice first presents itself as the answer (89), but natural justice standing isolated is ineffective. It must be incorporated by the very power it is supposed to judge: ' "Natural justice" is the slave of a ruling class. Where there is no such class (as in matters arising between nation states), then there is no natural justice to enact' (90).

Natural justice, then, is simply another myth, and far from being an independent judge of state power, is but state power under a smiling mask. Of course, such a contradictory conclusion was to be expected, for the True Conservative must at all costs support his central contention that state power is incontestable. The idea of natural justice as an independent criterion is for the True Conservative a conceptual nonsense, and so power stands supreme and beyond criticism, whether it be Thatcher-power, Soviet power, Ayatollah-power, or Junta-power in South America.

The unreality of anything except power, and the emptiness of the True Conservative's rhetoric, are again shown up in his remarks on *devolution*. Given his emphasis on the national focus of conservatism (36), and his remark that 'it is only an unfortunate society that cannot lay claim to nationhood' (186), it might appear that the True Conservative would be a ('natural') supporter of devolution — of the claims of the Welsh, Scottish and Irish peoples for their own nations. For why should they, with their different traditions, be subject to the

'English' constitution? But no. 'A nation must necessarily have a centre and a periphery, and unless the periphery is governed with the same strength and resolution as the centre, the nation falls apart' (67). So if you happen to be one of the marginal people of the periphery, hard luck. You must defer to the True Conservative's instinct that devotion to English imperialism comes before truth to the consequences of his own professed principles.

So in addition to the ultimate self-consuming contradiction that produces silence, the True Conservative contradicts himself on human nature, on consent, on natural justice and on devolution. In showing this, Scruton has obviously benefited from the recent French delight in discursive deconstructions: this has enabled him to construct the ultimate in deconstructive texts, a testament which finally expires in a torrent of self-destruction. Scruton shows how the True Conservative, realising that people don't *want* fascism, and that they can provide good reasons why they don't *need* it, has to blot out human reason in a welter of lies, which are then called ('natural') prejudice or instinct, when they are nothing but historically-distorting myths produced to support the True Conservative's own social dominance, his power and his privilege, myths hardly deserving to be dignified by the title 'ideology'.

Scruton's success in constructing and deconstructing the testament of the True Conservative, and showing it up as the pernicious rubbish it is, is considerable. Some might think that the construction is just *too* successful: it is almost as if Scruton really believed it. But this is a risk that a true satirist must take. And there certainly *is* a risk when we read the forceful expression of some of the True Conservative's more vicious visions:

'This decline in the very *idea* of sedition has been brought about not by popular agitation, but by the politics of power. The fact is, not that our society believes in freedom of speech and assembly, but rather that it is afraid to announce its disbelief. This disbelief is so entrenched in English law — in the common law as much as in statuory provisions — that it is impossible to doubt that it could be eradicated without wholly overthrowing the social order which the law enshrines . . . Modern parliaments therefore constantly enact new and selective laws against freedom of speech and assembly, each of which may reflect some serious view as to where evil lies, but none of which is so bold as to recognize that a society really does have enemies, that those enemies seek to undermine it, and that it is the duty of the government, as it is the expectation of the citizen, that they should be prevented by every means to hand. (18)

But while it is a long-standing principle of British law that the formation of hatred (and hence of racial hatred) is a serious criminal offence, it is not clear that illiberal sentiments have to be forms of hatred, nor that they should be treated in the high-handed way that is calculated to make them become so. On the contrary, they are sentiments which seem to arise inevitably from social consciousness: they involve natural prejudice, and a desire for the company of one's kind. That is hardly sufficient ground to condemn them as "racist". (68)

What form . . . should this "illiberal" system of punishment take? Are we to take our example from the cruel and emphatic law of Islam ,and institute flogging and maiming as expressions of civic virtue? The answer cannot be determined abstractly . . . Now the natural conclusion from these reflections is not always drawn, for fear of the barbarous and the primitive in men. But unfortunately, the barbarous and the primitive are there. (84)

The true civil servant is a servant. He may see himself, if the state allows, as a private employee, with private and contractual rights. He may exert against the state his "right" to strike. He (along with a million others) may engage in activities which, while legally sanctioned, are tantamount to rebellion. But when that is so the state is weak to the point of non-existence. What policy can restore its power? One answer suggests itself. Reward extravagantly those servants who are essential; but make them servants. As for the others, let them strike, and permanently. (111–12)

These passages are not exactly funny, but are clearly too ghastly to be taken seriously. It is this difficulty with the *tone* of the humour that is the main problem in this book. For a joke it is certainly humourless for long stretches, but then there are one or two excellent and explicit gags. There is the reference to '*soi-disant* conservatives' (sic) (16) — presumably something to do with the alienation that the True Conservative is concerned about later in the book. There is the use of a case from *Scottish* law to illustrate a claim about *English* self-consciousness [64]. There is a description of the 'degree' speech from *Troilus and Cressida* as one of Shakespeare's 'deepest reflections on the relation between public and private life' (179) — as if Shakespeare's own beliefs can be simply read off from the text, ignoring the role of the constructed 'Ulysses' in an artistic artefact. And then there are the women — or rather the lack of them. In spite of his constant emphasis on 'the family', the only three women in the life of the True Conservative are his Queen (38), his mother (144, 156) and his mistress (81), while his fantasy life is fully occupied by a vision of a 'willing' or even 'importunate schoolgirl' (77).

So much for the True Conservative's contact with reality — or rather his lack of it. He stands naked, surrounded only by myths, not only bankrupt but, in the word of Paul Jennings, 'bunkrapt'. Yet even though he may know the myths for the lies they are, he is a dedicated worshipper of power, and knows how important it is for his own privileged position that the rabble absorbs the myths and accepts the power. He is utterly barren, but appallingly barren, standing with gun in one hand and whip in the other, an image cloning itself throughout the torture-chambers of five continents.

Reprinted from *RP* 28

Edifying Discourses

Joe McCarney

Richard Rorty's book *Philosophy and the Mirror of Nature*[1] has already been the centre of a good deal of attention. It has been widely regarded by students and teachers of academic philosophy as saying important things about the past, present and future of their subject, and the paperback comes decked with tributes from notables, pointing to the same conclusion. This review will try to provide a backdrop to the debate by setting out and assessing the themes of the book.

They seem easy enough to state. The book is, above all, an attack on the tradition which sees philosophy as, essentially, epistemology. Its central concern on that view is the adjudication of claims to knowledge, and since culture is the assemblage of such claims, philosophy is foundational in respect to the rest of culture. Epistemology, since its invention in the seventeenth century, has been pursued as a general theory of representations, images in that great mirror of nature which is the human mind. The roots of this way of thinking go back, however, to the foundations of Western thought, to the Greek insistence that man's essence is 'to *know*', and that knowledge is to be conceived of by analogy with perception and explicated through the use of ocular metaphors. As against all this, Rorty's main philosophical thesis is that knowledge is a matter not of a certain relation between subject and reality, but of social justification, of what is endorsed by one's community or what one can get away with in conversation with one's peers. This in turn yields a conception of philosophy in which epistemology is succeeded by hermeneutics and knowledge by edification. It is no longer to be seen as foundational, as concerned to establish a permanent, neutral matrix for all inquiry, but rather as itself a particular cultural genre, a 'voice in the conversation of mankind'.

1. Basil Blackwell, London 1980.

The major difficulty with the book arises in regard to its positive aspect, its alternative vision of philosophy. Its incoherence shows itself in a straightforward way in the language of the presentation. Hermeneutics, we are told, is 'what we get when we are no longer epistemological' (p. 325). But the chapters which expand this idea do so in incompatible ways. In Chapter 7 it is consistently maintained that the epistemology-hermeneutics contrast/is one between 'discourse about normal and about abnormal discourse' (p. 346), so that hermeneutics is 'the study of an abnormal discourse from the point of view of some normal discourse' (p. 320). The doctrine of Chapter 8 is that hermeneutics is *itself* abnormal discourse. Moreover, 'to insist on being hermeneutic where epistemology would do' is to make ourselves able to view normal discourse 'only from within our own abnormal discourse' (p. 366). Hermeneutics is, it now appears, abnormal discourse about normal discourse, the mirror image, as it were, of the previous conception. Perhaps Rorty simply changed his mind between chapters, and it may be that the incongruity can, in any case, be resolved at some deeper level. But the puzzle should not be left to the reader to sort out.

There are other puzzles in this area. Hermeneutics is linked in Chapter 8 to the project of 'edification' — that is, of 'finding new, better, more interesting, more fruitful ways of speaking' (p. 360). Edifying philosophy, we are told, is *'supposed* to be abnormal' (p. 360), is 'peripheral' as opposed to 'mainstream' (p. 367), is 'essentially reactive' (p. 366) and 'can be *only* reactive' (p. 378). This line of thought is intelligible enough as it stands. But Rorty also wishes to take seriously the suggestion that epistemology-centred philosophy is merely 'an episode in the history of European culture', to be comprehensively superseded by edification: 'Perhaps philosophy will become purely edifying . . .' (p. 394). It is at best not obvious how all philosophy could conceivably be 'abnormal', 'peripheral' and 'reactive'. Once again the reader seems entitled to more guidance than the text provides.

The charge of incoherence can draw support from elsewhere. It arises also in connection with the idea of conversation. Edifying philosophy aims at 'continuing a conversation', and philosophy in general is best appreciated as a voice in the conversation of mankind. There are various grounds for misgiving here. For one thing, it is far from clear what taking part in a conversation involves. On the negative side, Rorty insists that it is not merely an 'exchange of views'; and on the positive side, that it is *'saying something'* (pp. 371–72). These are enigmatic clues, but they are all we get. Obviously there is an element of paradox in the fact that philosophy's credentials in the conversation of mankind rest on the superseded tradition of Aristotle, Descartes, Kant and Husserl. Moreover, the invocation of Dewey, Heidegger and Wittgenstein as the pillars of the edifying alternative seems adventitious and unconvincing. At any rate, all awareness of contemporary reports of what it was actually like to encounter the last two of these figures socially must be repressed, if one is not to find something risible in the idea of them as heroes of the cause of conversation. The real problem, however, lies elsewhere.

It lies in the fact that the image of the conversation of mankind is a deeply discordant element in the scheme of the book. The phrase itself and the inspiration behind it are, as Rorty acknowledges, derived from Michael Oakeshott. The implication is clear in Oakeshott, and is any case hard to avoid, that the conversation of mankind is a blending of past and present, a communion of the living and the dead to which all the 'voices' contribute in their own distinctive, unitary 'modes'. This is a wholly ahistorical conception, a paradigm of the 'attempt to escape from history' of which Rorty accuses traditional philosophy. As such, it is the characteristic product of the declining days of a school, English Idealism, which he explicitly recognizes as being, even in its best days, resolutely non-historicist (p. 165). How can it be reconciled with his own much-canvassed historicism, his feeling for the discontinuity and diversity of ages and cultures and his sense of the significance of abnormalities in discourse, of 'incommensurable aims in an incommensurable vocabulary'?

The conception is problematic in other ways. It is presented by Oakeshott in an idiom that straddles the language of aesthetics and that of etiquette. This aspect is whole-heartedly taken up by Rorty. Philosophical judgement becomes for him a species of connoisseurship, with terms such as 'tact' and 'civility' the key instruments. Thus, we are told: 'To think of Wittgenstein and Heidegger as having views about how things are is not to be wrong about how things are exactly; it is just poor taste' (p. 372). This is surely an admission of intellectual collapse. In the quasi-aesthetic mode, one might suggest that here American philosophy has achieved decadence at one bound. The question that arises is how it was possible for a tough-minded historicist to fall for a concept as precious and vapid as 'the conversation of mankind'. Why should a sophisticated, contemporary Mid-Westerner assume the persona of a fake eighteenth-century English gentleman? The answer must lie in something deeply congenial in the Oakeshottian vision. It may be poor taste to say so, but its appeal seems to be fundamentally ideological.

What is appealing is Oakeshott's conservatism. In this context the image of the conversation of mankind is wholly appropriate insofar as it sponsors a contemplative acceptance of the perennial riches of the human condition. Rorty's conservatism, however, is overlain with radical rhetoric. He likes to tease, but always with the final assurance that this philosophy too leaves everything as it is. The urge to have your cake and eat it finds expression in ways that are sometimes mundane, even slightly comic. Thus, it might be supposed that the thesis of the book has depressing implications for the practice of philosophy as a sociological reality. After all, it tells us that the analytic movement 'now has little more to do' (p. 173), and, more generally, that the professional philosopher's self-image collapses with the loss of the mirror of nature idea (p. 392). Perhaps, to put it crudely, we should start worrying about our jobs? It is hard not to feel that the *frisson* the book has induced in the profession has something to do with such suspicions. Rorty is sensitive to this aspect of the situation and at the end of the book takes steps to render it harmless. He notes that the rejection of the old professional self-image might seem to 'entail the claim that there can or should be no such profession'. But 'this does not follow', more especially because 'the need for teachers who have read the great dead philosophers is quite enough to insure that there will be philosophy departments as long as there are universities' (p. 393). The terms of this reassurance are precisely weighted. The residual need is for people to teach the writings of the mighty dead. This should indeed serve to secure philosophy a legitimate place in the academy, with the status of, say, classical philology. That is to say, it suffices to guarantee a philosophy department in Princeton, though not in Peoria. The expansion of the profession in recent years in the United States and Britain has been lubricated by the sense, obscurely felt and yet influential inside and outside the academy, that the philosophers were on to something important or, at any rate, prestigious. This generous view can scarcely be accommodated to the claim that their role is to be ex-positors of a handful of classic texts. Institutional arrangements can, of course, survive the loss of their legitimating ideas. Nevertheless, this loss must always be a serious matter, and Rorty's fellow profes-sionals do well to regard him as a dangerous person, for all his innocent airs.

His conservative instincts work against the grain of his thesis in more important ways. The tension shows itself in the way the argu-ment loses its grip whenever reassurance is being dispensed. Thus, we are told that 'the view that there is no permanent neutral matrix within which the dramas of inquiry and history are enacted has as a corollary that criticism of one's culture can only be piecemeal and partial — never "by reference to eternal standards" ' (p. 179). There is a false opposition here, and without it the claim that criticism must be piecemeal is merely gratuitous. If one has 'eternal standards' to refer to, criticism can be as piecemeal as one likes. The standards license it to home in on objects of any level of generality in the human world. The point is surely that in the light of such standards the distinction between what is and what is not piecemeal and partial, so significant for Rorty's 'holism', is of no theoretical interest. If, however, one takes him literally it becomes quite hard to see how piecemeal criticism is even possible, or, at any rate, how it can ever be justified. For, on his account, justification at this level must presumably be in terms of those culturally accepted practices which the criticism is calling into question. On the other hand, his historicism makes it easy enough to see how criticism can be directed to the whole. For it can appeal to the conception of a systematically different way of doing things. After all, the questioning of the philosophical tradition in the name of an edifying alternative shows what is possible. Moreover, Rorty's thinking in this area draws, as he explains, on the Kuhnian distinction between 'normal' and 'revolutionary' science. He should therefore have no difficulty in acknowledging the link between criticism and the kind of paradigm switch that Kuhn describes. He should be prepared, if ideology did not get in the way, to present himself as a prophet of revolutions in the realm of concepts.

This is to suggest that the logic of his theory makes him a kind of Young Hegelian. The idea is not as fanciful as it may appear. From one point of view the interest of the book lies in the way it displays the whole analytical movement struggling to catch up with Hegel, who figures as a discreet, yet powerful, presence throughout. He stands, as Rorty recognizes, at variance with the Kantian-epistemological tradition that is the chief target, and, perhaps for that reason, the references to him are by no means unsympathetic. Thus, there is something highly agreeable, at least to the present reviewer, in the explanation of why Hegelianism failed to appeal to the professors: it 'made philosophy too popular, too interesting, too important, to be properly professional' (p. 135). That history is currently permitting a second shot at the ivory tower is strongly suggested by Jay Rosenberg's conclusion, quoted by Rorty: 'We must come to see the physical universe as an integrated physical system which necessarily "grows knowers" and which thereby comes to mirror itself within itself' (p. 297). Moreover, Rorty keeps a careful eye on the links between Hegel and the heroes of analytical philosophy. Thus, he refers to the 'Hegelian implications' of Quine's behaviourism and holism (p. 195) and to Sellar's self-description of 'Empiricism and the philosophy of Mind' as 'incipient *Méditations Hégéliennes*' (p. 192). One can hardly help feeling that if only the closet Hegelians in the analytical movement would come out, the whole business might yet limp on to Feuerbach. All sorts of possibilities must surely then open up.

The opposition of historicism and conservatism is but one instance of a tendency to face different ways at once. Some others may be briefly noted.

(1) Rorty seems uncertain where he stands as regards the fact–value distinction. Thus, Sellars is commended for keeping it (p. 180, n. 13) and Gadamer for giving it up (p. 364). Moreover, their treatment of it is in each case taken to be central to their achievement.

(2) It is not clear how the various accounts of 'truth' fit together. It is referred to indifferently as 'what it is better for us to believe' (p. 10) and as 'what our peers will, *ceteris paribus*, let us get away with saying' (p. 176). These formulas, standing respectively, one might suppose, for Rorty's pragmatism and his epistemological behaviourism, do not obviously amount to the same thing. Neither can safely be identified with a third, 'the homely use of "true" to mean roughly "what you can defend against all comers" ' (p. 308). This use has nothing 'homely' about it, as anyone who tries it out on their nearest and dearest will surely discover. It is a philosopher's construct designed to flatter the professional debater who alone will find it plausible to think, as Rorty puts it elsewhere, of 'rational certainty' as 'a matter of victory in argument' (p. 156). It is not easy to see how one can simultaneously be pragmatist, behaviourist and sophist in this area.

(3) Structural uncertainties are reflected in the curiously short-winded character of the discussion at key points. For one who values continuing the conversation above all else, it is remarkable how often Rorty confesses to being able to see how something or other should be 'debated' or 'argued' (e.g. pp. 28, 97, 178, 364; cf. interview on the impossibility of arguing with Kripke). Perhaps the most important example of this enervation is the handling of Kuhn's suggestion that 'there is a serious and unresolved problem about why the scientific enterprise has been doing so nicely lately', in the sense of 'repeatedly producing powerful new techniques for prediction and control'. This is, of course, the central problem to which scientific realism addresses itself, and through which it has made its fortunes in recent years. Rorty's response is to recommend that we should not feel it acutely

and should not regret our inability to resolve it: here as elsewhere, the rule is that there is nothing to be done but describe 'what counts as justification within the various disciplinary matrices constituting the culture of the day' (p. 340). This laid back attitude will seem unimpressive if one allows that philosophy may, and should, be responsive to cultural concerns outside the academy. In our day nuclear issues are among the most pressing of these, and they provide also a spectacular illustration of the link between theoretical advance and technology. Rorty might have been expected to deal more responsibly with the intellectual challenge of understanding science as the voice in the conversation of mankind that makes it possible to put a stop to the conversation. But even if the whole enterprise, or at least the European role in it, now seems set to end with a bang, it is still a pity that analytical philosophy should go before with such a tiny whimper, however elegantly emitted.

The elegance, at any rate, is not in doubt. The literary merits of Rorty's book are substantial and do much to account for its impact. Its style is vigorous, supple, self-assured, with many incidental felicities of expression. More narrowly intellectual merits are evident chiefly in the treatment of the history of ideas. This displays mastery of the material, a fresh eye for its connections and disconnections and the ability to fix the results in striking generalizations. Admittedly, it is all done in terms of the achievements of Great Men, Descartes's 'invention of the mind' and so on, and this individualized historiography sits somewhat oddly with the socialized epistemology, the sense of the community as the source of epistemic authority. But within its familiar limits, it is a valuable and stimulating discussion. It is perhaps ironic that Rorty should be best at the broad historical sweep and fairly unimpressive, as this review has tended to show, as regards the feature for which he particularly commends the analytical movement, the 'insistence on detail and mechanics'.[2] But, of course, it is a commonplace enough sort of pathos to find individuals and movements priding themselves most on qualities they do not in fact possess.

In other ways Rorty is admirably self-aware. Behind the flamboyance, he is intelligently modest in his conception of the book, insisting that it adds little to the ideas of its heroes, but is concerned rather to present them in a therapeutically effective way (pp. 7, 13). As a cultural document which crystallizes certain tendencies of the day, its importance is indeed undeniable. It is essential reading for

2. See the interview with Richard Rorty in *Radical Philosophy* 32.

anyone who wishes to understand current stirrings in the academy, and, more especially, the rapprochement now in process between certain elements of the analytical and continental traditions. It does nothing, however, to ease suspicions that this development is being conceived along somewhat opportunist lines and is fuelled on one side by the simple discovery that Heidegger, Gadamer, Foucault and Derrida are eminently assimilable, and, once one gets over their exotic idiom, represent no threat to anything. There is obviously a negative lesson here, that of showing what radical philosophy in these times is not. But Rorty's pioneering efforts have also something positive to teach. Here one must return to the project of edification to note that he wishes to retain the implication of relevance to guiding moral choices (pp. 384, 388). If one combines this point with recalling the distinctive ideological cast of his own practical preferences, the contrast between knowledge philosophy and edification philosophy begins to sound like a variation on one of the oldest of themes, that of lordship and bondage:

> The toad beneath the harrow knows
> Exactly where each tooth-point goes;
> The butterfly upon the road
> Preaches contentment to that toad.

In the context of this dialectic Rorty's book appears as an attempt to unite the academy in the West behind the edifying discourses of the butterfly. Any alternative approach must try its stand on the knowledge of the toad, and seek to be the voice of that knowledge. It still has no better starting point than Hegel's treatment of the theme, with its assurance that the future belongs to the toad as the agent of spirit.

Reprinted from *RP* 32

Towards a Theory of Videotics

Richard Osborne

In the post-structuralist diaspora the search for a non-taxonomic 'truth', an understanding of the political history of the presentation of signs, demands that we interrogate our relationship to the notion of the materiality of the sign. From Copernicus to Warhol we have witnessed the destabilization of the subject-centred universe and the rise of a cultural physics that places the mobility of the sign at the (de-centred) centre of all discourses. Here we shall argue that all philosophy to date has signally failed to inaugurate a proper history of the materiality of the sign in cultural discursivity. Here nothing will be taken for granted, especially that phallo-centric notion of the link between sexuality and the search for truth. Indeed we shall necessarily construct a theoretical distance from the implications of the object of our inquiry and of all interjections by the discourses that write themselves in the interstitial moments of our lapses and aphasias. In the play of sliding signifiers that call our attention to the act of elision and confusion that constitutes the corpus of all writing we shall pursue, and be pursued by, that central question of the presence of the machine in the systems of discourse that constitute the 'social'. This 'logic of supplementarity', as Derrida describes the underlying theme of his work, is extended here to encompass the unknown limits of the post-filmic discourses of technological power.[1] Drawing upon recent advances in linguistics, semiology, criminology, biology, epistemology, gardening, electronics and robotics we shall here sow the seeds for an organic, and revolutionary, synthesizing of

---

1. *On Grammatology* in particular. We understand Derrida to mean that what we don't put in is just as important as what we do. Or alternatively that all meaning is impossible insofar as language is what it appears not to be.

modalities of thought that we have elsewhere described as a theory of videotics. The origins of videotic thought can be traced back to the pioneering work of the Australian Saufewer in his one lecture in 1968.[2]

Fundamentally videotics is a proto-science of electronic signs. This revolution in the way we think of images in a video-saturated society is based on Saufewer's ruptural insight that 'all images are constructed like an electric current'.[3] He is here gesturing to that fundamental, and irrevocable, distinction between *direct* and *alternating* current which is the very basis of the discursive opposition between Oriental and Occidental systems of power presentation. This opposition is the starting point of videotic analysis. The internal relations of the video derive from the distinction between *direct* current, the always pre-given potentiality of energy acts, the system that makes the video possible, and *alternating* current which re-presents the individual acts of energy consumption which a universal transformer makes possible. Saufewer's rejection of the origins of universal power and his insistence on the arbitrariness of the electronic sign have eternally displaced 'homo electronicus' and inaugurated an open-ended discursivity of power systems. The refusal of referentiality leads to the necessity of arbitrariness and a recognition that signs 'cannot be seen to represent what they represent except insofar as they are not other than that which they are in the necessity of materiality which is the precondition of the possibility of signification'.[4] In other words it is the either/or of the *alternating* current (on/off) that specifies the mode of signification of the electronic sign in its digital functionality as representation. The failure of linguistic theories to account for the complexity of the operation of electronic signs can be seen in their refusal of the notion of *direct* current, most particularly in their inability to analyse the effects of power blackouts in post-industrial society.

The search for a theory of signs immediately calls into being the elusive search for the fundamental unit of information upon which such a theory could build. Saufewer argued that it was the electronic

2. O. Saufewer. 'The trepidation of an out-back philosophy in the video revolution , given at Griffith University and recorded on video by the Queensland police.
3. Saufewer now denies having argued this, since it was said in the bar after the lecture and recorded for posterity by an undercover policeman. The balance of scholarship clearly points to Saufewer, however, although a certain Morris was standing next to him at the time.
4. Saufewer some ten minutes after the above. Police file S 14/56 page 112. QL/Archives 1968.

dot, but Brumsky has convincingly analysed the patterns of electronic transformation and switched to the 'frame' as the monodic
reference point of all science. The instance of the 'frame' implies the
totality of the video system, and vice versa, and its two sets of
instigmatic relations. These relations can be schematically represented as those of the *prostratigmatic* and the *syntapematic*. The
former refer, of course, to the contrast and opposition between
'frames', on/off, or being and not-being. The latter refers to the
possibilities of combination through which frames form larger units,
or tapes of meaning. The concept of the tape was first articulated by
EMI and has universally been adopted by videoticians, except in
filmology where the notion of the text is still mobilized in narrative
analysis. In the naturalized play of images created by the 'frame' in
motion we have the moment of the videological, the positioning of the
viewer as subject. The construction of the viewer, the voyeur as place,
through the (hidden) inflexion of social relations in the rapidity of the
repression of the origin of the electronic is the illusion of narrative that
gives rise to the notion of the subject.

The ghost in the machine of pleasure systems is of course the
autonomous subject rendered in the materiality of the tape as a
videological whole and rendered self-conscious in the 'play' mode.

The videological system re/presents television and the subject as
natural mythological entities and represses the entry into televisuality
which is the moment of acquisition of humanness through which
subjectivity is inscribed. The subject-for-itself is repressed in the
acquisition of televisuality when the 'mirror-phase' is negated in the
oedipal moment of the screen coming to life. This understanding
leads to further questions such as the class control of viewing practices
and the construction of genderized 'points-of-view' in the organization of programming. Residual counter-hegemonic practices such as
cinema-going and home movies clearly point to areas in which deconstructive techniques play an important role.

The realm of the videotic covers all spheres of human, and non-
human, activity and extends to the unconscious, which we now know
is structured like a video-tape. (Often badly worn and likely to play
erratically through constant repetition and sudden fast-forward and
reverse moves.) The role of the unconscious in the master-tape of
history, a history of difference rendered intelligible through man's
technological development, remains under-theorized in the web of
power relations which record history through man. In this analysis
we can see the state as the plane of relations on which the master-tape
is constructed and from which class copies are run to be distributed

through the system we know as IVAs. (Individual Videological Apparatuses).

We return then to Marx's stunningly prescient statement that history repeats itself, never in the same mode but always through the same images. Hegel's teleological epistemology is also exposed in his failure to predict the working out of the spirit in slow motion and freeze frame analysis, the videological mode of the synchronic. If we look at the video-tape of the Royal Wedding and examine its mythological status as a trans-cultural, trans-historical event then the full power of videological analysis can be seen. Chronologically, we would have said historically, we know that the video-tape came first and that constant repetition produced the illusion of the 'event', an 'event' only made knowable to the viewing subject by that prior body of discourse which constitutes tele-visuality. This itself explains the traditional playing out of the 'event' as it relates to, prolongs, reinforces and explains already given modes of signification. Barthes, Kristeva and others have somewhat inadequately referred to this process as 'intertextuality', demonstrating their failure to break from the idealist language of text-based criticism. A theory of videotics, emphasizing the materiality of the construction of the sign, more adequately refers to this process as one of 'forgery' or 'contrefaçon'.

The 'event' was forged to create the illusion of a history, of a past, of the diachronic, which could in itself be a teleological explanation for the presence of the Royal family as the (absent) centre of power in post-late-consumer monopoly capitalism. Prince Charles and Lady Diana were clearly produced as particular subjectivities to 'forge' the Royal Wedding as videological representations of the ordinary which, in their ordinariness, signified the historical transition from bourgeois royalty to the modern form of petty-bourgeois royalty. This reading is reinforced by the video recording of Elton John at a charity concert attended by the Royal subjectivities.

Here we have merely sketched the beginnings of a videological mode of analysis and posed the perennial question, 'What is the materiality of the sign in post-filmic, post-structuralist discourse?' in a revolutionary and electrifying way. As Saufewer put it, however, 'without the sign, no video, without the video, no sign.'

Reprinted from *RP* 36

Radical Philosophy Subscriptions.

If you want to keep up to date with philosophical debate in the English speaking world you may want to subscribe to Radical Philosophy. Subscriptions are for one year (three issues) and may be taken out from the current issue (39) and the one preceding it (38). All other issues are back issues. By subscribing you save money and receive Radical Philosophy more quickly.

ORDERS TO
Individual Subscriptions

Howard Feather	INLAND	£4. 00
General Education Department,	OVERSEAS	
Thurrock Technical College,	SURFACE	£6. 00
Woodview, Grays,	OVERSEAS	
Essex, U.K.	AIRMAIL	£10. 00

Institutional Subscriptions

John Fauvel	INLAND	£10. 00
Open University,	OVERSEAS	
Walton Hall,	SURFACE	£15. 00
Milton Keynes,	OVERSEAS	
MK7 6AA,	AIRMAIL	£20. 00
U.K.		

Complete Back-sets

Because of a constant demand for back issues we have reprinted many of the early numbers and can now offer complete back sets of Radical Philosophy. The sets will comprise Nos 1–40 & will be available from February 1985.

	INDIVIDUALS	INSTITUTIONAL
INLAND	£50	£100
OVERSEAS SURFACE	£75	£130
OVERSEAS AIRMAIL	£100	£150

Orders to the above addresses. All cheques payable to 'Radical Philosophy Group' and overseas orders in sterling please.